KENRICK-GLENNON SEMINARY LIBRARY
37050000291346

W9-BPO-088

THEOLOGY OF THE OLD TESTAMENT

I

GOD

DESCLEE COMPANY

New York - Tournai - Paris · Rome

P. VAN IMSCHOOT

THEOLOGY of the OLD TESTAMENT

I

GOD

PREFACE BY Msgr. LUCIEN CERFAUX

Translated by Kathryn Sullivan, R.S.C.J. and Fidelis Buck, S.J.

Theology of the Old Testament — Vol. I: God
is a translation from the French
Théologie de l'Ancien Testament — Vol. I: Dieu
(© 1954 by DESCLÉE & Co., Tournai), with adaptation and updating of the bibliography.

NIHIL OBSTAT
DONALD A. PANELLA, M.A., S.T.L., S.S.L.
Censor Deputatus

IMPRIMATUR
✠ FRANCIS Cardinal SPELLMAN
Archbishop of New York
February 10, 1965

The nihil obstat and imprimatur are official declarations that a book or pamphlet is free of doctrinal or moral error. No implication is contained therein that those who have granted the nihil obstat and imprimatur agree with the contents, opinions or statements expressed.

Library of Congress Catalog Card Number: 65-20538

Printed in Belgium

CONTENTS

PREFACE

St. Paul was eminently a man of both Testaments because he was a Jew by birth and a Greek by vocation. He has described, in the celebrated comparison of the olive tree, the relation between the two divine economies. The Christian Church, he explains, is the tree planted long ago by God, once and for all, and lovingly cared for and watered through the years; during all these centuries of growth the same luxuriant foliage rises from a single root.

The theology of the Old Testament, while adhering methodically to what is stable and capable of future growth in the religion of the chosen people and while describing the constants of revelation, cannot fail to suggest in the course of its expositions the unity and harmony of the two Testaments. No need to dream up theses that are alluring, if these theses remain unilateral; the simple reality is more eloquent than the fantasies of theologians.

It is a joy to discover in P. van Imschoot's book the classic sobriety of fundamental works. This learned Catholic renews a vanished tradition. Conversant with both texts and contemporary studies, he presents to us the biblical thoughts in outlines and depths.

Let no one think that such scrupulous exactitude has no place in theological knowledge or in piety. Christianity is a " historic " religion. St. Paul understood this well; that is why he chose the symbol of the single olive tree that was to cover the world, thanks to branches grafted on the original trunk.

A " historic " religion makes the present moment one with the whole past. The rhythm of life at the beginning still beats today and we may find it in the Christian Church; the mystery of the Church is, in a sense, but the love that has patterned from the beginning all the movements of the rhythm. One who would really understand the life of a plant cannot refuse to watch this life rising from the roots; the same is true of the life of the Church. One who would share in the abundance of its growth will strengthen his religious personality by connecting present graces with past experiences.

The God of the Christians is the God who revealed Himself in the Old Testament, the " personal " God who appeared to Abraham, who told His name to Moses, who spoke to the prophets. Some modern theologies seek to oppose to this God, the God of Greek reason.

Van Imschoot's pages will judge many approximations of this kind. The same revelation that puts humanity in contact with a personal God never ceases to purify and spiritualize a thought, a theology which, from the beginning and through God's power, strove to draw near its object. If it was the honor of Greek philosophy to give us our technical vocabulary, if it succeeded in expressing in abstract language such divine attributes as " independence, " the accents that move us are those of Isaias : " What care I for your sacrifices, for the fat of your calves and lambs ? Your new moons and festivals I detest ! "

Patriarcal monotheism and the prophetic message of divine holiness, united to the universalist dynamism that underlies the thought of Christ and of Paul, will continue until the end of time to give Christians a reason for living and an enthusiasm for spreading the faith.

The God who called the patriarchs and chose the people of times past, is still the God who calls His saints today and who creates grace in Christian souls. Perhaps this is understood in an abstract sense; it will be understood in another way, as the fruit of reflection, after reading this theology of the Old Testament. These pages clarify a number of ideas that were believed to be intangible, and which in fact were intangible only because excessive oversimplifications had turned them into caricatures. Let us give one example : to understand all the meaning of the miracles of the New Testament, those of the Gospel and those that come later in the history of the Church, is it not helpful to re-read the dense pages in which the author discloses to us the notion and varied forms of revelation ?

This is a book of rich and stimulating theology for which it is my privilege, on the basis of an old friendship, to write a preface. This book is a perfect answer to the exigencies of Christians today and it takes its place in the great theological movement that seeks more and more earnestly for an understanding of the divine plan.

The exegetes of Upsala chose for one of their recent publications, a little book in English, *The Root of the Vine*. This title would have been very appropriate for the work of P. van Imschoot; and the exergual inscription would have mentioned the allegory of the olive tree. But the author thought a text book should have a more serene and less publicity-minded title. He was right.

Lucien Cerfaux

FOREWORD

Few Catholic exegetes have until recently concerned themselves with biblical theology, especially of the Old Testament. With the exception of P. Heinisch, *Theology of the Old Testament*, Collegeville 1952; P. F. Ceuppens, *Theologia Biblica*, 4 vols., Rome 1938; the small volumes by A. Gelin, *Les pauvres de Yahvé*, Paris 1953; *The Key Concepts of the Old Testament*, New York 1955; J. Guillet, *Themes o the Bible*, Notre Dame 1960; J. Gillet, *The God of Israel, the God of Christians*, New York 1961, as well as some monographs that have appeared in biblical dictionaries, periodicals and in the collections *Études Bibliques*, *Biblische Zeitfragen*, *Biblische Studien*, and *Alttestamentliche Abhandlungen*, one can refer only to the outdated works of P. Scholz, *Handbuch der Theologie des Alten Testamentes*, 2 vols., 1861; H. Zschokkc, *Theologie der Propheten*, 1877, and *Der dogmatisch-ethische Lehrgehalt der alttestamentlichen Weisheitsbücher*, Vienna 1869; M. Hetzenauer, *Theologia biblica sive scientia historiae et religionis utriusque Testamenti catholica, I, Vetus Testamentum*, 1908, and some recent sketches of the religion of Israel, for example, by J. Nikel in J. Huby, *Christus. Manuel d'histoire des religions*, Paris 1912; J. Touzard in A. Bricout, *Où en est l'histoire des religions?*, 2 vols., Paris 1912; R. de Vaux in *Initiation biblique*, Paris 1948[2], and in *Supplément au Dictionnaire de la Bible*; A. Barrois in *Histoire générale des religions*, I, Paris 1948; and lastly that of N. Peters, "Die Religion des Alten Testamentes in ihrer Einzigartigkeit unter den Religionen des Alten Orients" in *Religion, Christentum, Kirche*, I, 1913[2].

The absence of any synthesis of the doctrine of the Old Testament and the obvious interest in a work that is concerned with the knowledge of the old revelation and the study of theology in general, justify, without doubt, the attempt the author has been making.

But is such an attempt not presumptuous, and even temerarious in the present state of biblical research?

As a matter of fact a synthesis of biblical theology presupposes the solution of a number of problems, many of which are far from being solved: problems of textual, literary and historic criticism, especially problems dealing with the authenticity, age and composition of the books of the Old Testament and their sources, and problems connected with the evolution of the religion of Israel which are so intimately linked with the social and political development of the chosen people, questions about the interpretation of texts and the appreciation of literary forms.

More than anyone else is the author of these pages aware of the difficulty of the project and the impossibility of satisfying all readers, above all those who are experts. But were it necessary to await the solution of all disputed and disputable questions in biblical matters, there would be no alternative but the renunciation of any attempt to reach a synthesis. The one here offered is only a provisional sketch which scholars perhaps may find unfinished and deficient, and the average reader will judge it as too technical and uninteresting.

Far from any big library and forced by circumstances to work under particularly disadvantageous and really painful conditions, the author has restricted the bibliography to well-known works which, with few exceptions, he has been able to study and which he has found profitable. He hopes he has neither omitted nor missed anything essential.

The present volume treats of God and God's relations with the world and its people. A second volume will deal with man; a third will have for its subject judgment and salvation.

If this work, in spite of its imperfections and lacunas, is being published, it is because the author has been encouraged by good judges and the pressing invitation of the Encyclical *Divino afflante Spiritu* which urges exegetes to bring out the theological doctrine of the inspired books:

> With special zeal they should apply themselves not only to expounding exclusively those matters which belong to the historical, archaeological, philological and other auxiliary services — as, to our regret, is done in certain commentaries — but having duly referred to these, insofar as they may aid the exegesis, they should set forth in particular the

> theological doctrine in faith and morals of the individual books or texts so that their exposition may not only aid the professors of theology in their explanations and proofs of the dogmas of faith, but may also be of assistance to priests in their presentation of Christian doctrine to the people, and may help all the faithful to lead a life that is holy and worthy of a Christian. [1]

If the present volume can contribute in some way to the realization of this program, the author will consider himself largely rewarded for all his trouble.

---

[1] Quoted from John E. Steinmueller, *A Companion to Sacred Scripture*, I, New York 1948, p. 471.

ABBREVIATIONS

The Books of the Old Testament

Genesis	Gn
Exodus	Ex
Leviticus	Lv
Numbers	Nm
Deuteronomy	Dt
Josue	Jos
Judges	Jgs
Ruth	Ru
1 Samuel	1 Sm
2 Samuel	2 Sm
3 Kings	3 Kgs
4 Kings	4 Kgs
1 Paralipomenon	1 Par
2 Paralipomenon	2 Par
Ezra	Ezr
Nehemia	Neh
Tobia	Tb
Judith	Jdt
Esther	Est
Job	Jb
Psalms	Ps(s)
Proverbs	Prv
Ecclesiastes	Eccl
Canticle of Canticles	Ct
Wisdom	Wis
Sirach (Ecclesiasticus)	Sir
Isaia	Is
Jeremia	Jer
Lamentations	Lam
Baruch	Bar
Ezechiel	Ez
Daniel	Dn
Osee	Os
Joel	Jl
Amos	Am
Abdia	Abd
Jona	Jon
Michea	Mi
Nahum	Na
Habacuc	Hb
Sophonia	So
Aggai	Ag
Zacharia	Za
Malachia	Mal
1 Machabees	1 Mc
2 Machabees	2 Mc

The Books of the New Testament

Matthew	Mt
Mark	Mk
Luke	Lk
John	Jn
Acts	Acts
Romans	Rom
1 Corinthians	1 Cor
2 Corinthians	2 Cor
Galatians	Gal
Ephesians	Eph
Philippians	Phil
Colossians	Col
1 Thessalonians	1 Thes
2 Thessalonians	2 Thes
1 Timothy	1 Tm
2 Timothy	2 Tm
Titus	Ti
Philemon	Phlm
Hebrews	Heb
James	Jas
1 Peter	1 Pt
2 Peter	2 Pt
1 John	1 Jn
2 John	2 Jn
3 John	3 Jn
Jude	Jude
Apocalypse	Ap

Bibliographic Abbreviations

AOB — H. Gressmann, *Altorientalische Bilder zum Alten Testament* [2], Leipzig 1927.
AOT — H. Gressmann, *Altorientalische Texte zum Alten Testament* [2], Leipzig 1927.
ARW — *Archiv für Religionswissenschaft.*
ATA — *Alttestamentliche Abhandlungen.*
Bb — *Biblica.*
BRL — K. Galling, *Biblisches Reallexikon*, Tübingen 1937.
BW — *Bijbelsch Woordenboek*, Roermond 1939 f.
BZ — *Biblische Zeitschrift.*
BZAW — *Beihefte zur Zeitschift für die Alttestamentliche Wissenschaft.*
BZfr. — *Biblische Zeitfragen.*
CBQ — *Catholic Biblical Quarterly*
Coll. Gand. — *Collationes Gandavenses.*
DA — *Dictionnaire Apologétique de la Foi Catholique.*
DB — *Dictionnaire de la Bible* (F. Vigouroux).
DBS — *Supplément au Dictionnaire de la Bible* (L. Pirot).
DTC — *Dictionnaire de Théologie Catholique.*
EB — *Encyclopaedia Biblica* (T. K. Cheyne).
El-Amarna — J. A. Knudzon, *Die El-Amarna Tafeln (Vorderasiatische Bibliothek)*, 2 vols., Leipzig 1915.
ERE — *Encyclopaedia of Religions and Ethics* (Hasting's).
ERS — M. J. Lagrange, *Études sur les religions sémitiques* [2], Paris 1905.
EThL — *Ephemerides Theologicae Lovanienses.*
Ges. B — W. Gesenius - F. Buhl, *Handwörterbuch über das Alte Testament* [16], Leipzig 1915.
Ges. K. — W. Gesenius - E. Kautzsch, *Hebräische Grammatik* [28], Leipzig 1909.
HDB — *Hasting's Dictionary of the Bible.*
JBL — *Jeurnal of Biblical Literature*
JNES — *Journal of Near Eastern Studies*
JThS — *Journal of Theological Studies.*
LThK — *Lexikon für Theologie und Kirche.*
RB — *Revue Biblique.*
RE — *Realencyklopädie der Klassischen Altertumswissenschaft* (Pauly-Wissowa).
RGG — *Die Religion in Geschichte und Gegenwart.*
RHPhR — *Revue d'Histoire et de Philosophie Religieuses.*
RHR — *Revue de l'Histoire des Religions.*
RLA — *Reallexikon der Assyriologie.*
RPT — *Realencyklopädie für Protestantische Theologie und Kirche* [3].
RScPT — *Revue des Sciences Philosophiques et Théologiques.*
RScR — *Recherches de Science Religieuse.*
ThG — *Theologie und Glaube.*
ThW — *Theologisches Wörterbuch zum Neuen Testament* (R. Kittel).
TS — *Theological Studies*
VB — *Vorderasiatische Bibliothek*, Leipzig 1907.
VT — *Vetus Testamentum*
ZA — *Zeitschrift für Assyriologie.*
ZAW — *Zeitschrift für die Alttestamentliche Wissenschaft.*
ZKTh — *Zeitschrift für Katholische Theologie.*
ZNW — *Zeitschrift für die Neutestamentliche Wissenschaft.*

OBJECT, METHOD AND DIVISION OF THE THEOLOGY OF THE OLD TESTAMENT

R. Kittel, "Die Zukunft der alttestamentlichen Wissenschaft," *ZAW* (1921), pp. 84-99; O. Eissfeldt, "Israelitisch-jüdische Religionsgeschichte und alttestamentliche Theologie," *ZAW* (1926), pp. 1-12; K. Steuernagel, *Alttestamentliche Theologie und alttestamentliche Religionsgeschichte* (*Marti-Festschrift*, Giessen 1925, pp. 266-273); W. Eichrodt, "Hat die alttestamentliche Theologie noch selbständige Bedeutung innerhalb der alttestamentlichen Wissenschaft," *ZAW* (1929), pp. 89-91; H. Gunkel, "Biblische Theologie und biblische Religionsgeschichte des Alten Testamentes," *RGG* ², I, cols. 1089-1091; A. Weiser, "Vom Verstehen des Alten Testamentes," *ZAW*, 61 (1945-48), pp. 17-30; G. E. Wright, *God Who Acts*, London 1952.

The term "theology of the Old Testament" includes some widely different ideas.

To some it means an exposition of the religion of the Old Testament, that is to say, the life, practices and religious beliefs of Israel throughout the centuries. [1] It is a description of their origin and evolution, the influences effected by social and cultural developments, by the political vicissitudes of the chosen people and by their contacts with neighboring nations and religions.

Understood in this way, biblical theology is a strictly historical discipline which belongs to the history of religion, even if one retains, as all Catholics and several Protestants do, the transcendent character that the religion of Israel owes to its divine origin and to the fact of revelation; for revelation, without doubt, is a fact of the supernatural order, though woven into the fabric of historic events, and this fact must be perceptible and effectively recognized as such by the human intelligence.

But if one wishes to write a history of the religion of Israel, it is arbitrary to stop at the time of the New Testament and to consider as sources only Jewish or Christian canonical books, for the evolution

[1] This is the method praised by H. Gunkel ("Biblische Theologie," *RGG*, I, col. 1090), and applied in the biblical theologies of R. Smend, B. Stade, A. Bertholet, K. Kautzsch, and in the histories of the religion of Israel of R. Kittel, G. Hölscher, E. Sellin, A. Loisy, A. Lods, A. Causse, E. Dhorme, W. O. E. Oesterley, T. H. Robinson, G. Toussaint, B. D. Eerdmans.

of the religion of Israel has continued until our own day. Its developments or deformations must be followed in the apocrypha, or to borrow the Protestant term, the pseudo-epigraphical and rabbinic writings. Therefore, no longer is it justifiable to speak of the theology of the Old Testament when making a purely historical study of facts, institutions and beliefs that go far beyond the frame of the Old Testament.

To question the right of using the title of theology of the Old Testament when making a study of the history of the religion of Israel, is not to cast a doubt on the legitimacy, the utility, or even the necessity for such a history. Such a study has this advantage : it highlights the various stages through which Israel's faith has passed.

It is important, nevertheless, that in our effort to discover the human factors, the influences of the ethnic milieu, the neighboring civilizations and religions which influenced the religion of Israel, we do not forget or neglect its own special and constantly affirmed character of a revealed religion. Furthermore, if this method can disclose the historic points of contact linking the religion of Israel with Christianity, it runs the risk of leaving in the dark the profound unity which binds the old revelation to the new.

A logical arrangement of the doctrines of the Old Testament brings into sharper focus the continuity and the likeness of the two revelations. It also casts a clear light on the lacunas and the imperfections of the Old Law.

The unity which joins the two revelations and the differences that separate them are strongly stated by the Epistle to the Hebrews (1:1.2). Their unity and continuity are manifest because they are both the work of God : formerly God spoke to the fathers and to the prophets ; at the end of time He spoke to us through His Son. It is the same God who has spoken through the prophets and through His Son, that is to say, it is the same God who has communicated His thought and especially His will to men. [2]

The new revelation is a continuation of the old, and therefore is its crown (cf. Mt 5:17).

Brought by the Son " in these latter days, " that is to say, at the period of consummation (Heb 9:26), the last period in which God's designs will be realized, and also the period to which the author and his readers belonged, this revelation, of which the Christians are the beneficiaries, is definitive and complete (cf. Jn 15:15 ; 16:13).

---

[2] The verb λαλεῖν is used several times in Hebrews to indicate communications made by God (Heb 2:2 ff. ; 3:5 ; 4:8 ; 5:5 ; 11:18 ; 12:25).

On the contrary, the revelation made through the prophets in ancient times " to the fathers, " that is to the Israelites (cf. Jn 7:22; Rom 9:5), the ancestors according to the faith of " the Israel of God " (Gal 6:16), was communicated by God at divers times (πολυμερῶς) and in divers manners (πολυτροπῶς).

If, in order to make Himself heard, God spoke in times past at various times and in various ways, it is because He divided revelation and communicated it in successive stages and in different ways according to the times and the development of the people to whom He spoke. In the course of centuries each of God's heralds delivered a part and contributed to its progress, but to no one was it given entirely. This evolution is still distinctly discernible in the books of the Old Testament which appeared between the thirteenth and the first century before Christ.

The old revelation was necessarily incomplete and imperfect because it was advancing toward the complete and final form which the Son was to give (cf. Mt 5:17). The old revelation was intended to give religious and moral education to " a stiff-necked people " (Ex 32:9; 33:3), consequently it was adapted and proportioned to what Israel could bear, according to the intellectual and moral development of a nation with " a hard heart " (Mk 10:5). That is why there are necessarily not only lacunas but also imperfections, nay even temporary concessions to the weaknesses of a crude people. As an example of this, let us take the permission granted for divorce (Dt 24:1); a permission that corresponds neither to God's first intention when instituting marriage (Mk 10:5 ff.), nor to the perfection exacted and reestablished by Christ (Mk 10:11 ff.; cf. Mt 5:31 ff.; 19:8 ff.).

Since the old revelation, as it is recorded in the sacred books, is the object of Old Testament theology, the latter must take into account the historic context and the various stages marked by the heralds of the divine word who succeeded one another from Abraham to the Precursor. To fail to do this would be to lose perspective and to falsify the thought of the inspired authors.

Biblical theology must also be mindful of the orientation of the old revelation towards the new. More than this, while paying scrupulous respect to the special characteristics of the Old Testament, biblical theology will bring about a synthesis of the doctrines of the Old Testament with a view towards the new revelation, since the new crowns the old and testifies to the final pattern God was following in the old economy and throughout the vicissitudes of Israel's religion. [3]

[3] Cf. E. Sellin, *Israelitisch-jüdische Religionsgeschichte*, Leipzig 1933, p. 2.

Although biblical theology is a systematic exposition of its doctrines, the theology of the Old Testament cannot ignore the history of the religion of Israel. On the contrary, it takes this history for granted, just as it takes for granted the exegesis and the literary and historic criticism of the books of the Old Testament.

But it can dispense itself from treating questions that are exclusively historical.

It is true that in the Old Testament the religion that comes from the heart plays a far more important role than theology properly so-called, that is to say, the scientific and rational elaboration of religion.[4] There is in fact in the books of the Old Testament no systematic statement of ideas about God and His relations with the world and men.

Yet certain categorical affirmations may be discovered, especially among the prophets, about the unity, the holiness, the metaphysical and moral attributes of God who had revealed Himself to Israel. Besides the élans of faith and confidence of the psalmists, the narratives of the Hebrew chroniclers, the legislative codes and the precepts of the sages spring from or are impregnated with living faith and open up a world of ideas about God's nature and His urgent demands on Israel. Without doing violence to Israelite thought, it is permissible to disengage and to group these ideas in order to unite them into a synthesis, which, while respecting the originality of each author and the differences which at times separate them, highlights both the basic unity of the revelation, that was entrusted to the chosen people and set down in their sacred books, and its continuity with the revelation of the New Testament for which it was the preparation.

In addition to these advantages, this method[5] also has the advantage of supplying theologians with the revealed facts which are the object of their science, and of giving the faithful the most essential principles that God has deigned to make known to men in the course of ages for their salvation.

Because the Old Testament has preserved divine revelation just as it was given, that is in a successive and fragmentary form, and has made no effort to present a systematic report nor an ordered plan, some pattern must therefore be introduced that will permit the logical arrangement of doctrines. At the same time no violence must be done

---

[4] H. Gunkel, *op. cit.*, col. 1090; cf. M. Burrows, *An Outline of Biblical Theology*, Philadelphia 1946, p. 4.

[5] This method is used by A. B. Davidson, E. König, E. Sellin, W. Eichrodt, J. Pedersen, P. Heinisch, A. Gelin, T. Vriezen, O. Procksch, J. Guillet; A. Burrows, E. Sellin, E. König, O. Procksch preceded their systematic exposition by a history of the religion of Israel.

to the structure of Israelite thought in order to adapt it to requirements of a more advanced theology.

A simple plan that seems most in conformity with this idea is the one adopted by E. Sellin and L. Köhler. They grouped the doctrines under three main headings :

I. God and His relations with the world in general and with Israel in particular.

II. Man, that is to say, ideas about nature and man's destiny, about his obligations and failings towards God and his neighbor, or the question of duty and sin.

III. Divine judgment and salvation, in other words, the general eschatology of the Old Testament.

CHAPTER I

GOD CONSIDERED IN HIMSELF

§ 1. *The existence of God*

The Old Testament accepts the existence of God as a self-evident fact which needs no demonstration. Only the Greek book of Wisdom (13:1-9), when arguing against idolatry, points out a proof of the existence of God the creator: man can and ought to recognize the Worker in His works. Elsewhere, when the wonders accomplished by God in nature or among men are described (for example Ps 19:6; 104:1-7; Jb 38; Is 40:25-31), it is not so much to prove that God exists as it is to praise Him (Ps 8; 19:8-10; 104), or to exhort to confidence in His power (for example Is 40:27-31); it is an effort to make Him known for what He is rather than to prove that He is.

Knowledge of God is not the fruit of reasoning but of revelation. God make Himself known because He appeared and spoke to man (Gn 18:1; Ex 3:2 ff.; 6:3; 33:11), or manifested His power to man (Is 19:21). To know God, is not only to know that He exists, it is above all to acknowledge His power, His goodness, His dominion and as a result to submit respectfully to His exigencies (Dt 11:2-8; Is 41:20; Os 11:3); " to know His name " is to have confidence in Him (Ps 9:11), it is to pay homage to Him and to obey Him (Ps 36:11; 87:4); sinners are those who " do not know Him " (1 Sm 2:12; Jer 2:8; 9:2-5). Knowledge of God is practically equivalent to submission to God or fear of God (Is 1:3; 11:2.9; Os 4:1.6; Prv 1:7) and may be paralleled with it (Prv 9:10; cf. Is 11:2). In the polemic against idolatry, it is invested with a special meaning; it signifies the acknowledgment of the one God and the non-existence of the gods (Is 43:10; 44:8.9; 45:5.6; Wis 13:1-9).

When the fool declares that there is no God (Ps 14:1; 53:2), he does not think of denying God's existence but only His action in the world. He declares that God is not concerned with man, that " He will do no good, nor will he do evil " (So 1:12), that is to say, He does nothing, He does not intervene in men's lives, He does not " punish " their crimes (Ps 10:4). To put it briefly, the fool wants to live in his own way, just as if there were no God to chastise him for his faults. The attitude of the impious is that of a practical atheist, but not that of a theoretical atheist. The latter is not to be found in the Old Testament nor in the entire Semitic ancient world.

§ 2. *The divine names*

M. J. Lagrange, *Études sur les religions sémitiques*, Paris 1905[2]; J. Hehn, *Die biblische und die babylonische Gottesidee*, Leipzig 1913; P. Kleinert, " El, " *BZAW*, 41 (1918), pp. 59-76; M. Noth, *Die israelitischen Personennamen im Rahmen der gemeinsemitischen Namengebung*, Stuttgart 1928; W. Baudissin, *Kyrios als Gottesname und seine Stelle in der Religionsgeschichte*, 4 vols., Giessen 1929; H. Bauer, " Die Gottheiten von Ras Shamra, " *ZAW*, 51 (1933), pp. 81-101; 53 (1935), pp. 54-59; O. Grether, *Name und Wort Gottes im A. T.*, Giessen 1934; J. W. Jack, *The Ras Shamra Tablets and their Bearing on the Old Testament*, Edinburgh 1935; D. Nielsen, *Ras Shamra Mythologie und biblische Theologie*, Leipzig 1936; R. de Vaux, " Les textes de Ras Shamra et l'Ancien Testament, " *RB*, 46 (1937) pp. 527-555; R. Dussaud, *Les découvertes de Ras Shamra et l'Ancien Testament*, Paris 1937; A. Bea, " Ras Schamra und das Alte Testament, " *Bb*, 19 (1939), pp. 435-453; O. Eissfeldt, *El im Ugaritischen Pantheon*, Berlin 1950 (*Berichte über die Verhandlungen der Sächsischen Akademie der Wissenschaften zu Leipzig*, Philol.-hist. Kl., 98, 4); A. Kapelrud, *Baal in the Ras Shamra Texts*, Copenhagen 1952.

Yahweh. M. J. Lagrange, " El et Jahve, " *RB*, 12 (1903), pp. 162-186; R. Kittel, " Jahwe, Jehova, " *RPT*, VIII, pp. 529-541; S. Landersdorfer, " Der Gottesname JHWH in den Keilinschriften, " *BZ*, 10 (1912), pp. 24-35; G. Breitschaft, " Ist der Gottesname JHWH in den Keilinschriften nachgewiesen?, " *BZ*, 10 (1912), pp. 238-241; H. Grimme, " Sind Jaho und Jahwe zwei verschiedene Namen und Begriffe?, " *BZ*, 17 (1925), pp. 28-42; R. N. Wambacq, *L'épithète divine Jahwe Seba'ot*, Paris 1947; G. R. Driver, " The Original Form of the Name Yahweh; Evidence and Conclusions, " *ZAW*, 46 (1928), pp. 7-25; O. Eissfeldt, " Neue Zeugnisse für die Aussprache des Tetragramms als Jahwe, " *ZAW*, 53 (1935), pp. 59-76; A. L. Williams, " The Tetragrammaton, " *ZAW*, 54 (1936), pp. 262-269; A. Vaccari, " Jahwe e i nomi divini nelle religioni semitiche, " *Bb*, 17 (1936), pp. 1-10; R. de Langhe, " Un dieu Yahweh à Ras Shamra?, " *EThL*, 19 (1942), pp. 91-101; K. G. Kuhn, *Ueber die Entstehung des Namen Jahwe*, (*Orient. Studien*, Enno Littmann, Leiden 1935, pp. 25-42); J. Oberman, " The Divine Name YHWH in the Light of Recent Discoveries, " *JBL*, 58 (1949), pp. 301 ff.; M. T. C. Vriezen, " 'Ehje 'ašer 'ehje, " *Fetsschrift Bertholet*, 1950, pp. 498 ff.; A. M. Dubarle, " La signification du nom de Jahweh, " *RScPT*, 35 (1951), pp. 3 ff.; E. Dhorme, " Le nom du Dieu d'Israel, " *RHR*, 141 (1952) pp. 5 ff.; G. Lambert, " Que signifie le nom divin YHWH?, " *NRTh*, 74 (1952), pp. 897 ff.

Adôn. L. Cerfaux, " Le titre Kyrios et la dignité royale de Jésus, " *RScPT*, 11 (1922), pp. 40-71; 12 (1923), pp. 125-153; *id.*, " Le nom divin Kyrios dans Bible grecque, " *RScPT*, 20 (1931), pp. 27-51; *id.*, " Adonaï et Kyrios, " *RScPT*, 20 (1931), pp. 417-452; G. Quell, " Kyrios, " *ThW*, III, pp. 1056-1060.

The Old Testament uses several different names to designate God. Most of these names are common nouns expressing an attribute or a function of the divinity, but when they are used in reference to the one God, they are proper nouns: for example El, Elohim, Adôn, Elyôn, Šadday. The proper name of the God of Israel is Yahweh.

1. EL designates the divinity among all the Semites, excepting only the Ethiopians. The eastern Semites write the word *'l* (*'êl* in

the massoretic Bible); in Accadian it takes the form *ilu*, in Arabic it is *il* or *ilah*.

The etymology of the word is uncertain. Among many solutions proposed, three are most widely supported. Some believe that the word is derived from a root meaning " to be strong, " *'wl*. To them the idea of power is primitive, the idea that is found in the expression *yêš lĕ 'êl yâdî* (Gn 31:29; Dt 28:32; etc.) and that is translated : " it is in the power of my hand, " [1] and in the names that designate mighty sacred trees *'êlâh, 'êlôn.* [2] Others hold that the root *'wl* originally meant " to be before. " To them the idea of primacy is primitive and *El* means " the leader. " This hypothesis is confirmed by the Hebrew and Accadian expression " to walk behind a god " which means " to honor a god. " [3] Finally, still others derive the word from the preposition *'el*, i.e., " towards. " To them *El* means " he toward whom one goes to pay homage, he from whom protection is sought, he to whom prayer is directed, " or rather " the goal of man's desires and strivings. " [4]

Nor is there any greater agreement about the value of the noun : is it ordinarily a proper noun [5] or an appellative? [6] Whatever it may have been originally, now it is incontestably an appellative noun, since it has a plural *'êlîm* (Ex 15:11; Dn 11:36) and a feminine form *'êlâh*, although these are never found in the Bible. It is used as a proper noun of a determined god by the Arameans, [7] the Arabs, [8] the Phoenicians, [9] the inhabitants of Ugarit (Ras Shamra), [10] perhaps

[1] This translation is contested. Others translate : " my hand is for god, " that is to say, " like god " (E. Sellin, *Theologie*, p. 4), or : " my hand belongs to a god " (W. Baudissin, *Kyrios*, III, p. 17, note 2).

[2] Dillmann, Nestle, E. Dhorme, *L'évolution religieuse d'Israël*, I, pp. 338 ff.; W. E. Albright, *Archaeology*, p. 72.

[3] Nöldeke, E. Sellin, *Theologie*, p. 4; W. Eichrodt, *Theologie*, I, p. 86; J. Hehn, *Die biblische und die babylonische Gottesidee*, pp. 200-213.

[4] P. de Lagarde, M.-J. Lagrange, *ERS*, pp. 79-81; O. Procksch, *Theologie*, p. 444.

[5] M. J. Lagrange, *ERS*, pp. 78 ff.

[6] J. Hehn, *op. cit.*, pp. 150 ff.

[7] Inscriptions of Hadad (1. 2) and of Panammu (1. 22), *ERS*, pp. 493-495.

[8] Inscriptions from southern Arabia cited by D. Nielsen, *Handbuch der altarabischen Altertumskunde*, Copenhagen 1927, I, p. 218.

[9] Inscription found at Oumm-el-ʿouâmîd (*Répertoire*, 504, 1), and the god Ἤλ or Ἦλος cited by Philo of Biblos (*Fragm. hist. gr.*, III, 570 b, 571 b, cited by W. Baudissin, *Kyrios*, III, p. 11).

[10] In Ugarit, El, the father of Baal and of Môt, heads the pantheon. He is " the king, the father of the years " (II *AB*, IV, 24, cf. Dn 7:9.10 : " The ancient of the days, " and Is 9:5 : " The father of eternity "), to whom belongs " the whole earth " (Canaan) and on whom all depends (cf. R. Dussaud, *Les découvertes*, p. 68).

also by the Accadians, [11] and in the Old Testament, where it frequently designates the one God. [12]

El is most often used in poetic language, sometimes as an appellative (for example, the God of thy father, Gn 49:25; the God who knows, 1 Sm 2:3; the jealous God, Ex 20:5; 34:14; Jos 24:19; another god, Ex 34:14; the just and succoring God, Is 45:21), sometimes as a designation for the one God (for example, Is 40:18; Ps 10:11.12; 16:1; 68:20). It can be identified in many theophoric names in every Semitic tongue: for example, *Yizreʿ-'êl* (may God sow), *Yišmaʿ-'êl* (may God hear), *Elî-'âb* ([my] God is father, Nm 1:9), *'Elî-hû* (He is [my] God, 1 Sm 1:1), *Elî-šâphât* (my God has judged, 2 Par 23:1), *Elî-šuʿa* (Eliseus, my God has helped), *Elî-melek* (Ru 1:2, my God is King, or Melek is [my] God [13]).

2. *El* is frequently accompanied by a determinative, the two words forming a composite name : *El-ʿôlâm* (Gn 21:33) is the ancient God or the eternal God who is adored at Bersabee; *El-rô'i* is the God who appears or sees me, that is to say, who looks at me benevolently (Gn 16:13); [14] *El Bethel* (Gn 35:7) is the God who manifested Himself at Bethel (Gn 28:12 ff.; 31:13). [15]

---

[11] The Accadians use the theophoric name *Ilu-ma-ilu* = Ilu (El) is god (W. Baudissin, *Kyrios*, III, p. 12); it is difficult to admit this interpretation : god is god, because it is pure tautology.

[12] The name *'Eli-'êl* = El is my god (1 Par 5:24; 8:20.22; 11:46.47) which can, strictly speaking, be interpreted " my god (protector) is god "; P. Lagrange (*ERS*, p. 71) translates Gn 46:3 : " I am El, the God of thy father "; Hehn (*op. cit.*, p. 190) : " I am the God (*hâ'êl* with the article), the God of thy father "; the presence of the article proves that here the noun is appellative.

[13] Cf. *Ili-milku* in the Amarna letters 286, 36. Accadian names formed with *ili* or *ilu* are frequent : for example *Ili-bani* (God is my creator); *Ili-ennam* (God has pity); *Ili-beli* (God is my lord). The same is true in Aramean : for example *Requb-el* (Requb is god); *Hazâh-'êl* (God sees, 4 Kgs 8:8); *Betû-'el* (Gn 22:22; cf. *Batti-ilu* in the Amarna letters 161, 20; 170, 5.28); *'Enî-'él* (God is my eye); *El-yâdâʿ* (God knows, 3 Kgs 11:23); *Tâbi-'êl* (Is 7:6, God is good; cf. *Tâb-ilu*, Assyrian). Arabic theophoric names signifying " El is bright, El shines, El rises, " suggest an astral god that is probably the lunar god; other names like " El remembers, El gave, El is lord, El is exalted, El hears, " indicate a lofty personal god who is well disposed (cf. W. Baudissin, *Kyrios*, III, pp. 292 ff.).

[14] A notice of an Egyptian official of the time of Menephta mentions the name of a Semite *Baʿal-roï* of Gaza in Palestine (*AOT*, p. 96).

[15] Others (Gressmann, Lewy, Dussaud) interpret : the god Bethel. Bethel is a divine name attested perhaps by Amos (5:5), certainly by the Ras Shamra texts (N. 14, 1.1, *Syria*, 1929, pp. 304-310), by a treaty concluded by Asarhaddon with the Baal of Tyre (681-669), by some theophoric names of the sixth century (Bethel knows, Bethel saves), by the Elephantine papyri, where Bethel is one of the divinities venerated by the Jewish colony, and by a Greek inscription of the third century A.D. found at Dura-Europos. It is not impossible for a place to bear the name of a god (cf. Gn 33:20; Ex 17:15; Jgs 6:24), (cf. A. Vincent, *La religion des Judéo-Araméens d'Eléphantine*, Paris 1937, pp. 562-582). However, the text of Gn 35:7 is not certain because the word El does not appear in the LXX. This reading, which eliminates

According to Ex 6:3 God made Himself known to the patriarchs under the name of *El Šadday* (cf. Gn 17:1; 28:3; 35:11; 43:14; 48:3). *Šadday* is a very old name (Gn 49:25; Nm 24:4.16) and occurs thirty-one times in the book of Job, where archaisms are freely used; it rarely appears in the other books of the Old Testament (Gn 49:25; Nm 24:4.16; Ru 1:20.21; Ps 68:15; 91:1; Is 13:6; Jl 1:15). The meaning of the word is uncertain. Several writers derive it from the root *šâdâd*, to be violent, and speak of the All-Powerful, as is done in certain passages of the LXX (παντοκράτωρ) and of the Vulgate (*omnipotens*).[16] Others derive it from the root *šdh*, to be damp, or from a verb meaning " to throw, " or finally from an Accadian word *šadù*, mountain, which also means " Lord, " " head, " and is applied to certain gods.[17] According to the last hypothesis *šadday* would mean the lofty God, the Most High, or the Lord, or perhaps the " God mountain, " that is to say, the secure refuge, just as He also is the rock (Dt 32:4; Ps 18:32).

EL-'ELYON is God most high.[18] According to Gn 14:8-20, the Canaanite king of Salem, Melchisedech, was priest of *El 'elyôn.* The most high God, who created the sun and earth, was honored at Salem (which Jewish tradition identifies with Jerusalem) before the Hebrews occupied Canaan. A God Elyon was known in Canaan[19] and in Phoenicia.[20] Originally God seems to have been called " most high "

---

the God of Bethel or the god Bethel, is preferred by P. Lagrange (*ERS*, p. 81, n. 2) and by O. Eissfeldt (" Der Gott Bethel, " *ARW*, 28 (1930), p. 9). " I am the God of Bethel " (Gn 31:13 : *hâ'êl*) is read by the LXX and the Targums : " I am the God who appeared to thee at Bethel. " This reading seems preferable to that of the *M.T.* because *hâ-'êl Bethel* is not correct.

[16] In other cases the LXX translate ὁ Κύριος, ὁ Θεός μου, ἱκανός, and once ὁ τὰ πάντα ποιήσας. The Vulgate is more consistent. The Syriac version most frequently interprets : God or the Powerful One (cf. F. Zorell, " Der Gottesname Saddai in den alten Uebersetzungen, " *Bb*, 8 (1927), pp. 215-219.

[17] J. Hehn, *Die biblische und die babylonische Gottesidee*, pp. 265-271; E. Sellin, *Theologie*, p. 5; G. R. Driver, in *The People and the Book*, Oxford 1925, p. 91; E. Burrows (*JThS* [1940], pp. 152-161) interprets *El Shaddai* in the sense of : God of the mountain, that is to say, God of the western country, *amurru*, according to the Babylonian meaning.

[18] The word *'elyôn* means " high, " as in the expressions : the upper door (4 Kgs 15:35), the upper pool (Is 7:3). *'Elyôn 'al* means " higher than " or " raised above " (Dt 26:19; 28:1). It is also the proper name of a Phoenician god (F. W. Albright, *JBL*, 14 [1935], pp. 180 ff.).

[19] If the Most High can be identified with " the Lord of the gods " invoked in a letter found at Ta'anach (*AOT*, p. 371, IId); the Moabite diviner Balaam is called " he who knows what 'Elyon knows " (Nm 24:16, where 'Elyon is parallel to Élohim and to Šadday).

[20] He is mentioned after Hadad and 'El in an eighth century B.C. Aramaean inscription that comes from the neighborhood of Aleppo and is published by P. S. Ronzevalle (*Mélanges de L'Université Saint-Joseph*, 15, p. 241, reproduced in *ZAW*, 50 [1932], p. 182), and by Philo of Byblos (Eus. *Praep. ev.*, 1, 10), who makes Elioun, called Hypsistos, the father of Phoenician gods, later supplanted by

because He dwelt in the heights of heaven (cf. Is 14:14,[21] because He is the Lord of heaven[22] or the God of heaven (Ezr 1:2; 5:11.12),[23] rather than because He was the highest of all gods (cf. Ps 97:9). In the Old Testament, the God of Israel is also called *'elyôn*, El 'elyôn (Ps 78:35), Elohim 'elyôn (Ps 57:3; 78:56), Yahweh 'elyôn (Ps 47:3), that is to say, the most high God, or most high Yahweh, or merely 'Elyôn, the Most High (Nm 24:16; Ps 18:14; 21:8; 46:5; 50:14; 73:11; ὕψίστος Sir 41:4; Wis 6:3, etc.), because " He is raised above the whole earth " (Ps 83:19; 97:9) and " above all the gods " (Ps 97:9). The word expresses the transcendence of the one God, although the old idea that He dwells in the heights of heaven is not altogether lacking (cf. Is 14:14; Ps 18:14), since Yahweh is also the " God of the heights of heaven " (Mi 6:6; cf. Ps 102:20; 2 Sm 22:17; Ps 18:17). To designate the one God, the Jews of the diaspora willingly made use of the name Hypsistos (the Most High), a term frequently employed in the Hellenistic world, especially in Syria and Asia Minor, where it designated the supreme master of the world, who dwelt in higher, heavenly spheres where he directed the movement of the stars and in this way controlled earthly events.[24]

3. ELOÂH is probably a derived form of *'êl* or *îl*. It is found in Hebrew, in Aramean *('élâh)*, in the Ras Shamra and North Arabic dialects (*al-ilâh :* Allah), but rarely in the dialects of southern Arabia or Accadian. The word *Éloâh* is used only 57 times in the Old Testament. In the book of Job it appears 41 times. All other cases are either in passages of poetry or recent prose. It is a synonym for *'El* and is sometimes an appellative (Is 44:8), more often it is the name of the one God. In Ugarit it seems to designate a god who is distinct from *'El*.

---

one of his descendants, Kronos (El) (cf. *ERS*, pp. 422 ff.). He was probably known at Ugarit (cf. *RB* [1949], p. 880). As for the god 'Elyon in Phoenicia, cf. R. Dussaud, in E. Dhorme, *Les religions de Babylonie et d'Assyrie*, Paris 1949², p. 360. As for Hypsistos, cf. F. Cumont, " Hypsistos, " *RE*, IX, pp. 444-448.

[21] Cf. the Babylonian expression " the Lord in heaven, " that is to say, " the Lord who reigns in heaven. "

[22] The cult of the " Lord of heaven " (Baàlšamên) is attested in Phoenicia in the twelfth and eleventh century B.C. (inscription of Jehimilk, *RB* [1930], pp. 321-331, where he holds the first place before the Ba'al of Byblos), in Syria (inscription of Zakir, king of Hamath, *AOT*, pp. 443 ff.), at Tyre (treaty of Asarhadon with Ba'al of Tyre, cited by A. Vincent, *op. cit.*, p. 122, n. 3), and in many more recent Punic and Aramean inscriptions (cf. O. Eissfeldt, " Ba'alssamên und Jahwe, " *ZAW* (1939), pp. 1-31; A. Vincent, *op. cit.*, pp. 120 ff., identifies Ba'alšamên with El Elyon).

[23] " The God of heaven " is the name by which the Jews of Elephantine designate Yahweh when they address the Persian authorities (similarly Ezr 5:11.12) (cf. A. Vincent, *op. cit.*, pp. 102 ff.).

[24] Cf. F. Cumont, *op. cit.*, p. 446.

4. ÉLOHÎM is the word most often used in the Old Testament to designate God (about 2,000 times). Its etymology is as uncertain as is that of *'êl*. Many derive it from *'êl* and explain it as a plural form which in Hebrew replaced the regular form *'êlim*.[25] Others think of the verb *'âlâh* which in Arabic signifies " to revere, " " to fear. "

The word *'élôhîm* frequently retains its plural meaning. In these cases it signifies a plurality of gods (for example, Ex 18:11; 12:12; 34:15; Dt 10:17; Jgs 9:9.13) and is followed by a predicate or by an apposition in the plural (for example, Ex 18:11; Dt 6:14). But more often it is used as a singular, either to designate a specific god, for example Chamos, the Élohîm of the Moabites (Jgs 11:24), Ištar of Sidon (3 Kgs 11:5), Ba'al Zebul of Accaron (4 Kgs 1:2), or the one God (with the article, for example, Gn 5:22; 6:9.11; 17:18; without the article as a proper noun, for example, Gn 1:1 ff.; 9:27; Am 4:11).[26] Ordinarily it is accompanied by an apposition or by a verb in the singular (for example, Ps 7:10; 4 Kgs 19:4; Gn 1:1 ff.; Jgs 11:24), rarely by an apposition or by a verb in the plural (Gn 20:13; 31:53; 35:7; 2 Sm 7:23; Dt 5:23; Jos 24:19).[27]

D. Nielsen[28] believes that *'élôhîm* originally is not a plural, but the noun *'élâh* with mimation, that is to say, with the addition of an m. Examples of this are often found in Arabic, especially in divine names of one syllable, and sometimes in the Ras Shamra texts. This hypothesis has won few supporters. Most philologists believe that *'élôhîm* was primitively a plural. Many say that it is a vestige of the polytheism of the ancient Hebrews: gradually they fused the many local divinities which they adored into one single god and came to use the plural as a singular to designate the unique God.[29] Yet the use of a plural to designate one god is not peculiar to the Hebrews; it is to be found in Canaan and in Phoenicia before the Israelite conquest, as the Amarna letters and the Ras Shamra texts prove. The lunar

---

[25] The plural *'êlîm* is found only in Ex 15:11; Dn 11:36. In Ps 29:1; 89:7 the expression *běnêy 'êlîm* should be understood as " sons of God, " just like *běnêy 'élôhîm* (cf. *Ges. B*, p. 37).

[26] The same is true of the Ras Shamra texts, where the word *'lhm* is used as the proper name of a specified god (Bauer, " Die Gottheiten, " *ZAW* [1933], p. 85). In Phoenicia, the plural *'êlîm* also serves as a generic noun designating the divinity, as *'êlîm* Nergal signifies the god Nergal (Bauer, *ibid.*).

[27] In several of these cases certain manuscripts have the verbs in the singular; *Ges. B* (p. 40) admits the plural is often a copyist's error.

[28] *Ras Shamra Mythologie*, pp. 18 ff. In the same way *'lm* would be *'êl* with mimation, that is to say, an m has been added which primitively had the value of a determinate article but whose meaning has been lost.

[29] R. Smend, *Lehrbuch*, p. 30, n. 4; E. Meyer, *Die Israeliten und ihre Nachbarstämme*, Halle 1906, p. 211, n. 1.

god Sin was called *ilani ša ilani,* "the gods of the gods," that is to say, the supreme god, and the Canaanite vassals of the king of Egypt spoke of Pharao as "their gods."[30] This plural is explained as an abstract-plural expressing a generic concept,[31] or better, a plural of intensity signifying that the individual so designated possesses to a high degree the specific characteristics of the species.[32] The Hebrews called Elohim the God who possesses in Himself alone all the characteristics of divinity. If they adopted this custom from the Canaanites,[33] perhaps they may have done so to contrast the one God who concentrates within Himself all that is divine with the multiple gods of the other nations. That is why the Old Testament mainly uses the appellative Elohim to designate the one God: "Yahweh is the God (*hâ'ělôhîm,* with the article) and there is no other like Him" (Dt 4:35; cf. Is 46:9). And because this word ordinarily designates the only true God, it is very often used without an article as a proper name (for example, Gn 1).

In some texts the word has a weakened meaning and is applied either to beings who belong to the divine sphere, to the *běnêy 'ělôhîm,* the sons of God, that is to say, the angels (Jb 1:6; 2:1), or on the contrary to the inhabitants of the lower world, the dead (1 Sm 28:13), or to men who possess divine power, like Moses (Ex 4:16; 7:1; cf. Nm 11:17.25), the king (Ps 45:7; Za 12:8; cf. 2 Sm 14:17; 3 Kgs 3:28), the judges (Ps 82:6; cf. Ex 18:15-19; 2 Sm 16:23). The same is true of the expression *'îš hâ 'ělôhîm* which is translated by "man of God," but designates a wonder-worker, for example: a prophet (1 Sm 2:27; 9:6; 3 Kgs 13:1 ff.; 17:18); the same is also true in the phrases "mountain of El" (Ps 36:7), "cedars of El" (Ps 80:11), "army of Elohim" (1 Par 12:23), which signify a high mountain, powerful cedars, a powerful army.

5. YAHWEH is the proper name of the God of Israel. The complete form is composed of four consonants *Y h w h.* It is used almost exclusively in the Old Testament and is attested in the ninth century B.C. by the inscription of Mesha, King of Moab.[34] The

---

[30] *Ilania;* Amarna letters 141, 2.10.16.32.37; 144, 2.6.8, etc.; cf. above n. 26, where Phoenician examples are indicated.

[31] In Hebrew the abstract concept is ordinarily expressed by the plural of the concrete word.

[32] In the same way the plurals *bě'âlîm, 'ădônîm* strengthen the idea of lordship, *qědôsîm,* that of holiness (Prv 9:10, where the word is parallel to Yahweh), *'elyônîm,* that of elevation (Dn 7:18, where the word designates the Most High; nevertheless the *qěrěy* is in the singular).

[33] This is the opinion of Bauer (*op. cit.,* p. 85) and Eichrodt, *Theologie,* I, p. 90.

[34] Text and translation is given by P. Lagrange in *DB,* IV, cols. 1014-1021; and in *AOT,* pp. 440-442.

form *Y h w* (yâhû or yâhô) is found as the second part of several theophoric names, such as *yĕšâ 'yâhû* (Isaias), *'Uzziyâhû* (Osias), whereas *Y h w* alone occurs in the Elephantine papyri, the Lachish letters (about 600 B.C.), on ostraca, and in some magic Greek texts as well as in others ('Ιαώ); [35] under the form *Yĕhô*, as the first part of proper names, for example *yĕhôyâkîn*. The form *Yw* (Yô) appears only in proper names, mostly in the beginning, for example *Yôkebed* (Ex 6:20), *Yôyâkîn*, rarely at the end, for example *'Aḥyô* (1 Par 8:14-31 and on ostraca). Finally the form *Y h* (Yâh) is found in several theophoric names, for example *'Abîyâh*, and used alone in several poetic texts (Ex 15:2) and some cultic formulas, such as *Hallĕlû Yâh* (praise Yâh; Ps 104:35; 106:1). Several philologists believe that *Y h w h* is the primitive form and the other forms are abbreviations; [36] other authors, on the contrary, think that it is derived from *Yh* or from *Yw*. [37]

The sacred tetragram *Y h w h* is pronounced Yahweh, according to the Greek transcriptions 'Ιαβέ, [38] 'Ιαουέ, 'Ιαυαί. [39] This is the general opinion. [40] The short form *Y a w*, pointed Jĕhû or Jĕhô by the Massoretes gave rise to the Greek transcriptions 'Ιαύ [41] and 'Ιευώ. [42] The pronunciation " Jehovah " dates from the thirteenth century and was generally adopted by Christians from the sixteenh century onward. It is certainly incorrect and was never used by the Jews. It is the result of Massoretic pointing, which placed the vowels of the word Adonay beneath the consonants of the sacred tetragram, because the Jews, out of respect, did not pronounce the divine name and in its place substituted the word Adonay, the Lord.

The etymology of the word is disputed. Some derive it from the root *hwh*, to fall, [43] or from *hwy*, to breathe, [44] thinking that primitively Yahweh was a god of the storm who made the wind blow and the lightning fall. Others are of the opinion that *Yâh* was

---

[35] Diod. of Sicily, *Hist.*, I, 94; Orig., *Joh.*, II.

[36] J. Hehn, *Die biblische un die babylonische Gottesidee*, pp. 228 ff.; A. Van, Hoonacker, *Une communauté judéo-araméenne à Eléphantine*, (*Schweich Lectures*) London 1915, pp. 67-73; W. Eichrodt, *Theologie*, I, pp. 92 ff.; G. R. Driver, *The Original Form*, pp. 23 ff.

[37] M. Noth, *op. cit.*, pp. 101-104; H. Bauer, *op. cit.*, p. 93.

[38] Theodoret, *Quaestiones*. 15 *in Ex.;* Epiphanius, 50, I; 40, I; Photius, *Ep.* 162; Jerome, *In Ps* 8.

[39] Clement of Alexandria, *Strom.*, V, 6, 34.

[40] A. L. Williams, *The Tetragrammaton*, on the contrary, claims that it was pronounced Yahwôh.

[41] Diod. of Sicily, Origen, Theodoret, Macrobius and certain magic texts. Cf. A. Vincent, *op. cit.*, pp. 39 ff.

[42] Porphyry.

[43] De Lagarde, B. Stade (*Gesch.*, I, p. 429).

[44] Ewald, Wellhausen.

originally an exclamation [45] by which the god was acclaimed during services. [46] Still others hold that the form *hw* was the pronoun *hû* of the third person singular: "he" or "to him." [47]

The account of Ex 3:14 ff. explains the name of Yahweh by the verb "to be" (in Hebrew *hyh*, or according to the ancient form *hwh*). When Moses asked the name of the God who was revealing Himself to him, God answered: "I am who I am," literally: "I shall be who I shall be," *'ehyeh 'ašer 'ehyeh*. And He said: "Thus shall you say to the Israelites: I am (or: I shall be, *'ehyeh*) sends me to you... Yahweh, the God of your fathers, the God of Abraham, the God of Isaac, the God of Jacob sends me to you. This is My name forever, this is My title for all generations." From this text it is clear that the divine name of Yahweh signifies: He is. [48] The verb "to be" is in the first person because Yahweh cannot say: "He is." God's answer is not a refusal to give His name. [49] In fact, when a similar refusal is expressed (Gn 32:30; Jgs 13:17.18), this is done in clearer terms. There is nothing in the context to suggest that the answer is evasive. God shows, in declaring His name, that He has nothing to fear from magic practices [50] and that He transcends the world. [51]

The words "I am who I am" must be understood in the light of analogous formulas, placed on God's lips [52]: "I say what I say" (Ez 12:25) and "I will show favor to whom I will show favor" (Ex 33:19); they insist on the reality [53] or rather on the efficacy and sovereign independence of the existence, of the word, and of the grace of God. [54] The verb *hyh* has the meaning of "to become,"

---

[45] The exclamation *Yâ* is common to all Semitic tongues.

[46] G. R. Driver, *The Original Form*, p. 24 and elsewhere.

[47] M. Buber-F. Rosenzweig, *Die Schrift*, II, p. 15; S. Mowinckel, cited by R. Otto, *Das Heilige*, 1932, pp. 326 ff.

[48] Cf. E. Dhorme, *RHR* (1952), pp. 5 ff.; he concludes that the name of Yahweh is the third person of the Canaanite verb *hwh* = to be, to exist, in the *Qal* form.

[49] As Volz, Gressmann, Gunkel, Balscheit, Köhler claim; A. M. Dubarle, *RScPT* (1951), pp. 11 ff. G. Lambert (*op. cit.*, *NRTh* [1952], p. 915) supports this opinion.

[50] According to the opinion of the ancients, knowledge of the name gives power over the holder of the name. That is why the name of the gods is kept secret in Egypt and elsewhere (cf. A. Erman-H. Ranke, *Aegypten und ägyptisches Leben im Altertum*, Tübingen 1923, p. 302).

[51] J. Hempel, *Gott und Mensch im A.T.*, Stuttgart 1936, p. 220.

[52] This is not true of any of the analogous formulas which, according to Dubarle *(op. cit.)*, indicate indetermination.

[53] J. Hänel, *Die Religion der Heiligkeit*, Gütersloh 1931, pp. 196 ff. Cf. T. C. Vriezen, *Festschrift Bertholet*, p. 498; he rightly insists on the intensive nuance in these expressions.

[54] O. Grether, *Name und Wort Gottes*, pp. 6 ff.; M. Buber (*Königtum Gottes*, Berlin 1932, p. 84) claims that the verb "to be" has only a copulative sense, never an existential sense; but he is wrong.

" to be in activity, " a meaning that is here strengthened by the imperfect which signifies that the action is not concluded; it expresses an existence that manifests itself actively, an operative being [55] rather than the absolute being. [56] The name of God must, according to the context, justify the mission to deliver Israel that was given to Moses as well as the promise of divine assistance that he received (" I shall be with you, " Ex 3:9-12); it was intended to remove the people's doubts, because they wished to know the name of the God who sent Moses so as to be sure that this God would be capable of achieving this deliverance. This name then must express the efficacy of the being of God the liberator: He who sends Moses is called " He is " (or " He will be "), Yahweh, that is to say, He who effectively manifests His existence. By the prodigies He will perform, " He will be recognized as Yahweh " (Ex 7:5; 9:14; 14:4.18; cf. Ez 13:23; 22:16; 25:11; 28:26). He is and acts with absolute liberty: " He is who He is. "

This interpretation is a development of the interpretation that stresses only the constancy of the aid and the fidelity of Yahweh toward His people; [57] this idea alone, which really is implied in the text, does not give the full content of the words of Ex 3:14.

Others read the word *hyh* as the causative form and translate: " I shall cause to be what I shall cause to be "; they conclude that Yahweh signifies the Creator. [58] But the word *hyh* is never used in the causative form. [59] Still others translate: " I shall be what I was, " which will give Yahweh the meaning of the Eternal. This interpretation is not valid: the verb in both cases is in the imperfect and each time must be translated by the same tense. Finally there are others [60] who understand the expression just as the LXX did; [61] they understand the verb " to be " as meaning " the absolute being. " From this they deduce that the words of Ex 3:14 reveal God's aseity: Yahweh would

---

[55] Cf. " I will be with you " (Ex 3:12).

[56] As the LXX have translated it: ἐγώ εἰμι ὁ ὤν... ὁ ὢν ἀπεσταλκέν με. This interpretation gives a philosophical nuance that is foreign to the Hebrew words and clouds the main idea conveyed by the expression: " I am who I am, " namely the efficacy and sovereign independence of the being of God.

[57] This interpretation is proposed by Davidson (*Theology*, pp. 45 ff.), J. Hehn (*op. cit.*, pp. 214 ff.), S. R. Driver (*The Book of Exodus*, Cambridge 1911, pp. 40 ff.), E. Sellin (*Theol.*, p. 8), W. Eichrodt (*Theologie*, I, p. 93), M. Buber, *Königtum Gottes*, Berlin 1932, p. 84.

[58] W. F. Albright, *From the Stone Age to Christianity*, Baltimore 1946, p. 198; J. Obermann, *op. cit.*

[59] Cf. H. Bauer, *ZAW* (1933), p. 93, n. 7.

[60] P. Karge, *Geschichte des Bundesgedankens im A. T.*, Münster 1909, p. 154; F. Ceuppens, *Theologia Biblica*, I, pp. 25 ff.; P. Heinisch, *Theologie*, pp. 19 ff.

[61] It seems that the Greek book of Wisdom gives the same interpration since it calls God τὸν ὄντα" (Wis 13:1).

mean : " He who is by Himself, " in opposition to every being that does not exist by itself and in opposition to the gods of the nations who are nothingness. This explanation attributes to the author of the account a philosophical view that is entirely foreign to the ancient Hebrews, and wrongly supposes that the verb *hyh* signifies the absolute being, whereas it expresses the active manifestation of existence. Besides, it is completely incompatible with the meaning of the imperfect, which indicates an action on the way of becoming.

The question of the antiquity of Yahweh's name is equally controversial : was it unknown before Moses, as the account implies in Ex 3:13-14 (this account is attributed to the Elohist) and as is affirmed in Ex 6:3 (this verse is attributed to the Sacerdotal Code)? Some prophets seem to support this hypothesis, especially Osee (12:10; 13:4) : " I am the Lord, your God, since the land of Egypt. " On the other hand, the accounts attributed to the Yahwist suppose that Yahweh was adored by the patriarchs (Gn 12:8; 13:4.18, etc.), even before the deluge by Enos, to whom the institution of the cult of Yahweh seems to have been attributed (Gn 4:26). In favor of this opinion may be alleged certain theophoric names belonging to the time before Moses : Yokebed, Moses' mother (Ex 6:20; Yo, that is to say, Yahweh is glory, or Yahweh is powerful), Abiyah (Yah is [my] father, 1 Par 7:8), Aḥiyah (Yah is [my] brother, 1 Par 2:25), and others. If the primitive form of the divine name is *Yhw* or *Yah*, it may be admitted that under this name, whose primitive meaning may have been lost, and before the time of Moses, the ancient Hebrews, or at least the tribe of Levi, to which Moses belonged, [62] adored Yahweh, whom they identified with El, Elohim, El Šadday. This hypothesis agrees with the Elohist account of Ex 3:13-15, which insists on the identity of God who manifested Himself to Moses and to the fathers, and therefore supposes that this God was not unknown to them. What God reveals is the meaning of the old name that has been modified to the form of Yahweh. Under this new form, enriched with a new meaning, God had not made Himself known to the ancestors (Ex 6:3 P). Beginning with Moses, or, as Osee said (12:10; 13:4), " since the land of Egypt, " Yahweh has become the God of Israel, the God of the covenant (Ex 24:3-8 E), the center of all the Israelite tribes (cf. Ex 17:15). [63]

---

[62] Cf. O. Procksch, *Theologie*, I, p. 75.

[63] This opinion is accepted by Lagrange (*RB* [1903], pp. 310 ff.), J. Hehn (*op. cit.*, pp. 229 ff.), A. Van Hoonacker (*Une communauté*, pp. 67 ff.), A. Vincent (*op. cit.*, pp. 27 ff.), E. König (*Theologie*, p. 140), W. Eichrodt (*Theologie*, I, p. 93). The contrary opinion is supported by F. Ceuppens (*op. cit.*, I, pp. 30 ff.) and P. Heinisch (*op. cit.*, pp. 16 ff.).

It is then probable that before Moses the divine name, at least in its shortened form (Yhw, Yahû or Yahô, or Jah), was known by some Hebrews or by some clans, for example, by the tribe of Levi, to which Moses belonged (Ex 2:1; 6:20). But was it also known by other Semites? Several authors declare that Jahû was adored in Babylon, Arabia, Ugarit, Canaan and among the Madianites (or Kenites).[64] They base this conclusion on the theophoric names which are found in Babylonia from the twentieth century before Christ. The element *Iau (Iaum, Iawi* or *Ia)*, at any rate, since it is never accompanied by the divine determinative, is not the proper name of a god, but a common name meaning "someone" and replaces a divine name or rather a verbal form[65] corresponding to that of the imperfect *hwh* (to be).[66] Theophoric names transmitted by Accadian documents, since the ninth century, are very probably Israelite names; even Yau-bidi, King of Hamat in Syria, could be a Hebrew.[67] The evidence found in Arabia and Canaan is not certain[68] and it has not been proved that the Ras Shamra documents contain the name of a god Yw.[69] The claim for a Madianite (or Kenite) origin of the cult of Yahweh is far from being proved. If it is true that Moses was influenced by the Madianite milieu when he lived in the desert, especially by his father-in-law, the Madianite priest (Ex 18:1 or Kenite, Jgs 1:16; 4:11), Jethro (Ex 18:13 ff.), and that later the descendants of the Madianites, allied to Israel, showed themselves to be Yahweh's fervent servants (Jos 14:6-12; 4 Kgs 10:15 ff.), the text of Ex 18:7-12 does not prove that they were such before Moses. Ex 18:11 rather suggests that Jethro knew Yahweh through the account Moses gave of the wonders worked by Yahweh for the deliverance of Israel. In fact it states: "Now I know that the Lord is a deity great beyond

---

[64] This is affirmed with slightly different nuances by Lagrange *(loc. cit.)*, E. König (*Theol.*, p. 140), S. Landersdorfer *(op. cit.)*, A. Vicent (*op. cit.*, pp. 27 ff.), who assembled the principal proofs, and other authors. The Madianite (or Kenite) origin of the cult of Yahweh is supported by C. P. Tiele (*Vergelijkende Geschiedenis der Egyptische en Mesopotamische Godsdiensten*, 1869, p. 588), B. Stade, F. Delitzsch, T. K. Cheyne, K. Budde, H. Gressmann, J. Meinhold, G. Beer, A. Vincent, H. H. Rowley (*From Joseph to Joshua*, London 1950, pp. 150 ff.). It is opposed by Lagrange, E. König, P. Heinisch, F. Ceuppens, R. Kittel, O. Procksch (*Theologie*, pp. 75 ff.), T. J. Meek (*Hebrew Origins*, London 1936, pp. 87 ff.), Buber (*Moses*, London 1957, pp. 94 ff.).

[65] J. Hehn, *op. cit.*, p. 243; M. Noth, *op. cit.*, pp. 108 ff.

[66] E. Dhorme (*art. cit.*, p. 16) sees in this the verbal form signifying "to be": Ya-wi-ilu = God exists (in a Mari tablet: Ya-wi-um = he exists).

[67] G. R. Driver, *The Original Form*, pp. 8 ff.; M. Noth, *op. cit.*, pp. 110 ff.

[68] The Canaanite name *Aḫi-Yami* (= *Aḫi-yah*, Yah is my brother), could be read *Aḫi-yawi*. Does Betia, a locality mentioned in an Egyptian document (about 1500), represent Beth-yah (= house of Yah)? Did Mori-yâh designate the hill of the temple of Jerusalem before the Israelite conquest?

[69] Cf. the advanced study of R. de Langhe (*EThL* (1942), pp. 91-101).

any other," because He has overcome the gods of Egypt. That is why he blessed Yahweh and offered sacrifices in which Aaron and the elders of Israel took part. Perhaps the words: "He offered sacrifices to Elohim" (Ex 18:12) suggest that he himself did not adore Yahweh, but God. If he used the word Yahweh when speaking to Moses, it may be that he did so out of courtesy to his son-in-law who had just made known to him the power of the God of Israel. This does not prove that he himself adored Yahweh. [70] Granted that the unification of the tribes of Israel had been made around Yahweh (cf. Ex 17:15), if Yahweh had been originally the god of the Madianites-Kenites, these tribes would have held a more important place in the confederation. They were, on the contrary, merely allies and, so to speak, subjects of Israel. It is, therefore, most improbable that Moses received from them their god.

Evidence so far presented does not prove the existence of a cult of Yahweh (or of Yah, Yahû), or of the knowledge of the divine name outside and independent of Israel. In the light of this evidence the hypothesis enjoys only a certain measure of probability. [71]

6. YAHWEH ṢEBA'OTH. The word *ṣâbâ'* (plural *ṣĕbâ'ôth*) means army (for example, Jgs 8:6; 9:29; 2 Sm 8:16; in the plural Dt 20:9; 3 Kgs 2:5), or troop, organized group (Nm 2:9.15). The tribes of Israel are often called "the armies of Israel" (for example, Ex 6:26; 12:17.51; Nm 1:3.52) and sometimes "the armies of Yahweh" (Ex 12:41; 7:4).

The expressions *Yahweh Ṣĕbâ'ôth* (217 times), *haṣṣĕbâ'ôth* (once), *Yahweh 'Élôhêy Ṣĕbâ'ôth* (11 times), *haṣṣĕbâ'ôth* (3 times), *Yahweh Ṣĕbâ'ôth 'Élôhêy Yśrâ'êl* (36 times), *'Élôhêy Ṣĕbâ'ôth* (9 times), *Yahweh 'Élôhîm Ṣĕbâ'ôth* (5 times), lastly *Yahweh 'Élôhêy Ṣĕbâ'ôth 'Élôhêy Yśrâ'êl* (twice) are very often found in the prophets, with the exception of Ezechiel, Isaias 56-66, Joel, Abdias, Jonas, Daniel, in the books of Samuel (11 times), in Kings (8 times), 1 Par (3 times) and in Psalms (15 times); never in the Pentateuch, Josue, Judges, Ruth, Proverbs, Job, Canticle of Canticles, Lamentations, Ecclesiastes, Esther, 2 Paralipomena, Esdras and Nehemias.

According to certain exegetes the expression *Yahweh Ṣĕbâ'ôth* is the primitive form and *Ṣĕbâ'ôth* is a proper name in apposition

---

[70] Similarly the Assyrian king, when he spoke to the besieged Hebrews of Jerusalem, declared that it was according to Yahweh's will that he had marched against the city (4 Kgs 18:25). These words do not prove that he adored Yahweh. Earlier than this, Mesa, the Moabite king, had boasted that he had carried off objects belonging to Yahweh.

[71] Cf. P. Heinisch, *Theologie*, p. 16.

with Yahweh.[72] But this hypothesis does not explain the origin of the expression *Yahweh 'Élôhêy Ṣĕbâ'ôth* which can only mean the God of the *ṣĕbâ'ôth*. How could a proper name become the name of a thing of which Yahweh is the God?[73] It must therefore be admitted that *Yahweh 'Élôhêy ṣĕbâ'ôth* is the primitive expression that designates Yahweh as the God of armies *(ṣĕbâ'ôth)* : from which has been derived by way of abbreviation, *Yahweh Ṣĕbâ'ôth.* The next question then is : to what armies is reference made—the armies of Israel, celestial armies, or those constituted by the stars?[74]

According to the first opinion,[75] the expression *Yahweh Ṣĕbâ'ôth*, or *Yahweh 'Élôhêy Ṣĕbâ'ôth* originally designated Yahweh as the warrior god (cf. Ex 15:3; 1 Sm 17:47; Nm 21:14). In fact *Yahweh Ṣĕbâ'ôth* is closely connected with the ark (1 Sm 4:3.5.7 ff.; 2 Sm 6:2), the sacred palladium, that was carried into battle (1 Sm 4:3 ff.; 2 Sm 11:11; 15:24) as the symbol or throne of Yahweh who was directing the campaign (1 Sm 15:2; 17:45; 2 Sm 5:10; 6:18). The *ṣĕbâ'ôth*, therefore, designate the armies of Israel that Yahweh commands: *Yahweh Ṣĕbâ'ôth* is " the God of Israel's batallions " (1 Sm 17:45) and these are " the armies of Yahweh " (Ex 7:4; 12:41). But this hypothesis does not explain why the primitive meaning is almost nowhere to be found among the prophets, yet they use the term 247 times. It is also most unlikely that, to designate Yahweh as the supreme master of nations and of the universe, the prophets would have chosen a term whose primitive meaning was so clearly nationalistic. Besides it is truly astonishing that the expression is never used in the very accounts of " the wars of Yahweh, " that is to say, the wars fought in the conquest of Canaan.

Others[76] believe that the word *ṣĕbâ'ôth* originally designated the armies of celestial beings that surround Yahweh. This opinion is based on the passages that mention Yahweh's heavenly hosts (Jos 5:13-16; Gn 32:2.3; 3 Kgs 22:19; 2 Par 18:18). But this does not seem very probable because wherever there is question of the heavenly army, the term *ṣâbâ'* is in the singular (Jos 5:14; 3 Kgs 22:19; 2 Par 18:18; Ps 148:2; cf. Jb 1:6; 2:1; 38:7; Dn 7:10).

---

[72] J. K. Cheyne, *The Two Religions of Israel*, p. 190.

[73] Cf. L. Köhler, *Theologie*, p. 32.

[74] Demons have been considered in this connection (Wellhausen, Schwally), but demons play almost no role in the O. T.; moreover, it is not likely that the prophets could have adopted and used with preference an expression designating Yahweh as the head of the demons.

[75] J. G. Herder, E. Schrader especially, cited by E. Kautzsch (*Theologie*, pp. 78 ff; " Sebaoth " in *PRE*, 17, pp. 423 ff.).

[76] Borchert, in *Theologische Studien und Kritiken*, 1896, pp. 619 ff.; G. Westphal, " Jahwes' Wohnstätte, " *BZAW*, 15, Giessen 1908, pp. 262-264.

The same objection opposes Köhler's interpretation.[77] To him *ṣĕbâ'ôth* means the army of stars (cf. Jgs 5:20). This army is always given in the singular (Dt 4:19; 17:3; 4 Kgs 17:16; Jb 38:7; Jer 8:2; Is 40:26, etc.). Besides, since the worship of astral divinities became popular in Israel after the time of Amos and Osee, it is hardly probable that these prophets would use a term derived from the polemic against the stars adored as gods in the east.

It seems, then, that from the beginning *ṣĕbâ'ôth* designate all the heavenly and earthly forces serving Yahweh and fighting for Him (cf. Jgs 5:20; Ps 18:8-16; Jos 10:10-15; Jb 38:7) and which are called in Ps 103:21 "His armies" (cf. v. 22 and Gn 2:1). This interpretation[78] is accepted by the LXX who translate Κύριος τῶν δυναμέων or παντοκράτωρ, and it expresses better the universal meaning given this term by the prophets who use it constantly to designate Yahweh as the sovereign master of heaven and earth (for example, Is 6:3; 9:18; 10:16.23.26.33; 51:15; 54:5; Am 4:13; 5:27; 6:8.14; 9:5.6; Jer 31:35) and who assume that this meaning is known to their hearers. This explains how the term was applied later to the almighty God who led Israel's armies in war. The expression is a favorite one of Jeremias (77 times), Aggeus (14 times), Zachary (44 times, in addition to 9 times in Za 9-14), and Malachias (24 times), that is to say, by the prophets who had to fight against Babylon's astral religion. It is likely that this use is somewhat polemic: it expressed Yahweh's dominion over the elements of the world, and this included the stars, which are not gods but the subjects of the only God, Yahweh, who orders them as part of His armies (Is 40:26; 45:12).

7. MELEK, BAAL, ADÔN. These three terms express God's sovereignty, an idea that is basic in the ancient East, especially among the Semites.

a) MELEK (= king) is a divine epithet often found among all the Semites, as many theophoric names testify,[79] in which the word *m l k* is either predicate[80] or subject;[81] in the first case the word

---

[77] *Theologie*, p. 33.

[78] It is proposed by R. Smend, *Lehrbuch*, pp. 210 ff.; J. Wellhausen, *Die kleinen Propheten*, Berlin 1898³, p. 77; J. Hehn, *op. cit.*, pp. 250 ff.; W. Eichrodt, *Theologie*, I, p. 95; cf. B. N. Wambacq, *op. cit.*, p. 279.

[79] Cf. W. Baudissin, "Moloch," *PRE*, pp. 269-303; *id.*, *Kyrios*, III, pp. 44-52; 97-104; O. Eissfeldt, "Jahwe als König," *ZAW*, 46 (1928), pp. 81-105; M. Buber, *Königtum Gottes*, Berlin 1932, pp. 47 ff.

[80] For example *ili-milku* = El is king; *abi-milki* = my father (= the god) is king, in the Amarna letters 146, 2; 152, 2; 286, 36; cf. Abi-melek (Gn 20:2; Jgs 8:31, etc.), Eli-melek (Ru 1:2); the same name is also found in Arabia.

[81] For example *Abdi-milki* (Amarna 203, 3) = one in the service of Mlk; Ahi-milki or *Ahî-melek* (1 Sm 21:2, etc.) = brother of Melek; *Mlk-ytn* = Mlk has given (Phoenician), *Nathan-melek* (4 Kgs 23:11 = Mlk has given); many Arabic names, for example: Mlk saves, Mlk is exalted, Mlk is gracious, servant of Mlk.

is an appellative, in the second it is employed as a divine proper name, [82] or at least as an appellative replacing a divine name. [83] It is very probable that this divine epithet goes back to a time when the Semitic tribes were not yet united in kingdoms. The god was then looked upon as guide, counselor or tribal prince; later he became the king of the people or the city.

A god *M l k* is attested by the Sumerian tablets of Drehem (2400-2300 B.C.) under the form *Ma-al-ku-um*; [84] in southern Arabia, *Mlkn* (*m l k* with nunation = the King), in Assyria, *Ma-lik*, [85] among the Ammonites, *Milkôm* (*M l k* with mimation = the King); at Ugarit, *Mlkm* (*M l k* with mimation); [86] in Phoenicia, *Melkart*, " the *Mlk* (= King) of the city (Tyre), " and the *Mlk* of Astarte; [87] finally in Israel, *Môlek* (Moloch, LXX and Vulg.), which was probably Phoenician in origin, the god to whom children were offered in sacrifice [88] (Lv 18:21; 20:2-5; 4 Kgs 23:10; Jer 32:35).

Since the epithet *Melek*, meaning guide, prince, or counselor, is very old among the Semites, there is no possible reason for doubting that, from the days of Moses, Yahweh was acknowledged as supreme head of the tribes (cf. Nm 23:21; 24:7.8; Ex 15:18; Dt 33:5). It was for this reason that Gedeon refused the title of king (Jgs 8:23; cf. 1 Sm 8:7).

It is as head and protector of Israel that Yahweh is called Melek in the oldest texts (Nm 23:21; 24:7.8; Ex 15:18; Dt 33:5) and in

---

[82] There are many examples of appellatives becoming proper divine names: among others, Mlk (Mlkart = the king of the city, the god of Tyre), Ba'alat (= lady) designating the " Lady " of Byblos, Bel designating Marduk, Marna (= our Lord) which became the name of the god of Gaza.

[83] Appellatives, such as brother, father, uncle, are often used in theophoric names, as substitutes for a divine name; for example *Aḥi-ram* (Phoenician) = (my) brother (that is to say, the god) is exalted; *Abi-ram* (Ab-ram) = the father (= the god) is exalted.

[84] N. Schneider, " Melchom, das Scheusal der Ammoniter, " *Bb* (1937), pp. 337-343; *id.*, " Melchom, " *Bb* (1938), p. 204.

[85] Cf. R. de Vaux, *RB* (1936), p. 281, n. 2, citing P. Jensen, *ZA* (1934), pp. 235 ff.

[86] H. Bauer, *ZAW* (1933), p. 93; D. Nielsen, *Ras Shamra Mythologie*, pp. 20,43.

[87] R. de Vaux, *RB* (1936), p. 281.

[88] O. Eissfeldt (*Molk als Opferbegriff im Punischen und Hebräischen und das Ende des Gottes Moloch*, Halle 1935) claims that the term molek designates not a god but a votive sacrifice. Albright adopts this view (*JPOS* [1935], p. 344), yet he admits the existence of a god Malik (alternating with Muluk), to whom Accadian texts refer beginning in 3000 B.C. (*Archaeology and the Religion of Israel*, Baltimore 1946², pp. 162 ff.); W. von Soden (*ThLZ* [1936], pp. 45 ff.) and R. Dussaud (*Syria*, 1935, pp. 407 ff.) also hold this view. This view, however, is attacked by R. de Vaux (*RB* [1946], pp. 278-282), A. Bea (" Kinderopfer für Moloch oder für Jahwe?, " *Bb* [1937], pp. 95-107), N. Schneider (*Bb* [1937], pp. 337-343), E. Dhorme (*L'évolution religieuse d'Israël*, Bruxelles 1937, I, pp. 213 ff.), and A. van den Born (" Molek " in *BW*).

several theophoric names.[89] This idea is found in every epoch (Ps 5:3; 74:12; Mi 2:13; 4:7; So 3:15; Is 33:22; 44:6; Jer 8:19). Beginning with the period of the monarchy, Yahweh is described as the all-powerful (Is 6:5) and glorious King (Ps 24:7-10), the king of the world (Ps 29:10; 93:1-4; 95:3-5; 96:10; 97:1), and finally the king of heaven (Dn 4:34). Several texts contain a promise of salvation (Is 33:22; Mi 4:7; So 3:15) and thus acquire an eschatological meaning. This is especially marked during and after the exile : the royal power exercised by Yahweh from days of old (Ex 15:1-8), or at all times (Ps 146:10), is the guarantee of future salvation. It is frequently presented as the definitive establishment of Yahweh's kingship (Is 24:23; 43:15; 44:6; 52:7-10; Ps 22:29). Yet the expectation of God's future kingdom did not obliterate the idea of Yahweh's rule over this world (Ps 103:19; 145:11-13; Dn 4:31.34; 1 Par 29:11; Sir 51:1; Ps. Sal. 2:30, etc.).

b) BAAL is a divine epithet common to all the Semites. In profane language *ba'al* (Accadian : *bêl*) means lord or owner. In Hebrew the second meaning predominates : *ba'al kânâph* = owner of a wing, *ba'al 'iššâh* = owner of a woman, a married man (Ex 21:3), *ba'al habbayit* = the master of the house (Ex 22:7). As a divine epithet, *ba'al* means lord rather than owner.[90] Frequently the word is qualified by the name of the place or the thing that constitutes the god's domain : for example, Baal Lebanon is the Lord of Lebanon,[91] Baal Saphon is the Lord of the North,[92] Baal Gebal is the Lord of Gebal and Baalat Gebal is the Lady of Gebal,[93] Baal Berit is the Lord of the covenant (Jgs 8:33; 9:4), Baal Šamên is the Lord of heaven,[94] who dwells in heaven;[95] Enlil, the god of Nippur, bears the title of *bêl šame u irṣitim*,

---

[89] For example : *Melkišu'a* (1 Sm 14:49 = the King is help), *Malki'êl* (1 Par 7:31 = El (God) is (my) king), *Aḥimelek* (1 Sm 21:2 = brother of Melek). Several critics believe that the majority of these names are Canaanite in origin and that Melek primitively designated a god different from Yahweh. Yet it is probable that in the eyes of the Israelites who bore this name, it was meant to apply to Yahweh.

[90] W. Baudissin, *Kyrios*, III, pp. 29 ff.; D. Nielsen, *Der dreieinige Gott*, Berlin 1922, pp. 108 ff.; Lagrange writes in *ERE*², p. 83 : "the precise idea is neither real ownership, nor personal ownership, but real dominion." B. Stade, E. Meyer, R. Smith maintain that the fundamental meaning is "possessor."

[91] *Corpus Inscriptionum Semiticarum*, I, 5.

[92] This is mentioned in the Ras Shamra texts (cf. H. Bauer, *ZAW* [1933], p. 86). According to O. Eissfeldt (*Baal Zaphon, Zeus Kasios und der Durchzug der Israeliten durchs Meer*, Halle 1932), Saphon stands for mount Casios which rises near the site of Ugarit.

[93] *Syria*, 1925, p. 109, pl. XXV.

[94] He is named in the Phoenician inscription of Jehimilk of Biblos, 12th or 11th century (*RB* [1930], pp. 321-331), in the inscription of Zakir, king of Hamath (*AOT*, pp. 443 ff., about 800), and other less ancient texts (cf. O. Eissfeldt, "Ba'alšamen und Jahwe," *ZAW* [1939], pp. 1-31).

[95] *Ba'alu ina šamê*, Baal in the heaven, in the Amarna letters; cf. H. Gressmann, "Hadad und Baal," *BZAW*, 33 (1918), p. 213.

Lord of heaven and earth, and several gods in Babylonia, that of *bêl ilê*, Lord of the gods. [96] But it also occurs as the proper name of a god at Ras Shamra [97] and probably in certain theophoric names, for example *Bel-râm* (= Bel is exalted). [98] Canaanite gods bore the name of Baal, often with the article : " the Lord " (for example Jgs 6:25; 3 Kgs 16:31; 18:26; 19:18). [99] The plural form is given in other texts (*habbĕʿâlîm*, Jgs 2:11; 3:7; 8:33; 1 Sm 7:4; 3 Kgs 18:18; Jer 2:23; 9:13, etc.).

After the conquest of Canaan, Baal's name is found in several Hebrew proper names : Gedeon is surnamed Yerubbaal (Baal contends, Jgs 6:32), one of Saul's sons is called Ešbaal (man of Baal, 1 Par 8:33), one of David's sons is called Beʿelyâdâ (Baal knows, 1 Par 14:7), one of Jonathan's sons is called Meribaal (perhaps : Baal is my lord, 1 Par 8:34). Other names formed with Baal have been discovered on Samarian ostraca, dating from the reign of Achab. [100] This is no proof that the Hebrews borrowed this divine epithet from the Canaanites, it was used by all Semites. This epithet designated their God Yahweh as the Lord. [101] This would explain the many names formed with Baal in the families of Saul and David, who were loyally devoted to the cult of the God of Israel. [102] Later, after the polemics of the prophets, especially of Osee (2:10.15.19; 13:1) and of Jeremias (2:23; 11:13), against the Canaanite god, editors, when writing proper names, often substituted *bošet* (= shame) for baal. [103]

c) ADÔN means lord, someone who exercises authority. The word is occasionally used alone (Ps 12:5), more frequently with a possessive pronoun. In the latter case it expresses acknowledgment of the authority exercised by the superior; *'ădonî*, my lord, is the title by which a servant addresses his master (Gn 24:12; 25:65; Ex 21:5), a wife addresses her husband (Gn 18:12), a subject addresses his sovereign (1 Sm 24:11; 25:28 ff.; 26:17, etc.). When it is used in reference to the King, it has the value of a royal title (3 Kgs 1:36.37; Jer 22:18; 34:5). On the other hand, it may also be used as a polite formula in which the

---

[96] W. Baudissin, *Kyrios*, III, pp. 33 ff.
[97] In the Ras Shamra texts, cf. H. Bauer, *ZAW* (1933), p. 85.
[98] In a Taʿanach tablet, cf. Noth, *Geschichte*, p. 114.
[99] Lagrange (*ERS*, 93 ff.) and O. Eissfeldt (*op. cit.*, *ZAW* (1939), pp. 1-31) think that in the O. T. " the Baal " designates Baal šamên, the Lord of heaven. Lagrange holds the opinion that " the Lord of heaven, " originally one, later became the local god, the author of fertility, and that this was the origin of the multitude of Baals against whom Osee (2:15.19; 11:2) and Jeremias struggled (2:23; 9:13).
[100] H. Gressmann, " Die Ausgrabungen in Samaria, " *ZAW* (1925), pp. 147 ff.
[101] Cf. the name *Baʿalyâh* = Yahweh is lord (1 Par 12:5).
[102] W. Baudissin, *Kyrios*, III, pp. 89 ff.; W. Eichrodt, *Theologie*, I, pp. 99 ff.
[103] *Mephibošet* (2 Sm 4:4), *Išbošet* (2 Sm 2:10 ff.), *Yerubbešet* (2 Sm 11:21).

meaning of the possessive pronoun is lost as in the French: Monseigneur, Monsieur (for example Gn 23:6; 33:8; Jgs 4:18).

Only in Hebrew, Canaanite and Phoenician [104] is adôn found as a divine epithet. In the Old Testament Yahweh is called the Lord (*hâ'adôn*, for example, Ex 23:17; 34:23; Is 1:24; 3:1; 10:16.33; 19:4); He is the Lord of the whole earth (Jos 3:11-13; Mi 4:13; Za 4:14), "the Lord of Lords" (Dt 10:17; Ps 136:3), and more often with a possessive noun "my Lord, our Lord" (Ps 8:2; 147:5, etc.). In these expressions the primary meaning of the word adôn and of the possessive pronoun are still clearly evident.

Ordinarily the Massoretes vocalized *'Ădonây* whenever the title applied to Yahweh. This form is probably a simple variant of the plural [105] with the possessive pronoun (*'ădonay*, with short *a* = my lords). In this expression the value of the possessive pronoun is slight. Adonay (My Lord) becomes a divine title frequently attached to Yahweh (My Lord Yahweh), or it is used instead of Yahweh and has the value of a proper noun. Eventually it completely replaced the sacred tetragram which the Jews avoided pronouncing out of respect for the divine name. According to Baudissin, [106] the substitution or addition of Adonay to the tetragram in the Hebrew text, at least in the prophets, was not made until the beginning of the first century B.C. through the influence of the LXX who translated Yahweh by Κύριος. The general opinion, which is based on good reasons, [107] admits that the title Adonay (My Lord), long ago attributed to Yahweh, especially by the prophets, His servants (Am 3:7; 3 Kgs 18:15), replaced the tetragram, as its profane use decreased. Eventually it was substituted for the tetragram in the reading of the sacred text, perhaps from the third century B.C. onward, and it seems to have given the term Κύριος to the LXX, for this is the Greek equivalent which replaced the tetragram in the Greek Bible.

8. The Old Testament knows other divine names, some of which are rarely used or appeared late. For example: The Holy One of Israel (Is 1:4; 5:19; Ps 71:22; 78:41, etc.), of the Holy (Hb 3:3; Jb 6:10) — to this we will return later; [108] the Most High (*'Elyon*

[104] W. Baudissin, *Adonis und Esmun*, pp. 66 ff.; *id.*, *Kyrios*, III, p. 52, n. 2, where many Phoenician examples are given.

[105] This plural is explained as a plural of intensity, as in Elohîm.

[106] *Kyrios*, 4 vols., Giessen 1926-1929; he was followed by W. Eichrodt (*Theologie*, III, p. 101), E. Sellin (*Theologie*, pp. 6,9).

[107] Cf. L. Cerfaux, "Le nom divin Kyrios," *RScPT* (1931), pp. 27-51; 417-452.

[108] Cf. § 6.

and later ὕψιστος); [109] the God of heaven (Jon 1:9; Dn 2:18.19.37.44; Ezr 1:2; 6:9.10). [110] Yahweh, the God of heaven and earth (Gn 24:3.7, LXX); later the Heaven (Dn 4:23; 1 Mc 3:18.19.60, etc.), the Great *(ribbôn)*, the Glorious, the Eternal. [111] Because Yahweh is the assured refuge of those who are faithful to Him, He is also called the Rock of Israel (2 Sm 23:3; Is 30:29), my, our, his Rock (Dt 32:30; 2 Sm 22:3.47 = Ps 18:3.47; 19:15, etc.) or the Rock (Dt 32:4).

He also is the Strong One or the Lord of Israel or of Jacob (Gn 49:24; Is 1:24; 49:26; 60:16; Ps 132:2.5). The Massoretes pointed the word *'âbîr* (from the root *'br* = to be strong) when it is applied to God, and *'abbîr* when it designates robust or powerful men (for example, Jgs 5:22; Lam 1:15) or a species of bulls (Is 34:7; Ps 22:12; 50:13). This distinction seems to have been the result of a theological scruple. But it does not mean that primitively Yahweh was a god-bull or that the bull was His symbol (cf. Ex 32:4; 3 Kgs 12:26.32), [112] because the word expresses strength or primacy (cf. 1 Sm 21:8; Jb 34:20) and most often is used in reference to men, once to angels (Ps 78:25), rarely to animals. [113] Furthermore, while the prophets compare Yahweh to a lion, a wolf, or other animals, they carefully avoid comparing Him to a bull, [114] very likely because of hostility to the bull-cult of Bethel. So if they have preserved this ancient epithet, it is because it did not suggest to them the image of a bull.

Gn 31:42.53 has preserved an ancient name of the God of the Fathers, "the Terror of Isaac," that is to say, the God who inspires terror in Isaac [115] rather than "the terror that Isaac inspires." [116] Jacob, in fact, does not swear by the terror that Isaac inspires, but by the divinity that makes his father tremble (31:53).

---

[109] Cf. above § 2, 2.

[110] This is found fairly frequently in the Elephantine texts, cf. above n. 23.

[111] Circumlocutions designating God multiplied in rabbinism. In addition the following terms were used: the Place, the Name, the Glory, the Dwelling, the Word.

[112] K. Budde, "Ephod und Lade" (*ZAW* [1921], p. 38); H. Gressmann, *Die Lade Jahwes*, Stuttgart 1920, pp. 28 ff.

[113] Cf. H. Torczyner, "Abir kein Stierbild," *ZAW* (1921), pp. 296-300; J. Hempel, "Jahwesgleichnisse der israelitischen Propheten," *ZAW* (1924), pp. 100 ff.; W. Baudissin, *Kyrios*, III, pp. 118 ff.

[114] This epithet is frequently applied to the Babylonian gods (cf. J. Hehn, *op. cit.*, p. 298).

[115] Cf. O. Procksch, *Die Genesis*, Leipzig 1913, p. 181; A. Alt, *Der Gott der Väter*, Stuttgart 1929, pp. 27 ff.; P. Heinisch, *Genesis*, Bonn 1930, p. 318.

[116] E. Meyer, *Die Israeliten und ihre Nachbarstämme*, Halle 1906, pp. 254 ff., where the conclusion is reached that Isaac was the god who inspired terror.

§ 3. *Anthropomorphisms*

J. Hempel, " Die Grenze des Anthropomorphismus Jahwes im Alten Testament, " *ZAW*, 57 (1939), pp. 75 ff.; F. Michaeli, *Dieu à l'image de l'homme*, Neufchâtel 1950.

Very frequently the Old Testament speaks of God as of a man: eyes are attributed to Him (Am 9:4), hands (Am 9:2), fingers (Dt 9:10), arms (Jer 27:5), feet (Na 1:3), face and back (Ex 33:23), mouth (Jer 9:11), nostrils (Ps 18:16), lips and tongue (Is 30:27), breath (Is 30:28). God speaks (Lv 4:1), cries (Lv 1:1), roars (Am 1:2), listens (Gn 17:20), looks (Gn 6:12), smells (1 Sm 26:19), laughs (Ps 2:4), whistles (Is 7:18), walks (Mi 1:3), sleeps (Ps 44:24) and awakes (Ps 78:65). He strolls in the garden of Eden (Gn 3:8) which He has planted (Gn 2:8); He fashions, like a potter, the body of man and breathes into him the breath of life (Gn 2:7); He comes down to see the tower of Babel (Gn 11:5), goes forth from the mountains of Seir and advances through the countries of Edom (Jgs 5:4); He closes the ark containing Noe and his family (Gn 7:16); He stretches Juda like a bow and places Ephraim like an arrow (Za 9:13); He is a valiant warrior (Ex 15:3; Ps 24:8); He waits like a panther (Os 13:7), devours like a lion (Os 5:14), or consumes like a worm (Os 5:12). He is given all the sentiments that disturb men (anthropopathisms): complacency (Jer 9:23), joy (So 3:17), anger (2 Sm 24:1), hatred (Dt 12:31), aversion (Ps 106:40), distaste (Lv 20:23), jealousy (Ex 20:5), vengeance (Is 1:24), repentance (Gn 6:6).

There are many anthropomorphisms in all the Old Testament books. They abound in the narratives attributed to the Yahwist and in the works of most of the prophets, who have nevertheless, a very high idea of God. They are less frequent and less pronounced in the parts attributed to the Elohist and in the Sacerdotal Code. They are restrained, in fact they are effaced as far as possible in the Greek version of the LXX and in the Aramic versions. Some of the prophets and psalmists protest against the anthropomorphization of Yahweh: " He has no eyes as men have " (Jb 10:4); " He is God and not man " and does not grow angry (Os 11:9); He does not change His mind as men do (1 Sm 15:29; Nm 23:19); He neither slumbers nor sleeps (Ps 121:4); He does not tire (Is 40:28). Yet no one stopped using anthropomorphisms, nor tried to spiritualize them.

This is due to many causes. The first is of a general nature: the basic inability of the human mind to represent God as He is in Himself, so that the most advanced theology is unable to free itself completely from anthropomorphisms. Even the New Testament is not without them.

The second cause is the concrete character of the God of the Old Testament whose knowledge is not the fruit of philosophic reflection but of revelation. The whole Old Testament presents God as the living God, active and personal, who made Himself known to Israel and continues to manifest Himself by His interventions in the history of His people. God was perceived by the religious geniuses of Israel as a personal being, accessible to man, as an acting will, intervening in life. As in every lived religion which is not a pure intellectual speculation, this concrete and personal God is necessarily described by the more or less numerous and accentuated anthropomorphisms that serve to express the individuality of the divinity. In Israel they abounded because the philosophic spirit was not highly developed there.

The third cause is the practical nature of the Hebrew mind and language, which is so poor in abstract terms. The Israelite loves the concrete word, the picturesque expression that strikes the imagination. Even when he refers to man, he likes to speak of the arm or hand to express power, of his gasping or fiery breath to express impatience or anger, of the face that is inclined or is averted to express benevolence or aversion, and so forth. Is it any wonder that he speaks of God in the same way?

But it is God's holiness that has prevented anthropomorphisms from bringing God down to the human level, like the gods of the pagan mythologies. It is His holiness that preserves Him on the level of the totally other, infinitely elevated above all other beings and all that is weak and sinful.

§ 4. *God's personal character*

God's personal character is evident on every page of the Old Testament; it is strongly stressed by the numberless anthropomorphisms that are to be found in texts of every epoch. God is, like many Semitic divinities, the lord and master of His people. This is proved by the names of Melek (guide, counselor, king), Baal (master), Adon (lord): [1] indeed, the God who exercises sovereignty is necessarily

[1] Cf. above I, § 2, 7.

conceived as an individual, as a will which imposes itself upon those who are subject.

In the Old Testament this is all the more evident in that the relation of lord to subject is everywhere presented as having been established in time and through an act of the free will of God, who among all the peoples (Ex 19:5; Am 3:2) has chosen Israel to be His servant (Is 41:8; 44:1, etc.), His possession (Ex 19:5; Dt 7:6; 26:18.19, etc.), His community (Mi 2:5; Ps 74:2). This election is expressed by the verbs " to choose " *(bâhâr)*, " to know " *(yâdâ')*, " to acquire " *(qânâh)*, and was carried out when Yahweh delivered His people from the servitude of Egypt in order to settle them in Canaan (Ex 15:13; Dt 26:7-10; Am 2:9.10; Os 13:4, etc.). Another tradition traces this election to the days of the patriarchs, especially to the time of Abraham, the father of the Chosen Race (Gn 12:2.3; 15:7; 17:1), with whom God concluded an alliance (Gn 15:9-18; 17:2-21). This election or this alliance is always shown to be a historic fact, a divine initiative and a grace. [2] This gives the God of the Old Testament a character much more personal and moral than that of any of the national or local Semitic gods. It makes Him a God of history and not a God of nature or the personification of a force of nature, as were the majority of the divinities of the ancient East. When Yahweh is represented in relation to nature, it is as the sovereign master of the world that He has created, and that He conserves and rules. [3]

Lastly the God of the Old Testament is " the living God, " for example in Ps 42:3; 4 Kgs 19:4; Dt 5:23. This expression is surely very old because it is one of the formulas most frequently used in oaths : " Yahweh lives " (Jgs 8:19; 1 Sm 14:39.45; 19:6; 20:3.21; 2 Sm 4:9; 12:5; 14:11, etc.); more rarely " Elohim lives " (2 Sm 2:27) or " El lives " (Jb 27:2). Yahweh Himself swears by His own life : " I live " (Nm 14:21.28; Dt 32:40; Jer 46:18, etc.). Originally this term expresses faith in the vitality and power that manifests the redoubtable God, before whom foreign nations flee (Jos 3:10), whose voice no man dares to hear (Dt 5:23), and whom no one can insult with impunity (4 Kgs 19:4.16; 1 Sm 17:26). [4] In Psalms 42:3 and

---

[2] Cf. below IV, § 1.

[3] Cf. below II, § 3 and 4.

[4] J. Hempel, *Gott und Mensch im A. T.*, Stuttgart 1936², p. 34. W. Baudissin (*Adonis und Esmum*, Leipzig 1911, pp. 450-510) thinks that this expression was originally applied to nature divinities, for example to Adonis in Phoenicia. The permanent power, which is manifest in nature, was attributed to Adonis or to some similar divinity, but also to the divinity in general; and one expresses this belief

84:3 " the living God " is the God who manifests Himself in the life of the devout psalmist who seeks to enjoy Yahweh's presence in His temple. Later, " the living God, " that is to say, the only God, Yahweh, is often placed in opposition to the gods of the peoples (Jer 10:1-10; Dn 14:4.5.24.25, V) who are only " dead gods " (Ep. Jer 26.70), " powerless gods " (Is 44:18; Ps 135:15-17), lacking all life (Wis 15:17). It is mostly in this sense that the expression survives in Judaism and in the New Testament (for example, Mt 16:16).

§ 5. *The One God*

J. Hehn, *Die biblische und die babylonische Gottesidee*, Innsbruck 1911; W. Schmidt, *Der Ursprung der Gottesidee* (5 vols.), Münster im W. 1926 ff.; *id.*, *Origine et évolution de la religion*, Paris 1931; K. Holzey, " Jahve der Gott Israels " (*ATA*, XII, 4), Münster im W. 1936; N. Söderblom, *Das Werden des Gottesglaubens*, Leipzig 1926²; B. Balscheit, " Alter und Aufkommen des Monotheismus in der israelitischen Religion " (*BZAW*, 69), Tübingen 1938; A. Alt, *Der Gott der Väter. Ein Beitrag zur Vorgeschichte der israelitischen Religion*, Stuttgart 1929; W. F. Albright, *From the Stone Age to Christianity*, Baltimore 1946².

Monotheism is the belief in one unique god to the exclusion of any other divinity. Its absolute and exclusive character distinguishes it from monolatry which is the belief of a group of men in a god, recognized as the only legitimate god of the group, but who concede the existence of other divinities adored by other peoples. Some authors identify monolatry with henotheism. It would seem better to reserve the latter term for the attitude of those who, while they admit the existence of several gods, address themselves to one of these gods, as if he were the only god, or who attribute to him all the titles and attributes of the other gods as if he alone possessed all the marks and power of the other divinities. [1] Many examples of this attitude can be found in Vedic, Babylonian and Egyptian hymns. For example, a hymn to Nabu declares: " Have confidence in Nabu and in no other god. " [2] A psalm in honor of the lunar god, Nannar,

---

by saying to the divinity: " it lives " (p. 490). The Hebrews probably borrowed the expression from the Canaanites. Against this position, it may be objected that, according to Baudissin himself, the God of Israel had in primitive times the character of a " tribal god " and that such a god does not die and rise, as does a nature god. " It is to be expected that a tribal god will manifest the permanence of his life " (p. 490). This remark brings us back to Hempel's interpretation. In fact, the expression " the living God " is applied to Yahweh when He manifests Himself, not in the phenomena of nature, but rather in favor of His people.

[1] Cf. A. Bertholet, " Henotheïsmus, " *RGG*, II, cols. 1802-1803.

[2] Rawlinson, *Cuneiform Inscriptions of Western Asia*, I, 2, 12.

uses these terms : " Lord, conqueror of the gods, who alone is exalted in heaven and on earth. "[3] Another psalm, addressed to Marduk, attributes to this god all the characteristics of the other divinities and identifies him with them.[4] These enthusiastic formulas denote confidence in a specified god but are not to be understood as monotheistic affirmations that exclude the existence of other divinities.

Here we need not give the history of monotheism in Israel, but we must briefly indicate its stages. A quick survey of the historic and prophetic books of the Old Testament reveals that monotheism made its way into the people of Israel only painfully and slowly (after the return from the exile). The masses were always inclined to a naturalistic and polytheistic religion. Even in the fifth century B. C., the Elephantine Jews adored, besides Yahu, the goddesses Anath-Yahu and Anath-Bethel, as well as other divinities they had carried from their homeland, the region of Bethel and Samaria. Therefore a distinction must be made between the religion of the people, the religion of religious leaders (cf. Jer 7:25.26), and the doctrine laid down in the sacred books.

According to the first chapters of Genesis the one God manifested Himself from the beginning of mankind. The first account (Gn 1:1-2:4) describes the creation of the world and of man as the work of God (Elohim) who created heaven and earth and all that is in it in six days by His all-powerful word, and rested on the seventh day, thereby instituting the Sabbath. For the author of this account Elohim is evidently the one God on whom the whole universe depends. A second account (Gn 2:4 b-3:24) is more interested in the creation of man than in the creation of the world. Yahweh is shown fashioning man's body and breathing into his body life-giving breath. He provides for the man's needs by planting a garden, by creating animals and finally the woman, and forbidding him, under pain of death, to eat the fruit of the tree of good and evil. The man and the woman, deceived by the serpent, transgress the divine order. The man is condemned to painful labor on an earth now unfruitful and cursed. The woman is condemned to the pain of childbirth and is made subject to man. Both are condemned " to return to the dust from which they were taken. " Then they were driven from the garden where they had enjoyed happiness and intimacy with their creator. In this account Yahweh appears, in spite of anthropomorphisms, as the

---

[3] *AOT*, p. 241.

[4] *AOT*, p. 329. Cf. the rather one-sided article of Morton Smith " The Common Theology of the Ancient Near East, " *JBL*, 71 (1952), pp. 135 ff. He stresses the tendency to monotheism in ancient oriental religions.

creator and absolute master of man's life and destiny and is obviously represented as the only God.

Many consider that these accounts are the echo of a tradition that goes back to the first days of mankind and was faithfully preserved by that branch of the Semites whence sprang Israel. They hold that Israel was the heir and guardian of primitive monotheism and that traces of this belief are also to be found among many peoples of inferior culture who recognize the existence of a supreme being, the author of the world and men. This view seems to be oversimplified. Scripture itself (Jos 24:2.14.15; Jdt 5:7-9) declares that the ancestors of Abraham, the father of the Hebrew people, " served other gods, " that is to say, they were polytheists. So it is believed that the doctrine of Gn 2:4 b-3:24 was revealed at a later date and probably to the author of the account.

Popular traditions assembled in Genesis give different names to the God of the patriarchs: Yahweh, according to the accounts attributed to the Yahwist (Gn 12:8; 13:4, etc.), El, Elohim, El Šadday, according to the Elohist (for example, Gn 20:3.6) and the priestly Code (Gn 17:1; 28:3; Ex 6:3), and especially " the God of Abraham " (Gn 26:24), " the God of Isaac " (Gn 28:13), " the God of my father Abraham and the God of my father Isaac " (Gn 32:10), " your God and the God of your father " (Gn 43:23), " the God of your father " (Gn 49:25), occasionally " the Terror of Isaac " (Gn 31:42), " the Powerful One " or " the Lord of Jacob " (Gn 49:24), El 'Olâm (the ancient or eternal God, Gn 21:33), El 'Elyôn (the Most High God, Gn 14:18.20), El rô'î (the God who sees me, Gn 16:13), El Bethel (the God of Bethel, Gn 28:12-22). [5]

The majority of non-Catholic historians conclude from the plurality of divine names that the Hebrews before the days of Moses were polytheists and adored as many local or family gods as there were different names (cf. Gn 31:19; 35:2.4). This conclusion is not inevitable, because none of these names, with the exception of Yahweh whose worship might have been attributed anachronistically to the patriarchs, is a proper name. El and Elohim are generic names of the divinity, and the different determinatives which were added can be understood as the expression of different aspects of one and the same God. [6] It is obviously in this sense that the accounts, in their

---

[5] For the meaning of these words see above § 2.

[6] Cf. A. G. Barrois (*Manuel d'archéologie biblique*, II, Paris 1953, p. 402): " The many epithets bestowed on the gods of Ugarit and the various titles by which Ašérah was invoked suggest that we should see in the elements *šaddaii*, *'elyôn*, etc., simple surnames of the same divinity, El, adored under different names. "

present form, interpret these names. They identify "the God of Isaac" with "the God of his father" (Gn 26:23.24), "the Powerful One of Jacob" with El Šadday and "the Rock of Israel" (Gn 49:24.25), the God who manifested Himself to Moses with "the God of the fathers, the God of Abraham, the God of Isaac, the God of Jacob" (Ex 3:15).

It will be observed that the God of the patriarchs is not connected with special sites, save in the expression El Bethel, but with individuals (the God of Abraham, Isaac, Jacob) or with a group (the God of the fathers, the God of Israel, Gn 33:20). He appears, therefore, as the God who revealed Himself to Abraham, to Isaac and to the fathers, who remains in contact with them, who concludes a covenant with them (Gn 15:7-17; 17:1-14), who protects [7] them in their wanderings not only in Canaan but also in Egypt and in Aramean territory (Gn 12:17; 15:7; 24:28; 30:27.30; 39:2.3.21-23). His power is not limited to one place or to a specific region. Therefore He is not a local god, nor is He, strictly speaking, a tribal god, since His benevolence and His power go beyond the tribe of Abraham or of Isaac (Gn 12:3), for example, to Laban who is an Aramean (Gn 30:37), and to Abimelech, the king of Gerara (Gn 20:17.18).

He has none of the characteristics of a nature god: He has no goddess with whom He shares His throne, nor is He associated in any special way with any of the forces of nature. On the contrary, He is the Most High God (Gn 14:18-20.22), that is to say, He who dwells in celestial heights (Gn 19:24; 21:17; 24:7) and "who has created heaven and earth" (Gn 14:19.22), the almighty God (or Most High, El Šadday). In all these ways He is related to the supreme God *(Allfather)* of many primitive people, [8] with the difference that He is closer to man and more active than the *Allfather* of most primitives. "El, the God of Israel" (Gn 33:20) is "the God" (*hâ'élôhîm*, Gn 20:6) and allows no "strange god" beside Him (Gn 35:2.4). His moral character, His benevolence and His power are attested not only by several accounts (for example, Gn 12:17; 19; 20:3-18) but also by old theophoric names, for example *Yšmâ'-'êl* (Ismael, May God hear!, Gn 16:15), *Yerahmě'êl* (May God have pity!, 1 Par 2:9), *Eli-'âb* ([my] God is father, Nm 1:9), *Elî-hû* (= He is [my] God, 1 Sm 1:1), *Yabně'êl* (May God build!, Jos 19:33), *Elî-šâphaṭ* (= [my] God has judged, 2 Par 23:1), *Elyâdâ'* (God knows, 2 Sm 5:16), *Eliphelet* (God saves, 2 Sm 5:16), *'Azěrî'el* (God is my help, 1 Par 5:24), *Ab-râm* (= the father, that is to say, God, is exalted), etc.

[7] This is probably the meaning of El rô'î which signifies "the God who sees me," that is to say, who looks at me benevolently.

[8] N. Söderblom, *Das Werden des Gottesglaubens*, Leipzig 1926 [2], p. 273.

All the books of the Old Testament make Moses the true founder of the religion of Israel : Yahweh is the God of Israel " since Egypt " (Os 12:10; 13:4). Most modern critics recognize the solid foundation of this tradition; but several claim that monotheism appears only with the eighth-century prophets and is stated clearly only at the time of the exile. This opinion is contrary to the attitude of the prophets who pose, not as innovating, but as continuing the work of Moses; for example, Elias who walks unto " the mountain of God " on which Yahweh showed Himself to Moses (3 Kgs 19:4-18), Amos (2:10.11; 9:7), Osee (2:16.17), Jeremias (7:22.25; 15:1). In their eyes the days of Moses and the sojourn of Israel in the desert is the time of the ideal religion to which they wish to recall Israel, the time of Yahweh's first love for His people (Os 2:16.17; Jer 2:2; Ez 16:3-14).

The God who revealed Himself to Moses in the desert calls Himself the God of the ancestors (Ex 3:6.13.15; 6:3.4), but He makes Himself known as He whose existence manifests itself actively and with a sovereign independence: " I am who I am " (Ex 3:14). [9] By the power which He gave proof of when He delivered the Hebrew tribes from servitude, He won this people as His spouse (Os 2:16; 9:10; Jer 2:2; 7:22; Ez 16:8 ff.), His kingdom, His own possession, a holy nation (Ex 19:5.6). With them He concluded a covenant (Ex 24:3-8; 34:1-35) which carried with it grave moral obligations formulated in the decalogue (Ex 20:2-17; Dt 5:6-18). He reveals Himself as a God essentially moral and sovereignly free, as a Lord (cf. Ex 15:18; 19:6; Nm 23:21) who exacts the total submission of His subjects. For He is a " jealous God " (Ex 20:5; 34:14), who tolerates no rival : " You shall not have other gods beside me " (Ex 20:3; Dt 5:7; cf. Jgs 5:8). This exclusivism is altogether characteristic of the God of Moses and is found in no other ancient god, not even in the solar god Aton, whom Amenophis IV sought to impose as the only god in Egypt. [10] Moreover, Yahweh is the holy God, inaccessible to the profane (Ex 3:5; 19:12.24) and invisible : no one can see His face " because man cannot see Me and live " (Ex 33:20; Jgs 6:23; 13:22;

---

[9] See above § 2, 5.

[10] On the so-called monotheistic reform of Amenophis IV (1375-1360 B.C.) cf. A. Moret, *Le Nil et la civilisation égyptienne*, Paris 1926, pp. 373-379; J. H. Breasted and T. E. Peet, *Cambridge Ancient History*, II, pp. 109 ff. and pp. 203 ff.; Wardle, " The Origins of Hebrew Monotheism, " *ZAW* (1925), p. 43 and pp. 207 ff.; A. Erman, *Die Religion der Aegypter*, Berlin 1934, pp. 110-130. Amenophis IV called himself " the favorite of two goddesses, " the son who came from Aton's flesh, and he required his courtiers to address him as " god. " This indicates the distance that separates the Egyptian god from Yahweh whom no man can see without dying (Ex 33:20) and who allows neither any other god nor any divine image (Ex 20:3.4).

Is 6:5, etc.), except by a very special grace accorded to the rarely privileged (Ex 24:11; 33:11; Dt 34:10). Although He has manifested Himself in the tempest, the storm, the cloud, the earthquake (Ex 19:16; 24:15-17; 34:5), He is not a god of the tempest. He is exalted above the elements, He commands them and disposes them as He pleases (Ex 15:8.11; Nm 16:30; Dt 33:13-16; Gn 49:25; Jgs 5:20; Jos 10:12-14). From all this it follows that the religion of Moses is monotheistic, [11] even though the denial of the existence of " strange gods " (cf. Ex 12:12) is never explicitly formulated (yet cf. Jgs 6:31), which constitutes a monotheism that is rather practical than theoretical.

It may be objected, however, that the God of Israel has a proper name, Yahweh. This seems to point to the fact that the Hebrews thought that they had to distinguish Him by this name from other gods. The conclusion would be that they acknowledge the existence of these gods. This is in fact what Jephte declared: the Moabites legitimately possess the land which their god Chamos gave them, just as Israel possesses the land which Yahweh granted them (Jgs 11:24). David complained that he had been driven from " the inheritance of Yahweh, " that is to say, from the land of Israel, and sent " to serve strange gods " (1 Sm 26:19). Achaz believed that he was obliged to offer sacrifices to appease the gods of Damascus (2 Par 28:23).

In the eyes of the ancients the name is not a simple label distinguishing one individual from his kinsmen. It is an integrating part of the person; what has no name is, so to speak, non-existent. This is the reason why the God of Israel, since He is thought of as a personal being, bears a proper name, although He is alone of His kind. Moreover, the name is supposed to correspond to the essence of the object, and consequently reveals it. For this reason the people expressed a desire to learn the name of the God who manifested Himself to Moses (Ex 3:13). Lastly, according to the opinion of the ancients, the knowledge of God's name was necessary in order to enter into relations with Him. The god's name had to be invoked in any cultic act, [12] either to attract his attention or, if he has gone away, to make him come near (cf. 3 Kgs 18:27). The revelation of God's proper name (Ex 3:14) corresponds to the exigencies of the ancient mentality that attached great importance to the " name. "

---

[11] Cf. W. F. Albright, *From the Stone Age to Christianity*, Baltimore 1946², p. 207.

[12] Cf. the expression " to invoke the name of Yahweh " (Gn 4:26; 12:8, etc.) that literally means " to call by name " the God whom one addresses.

This does not imply, in any way, that the proper name is necessary to distinguish an individual among several of the same kind.

The words of Jephte (Jgs 11:24) and of David (1 Sm 26:19) as well as the attitude of Achaz (2 Par 28:23) prove how difficult it was for monotheism to make progress in Israel even among the ruling classes. They do not prove that Moses or the prophets, living at the time of David and of Achaz, did not profess the strictest monotheism. Jephte, dealing with the king of Moab, employed the usual diplomatic language [13] of naming the gods of the two parties present (cf. Gn 31:53). He was little aware of Yahweh's demands, since in good faith he offered Him his daughter in sacrifice (Jgs 11:34-39), in spite of Yahweh's horror of human sacrifices (Gn 22; Lv 18:21; 20:2.3; Dt 12:31; 18:10). The attitude of Achaz is a typical example of the religious syncretism that prevailed in Israel as a consequence of relations with neighboring nations, despite the protestations of the prophets and of all Yahweh's faithful followers (cf. 4 Kgs 16; Is 7:4-17). As for David's words (1 Sm 26:19), they express the widely held belief that the cult of Yahweh could not be celebrated outside the land that was His own (cf. 4 Kgs 5:17.18), so that in foreign countries one was obliged to venerate " strange gods " (cf. 4 Kgs 17:25-28). [14] There is no proof that David shared this opinion; on the contrary, according to 2 Sm 7:22, he professed the purest monotheism. [15]

The passage containing the prohibition to represent Yahweh by any kind of image, Dt 4:15-19, warns Israel against star-worship. This cult was widely practiced in the East, especially in Babylonia and Assyria. The passage states that Yahweh " gave them (the stars) to be shared by all peoples, " while He has chosen Israel as His own good. According to the opinion of the ancients, the stars were not inanimate heavenly bodies but living beings (cf. Dt 32:9, LXX; Jb 38:7) whose action affected nature and man. From this point of view, the existence of these beings could not be denied. But here their power is subject to Yahweh who divided them among the nations and kept Israel for Himself. This text stresses the supereminent dignity and universal power of Yahweh who disposes all peoples as He wishes: He has chosen Israel for Himself and He allows the other nations to adore the stars which are not gods (cf. Dt 4:35; " It

[13] W. F. Albright (*Archaeology and the Religion of Israel*, Baltimore 1948, p. 118) sees in this a typical argument *ad hominem* meant to impress the Ammonites.

[14] W. F. Albright (*op. cit.*, p. 118) notes that it was practically impossible for an Israelite to remain faithful to Yahweh in a foreign land because there was no cultic organization nor social milieu to assure his fidelity.

[15] Cf. P. Heinisch, *Theologie des A. T.*, p. 26.

is Yahweh who is God and there is no other God but He"). The Hebrews made no distinction between what God does and what He permits, so thay attributed evil to Him, as in the present case they attributed to Him the idolatry of the nations because He is the author of all things (cf. Am 3:6; Is 6:9; 1 Sm 26:19; 2 Sm 16:10; 24:1).[16]

As early as Moses' time the innate tendency of the Israelite tribes to a naturalistic religion showed itself in the incident of the golden calf (Ex 32) and of Baal-Pé'or (Nm 25:1-3). The tendency became more pronounced when they occupied Palestine, settled among the Canaanites, and adopted their civilization which was far higher than their own. With this civilization they embraced many of the ideas and religious institutions of the former occupants of that region. There can be no doubt that the great majority never totally abandoned their national God, because Yahweh was the principal link that united the tribes to one another (Jgs 5; 1 Sm 11:7-15; 2 Sm 3:17-19); but many also offered homage to the regional deities, Baal and Astarte, and later to the gods of Babylonia and Assyria (Jgs 2:11-13; 3:7; 3 Kgs 14:22-24; 16:31-34; 4 Kgs 21:2-7, etc.); several kings even went so far as to admire or worship for political reasons the deities of neighboring nations (Solomon, 3 Kgs 11; Achab, 3 Kgs 16:31-33; 18:18; Achaz, 4 Kgs 16; 2 Par 28; Manasses, 4 Kgs 21:3-7). Others, on the contrary, such as Jehu in the northern kingdom (4 Kgs 10), Ezechias (4 Kgs 18:4) and Josias (4 Kgs 23) in the kingdom of Juda, tried to oppose this syncretism by religious reforms which were at times violent. All in vain; until after the exile "strange gods" were adored in Israel. Not until the fifth century B.C. did monotheism penetrate the popular masscs.

Against this syncretism, against this infidelity of many in regard to Yahweh, against the "Canaanization" of the worship and of the holy God, who was reduced to the level of a Baal (Os 2:18), rang out the indignant protests of the prophets, all of whom professed strict monotheism. Samuel, who had been brought up in the sanctuary of the ark at Silo, appeared as a representative of pure tradition. He declared: "Obedience is better than sacrifices and to hearken is better than to offer the fat of rams." He condemned rebellion with the same severity as divination and the use of teraphim (1 Sm 15:22.23; cf. Os 6:6). He demanded the departure of the "strange gods,"

[16] Cf. A. Junker, *Das Buch Deuteronomium*, Bonn 1933, pp. 37 ff.; A. Clamer, *Le Deutéronome (La Sainte Bible)*, II, Paris 1938, pp. 541 ff.

which he called " vain things " (1 Sm 12:21), [17] and a return to Yahweh alone (1 Sm 7:3). Elias, who obviously associated himself with Moses (3 Kgs 19), fought vigorously against the Baal of Tyre and placed this alternative before the people : either Yahweh or Baal (3 Kgs 18:21). He scoffed at Baal who could not send fire to burn the sacrifice that had been prepared nor hear the noisy supplications of his worshippers (3 Kgs 18:24.27); he proclaimed and made men acknowledge that Yahweh is God in Israel (3 Kgs 18:36), the God (*hâ'élôhîm* with the article, 3 Kgs 18:21.37.39), that is to say, the only God. [18]

To Amos, Yahweh is the God of Justice, the Lord, not only of Israel, whom He has freely chosen and whom He can reject for its faults (Am 3:2; 9:7.8), but also of strange peoples (Am 1:3-15; 9:7), of heaven and of earth (Am 5:8; 7:4; 8:9) and of the lower world (Am 9:2), while the other gods are nothing but " lies " (Am 2:4). [19] Osee places greater stress on Yahweh's love for His people (Os 3:1; 11:1), who owe Him in return exclusive love and undivided service (Os 2:4-7; 6:1.2; 12:7) : to serve other gods is to commit adultery (Os 2:4-7). It is Yahweh, and not Baal, who makes flourish the wheat, the vine and the olive tree (Os 2:10), who assures peace and prosperity (Os 2:20); besides Yahweh there is no other Savior (Os 13:4). Osee fought violently against the worship of Baal and the worship of Yahweh as Israel practised it, when it treated its God as a Baal (Os 4:12.13.15.17-19; 5:6; 11:2) and adored Him under the form of a " calf " (Os 8:5.6; 13:2).

Isaias stressed God's holiness. Yahweh is " the Holy One " (Is 1:4; 5:19.24; 6:3; 10:17). He alone is exalted above all that is weak and sinful (Is 1:4; 5:24.25; 10:17). He is " God " (El) and " spirit, " that is to say, powerful and everlasting, while all the power of a great kingdom like Egypt is but " man " and " flesh, " that is to say, weak and mortal (Is 31:3). Idols are " nothings " *('êlîlîm)*, the products of artisans, that shall be cast to rats and bats when Yahweh shall appear in redoubtable majesty (Is 2:8.18.20). Jeremias reproaches Israel for abandoning Yahweh in order to follow gods " which are no gods " (Jer 2:11; 5:7; Dt 32:21), which are but " vanity " (Jer 2:5), which are of no help (Jer 2:8). The teaching of the prophets on

---

[17] There is evidence that this verse is a relatively recent gloss.

[18] Cf. E. Kautzsch, *Biblische Theologie des A. T.*, p. 135; E. Sellin, *Der alttestamentliche Prophetismus*, Leipzig 1912, pp. 23 ff.; R. Kittel, *Geschichte des Volkes Israel*, II, Berlin 1917, p. 389; H. Gunkel, " Elias, " in *RGG* [2], II, p. 608; W. Eichrodt, *Theologie*, I, p. 112, and all Catholic commentators; O. Procksch, *Theologie*, p. 139.

[19] The authenticity of Am 2:4.5 is questioned by several critics. A. Van Hoonacker (*Les douze petits prophètes*, Paris 1908, p. 218) accepts it.

God's unity can be summed up in this formula from Deuteronomy: "Yahweh is God; there is none else beside Him" (Dt 4:35.39; 6:4; 32:39; cf. Jer 2:11-13; Is 41:4.29; 44:6; 46:9, etc.).

Although the prophets sought to bring the people to the one God who had revealed Himself to Moses, it cannot be denied that they helped to strengthen and develop monotheism: they cast light on the universality of Yahweh's power (for example Am 1:2-2:3; 9:7; Is 2:2-4; 7:18-20; 8:7-10; 13; Jer 46:25) and His essentially moral character. Yahweh exacts above all the observance of His moral precepts, justice, mercy, forthrightness, fidelity (Am 5:4.5.24; Os 6:6; Is 1:17; 11:9; Mi 6:8, etc.), and rejects all worship which is not the expression of a total inner submission, of a conversion of heart (Am 5:21-23; Os 6:6; Is 1:11-17; Mi 6:6-8) or, as many call it, "the knowledge" of God (Os 4:1.6; Is 1:3; 11:2.9; 41:20; Jer 2:8; 9:2-5; 22:16).

The doctrine of the prophets is to be found in all the later books of the Old Testament. Numerous psalms, all the sapiential as well as other books honor the one God, the creator of heaven and earth (Gn 1; Ps 8; 93:2; 96:10; 104; Jb 38; Prv 8:23-30; Sir 24:3-8; Wis 9:1-3; Neh 9:6; Jdt 9:17; 16:15-19, etc.). His omnipotence and holiness, which differentiate Him from every other being, and His moral character are universally recognized (for example, Ps 40:7-11; 50:14.15; 51:17.18; 69:32; 93; 95:3-5; 97). No god exists except Yahweh (Dt 4:35; 3 Kgs 8:60; 4 Kgs 19:15; Is 41:29; 45:6; 46:9, etc.). From the time of Jeremias, the struggle against the gods "who are not gods" (Jer 2:11; 5:7) and against every form of idolatry became an oft-repeated theme (Jer 2:13.28; 10; Is 40:18-20; 41:6.7; 44:10-20; 46:6.7; Hb 2:18; Ps 115:4-8; 135:15-18; Wis 13:9-14:11; 14:12-21; Bar 6, etc.).

Nevertheless, even in those books which give energetic affirmations of God's unity, expressions are found that seem to admit the existence of other gods (for example, Dt 4:19; Ps 81:10; 82:1-7; 86:8; 95:3; 96:4; 97:7.9; Is 41:21-23). This antinomy is to be explained by Israel's polytheistic milieu: the struggle against false gods and the desire to raise Yahweh above all that the gentiles honored or adored gave life to these "nothings."[20] Thus in Is 41:21-23, for example, Yahweh challenges these gods who do not exist to prove their existence by their prophecies (cf. also Ps 86:8-9). Moreover, despite the irony with which Israel referred to the divine images and statues of the pagan

[20] J. Hempel, *Gott und Mensch im A. T.*[2], p. 72.

world (for example, Is 44:15-18; Wis 13:10), it never knew how to free itself from the opinion commonly held in the ancient world which considered the image not as a simple figure, but as a double of the being it represented. Judaism eventually reduced the gods to the level of demons; so, according to Ps 106:37, it is to demons (šêdîm), and not to Moloch, that Israel sacrificed its children (cf. also Dt 32:17; Bar 4:7; Enoch 19:1; Jubilees 15:30 ff.; 1 Cor 10:20). All this goes to show that in Israel monotheism is neither the conclusion nor the object of philosophic reflection.

§ 6. *The Holy God*

W. Baudissin, *Studien zur semitischen Religionsgeschichte*, II, Berlin 1878; R. Kittel, "Heiligkeit Gottes im A. T.," *RPT*[3], VII, pp. 566-573; J. Skinner, "Holiness," *HDB*, II, pp. 394-399; H. Delehaye, *Sanctus*, Brussels 1927; O. C. Whitehouse, "Holiness," in *ERE*, VI, pp. 750-759; M. Schumpp, "Das Heilige in der Bibel," *ThG* (1930), pp. 331-343; Fr. Pfister-Begrich, "Heilig und Profan," in *RGG*[2], II, cols. 1714-1721; J. Hänel, *Die Religion der Heiligkeit*, Gütersloh 1931; O. Procksch, "Hagios," in *ThW*, I, pp. 87-116; W. Grossouw, "Heilig, heiligheid," in *BW*, cols. 625-630; R. Otto, *Le Sacré*, Paris 1929; F. S. Leenhardt, *La notion de sainteté dans l'Ancien Testament*, Paris 1929.

In the Old Testament, as in other ancient religions, holiness is what characterizes divinity to the point that holiness constitutes the essence of divinity. As it is said: Yahweh swears by Himself (Am 6:8), so it is said in the same sense: He swears by His holiness (Am 4:3; Ps 89:36; cf. Ps 60:8; 108:8). According to Nm 20:12, to believe in Yahweh is "to sanctify Him," that is to say, to acknowledge Him for what He is, the Holy One. He is "the Holy" *qâdôš* (Is 40:25; Hb 3:3; Jb 6:10), or *qĕdôšîm* as a plural of intensity (Jos 24:19; Os 12:1; Prv 9:10; 30:3), "the Holy of Israel" (Is 1:4; 10:17; 30:11.12, etc.). He alone is holy because He alone is God: "Who is holy like Yahweh?" (1 Sm 2:2; cf. 2 Sm 7:22), while other Semites have several "holy gods" (Dn 4:5.6; 5:11).[1] His name, which is the expression of His essence that was revealed to Israel, is "holy," that is to say, divine (Am 2:7; Ez 20:39; Lv 20:3, etc.); in like manner the expression "His holy arm" (Is 52:10; Ps 98:1), "His holy word" (Jer 23:9; Ps 105:42), "His holy spirit" (= Is 63:10; Ps 51:13) designate the divine arm, the divine word, the divine spirit.

---

[1] The inscription of Echmounazar (line 9) uses the same expression (*ERS*, pp. 483 ff.).

The etymology of the Hebrew word (*qôdeš* = holiness; *qâdôš* = holy) is disputed. Some derive it from the root *qâdad* which signifies "to sever," "to separate by cutting." Others derive it from *ḥâdaš*, "to be new, pure, shining." The opposite of *qôdeš* (sacred) is the *ḥol* (from the root *ḥll* = to untie, to free), the profane (1 Sm 21:5.6; Ez 22:26; 42:20; 44:23), that is to say, that which is free from interdict, and is consequently given for common use; the *qôdeš* is that which is withdrawn from common use. The sacred *(qôdeš, qâdôš)* and the pure *(ṭôhar, ṭâhôr)* are related ideas, although they are distinct. Only the pure can be sacred or approach the sacred; that is why the verb to sanctify is sometimes used in the sense of "to purify" (Jos 7:13; 2 Sm 11:4; Jb 1:5; 2 Par 30:17) and the word "profane" in the sense of the impure (1 Mc 1:47.62; Mk 7:2.15; Rom 14:14; Heb 10:29). Purity, at all events, is the condition or the necessary preparation for access to the sacred. Holiness contains two elements which are not part of the notion of the pure, namely, a mysterious power and acceptance of the divinity or possession by the divinity. But the sacred is contagious (Ez 44:19; Ex 29:37; 30:29) like the impure (Lv 11:31-40; 15:4-12.20-28) which makes him who touches it "impure" (Nm 19:1-8). The sacred and the impure have a common character: both are charged with awesome power. Yet the sacred is distinct from the impure because it always has a relation to the divinity, while such a relation is not included in the notion of the impure.

Holiness is ascribed to objects, places, times, persons, and to God. It follows that of itself it does not include moral perfection. According to the oldest concept, holiness includes the presence of a mysterious and awesome power which manifests itself in all that is connected with worship.

Ritual garments worn by priests during liturgical functions are considered charged with a mysterious power which can be communicated and render unfit for profane use all that they touch: for this reason priests will lay aside their sacred garments in the temple and will don others out of fear "lest they sanctify the people with their garments" (Ez 44:19; cf. 42:14; Ex 29:37; 30:29). Sacred vessels used in worship cannot be touched by the levites who are charged with their transportation "lest they die" (Nm 4:15.20).

The place where Yahweh showed Himself in dream to Jacob is "awesome," because it is "the house of God" and Jacob is seized with terror before the revelation of the sacred nature of the place (Gn 28:17).

Moses received the order " to sanctify " *(quiddeš)* the people in order to prepare them for the " descent " of Yahweh on Sinai, and he exhorted the priests " to sanctify themselves " *(ytqaddešû)* " for fear lest Yahweh strike them " (Ex 19:10.22), that is to say, to put themselves in such a condition as to be able to approach the holy and awesome God (cf. Jos 3:5; 1 Sm 16:5; 2 Par 5:11; 29:5.34; 30:15.24) for fear lest they be struck down (cf. Ex 19:21).

The sanctuary, the abode of Yahweh, seemed to be filled with an awesome power, and it was the sound of the little bells sewn unto the garments of the high priest that protected him when he officiated before Yahweh; " that its tinkling (of the little bells) may be heard as he enters and leaves the Lord's presence in the sanctuary, else he will die " (Ex 28:35; cf. Lv 16:2.12 ff.) [2].

Eliseus is called " holy " because he is " a man of God, " that is to say, a wonder-worker exercising a superhuman power (4 Kgs 4:9; cf. Jgs 13:6) and possessing the spirit of God (4 Kgs 2:15).

The holy ark (2 Par 35:3) is charged with a mysterious and awesome power which protects it from all profane contact (1 Sm 6.19.20; 2 Sm 6:7.8), because it is the ark of Yahweh (Jos 3:13; 1 Sm 4:6, etc.), the symbol and the throne of " the holy God before whom no man can live " (1 Sm 6:20). To this point we will have to return. According to this concept, holiness appears to resemble an extraordinary power inherent in the object, the place, the person because of the bond that unites them to God.

In many texts, especially the legislative ones that ascribe holiness to objects, places, times or persons, the idea of a mysterious and awesome power recedes and the idea of relation to worship or to the divinity takes the first place. In these cases, anything is holy that is withdrawn from profane use and is set apart for or belongs to the divinity. To express this idea the Hebrew employs the noun *qôdeš* (holiness), when it is a question of objects, places, or sacred times, and the adjective *qâdôš*, when it is question of persons.

---

[2] Most modern commentators explain that these little bells were the instruments whose sound protected the high priest from the actions of malevolent demons. (Cf. J. Dölger, *Antike und Christentum,* IV (1934), pp. 233-242). But is it to be supposed that the sanctuary, the abode of Yahweh, was haunted by demons? It is not only a question of protecting the high priest against the spirits who guard the threshhold of the sanctuary (A. Jirku, *Die Dämonen und ihre Abwehr im A. T.*, Leipzig 1912, pp. 82, 85), but also to protect him throughout the entire duration of his service in the temple (J. Dölger, *op. cit.*, p. 240).

Objects used in worship are " holy, " for example, the ritual garments of the priests (Ex 28:2.4.36; 29:6, etc.), the oil used in ritual anointings (Ex 30:25.31.32), the sacrificial offerings and victims (Ex 28:38; 29:33.34; Ez 44:13; Ag 2:12; 2 Par 29:33, etc.), the tithes (Lv 27:30.32; Dt 26:13), the first-born of pure beasts (Nm 18:17), the loaves of proposition (1 Sm 21:5) and, in general, all that is offered to God or to the sanctuary (Jos 6:19; Is 23:18; Ez 20:40; 3 Kgs 7:51; 15:15, etc.).

Holy are the places where Yahweh dwells (Ex 15:17), such as the tabernacle (Ex 25:8; *miqdâš* = sanctuary, Ex 28:29.35.43, etc.; *qadeš;* Ex 29:31, etc.; *mâkôm qâdôš* = holy place), the temple (Ez 42:20; Is 64:10; Ps 5:8, etc.),[3] the temple hill (Jl 2:1; 4:17; Is 11:9, etc.), and the whole city of Jerusalem (Is 48:2; 52:1), which is " the city of God, the holy dwelling place of the Most High " (Ps 46:5), the heaven (Dt 26:15; Mi 1:2) and those places where He reveals Himself (Ex 3:5).

" Holy " days (Neh 10:35) or days " consecrated to Yahweh " (literally: " holy for Yahweh, " Neh 8:9-11) are days consecrated for worship, especially the Sabbath (Ex 16:23; 31:14.15; 35:2; Is 58:13) which God Himself " has sanctified " (Gn 2:3), that is to say, has reserved for Himself alone and for His worship, and consequently has withdrawn from men's work. The " holy assemblies " (Ex 12:16; Lv 23:2-4) are the reunions convoked for worship on feast days.

As for persons, they may be " holy ": 1) as in the case of objects because of their relation to worship or on account of their belonging to God; or 2) by reason of a quality intrinsic to the individual.

1) Priests and levites are holy (2 Par 23:6; 35:3) because they have been set apart for the worship of Yahweh (2 Par 26:18; Ez 48:11) and consecrated to Him by appropriate rites (Ex 29:1.21.33.44); they are to be looked upon as holy (Lv 21:8), that is to say, considered as belonging to God and consequently inviolable. Nazarites are holy because of their vow which sets them apart and by which they are consecrated to Yahweh (Nm 6:5). Combatants are " consecrated "[4] (Is 13:3; Jer 22:7; 51:27; So 1:7), because they fight a holy war, Yahweh's war, or, as it is said in Hebrew, because they " sanctify

---

[3] In the temple a distinction was made between " the Holy Place " (Ex 26:33; Lv 4:6) and " the Holy of Holies " (Ex 26:34) in which the Ark of Yahweh was kept.

[4] For this reason the warriors were subject to certain restrictions, especially in sexual matters (1 Sm 21:6; 2 Sm 11:11), and in regard to ritual purity (Dt 23:11). The camp had to be " holy, " that is to say, free from all uncleanness and excrement, because Yahweh was there (Dt 21:13-15).

the combat " (Mi 3:5; Jer 6:4; Jl 4:9), preparing for it by religious rites and sacrifices (1 Sm 7:8.9; 14:24; So 1:7). Terms *(qĕdêšîm, qĕdêsôth)* derived from the root *qdš* (to be holy) were even used to denote men and women who gave themselves up to sacred prostitution in Canaanite sanctuaries (Dt 23:18; 3 Kgs 14:24; 22:47) and who dared to enter those of Yahweh (3 Kgs 14:24; 22:47; cf. 1 Sm 2:22; Os 4:14). Jeremias was sanctified by Yahweh from his mother's womb, that is to say, he was set apart and vowed to God's service (Jer 1:4). Finally the whole people of Israel is holy, because it was set apart by God to be His possession (Ex 19:5.6). Since it is the people of Yahweh, it shares in the character of the holy God, in His essential holiness, and, at least in principle, in His moral holiness; and in this sense it is " His holy people " (Is 63:18), the holy people (Dn 12:7), " the holy seed " (Ezr 9:2), the people of saints (Dn 8:24), " the people of the saints of the Most High " (Dn 7:27), the saints of the Most High (Dn 7:18.22.25).

2) But because Israel is holy, inasmuch as it is set apart from all other peoples and belongs to Yahweh (Lv 20:26), it must also be holy intrinsically after the example of its God: " Be holy, because I am holy, I, Yahweh, your God " (Lv 11:44; 19:1; 20:26). This required holiness includes ritual purity (Lv 11:43-44; 20:25.26) and religious purity (Dt 14:1.2) and moral purity (Lv 19:1-37; Ps 15; 24:3-6), that is to say, the observance of all divine precepts (Nm 15:40). More than all other Israelites, the priests are held to religious and ritual holiness, because Yahweh " sanctifies them, " that is to say, consecrates them to His service and makes them His own in a quite special manner (Lv 21:1-23). Holiness in the Old Testament acquires thus a personal and moral character that distinguishes it from the holiness recognized by other ancient religions.

Although the God of Israel has always been a moral God, as many old accounts and ancient theophoric names attest, [5] the holiness which characterizes Him does not denote, in all the texts, Yahweh's moral perfection. Several — and this is largely true of the oldest ones — denote only the " numinous " aspect which characterizes the divine or the sacred in all religions. The " numinous " embraces several elements: it is " the wholly other, " that is to say, that which is totally different from and above all other being, that which is powerful and majestic, mysterious and terrifying, but at the same time fascinating. Before the " numinous " man is keenly conscious of his own nothingness,

---

[5] See above, p. 33.

he trembles, is startled and is filled with a reverential fear composed of dread and confidence.

Before Yahweh, Abraham is filled with terror (Gn 15:12; 28:17) and feels himself to be " dust and ashes " (Gn 18:27; cf. Jb 42:6); Job cannot speak, he is overcome by fear and the consciousness of his own nothingness (Jb 40:3-5); Moses and Elias hide their faces (Ex 3:6; 33:22; 3 Kgs 19:13); Isaias believes himself lost (Is 6:5); Daniel grows weak and falls with his face to the ground (Dn 10:8.9); even the Seraphim cover their faces with their wings (Is 6:2), because " no one can see God and live " (Ex 33:20; 19:21; Jgs 13:22); " Who is able to stand before the Lord, this holy God? " (1 Sm 6:20).

No one who is profane can look at Him (1 Sm 6:19.20), nor touch Him (2 Sm 6:7.8), nor approach Him (Ex 19:21), nor hear Him (Dt 5:22), without risking his life (cf. Ex 24:10.11). The old poem of Ex 15:11 gives concise expression to the different elements of the numinous: the wholly other character, the mysteriousness, the awesomeness, the majesty, the power of Yahweh: " Yahweh, who is like you among the gods? Who is like you magnificent in holiness, awesome in striking deeds, worker of wonders? " Isaias 40:25 insists on the unique character that differentiates Yahweh from every other being: " Whom would you compare Me with, as an equal? says the Holy One " (cf. 46:5; Os 11:9; Ps 89:7). And Is 8:12-14 stresses the awesome character of " the Holy One of Israel " whose wrath is about to fall on a guilty people: " Do not call conspiracy all that this people calls conspiracy, and do not fear what they fear, nor be in dread. But Yahweh Sabaoth, Him you shall regard as holy; let Him be your fear, and let Him be your dread. And He will become a sanctuary, and a stone of offense, and a rock of stumbling to both the houses of Israel, a trap and a snare to the inhabitants of Israel " (Is 8:12-14). [6] " To sanctify Yahweh, " that is to say, to hold Him for what He is, namely holy, is to fear Him, to be in awe of Him. He does, indeed, become " a sanctuary, " that is to say, He proves by His acts that He is a mysterious and awesome force which closes like a trap on its prey. The same idea recurs again in Is 10:17: " The

---

[6] Instead of *qešer* (conspiracy) several critics propose the reading *qodeš* (holy); others, on the contrary, correct the verb *taqdišû* (sanctify) into *taqširû* (hold him as a conspirator). These corrections (the first is attractive) are not necessary. There is no more reason to suppress, as do most critics, the word " a sanctuary, " which joins v. 14 to the verb of v. 13 " sanctify. " Yahweh would be a sacred object, that is to say, something awesome, a trap, a snare for Israel (cf. F. Feldmann, *in h.l.*, and J. Hänel, *Die Religion der Heiligkeit*, pp. 111 ff.). F. Leenhardt (*La notion de sainteté dans l'Ancien Testament*, pp. 177 ff.) retains the word and interprets it as " a refuge, " because a sanctuary is a place of refuge; but this meaning does not suit the context.

Holy One of Israel will be a flame which will consume and devour his thorns and briers in a single day." The holiness of Yahweh is often associated with His awesome, fear-inspiring character (for example, Ex 15:11.12; Is 29:23; Ps 99:3; 111:9). Other texts connect it with the elevation of the Most High who lives in a lofty and holy place (Is 40:25; 57:15; 63:15); or it is connected with His jealousy which signifies the exclusive character of the God of Israel (Jos 24:19; Ez 39:25.27; cf. Na 1:2-6). Before the royal majesty of Yahweh, the holy God, "the peoples tremble," "the earth quivers," His faithful ones prostrate themselves before His footstool (Ps 99:1-5). [7]

Yahweh manifests what He is, or, as it is expressed in Hebrew, "He sanctifies Himself," [8] that is to say, He manifests His holiness by showing His power through His great deeds (Lv 10:3; Nm 20:13; cf. Ex 15:11; 1 Sm 2:2; Ps 77:14.15), by the work of creation (Is 41:20; 45:11.12), by the grandiose and terrifying phenomena that accompany His arrival (Hb 3:3-15; Ps 29:3-9; 77:12.17), by the deliverance and restoration of His oppressed and scattered people (Ez 20:41;28:22.25; cf. Is 41:14; 43:3; 47:4). It is also said that He "sanctifies His great name" (Ez 36:23), because His name manifests what He is: great, powerful and holy, three terms that are intimately associated in the passage of Ez 36:17-32. Because of Israel's exile among the Gentiles "His holy name has been profaned" (Ez 36:20.21.23); in fact, the Gentiles, because they conquered and subdued Israel, believe that Yahweh is a God less powerful than their gods and unable to protect His people (36:20). Not esteemed for what He is, the holy God is dishonored, "His holy name is profaned" (cf. 20:9.14.22). Yahweh cannot tolerate this profanation: "He has had pity on His holy name" which has been profaned, and for the honor of His name He will restore Israel (36:22). He "will sanctify His great name which has been profaned" by bringing Israel into its own land from all the nations where it had been scattered; "He will sanctify Himself" in His people, before the eyes of the nations, that is to say, He will manifest what He is, the holy God, in the sight of the nations "so that they may recognize that He is Yahweh," that is to say, He who efficaciously manifests His existence (cf. 20:9 and Ex 3:14) by His all-powerful intervention in favor of His people (36:23).

---

[7] In Ps 99:1-5, the acclamation "He is holy" is a response to the strophes of the hymn to King Yahweh, elevated, grand, awesome, powerful, just and true, who is at once feared and admired. Here are found all the elements that constitute holiness, including its moral aspect.

[8] The verb employed in the *Niphal* (passive) form has always Yahweh for its subject.

Because holiness constitutes in some way, according to the Hebrews, the divine essence, it is frequently associated with God's glory (in Hebrew *kâbôd* from the root *kbd* which means " to be heavy "). It is something that gives importance and weight and inspires respect and fear (Ps 102:16). To give glory to God means, therefore, to recognize God's importance, to acknowledge Him for what He is — holy and powerful. For Yahweh, " to sanctify Himself, " that is to say, to manifest what He is, the Holy One, is also " to glorify Himself " (Ez 28:22); these two expressions are parallel and practically equivalent. Israel's sins are a challenge " to His glory " (Is 3:8), because they are an affront to His awesome holiness; Yahweh cannot surrender " His glory " to any one (Is 42:8; 48:11), because He cannot surrender what gives Him His worth, His holiness by which He is God. Nevertheless, glory is not identical with holiness; it stresses power which is included in holiness; furthermore glory is often the exterior manifestation of power and holiness or of Yahweh Himself, [9] while holiness always denotes Yahweh's intimate nature and has often a moral aspect which is not formally included in the concept of glory.

Among the prophets, God's holiness often assumes a very marked moral aspect: Yahweh is not only totally different and far above that which is created and physically weak, He is also far above that which is morally weak or imperfect. Amos (2:7) considers Israel's moral deviations as a profanation of the holy name, that is to say, of Yahweh's essentially holy person. Osee (11:8.9) explains by Yahweh's holiness, that is to say, by what distinguishes God from man and from every creature, the incomprehensible love of Yahweh for His people, that love which confounds the human spirit and defies every juridical form governing Yahweh's union with Israel: " because I am God (El), and not man, a holy one in your midst. " This love, which continues despite Israel's infidelities (cf. 11:1-4) and forgives them, shows that Yahweh is He who is " wholly other, " totally different from this earthly world and from every creature.

At the sight of the Yahweh of hosts, before whom the Seraphim veil their faces and the lintels of the temple gates shake, Isaias (6:5) feels he must perish, " because he is a man of unclean lips and dwells in the midst of a people of unclean lips. " It is, then, his sins (cf. Is 6:6), much more than his nothingness that separates the prophet from the Holy One of Israel and causes him to tremble before the moral grandeur and the awesome majesty of the Lord. The Holy One of Israel is profaned by the iniquities of His people (Is 1:4; 5:18.19); He will

[9] See III, § 10.

manifest His greatness in the judgment and in the justice that He will exercise against the pride of mortal men (Is 5:15.16). Habacuc (1:12.13) appeals to the " Holy One " in these terms : " Are you not from eternity, Yahweh, my holy God? Your eyes are too pure to look upon evil; You cannot endure the sight of misery. Why, then, do You gaze on the faithless in silence while the wicked man devours one more just than himself? " Here the Holy One is the eternal God who rules from above and who causes men and the world to tremble (cf. 3:3-6) and cannot allow oppression and injustice to triumph. Job 15:14-16 (cf. 25:4-6; Ps 143:2) gives vigorous expression to the consciousness of nothingness, impurity and guilt of man before God who cannot even rely upon His holy ones (that is to say, upon the angels). [10]

In sacerdotal environments the moral aspect of God's holiness is not obliterated by cultic considerations; although much insistence is placed there on ritual purity, moral purity is also exacted (Lv 19:2-37) as the condition of access to Yahweh, to sacred things and to His sanctuary, because Yahweh is holy (Lv 19:2).

Certain liturgical psalms (Ps 15; 24:3.4) require from pilgrims who present themselves at the gates of the temple on the holy mountain nothing less than conditions of the moral order.

The expression " the Holy One of Israel, " coined by Isaias, contains a paradox : Yahweh is distinct from every creature inasmuch as He is holy. Yet if He is bound to Israel inasmuch as He is " the Holy One of Israel, " it is because He established a relation which has for its goal the sanctification of Israel. But this goal will be attained only by " a remnant " of the people (Is 4:2.3), [11] by those who will have been purified by cataclysms which will befall the whole nation. According to Ezechiel (36:22-27), the sanctification of Israel will bring about not only the restoration of the scattered nation, but, above all, a purification from all its stains and defilements as well as a true interior regeneration of its members : Yahweh will " sanctify Himself " in Israel in the sight of the nations, that is to say, He will manifest His holiness by gathering together all those who are scattered in many lands, by cleansing them from all their impurities, by giving them a new heart and a new spirit, and finally, He will give them His own spirit, that is to say, His own strength which will enable them to observe His laws. In this new and eternal covenant (37:26), which

[10] The angels are " the holy ones " (Jb 5:1; 15:15; Ps 89:6-8), because they are " the sons of God " (Ps 29:1; 89:7; Jb 1:6; 2:1; 38:7), that is to say, they are divine beings who form Yahweh's council (3 Kgs 22:19) and are His servants and messengers.

[11] O. Procksch, *Theologie*, p. 93.

will replace the old one that was broken by Israel's faults, the Holy God will communicate a principle of moral perfection to His people (cf. Jer 31:31-34) and make them, in the highest meaning of the word, a holy people.

§ 7. *The spirituality of God*

The Hebrew, unlike the Greek philosopher, does not place spirit in opposition to matter and has no understanding of pure spirit, that is to say, of a substance that is purely spiritual and simple and excluding all composition. The term he uses to express spirit *(ruaḥ)* signifies wind, breath or spirit. Spirit is for him not a simple, immaterial substance, but a concrete power which he conceives as wind and which he opposes to "the flesh" (Is 31:3), as something which is powerful and durable (the spirit) to that which is weak and perishable (the flesh).[1] It is not said that God is spirit, but that He has spirit. The Hebrew does not speculate about God's nature; he believes in God who has revealed Himself and whose action is manifest in nature and the history of Israel. It is enough for the Hebrew to know that God is and what He is, and what He does for him and for his people. It is not to be expected, therefore, that we find in the Old Testament an exact notion of God's spirituality.

Nevertheless, since the God of the Old Testament is a personal being, totally different from and sovereignly raised above all other being, and since He is, as we shall see later, eternal, immutable, all-powerful, omnipresent, it is clear that He is neither corporeal nor material. The innumerable anthropomorphisms of the sacred books do not prove the contrary; they are meant to throw light on the personal character of the living God who manifests Himself to man as God the redoubtable, but also as God the accessible and compassionate. Even the popular accounts in which Yahweh is described as fashioning man as a potter (Gn 2:7), as walking in the Garden of Eden (Gn 3:8), sewing loin cloths (Gn 3:21), shutting the door of the ark after Noe has entered (Gn 7:16), smelling the odor of victims burned in sacrifice (Gn 8:21), coming down from heaven to see the tower of Babel (Gn 11:5), represent Him at the same time as the creator, the sovereign master and the supreme

[1] On the notion of spirit in the Old Testament, see P. van Imschoot, "L'action de l'esprit de Jahvé dans l'Ancien Testament," *RScPT* (1934), pp. 533-588; and the articles "Geest," "Heilige Geest," *BW*, cols. 470-485.

judge of man, and consequently exalted above all human limitations and deficiencies. [2]

According to certain accounts of theophanies, Yahweh or His angel appears under human form (Gn 18; 16:7-13; Jgs 6:11-23; 13:3-23), but no description of His exterior is given. Moses cannot see His face, [3] but only His back (Ex 33:22.23) and He veils His face when He appears (Ex 3:6; cf. 3 Kgs 19:13; Elias). If certain privileged ones have been able to see Yahweh (Gn 32:31; 33:10; Ex 24:10.11; Jgs 6:11-23; 13:3-23), they are amazed to find that they are not dead (Gn 32:21; Ex 24:11; Jgs 6:23; 13:22), because all agree that "man cannot see God and live" (Ex 19:21; 33:20; cf. Is 6:5), so awesome is the holy God. Usually He manifests Himself only by a voice that can be heard, but He who speaks is not seen (Gn 12:1; 13:14; 15:1; 21:17; 22:11.15; Dt 4:12; 5:20; 1 Sm 3:4.6.8, etc.); or He manifests Himself by His glory (Ex 16:7.10; 24:15.16; 29:43; 40:34.35; Lv 9:6; Nm 14:10; 16:19; 17:7; 20:6; Dt 5:23.24; 3 Kgs 8:11, etc.), by visions and dreams (Nm 12:6; Gn 20:3; 31:11.24; 37:5.9; Nm 22:8.20; Jos 5:13; 1 Sm 28:6.15; Is 6:1; Am 7, etc.).

And the prophets who declare that they have seen Him, take care not to describe Him: Amos (9:1) says simply that Yahweh remained standing beside the altar at Bethel; Isaias (6:1-13) speaks of Yahweh seated on a raised throne, the train of His robe filled the temple, winged Seraphim surrounded Him, smoke filled the sanctuary: all else was for him indescribable. [4] Ezechiel (1:4-2:9) gives a detailed description of the light, fire, Cherubim, chariot, firmament and throne of Yahweh, but he speaks with extreme reserve of the luminous figure under which Yahweh appears to him: "And above the firmament that was over their heads something like a throne could be seen, looking

---

[2] Cf. W. Eichrodt, *Theologie*, I, p. 106.

[3] According to another and probably more recent tradition, Moses was privileged to see the figure *(tĕmûnâh)*, the face *(pânîm)* of Yahweh (Ex 33:11; Nm 12:8; Dt 34:10). Those texts seek to stress the intimacy of Moses' relations with God who showed Himself to him without any intermediary. He spoke to him, mouth to mouth, or "face to face" (Ex 33:11), that is to say by showing Himself, and not by enigmas, that is to say, not by visions and dreams as He revealed Himself to the other prophets (Nm 12:6-8). The expressions "to speak face to face" (Ex 33:11; Dt 5:4), or "mouth to mouth" (Nm 12:8), or "eye to eye" (Nm 14:14), indicate a personal and immediate revelation of God, but they do not imply a vision of God who speaks (cf. F. Nötscher, *Das Angesicht Gottes schauen*, Würzburg 1924, p. 54). The expression "to see the face of Yahweh" may mean to visit the sanctuary (Ex 23:15.17; 34:20.23; Is 1:12; Ps 42:3), or to experience divine benevolence (Ps 17:15; cf. Nm 6:25.26). To seek Yahweh's face is to speak to Him in order to obtain His help (Ps 27:8), or to go to His sanctuary (Ps 24:6); to caress His face means to appease Him, to make Him benevolent (1 Sm 13:12) (P. Heinisch, *Theologie*, p. 31; F. Nötscher, *op. cit.*).

[4] J. Hänel, *op. cit.*, p. 246.

like sapphire. Upon it was seated, up above, one who had the appearance of a man. Upward from what resembled His waist I saw what gleamed like electrum; downward from what resembled His waist I saw what looked like fire; He was surrounded with splendor. Like the bow which appears in the clouds on a rainy day was the splendor that surrounded Him. Such was the vision of the likeness of the glory of the Lord" (Ez 1:26-28). The prophet's hesitation and the multiplication of terms expressing the resemblance and similitude with a human figure or brilliant objects clearly indicate that Ezechiel had a deep realization that God whom he perceived in a vague way cannot be described in human terms because He is totally different from and infinitely above every creature.

God's totally different nature is formally expressed by many prophets: "I am God and not man" (Os 11:9). Is 40:12-18 declares that no image can represent God because He resembles no other being (cf. Is 46:5; Ps 89:7). Dt 4:15.16 justifies the prohibition of images referring to the fact that Yahweh has not manifested Himself under any figure. Several texts formally disapprove of making God like unto man: He neither sleeps nor slumbers (Ps 121:4), He does not grow weary (Is 40:28), He does not repent as a man does (1 Sm 15:29; Nm 23:19), He has no eyes as men have (Jb 10:4). Isaias (31:3) believes the antithesis between God and man to be of the same order as that which exists between spirit and flesh; the parallelism established between the two antitheses supposes that God is spirit, that is to say, powerful and incorruptible, while man is flesh, that is to say, weak and perishable.

Finally, only a spiritual God can fill earth and heaven (Jer 23:24), have heaven as His throne and the earth as His footstool (Is 66:1), be too great to be contained in heaven and earth (3 Kgs 8:27), penetrate minds and hearts (Prv 16:2; Jer 17:10). [5]

§ 8. *The attributes of God*

God manifests His attributes by His works. In God, His attributes are not distinct from His nature; but because man has only an analogical and imperfect knowledge of God (Wis 13:5), he is forced to consider them separately. This is what happens in the Old Testament which, however, does not always give to these attributes the sharply defined outlines which they have in a more advanced theology. Yet it is

[5] Cf. J. Hänel, *op. cit.*, p. 246.

possible, without doing violence to Israelite thought, to group them in two categories :

A. Metaphysical attributes. B. Moral attributes. [1]

A. Metaphysical attributes of God

1. *God's omnipotence.* — Yahweh's power is sung with enthusiasm in the oldest poems of the Bible which exalt the warrior God, the victor over the enemies of Israel : " Yahweh is a warrior, Yahweh is His name " (Ex 15:3) ; " Sing to Yahweh, for He is most high ; He has cast horse and rider into the sea " (Ex 15:1). " Who is this glorious king ? It is Yahweh, the mighty, the valiant ; it is Yahweh, mighty in battle " (Ps 24:8). When he advances to succor His people " the earth quakes, the skies shake, [2] clouds turn into water, mountains tremble " (Jgs 5:4). At His command, stars (Jgs 5:20 ; Jos 10:12.13) and elements (Ex 14:21 ; 15:5.8 ; 1 Sm 12:18) fight for Israel (cf. 1 Sm 7:10 ; 4 Kgs 19:35, etc.). The strength of His arm or His right hand, raised on behalf of His people, is proudly vaunted (Ex 6:6 ; 14:31 ; 15:6 ; Dt 4:34 ; 6:21 ; Is 40:10 ; 51:5 ; 52:10, etc.). The old names of the God of Israel, " the Powerful One of Jacob " (Gn 49:24 ; Is 1:24 ; 49:26 ; 60:16 ; Ps 132:2.5), perhaps El Šadday (Gn 17:10 ; Ex 6:3) and El (for example, Gn 33:20) [3] attest that power is the divine attribute that seems to have most impressed the ancient Hebrews. The strongest army is but " flesh, " that is to say, weak and perishable, before God (Is 31:3 ; cf. 2 Par 32:8 ; Jer 17:5 ; Ps 20:8 ; 33:16.17). He is " the rock " (2 Sm 23:3 ; Is 30:29 ; Dt 32:30, etc.) and " the shield " of Israel (Gn 15:1 ; 2 Sm 22:3.31, etc.). He commands as master the greatest foreign empires (Is 7:18 ; 9:10.11), whose kings are His instruments and carry out His decrees (Is 10:5.15 ; 41:4 ; 44:8 ; Jer 25:9 ; 27:6).

God's omnipotence manifests itself brilliantly not only in the history of Israel but also in the creation of the world (Gn 1 ; Ps 19 ; 33:6 ; 104 ; Jb 38, etc.). He it is who set the stars moving in order and calls them by their name (Is 40:26). He created the universe by His all-powerful word (Ps 33:6), and this word does not return to Him empty but it does all that He wishes (Is 55:11) ; no one can prevent Him from carrying out what He has decided (Is 43:13) and no prodigy He performs can come as a surprise (Gn 18:14). Even the most fearsome monsters of oriental mythology, such as Leviathan, [4]

---

[1] As Sellin does (*Theologie*, pp. 23-30).

[2] Read with LXX *nâmogû* instead of *nâtâphû* (pour out).

[3] For the meaning of *El Šadday* and of *El*, see above § 2.

[4] On Leviathan, cf. " Liwjathan, " *BW*, cols. 961-962.

the seven-headed sea beast (Is 27:1; Ps 74:13.14) and the sea dragons (Ps 74:13; Jb 7:12; Is 51:9), are pierced by Yahweh with a glance or He masters them to use them as His toys (Ps 104:26).

2. *God's sublimity.* — The sublimity of God is already indicated by the ancient names of El Elyôn, the Most High God (Gn 14:18; Ps 57:3; 78:35) or the Most High, or simply Elyôn (Nm 24:16; Is 14:14; Ps 18:14; 21:8, etc.). Originally these words seem to have signified that God dwells on heavenly heights (cf. Mi 6:6 : the God of heavenly heights), but prophets and psalmists frequently used them, as did later the Jews of the Dispora, to designate the transcendent God who is "raised above the entire earth" (Ps 83:19; 97:9) and above all the gods (Ps 97:9), Yahweh, the awe-inspiring Most High, a great king over all the earth (Ps 47:3). Yahweh alone is lifted up (Is 2:11); "Who is like Him magnificent in holiness, terrible in glorious deeds, worker of wonders?" (Ex 15:11; cf. Ps 66:3.5); He is "the high and lofty one and inhabits eternity; His name is Holy, He dwells in the high and holy place" (Is 57:15). "The Lord reigns: the people tremble; He sits above the Cherubim; the earth quakes. The Lord is great in Sion, He is high above all the peoples. Let them praise your great and awesome name: He is holy....Extol the Lord, our God, and worship at His footstool: He is holy!" (Ps 99:1-3.5). Here it is seen how infinite elevation of the Most High is intimately bound up with His holiness, of which it is, in fact, an element. "There is none like you, O Lord: You are great, and great is Your name and mighty. Who would not fear You, King of the nations?" (Jer 10:6.7). "Great is the Lord and greatly to be praised, His greatness is inscrutable" (Ps 145:3; cf. Sir 18:1-4). Hymns delight in exalting the greatness and the elevation of God the creator above all creatures (Ps 95:3-5; 96:4-6; 97:9); and Isaias (2:6-21) describes in striking terms the abasement of human pride before the Most High "when He shall rise up to strike the earth": "Human pride will be abased, the arrogance of men brought low, and the Lord alone will be exalted, on that day" (2:17; cf. also Is 40:15-18; Jb 37:22-24).

Raised up above all creatures, Yahweh is absolutely independent and has no need of any one of them (2 Mc 14:35). The richest sacrifices are not worthy to be offered to Him : all the forests and all the animals of the Lebanon do not suffice for a holocaust (Is 40:16). Since the whole earth and all that is in it belongs to Him (Ex 19:15; Dt 10:14), He has no need of the offerings of men: "I take from your house no bullock, no goats out of your fold: for Mine are all the animals of the forests, beasts by the thousands on My mountains. I know all the birds of the air, and whatever stirs in the plains, belongs to Me. If I were hungry, I should not tell you; for Mine are the world and its fullness" (Ps 50:9-12). Even man's piety and virtues add nothing to God's perfection or happiness; piety and virtues are necessary only for man himself. "Can a man be profitable to God? Surely he who is wise is profitable to himself. What does it profit Šadday if you are righteous, or is it gain to Him, if you make your ways blameless?" (Jb 22:2.3; cf. 35:7). In a similar way man's sin takes nothing from Him and impairs Him in nothing: "If I sin, what do I do to You?" says Job (7:20; cf. 35:6). Sin harms only man: "If you are wise, it is to your own advantage; and if you are arrogant, you alone shall bear it" (Prv 9:12).[5] The Lord laughs at the plotting of the wicked because He sees that His day will come, that is to say, the day will come when He will have the last word (Ps 37:13; cf. 2:4; Prv 3:34).[6]

3. *The eternity and immutability of God.* — The words *'ôlâm* and *qedem* very often signify a long period of time belonging either to past or future (for example, Gn 6:4; Dt 32:7; Ex 12:14; 27:21). The wish addressed to the king: "Live forever" (3 Kgs 1:31; Dn 2:4) is only a court formula and is not to be taken literally. But applied to God, these words take on a deeper meaning, because the God of Israel has neither beginning nor end. This sharply distinguishes Him from the gods of Babylon, Egypt, Phoenicia and Greece. Israel never knew the theogonies which are part of most mythologies in the ancient East.

Nor is Yahweh a god who dies and rises as do gods like Adonis, Tammuz, Osiris, etc., who personify the vegetation that dies and lives again each year. He is the God who has always been and who does not die: "Are you not from eternity, Yahweh, my holy God, who does not die?" (Ha 1:12).[7] The "eternal God" (or ancient: *'ēl 'ôlâm*, Gn 21:33), who was already venerated by the patriarchs, is the living God,[8] "living eternally" (Dt 32:40), whose protection and power are exercised always and unendingly, from generation to generation (Ex 15:18; Dt 33:27; Is 9:5; Ps 103:17; 145:13). He is "an eternal rock"

---

[5] In the sapiential books, the wise man is one who is prudent and virtuous; the scorner is one who mocks God and man (cf. Prv 21:24; 22:10; 29:8.9).

[6] "His day" may be understood as a reference to the day of the wicked (cf. Prv 1:26; Jer 50:27-31), that is to say, the day when the accounts of the wicked are settled, the day when evil, the normal consequence of sin (Prv 1:18.19; 2:18.19.22), will surprise him (Prv 6:11.15).

[7] Read *'élohêy qodši* instead of *'élohay qĕdôšî* (= my God, my Holy One) and *tâmût* (thou diest) instead of *nâmût* (we die).

[8] Cf. above § 4; cf. R. Kittel, *Die hellenistischen Mysterienreligionen*, Stuttgart 1924, pp. 77 ff.

(Is 26:4). He has created heaven and earth (Gn 1:1); He was in existence, therefore, before the world was. "Before the mountains were begotten and the earth and the world were brought forth, from eternity to eternity You are God. For a thousand years in Your sight are as yesterday, now that it is passed, and as a watch of the night" (Ps 90:2.4). Time does not count for God: ten centuries pass as quickly for Him as does one day, or as the three or four hours of a night watch.[9] His days are from generation to generation (Ps 102:25).

The book of Isaias which proclaims so insistently the unicity of God (Is 41:29; 44:6; 46:9), teaches no less clearly His eternity: "I, I Myself call forth the generations since the beginning. I am the first and with the last I will also be" (cf. Is 41:4).[10] "I am the first and I am the last; there is no God but Me" (cf. Is 44:6; 48:12). "You are My witnesses...so that...you may know that it is I (that is to say, that I am God)" (cf. Is 43:10). "Before Me no god was formed, and after Me there shall be none. It is I, I the Lord; there is no savior but Me" (Is 43:10.11).

Just as God is without beginning and without end, so is He without change; heaven and earth pass but He remains the same: "Of old You established the earth, and the heavens are the work of Your hands. They shall perish, but You remain, though all of them grow old like a garment. Like clothing You change them, and they are changed, but You are the same, and Your years have no end" (Ps 102:26-28). Similarly divine wisdom "while herself perduring, renews everything" (Wis 7:27), and the divine word lasts forever: "Though the grass withers and the flower wilts, the word of God stands forever" (Is 40:8).

God is immutable in His being and also in His will: "He does not call back His words" (Is 31:2). He has spoken and has not repented, He has resolved and has not gone back on His word (Jer 4:28). "The heavens shall vanish like smoke, and the earth shall be worn away like a garment, and the inhabitants thereof shall

[9] The Hebrews divided the night into three watches: each one three or four hours long.

[10] In the expression *'ănî hû, hû* signifies: the same (cf. Ges.-K, § 135, a, n. 1). This expression recurs several times: Is 43:10.13; 46:4 (cf. Ps 102:28; Jer 5:12); P. J. Beveridge ("*I am" in the Fourth Gospel*, Expositor 26 (1923), pp. 418 ff.) interprets this as an affirmation of God's eternity (cf. Dt 32:39); P. Volz (*Jesaia*, II, Leipzig 1932, p. 16) and J. Fischer (*Das Buch Isaias*, Bonn 1939, p. 42) interpret it as an affirmation of Yahweh's divinity (cf. Ex 6:7: you will recognize that I am Yahweh; Ez 6:7.13, etc.); cf. also E. Schweitzer, *Ego eimi*, Göttingen 1939.

perish (like gnats) [11]; but My salvation will be forever and My justice shall not fail" (Is 51:6; cf. 51:8). If Israel was not consumed because of its faults, it is because "Yahweh does not change" (Mal 3:6). This means that He is constant in His plans of salvation, because He is "the eternal rock" (Is 26:4) of His people.

On the other hand, other texts attribute to God either repentance, [12] or a change of attitude or of plan. When Yahweh decides to destroy His people in the desert as a result of the golden calf incident, He allows Himself to be swayed by the supplications of Moses: "And the Lord repented of the evil that He said He would do to His people" (Ex 32:10-14). Amos (7:3.6) obtains the retraction of the decrees of extermination that Yahweh had issued against Israel. Osee (11:8.9) describes the struggle that takes place in Yahweh's heart, the struggle between wrath and pity, between the will to pardon Israel and the will to chastise this faithless nation according to its merits: "How can I hand you over, O Israel? My heart is turned within Me, My repentance is stirred up. I will not execute the fierceness of My wrath; I will not return to destroy Ephraim, because I am God and not man: the Holy One in your midst (and I do not take pleasure in destruction)." [13] These passages show forth the power of prayer and intercession of the prophets over God's heart and the infinite mercy of Yahweh who allows Himself to be swayed and who forgives sinners. Intimately convinced of the efficacy of prayer and of divine mercy, the Hebrews did not try to reconcile these truths of experience with God's immutability. Yet the problem did not altogether escape Osee, because he tried to explain Yahweh's incomprehensible mercy towards His guilty people by Yahweh's holiness, that is to say, by what differentiates God from man and places Him above every created being. The prophet very plainly was aware of the mystery of God, of One who is totally different from and is elevated above all that man knows, and who is able to unite in Himself seemingly irreconcilable attributes.

4. *The omnipresence of God.* — The omnipresence of God is deduced directly from His spirituality. But as the Hebrews had only a very vague notion of spirituality, [14] the people were very slow to rise to the concept of God's ubiquity. It is not surprising, therefore, that

---

[11] Read *kinnîm* = little flies, instead of *ken* = also.

[12] Cf. below §9, 2.

[13] The text is corrupt. We have adopted the reading of A. Van Hoonacker (*Les douze petits prophètes*, Paris 1908, p. 108).

[14] Cf. § 7.

the Bible contains traces of a fairly large number of popular opinions concerning Yahweh's dwelling places.[15] According to the commonly held opinion Yahweh dwelt in the territory of Israel, while beyond its boundaries homage had to be paid to other gods (Jgs 11:24; 1 Sm 26:19; cf. 4 Kgs 5:17.18). He dwelt on holy mountains, on Sinai, Horeb, the heights of Seir (Jgs 5:4) and lastly on Mount Sion, or He made His home in ancient sanctuaries, such as Bethel (Gn 28:16.17; 31:13), Bersabee (Gn 21:33) and later in the temple of Jerusalem (Mi 3:11; Jer 7:4). Men swore by the God of Dan or by the tutelary divinity of Bersabee (Am 8:14).[16] And several believed that Yahweh " who is seated upon the Cherubim " (2 Sm 6:2) was present only there where His ark was (1 Sm 4:6.7).

Besides these earthly dwelling places, Yahweh also dwelt in heaven. According to some of these popular accounts this localization of Yahweh in heaven seems to have been understood in the proper sense (for example, Gn 11:5.7; 21:17; 22:11; 28:12). The ancient Hebrews, it seems, never realized that there is a contradiction in localizing God both in heaven and in a place on earth. Thus in the account of Jacob's dream (Gn 28:11.12.17.18), Elohim is supposed to dwell in heaven because His angels descended from there on a ladder to the place where Jacob had fallen asleep; but God also dwells in that place, because the patriarch recognized that that place is " the house of God and the gate of heaven " by reason of the ladder that connected that place with heaven. May one not see in this contradiction an attempt, although an awkward one, to free God from all localization and to suggest His transcendence?

In opposition to these popular ideas there is from the beginning another current of thought which places Yahweh above local contingencies. Already early accounts concerning the patriarchs represented Him as exercising His power in all regions of Palestine as well as in those neighboring lands through which Israel's ancestors had passed. He made Abraham leave Ur of the Chaldees; and from Haran in Mesopotamia He led him into the land of Canaan (Gn 11:31-12:4); He protected him in Egypt (Gn 12:10-20; cf. 39 ff.),

---

[15] Cf. C. Westphal, " Jahwes Wohnstätten nach den Anschauungen der alten Hebräer " (*BZAW*, 15), Giessen 1908.

[16] The God of Dan is Yahweh who was represented at Dan under the form of a bull (3 Kgs 12:29). The massoretic text reads " by the way of Bersabee. " The parallelism of this verse with the preceding one supports the correction proposed by several critics who, instead of *derek* (way) read *dôdĕkâ* (thy Dôd). Dôd designates the tutelary divinity of the city, as in line 12 of the Mesha stone (cf. A. Van Hoonacker, *op. cit.*, p. 277).

in the region of Gerara (Gn 20; 26) and in Aramean territory (Gn 24:10-67; 29-31). He obliged Pharaoh to release Israelite tribes that had been reduced to slavery in Egypt (Ex 6 ff.) and hurled his army into the Red Sea (Ex 15:1.2); He guided the tribes across the desert and opened to them at last the Promised Land. It is clear that Yahweh had never been a local god; and if He had been given special veneration in certain sanctuaries, it was because of the revelations with which, according to tradition, He had honored Israel's ancestors in those places.

Inevitably worship became localized in certain sanctuaries and was later centralized in the temple of Jerusalem. It does not follow, however, that the God who was adored there had ever been considered to be a local god. So true is this that the sacred writers, who have most clearly affirmed Yahweh's omnipresence, continue to speak of His dwelling on Sion, the holy mountain (for example, Ps 46:5; Am 1:2; Is 2:2.3; 11:9; 48:2; 52:1), or in the temple of Jerusalem (for example, Is 2:3; 64:10; Jer 7:10.11; 3 Kgs 8:26-53) where the faithful come " to see His face " (Is 1:12; Ps 24:6; 42:3).[17] They also mention, without the slightest hesitation, Yahweh's presence in heaven (Ps 2:4; 11:4; 68:6; 103:19; 3 Kgs 8:34.39; Am 9:6; Is 63:15), because this manner of speaking enables them to express the transcendence of the Most High who rules the world: " the heaven is My throne and the earth My footstool " (Is 66:1; cf. Jer 23:24).

Solomon's prayer (3 Kgs 8:27)[17*] states very clearly God's immensity: " For if heaven and the heavens of heavens cannot contain You, how much less this house, that is to say, the temple, which I have built? " (cf. Is 66:1). Amos 9:2-4 declares that Yahweh will reach sinners as easily in the depths of Sheol or of the sea, as in the heavens or the caves of Carmel. According to Isaias (6:3), the glory of Yahweh, that is to say, His holiness and His power in their manifestations, fills the universe. According to Jeremias 23:23, He fills heaven and earth (cf. Wis 1:7; 8:1) and His eyes penetrate the most secret hiding places. Finally Ps 139:7-10 gives a magnificent description of God's omnipresence: " Where can I go from Your spirit? from Your presence where can I flee? If I go up to the heavens, You are there; if I sink to the nether world, You are present there. If I take the wings of dawn, if I settle at the farthest limits of the sea, even there Your hand shall guide me, and Your right hand hold me fast " (cf. Jb 23:8.9).

---

[17] For the meaning of this expression, cf. p. 50, note 3.
[17*] This verse is a late addition.

" Longer than the earth is His measure, and broader than the sea " (Jb 11:9).

5. *The omniscience of God.* — Although the omniscience of God is intimately linked to His ubiquity, omniscience was earlier recognized by the Israelite people, at least inasmuch as they attributed to Yahweh the knowledge of things beyond man's grasp, especially the knowledge of the future; this is evident from the old custom of consulting God (Gn 25:22; Ex 18:15; Nm 27:21; Jos 9:14; Jgs 1:1; 18:5; 20:18.23.27; 1 Sm 9:9; 10:22; 14:37) in order to learn the future or some secret thing.

" The eyes of Yahweh are in every place, keeping watch on the evil and the good " (Prv 15:3); nothing on earth can escape them (Jb 28:24; Za 4:10); they penetrate even to Sheol (Prv 15:11; Jb 26:6) and into men's hearts (Prv 15:11; Ps 11:4; 33:15; 3 Kgs 8:39; Prv 16:2; 21:2). God knows all men's thoughts (Ps 94:1.2), their intentions (Ps 139:1-4) and their most secret plans (Ps 44:22; 139:2); He sounds men's reins and hearts (Jer 11:20; 17:10). He knows the future of men (Ps 139:15.16) and of peoples and announces it to His prophets (Am 3:7; Is 5:19; 14:26; 19:17; Mi 4:12): " Behold the former things have come to pass: and new things I now declare; before they spring forth, I tell you of them " (Is 42:9; cf. 44:7; 45:21). He alone knows the future because He alone is God: " Who has told this long ago? Who has declared it of old? Was it not I, the Lord? And there is no other god besides Me " (Is 45:21; cf. 41:23). " Yes, I am God, and there is no other god besides Me. I am God there is none like Me, declaring the end from the beginning, and from ancient times things not yet done " (Is 46:9.10). The gods of the Gentiles, on the contrary, are incapable of knowing the future; and Yahweh ironically provokes them: " Tell the things that are to come hereafter, and we shall know that you are gods... Behold, you are nothing, and your work is nought " (Is 41:23.24).

6. *The wisdom of God.* — Wisdom comprises the perspicacity of the intelligence that grasps things, situations, the end to be reached and the art of choosing the means that lead to the end: wisdom consists in understanding one's way (Prv 14:8); " the wise man measures his steps " (Prv 14:15). The height of wisdom is to be " wise like the Angel of God and to know all that happens on earth " (2 Sm 14:20), or, what amounts to the same things, " to understand good and evil " (2 Sm 14:17), that is to say: to grasp all and to understand all. From this very ancient text it follows that God possesses wisdom in the highest degree.

The old account of Gn 2 and 3 supposes even that Yahweh alone is in this possession because He has reserved for Himself "the knowledge of good and evil" and has forbidden it to man, because it would make man like unto God (Gn 2:17; 3:5.22).[18] To seize upon wisdom (Jb 15:8) is to exalt one's self against Yahweh who alone is exalted (Is 2:11; cf. 10:12-16; 14:12-15). The king of Tyre who prided himself on his wisdom and made his heart like that of a god, will be punished for his blasphemous pretention by an ignominious death (Ez 28:1-10; cf. Is 14:12-15). This idea also dominates the description of Job 28:12-27: the wisdom, which God alone from the beginning of the world has established and investigated (v. 27), has been "hidden from the eyes of all living" (v. 21) and is to be found neither in the land of the living nor in the abode of the dead (v. 13 ff.). Similarly Baruch (3:15-38) declares that wisdom is inaccessible to man: neither those who interpret fables nor those who search for intelligence, nor those who dwell in Theman, nor the Arabs who are quite famous because of their wisdom (Jer 49:7; Abd 8; Jb 2:11), nor the giants of ancient days (cf. Gn 6:4) have found "the way of wisdom" (vv. 22-27), because "no one has gone up into the heavens and brought it down from the clouds" (v. 29; cf. Sir 1:5.8).

Prophets and wise men exalt Yahweh's wisdom (Is 28:29; 31:2; 40:13.14; Dn 2:20-23; Jb 9:4; 11:6-8; 12:13; 21:22; Sir 1:1-10) and love to point out how His wisdom overwhelms and surpasses human wisdom (Is 10:12-16; 19:11-15; 28:9-13; 29:14; 31:2.3; Jer 10:12-14; Dn 2:20-23; Jb 12:13-25; Ps 94:10-12; 139:6; Prv 19:21; 21:30). God's wisdom is not an acquired quality because no one could have taught it to Him, nor showed Him the way of knowledge (Is 40:13.14). Divine wisdom is unfathomable for man (Is 40:28; Jb 11:6-9; Ps 92:6; 139:17.18) and infinitely surpasses human wisdom. "For My thoughts are not your thoughts; nor your ways My ways, says the Lord. For as the heavens are exalted above the earth, so are My ways exalted above your ways, and My thoughts above your thoughts" (Is 55:8.9).

Yahweh is the possessor of wisdom and communicates it to whomever He wishes: to certain privileged ones, like Joseph (Gn 41:25.38) and Daniel (Dn 1:17; 5:11), who receive it in order to interpret dreams; but especially to leaders (Dt 34:9), to judges (Ezr 7:25), to kings, like David (2 Sm 14:20) and Solomon (3 Kgs 3:11.28), and most abundantly to the messianic king (Is 11:2.3), because the kings are

[18] On the controversies connected with this expression, cf. J. Coppens, "Publications récentes sur l'A. T.," *EThL*, 11 (1934), pp. 594 ff.

the guardians of the law and the defenders of justice. Finally, according to the later sapiential books, the wise men themselves hold their wisdom from God (Jb 32:8; Sir 1:1.10; 39:6; 51:17; Wis 7:7; 9:17).[19]

God manifests His wisdom by His Law, which He has given to His people to make them wise (Dt 4:5.6; Ps 19:8), but above all by the creation and government of the world: each one of His works is good (Gn 1:10.12.25) and all His works together are "very good" (Gn 1:31), that is to say, in conformity to their author's plan. Poets are pleased to praise the wisdom with which God made and ordered the universe (for example, Jb 36:23-37:24; 38-41; Ps 8; 104; Prv 8:22-31), and the sapiential books delight in describing the interventions of divine wisdom in the work of creation (Prv 3:19.20; Jb 26:12; 28:20-27; Wis 9:1.2; 14:4; and especially Prv 8:22-31; Sir 24:3-6; Wis 7:22.27; 8:1.6).[20]

B. Moral attributes of God

F. Nötscher, "Die Gerechtigkeit Gottes bei den vorexilischen Propheten" (*ATA*, VI, 1), Münster im W. 1915; J. Ziegler, "Die Liebe Gottes bei den Propheten" (*ATA*, XI, 3), Münster im W. 1930; E. Tobac, "Grâce," *DA*, II, cols. 325-344; P. Bonnetain, "Grâce," *DBS*, III, cols. 701-1319; P. van Imschoot, "Genade," *BW*, cols. 497-506; *id.*, "Liefde," *BW*, cols. 951-960; J. Köberle, *Sünde und Gnade im religiösen Leben des Volkes Israel bis auf Christum*, Munich 1905; J. Moffat, *Grace in the N. T.*, London 1930; N. Glueck, "Das Wort Ḥesed im alttestamentlichen Sprachgebrauch" (*BZAW*, 47), Giessen 1927; W. E. Lofthouse, "Ḥen and Ḥesed in the O. T.," *ZAW* (1933), pp. 29-35; G. Quell–G. Shrenck, "Dikaios", *ThW*, II, pp. 176-214; R. Bultmann, "Eleos," *ThW*, II, pp. 475-479; H. W. Hertzberg, "Die Entwicklung des Begriffes Mišpat im A. T.," *ZAW* (1922), pp. 256-287; H. J. Stoebe, "Die Bedeutung des Wortes Ḥäsäd im A. T.," *VT* (1952), pp. 244 ff.

Several authors hold that the God of the most ancient Hebrews had no moral character,[21] or at least that He was principally a redoubtable God whose power and anger were released like a force of nature, without any apparent reason.[22] These opinions, expressed in such terms, are inexact. If it is true that adjectives denoting Yahweh's moral attributes are found most often in relatively recent books, they are not altogether missing in the older

---

[19] This idea is not found in the earlier sapiential books (cf. P. van Imschoot, "Sagesse et esprit dans l'A. T.," *RB*, 1938, pp. 23-49).

[20] The question of the personification of wisdom will be treated later, III, § 12. Cf. P. van Imschoot, *La Sagesse dans l'A. T. est-elle une hypostase?*, *Coll. Gand.* (1934), pp. 1-8; 85-94.

[21] J. Wellhausen, B. Stade, R. Smend and others.

[22] H. Gressmann, *Palästinas Erdgeruch in der israelitischen Religion*, Berlin 1909, p. 78; H. Gunkel, *Die Propheten*, Göttingen 1917, p. 81; P. Volz, *Das Dämonische in Yahwe*, Tübingen 1924.

books,[23] and the moral qualities they express have always been recognized in the God of the Hebrews. This is plain from the evidence of the old accounts describing Yahweh's justice and benevolence toward the patriarchs and of several old theophoric names, such as 'El-yâda' (= God knows, 2 Sm 5:16), 'El-ḥânân (= God is gracious or merciful, 2 Sm 21:19), 'Elî-'êzer (= my God is help, Gn 15:2; Ex 18:4), 'Eli-'âb (= my God is father, Nm 16:1; 1 Sm 16:6), Yišmâ-êl (= God understands, hears, Gn 16:15), Yĕraḥmĕ-'êl (= God has pity, 1 Par 2:9).[24] Furthermore, despite His awesome character, the God who revealed Himself to Moses is also the benevolent and merciful God (Ex 20:6; 34:6.7) who took pity on the people oppressed in Egypt (Ex 3:7).

1. *The kindness and mercy of God.* — To express the kindness and mercy of God, the Old Testament makes use of several different terms whose meaning is not always clearly distinct.

a) The term *ḥesed* occurs many times. The LXX and the Vulgate usually translate it by ἔλεος, mercy; but its meaning is more complex; it denotes the sum total of duties incumbent on those who are united by the bond of blood (for example, Gn 47:29), of kinship (Gn 20:13), of friendship (1 Sm 20:8.14.15), of hospitality (Gn 19:19), of covenant (Gn 21:23; 1 Sm 20:8.14.15). *Ḥesed* includes assistance, fidelity, loyalty, solidarity, love that members of a community owe one another, whether the community be a natural one, such as the family, or the result of an alliance or by reason of hospitality. The word denotes concrete manifestations of assistance and of fidelity rather than sentiments or dispositions that inspire them; this is clear from the use of the word in the plural (for example, Gn 32:11; Is 63:7; Ps 25:6; 89:50) and from the expression " to do *ḥesed* " (for example, Gn 24:12; 40:14; 1 Sm 20:8.14.15), which means to lend aid, to act loyally or faithfully towards others. Because the help (the loyalty, the fidelity, *ḥesed*) is a duty imposed by the bond uniting the members of a community, *ḥesed* is often asked for at the same time as right (*mišpaṭ*, for example, Os 12:7; Mi 6:8; Jer 9:23; Za 7:9; Ps 101:1) or justice (*ṣĕdâqâh*, Jer 9:23; Ps 36:11; 40:11; 143:11.12); for the same reason *ḥesed* is frequently associated with covenant *bĕrît* (Dt 7:9.12; 3 Kgs 8:23; 2 Par 6:14; Ps 50:5.6; 89:29; 106:45, etc.): " to keep the covenant and the *ḥesed* " is " to observe the covenant faithfully. " And since *ḥesed* is close to fidelity *('émet)*, the two terms are often

[23] Cf. for example : Ex 22:26; 34:6.7; 1 Sm 24:14.

[24] Cf. above § 2, 1, and the article " El, " *BW*, cols. 368-370.

united. So true is this that they form, so to speak, a single expression: *'âṣâh ḥesed wĕ-'émet* means to give faithful aid, to show a faithful attachment (Gn 24:49; 47:29; Jos 2:14, etc.).

In a community, nevertheless, help and loyalty *(ḥesed)* must exist not only between equals or between inferiors and superiors (for example, Gn 21:23), [25] they may also be found in a superior with regard to inferiors. In that case *ḥesed* has the meaning of favor, grace (Est 2:9.17; Ezr 9:9).

This is the case when it is a question of God's *ḥesed*, because this *ḥesed* is based on the covenant (Dt 7:9.12; 3 Kgs 8:23; Is 55:3, etc.), which is a purely gratuitous initiative on the part of Yahweh. [26] In fact, if Yahweh has made a covenant with Israel and has promised "to observe the covenant and the *ḥesed*" (Dt 7:9; 3 Kgs 8:23, etc.), it is because He has loved the people (Dt 8:7.8; 10:15; Os 11:1; Jer 31:3), not for the latter's merits (Dt 7:7; 9:4.6), but gratuitously (Am 3:2; 9:7; Ez 16:3-14). When the Old Testament attributes *ḥesed* to God, the idea of kindness prevails, while the idea of help that is due diminishes. That is why God's *ḥesed* is often made parallel to His love (*'ahăbâh*, Jer 31:3), or especially to His compassion, His mercy (*raḥămîm*, Jer 16:5; Is 63:7; Ps 25:6; 40:12; 51:3; 69:17, etc.).

The Israelite knows that he can count on the help and kindness of Yahweh; he asks for it with confidence, but he does not exact it as a due (Ps 6:5; 25:6.7; 119:149; 143:12). He also knows that to obtain it he himself is obliged to fulfill the conditions of the covenant, that is to say, he must observe the precepts of His God (Ex 20:6; Dt 7:12; 3 Kgs 8:23; Os 10:12, etc.). Yet when Israel transgresses the terms of the covenant, Yahweh does not withdraw His *ḥesed* at once, because He is a merciful and gracious God, slow to anger, rich in kindness *(ḥesed)* and fidelity *('émet)*, continuing His kindness *(ḥesed)* for a thousand generations, forgiving wickedness, crime and sin (Ex 34:6.7; Nm 14:18; Ps 86:15; 103:8; Jl 2:13; Jon 4:2; Neh 9:17). Here *ḥesed* denotes mercy which gives grace and pardon to the sinner (cf. Ps 51:3); the word becomes a synonym of *raḥămîm* (=mercy, compassion), to which it is often made parallel (Jer 16:5; Is 63:7, etc.).

b) The mercy *(raḥămîm)* [27] of God is mainly the pity He shows to the unfortunate and the weak (Ps 69:17; 79:8; 103:13.14; 119:77;

---

[25] Abraham dwelt as a client in the territory of king Abimelech (Gn 21:23).

[26] Cf. below IV, § 1, 2. Cf. Ps 89:4.50; 3 Kgs 3:6; Is 55:3.

[27] *Raḥămîn* means in the first place the bowels which to the Hebrews were the seat of sentiments: when Joseph was overcome with compassion, it was said "his bowels were stirred" (Gn 43:30; cf. 3 Kgs 3:26). The word is most often understood as an abstract plural meaning compassion or pity. In the singular *reḥem* signifies

cf. Is 9:16), in particular to His oppressed people (4 Kgs 13:23; Ps 106:46; Is 14:1; 30:18; 49:13; 54:8, etc.). Just like *ḥesed*, the word *raḥămîm* signifies the concrete manifestation of pity rather than the sentiment and is frequently associated with grace (*ḥen*, for example, Ex 33:19; 4 Kgs 13:23; Ps 102:14); when the pity of God has as its object the guilty but repentant people, pity takes the meaning of mercy which pardons sin (for example, Os 2:25; Jer 31:18-20; Is 55:7; Mi 7:19; Ps 51:3; 79:8; 103:8-10).

c) For the God of Israel is long-suffering (*'erek 'appîm*),[28] that is to say, slow to anger, patient (Ex 34:6; Jl 2:13; Jon 4:2; Ps 86:15; 103:8; 145:8; Neh 9:17); because He is " great in strength " (Na 1:3), He can wait for His hour to chastise the guilty, He does not take pleasure in the death of the wicked, but wishes him to be converted and live (Ez 18:23). He gives man time to be converted. Yahweh is merciful (*raḥûm*), long-suffering and rich in kindness (*ḥesed*). He does not seek revenge indefinitely and does not hold rancor forever; He does not treat us according to our sins and does not punish us according to our faults. Just as a father has pity (*riḥam*) on his children, so Yahweh has pity on those who fear Him. For He knows of what we are made and He is mindful that we are dust (Ps 103:8-10, 13.14).

d) The verb *ḥânan* is often used. Its primary meaning is " to lean over, to be inclined "; from this comes the idea of " being gracious, showing favor " (for example Nm 6:25), of granting favor (for example, the favor of having children, Gn 33:5.11). In all his needs the Israelite implores the favor of His God: " be favorable to me " or " have pity on me " (Ps 4:2; 6:3; 25:16; 26:11; 27:7, etc.). Yahweh shows grace to the repentant sinner, that is to say, He pardons him (Ps 51:3; Am 5:15); in this case grace is practically synonymous with mercy (*raḥămîm*) and is often coupled with it (for example, Is 27:11; 30:18;

---

the maternal bosom (Gn 20:18; 29:31, etc.) and is regarded as the seat of the mother's pity for her children. The verb *riḥam* means to have pity; the primitive sense appears in Is 49:15: Can a mother forget her child? Can she cease to feel pity (*mêraḥêm*) for the fruit of her womb? The meaning was extended to pity in general (cf. P. Dhorme, *L'emploi métaphorique des noms de parties du corps en hébreux et en accadien*, Paris 1923, pp. 134 ff.; or in *RB*, 1922, pp. 514 ff.). The verb *rḥm* is applied to God in the old tribal name *Yeraḥme'êl* (1 Sm 27:10; 30:29).

[28] The word *'aph* means nose, in the plural *'appîm*, nostrils, that is to say, the organ of respiration: he who breathes, that is to say, he who lives has breath in his nostrils (Is 2:22). Anger affects respiration or the nose, and to indicate anger, it is said: he is " short of nose " (Prv 14:17), or " short of breath " (Mi 2:7; Ex 6:9); he is " long of nose " (Prv 14:29; Ex 34:6) or " long of breath " (Eccl 7:8; Sir 5:11) is said to indicate longanimity and patience. For the same reason, the word *'aph* or *'appîm* often means anger, for example in the popular expression " his anger blazed " (Gn 39:19; Ex 4:14; cf. P. van Imschoot, " L'esprit de Yahweh, source de vie dans l'A. T., *RB*, 1935, p. 484, note 1).

4 Kgs 13:23). Similarly the adjectives *ḥannûn* and *raḥûm* are often joined (Ex 34:6; Jl 2:13; Jon 4:2; Ps 103:8.13.14, etc.). The noun *ḥen* (grace, favor) which the LXX ordinarily translate by χάρις has the various meanings of the Greek word and of the word " grace ": it means beauty (Prv 31:30), amiability, grace (Ps 45:3; Prv 4:9; 5:19), favor (Est 2:15); " to find grace in the eyes of someone " (Gn 19:19; 30:27; 32:6, etc.) is to obtain his favor, or better, to obtain a favor, because *ḥen*, just like *ḥesed*, denotes a concrete benefit rather than a sentiment, as is proved by the expression " to procure the favor of someone " (Gn 39:21; Ex 3:21; 11:3, etc.), which means to obtain for another someone's good offices.

e) Two other words *(ḥûs* and *ḥamal)* which mean to have pity, compassion, are employed more rarely with Yahweh as subject (Jl 2:18; cf. Mal 3:17), at least in affirmative propositions. In the prophets, these verbs are met more frequently in negative propositions: " Yahweh will not have pity, He will not spare " (for example, Jer 13:14; 21:7; Ez 5:11; 7:4.9; 8:18, etc.).

f) God's goodness is often expressed by the root *ṭôb* and its derivatives. The verb *yṭb* in the *Hiphil* form is used to designate God's beneficent action toward men; it means to do good, to make happy (for example, Gn 32:10.13; Ex 1:20; Dt 8:16; 28:63; 30:5). Ordinarily it refers to earthly benefits granted by God (Gn 32:10.13; Dt 28:63; 30:5; Jer 18:10; 32:40; Ez 36:11, etc.).

The adjective *ṭôb* (good, benevolent) is rarely applied to God by the prophets (Jer 33:11; Na 1:7), but frequently by the psalmists (for example, Ps 25:8; 34:9; 106:1; 107:1).

The noun *ṭûb* (goodness) is used by the prophets to denote divine benefits, especially those that belong to the final restoration of Israel (Os 3:5; Jer 31:12.14; Za 9:17). In Jer 31:12 the *ṭûb* of Yahweh obviously refers to the blessings mentioned in the following verse: they shall be radiant at the blessings *(ṭûb)* of Yahweh, at the grain, the new wine, the oil, at the sheep and the cows.[29] His blessings are placed parallel to " the fat " with which He satisfies: " And I will satisfy the soul (or the throat, *nepheš*) of the priests with fat things and My people shall be filled with My blessing *(ṭûb)* " (Jer 31:14).

---

[29] P. Volz (*Der Prophet Jeremias*, Leipzig 1922, pp. 276, 278) and F. Nötscher (*Das Buch Jeremias*, Bonn 1934) translate: " They shall shine (because of joy) over salvation " (cf. Is 60:5; Ps 34:6) and consider the words " over the wheat," etc., to be a gloss. A. Condamin (*Le livre de Jérémie*, Paris 1920, p. 222) translates: " They shall stream to the blessings " (cf. Is 2:2). We adopt the correction proposed by W. Rudolf (*Biblica Hebraica*, II) according to the Syriac version and the Targum.

The abstract meaning "goodness" appears only in relatively recent works (Is 63:7; Ps 25:7; 27:13; 31:20; 145:7). [30]

2. *The truth and fidelity of God.* — The Old Testament very frequently associates, with regard to God, the terms *ḥesed* and *'émet* (Ps 25:10; 26:3; 40:11.12; 57:4.11; 61:8; 69:14; 85:11; 86:15; 89:15; 108:5; 115:1; 117:2; 138:2), *ḥesed* and *'émûnâh* (Ps 36:6; 88:12; 89:2.3.25.34; 92:3; 98:3; 100:5). The two words are derived from the root *'mn*, which means to be firm, stable, sure; *'émet* expresses that the thing or the person is as it should be, that it is true : "a true seed" (Jer 2:21) is a seed of good quality, a good plant, in contrast with a bad seed, a degenerate plant. From the prodigy which Elias had worked, the woman whose son he had restored to life recognizes that he is a man of God and that the word of Yahweh in his mouth is truth (3 Kgs 17:24), that is to say, is truly in him and is efficacious, as might be expected. This is the reason why *'émet* often denotes truth : "You are the God *(hâ'élohîm)*, that is to say, Your words are truth." [31] He is *'élohêy 'émet*, the true God (2 Par 15:3; Jer 10:10; 2 Sm 7:28). In the moral sense *'émet* means veracity, surety; a truthful man, a sure man, on whom one may count, is called *'îš 'émet ;* this supposes also constancy: for this reason *'émet* is often translated by fidelity which is also expressed by *'émûnâh; 'émet* is opposed to *šeqer* (lie, falsehood, for example, Prv 12:19; Jer 9:4), but also to *reša'* (naughtiness, impiety, Neh 9:33). This shows that the word not only designates logical truth, but also moral rectitude.

Yahweh is "rich in *ḥesed* and *'émet*" (Ex 34:6) : He possesses goodness and truth to a high degree, that is to say, veracity and constancy, in a word, fidelity; His fidelity *('émet)* is a shield (Ps 91:4), that is to say, an assured protection; it is a sure guide (Ps 43:3); all His paths are goodness and fidelity (Ps 25:10), that is to say, His whole way of acting is inspired by benevolence and fidelity to His promises. He makes His faithful ones walk in His truth and He teaches them His paths, that is to say, He teaches them to be guided by His directives, which assure salvation (Ps 25:4.5); His judgments are truth (Ps 19:10), His decrees teach true piety and assure happiness (v. 12); His words are truth (2 Sm 7:28), His promises do not deceive, but will be fulfilled; His truth is established in the heavens (Ps 89:3), that is to say, His veracity and His fidelity in keeping His promises have the solidity of the firmament and guarantee the perpetuity of

[30] Cf. J. Ziegler, *Die Liebe Gottes*, pp. 46-48.

[31] The *vaw* (= and) is explicative (Quell, *op. cit.*, p. 237): Yahweh is the only true God, which is equivalent to saying that His words are truth.

His protection (Ps 89:25; cf. Mi 7:19.20), because He does not lie nor repent (1 Sm 15:29; Nm 23:19). Yahweh abhors lying and perjury, because His eyes are turned toward truth *('ĕmûnâh)* (Jer 5:2.3).

3. *The justice of God.* — The fundamental meaning of the Hebrew word *(ṣĕdâqâh, ṣedeq)*, which we translate by justice, is : conformity to a rule. *Ṣedeq* is sometimes used for objects, for example *mo'zĕnêy ṣedeq*, "just balances," *'abĕnêy ṣedeq*, "just weights" (Lv 19:36), that is to say, in conformity with the norms that regulate instruments of weight and measurement. More often it is used of persons and of God. He is "just" who acts according to the norms that flow from his nature and his social relations. To be just is to act according to the right *(mišpaṭ)*, that is to say, not according to an abstract and ideal rule, but according to concrete norms and duties resulting from the social relations in which each is involved. God is just, that is to say, He acts always according to the norms that flow from His nature and the covenant that unites Him to Israel; He complies with what is rightly expected of Him, insofar as He is God and the God of the covenant. "He who judges the whole earth, will He not act justly?" (Gn 18:25). "His works are perfect" *(tamîm)*, for all His ways are right *(mišpat)*; He is a faithful and faultless God, He is just *(ṣaddîq)* and right (*yâšâr*, Dt 32:4; cf. So 3:5).

Although the adjective *ṣaddîq* is rarely found except in recent texts, the idea it expresses is very old. Baudissin [32] has shown that it belongs to the oldest Semitic times because all the Semites consider the god of the tribe, who is also the chief, as the judge, for he maintains the right of the group against strangers and the right of each member of the tribe. It is this idea which is expressed in very old Babylonian theophoric names (*Belî-da-a-an* = Bel is judge, *Šamaš-da-a-an* = Šamaš is judge), in Canaanite names (*šâphaṭ-Baal* = Baal judges, *šipṭi-baalu*, Amarna 333), as well as in Hebrew names (*šĕphâṭ-yâhû* = Yahweh judges, the name of one of David's sons, 2 Sm 3:4; *Yĕho-Šâphaṭ*, 2 Sm 8:16) [33] and in the name of the god of Ugarit, *Dan-el* (El is judge, cf. Daniel). Now when the god is considered as judge, he is also held to be equitable, since he is the defender of right. That is why the Semites willingly attribute to him the qualification of "just." The term *ṣdq*, which is common to western and southern Semites, expresses this quality which is manifested principally in

---

[32] W. Baudissin, *Kyrios*, III, pp. 379 ff.

[33] Reference may also be made to the old expression "may Yahweh be judge between thee and me" (for example, Gn 16:5, 1 Sm 24:13), and to the custom of settling differences by a decision of God (Ex 22:7.8), that is to say, a divine oracle pronounced by the priest (cf. Ex 18:15.16; Dt 33:8).

the exercise of the judiciary function. Several theophoric names attest this idea that was held of the god-judge: for example, the old West Semitic name *ammi-zaduqa* (= my uncle, that is to say, the god, is just), [34] *aḫi-ṣaduq* (= my brother is just) in the time of Hammurabi, [35] *Ṣidqî-yâhû* (= Yahweh is just, 4 Kgs 24:17) in the time of Achab, *Ṣâdôq* (2 Sm 8:17) in the time of David. [36]

It is wrong, therefore, to claim, as the Wellhausen school does, that the God of Israel became a just God, in the moral sense of the word, only in the teaching of the prophets. Although Amos, Osee and Isaias do not apply the adjective *ṣaddiq* to Yahweh, they suppose not only that Yahweh is just and equitable but also that the people must have recognized Him to be so, because they vigorously rebuke the people for having committed social injustices in Israel, a crime that Yahweh will punish with rigorous punishments (Am 2:6; 3:10; 4:1-3; 5:7.10.12; Os 10:4; Is 1:16.17.23; 3:13-15; Mi 3:1-4.9-12). Ancient popular traditions found in Genesis, furthermore, describe many cases in which God's justice chastises men's faults: the ancestors of mankind are driven from the garden of Eden because they transgressed God's order. Yahweh decides to destroy mankind by the deluge (Gn 6:11.12; 7:1), and to save Noe because he was just (Gn 6:8; 7:1). The people of Sodom and Gomorrah perish by fire from heaven for their crimes while Lot is spared (Gn 19). Abraham is unable to admit that Yahweh can make perish the just with the guilty (Gn 18:23), and Yahweh shows Himself disposed to pardon these towns in favor of a few just men who are to be found in them (Gn 18:26.28-32). Ruben declares to his brothers that they were expiating the death of Joseph (Gn 42:22). David expects Yahweh to punish the murder of Abner (2 Sm 3:39). Nathan reproaches David, in Yahweh's name, for the adultery and murder he has committed and announces the divine chastisement (2 Sm 12); and the king recognizes that he has sinned against Yahweh (12:13). Elias declares to Achab, who was guilty of Naboth's murder, that Yahweh would make him expiate his crime by death (3 Kgs 21:1-19).

It has been objected, it is true, that Yahweh is partial to his protégés, the patriarchs of Israel: He takes the side of Abraham, when he lied and made his wife pass as his sister (Gn 12:10-20; 20; cf. 26:6-10), of Jacob, when he obtained the paternal blessing by fraud (Gn 27)

---

[34] W. Baudissin, *op. cit.*, III, p. 411.

[35] W. Baudissin, *op. cit.*, IV, p. 50.

[36] Cf. the name *ṣa-du-uq* in the Amarna letters (287, 1.32). The name is a hypocoristic form of a theophoric name (*Kyrios*, p. 404).

and enriched himself at the expense of his father-in-law (Gn 30:25-31:13), of the Israelite tribes, when they plundered the Egyptians (Ex 3:21.22; 12:35.36). He ordered the total destruction of the Canaanites (Dt 7:1-11.16). He incited the Sichemites to revolt against their king, Abimelech (Jgs 9:23); He aroused David against the people when He ordered him to take a census of Israel and then punished the people for the king's fault (2 Sm 24). David believed that it was perhaps Yahweh who stirred Saul against him (1 Sm 26:19) and that He caused Shimei to curse him (2 Sm 16:10). Yahweh deceived Achab by the false predictions of the prophets in order to bring him misfortune (3 Kgs 22:10-23); He hardened Pharao's heart (Ex 4:21; 7:3, etc.), and the heart of His people (Is 6:10; cf. 29:10, etc.). He gave Israel precepts that were not good in order to ruin them (Ez 20:25.26).

Yahweh, without doubt, who chose Israel from all the nations (Ex 19:5; Am 3:2) and concluded an alliance with them and with their ancestors (Ex 24:8; Gn 15:8; 17:1, etc.), bound Himself to protect His people in a very special way, on condition, however, that in exchange they observe the stipulations of the moral and religious order which Yahweh had imposed on them (Ex 19:5; 24:3; Dt 11:13-17.26-32; 26:17-19; 28:1-68). But since the covenant is an act of pure benevolence on God's part (Am 9:7; Os 11:1; Jer 31:3; Ez 16:3-14; Dt 7:7-9; 10:15), it does not violate the rights of any other people and is not contrary to God's justice; it is uniquely an act of Yahweh's sovereignty, " who shows favor to whom He shows favor " (Ex 33:19), that is to say, He grants favors to those whom He wishes. It cannot be said that in the Genesis accounts Yahweh takes simply the side of the patriarchs when they dissemble or act fraudulently; lying, in fact, is condemned (Gn 12:18; 20:9). Yahweh prevents, by punishments or threats, the kings of Egypt and Gerara from committing adultery, and He makes Jacob expiate his fraudulent schemes by exile and many tribulations. According to Ex 3:21.22 Yahweh will dispose the Egyptians to be favorable to the Israelites, so that the latter may obtain from the former precious objects which they will take along on their flight. In this there is neither fraud nor injustice. The author of the book of Wisdom (10:17) sees in it only a compensation for the work the Hebrews did during their sojourn in Egypt (cf. Jub. 48:18).

As for the *ḥerem,* [37] decreed by Yahweh against the Canaanites

---

[37] *Ḥerem,* from the root *ḥrm* which means " interdict, " is usually ordered by the chief or by Yahweh, who delivers the town or enemy tribe to Israel (for example, Dt 2:24.31; 3:2-6; Jos 6:16.17; 8:1-2; 1 Sm 15:3). What is *ḥerem,* is reserved for

(Dt 7:1-11.16) and against certain cities and tribes (Dt 2:23-35; Jos 6:2.20.21; 7; 8:1.2.24-29; 1 Sm 15), it must be judged, not according to present laws governing warfare, but according to the old law that considered the total destruction of conquered cities to be normal, even obligatory, at least in holy wars. Granted that Yahweh is the leader who conducts the war,[38] all the booty, including the conquered, men, women and children, are His by every right. For this reason the booty is *ḥrm*, reserved, and cannot be given to men for their use; it must, therefore, be totally destroyed (cf. Jos 7:10-26; 1 Sm 15:18-23.32.33). The Canaanites, furthermore, and the Madianites were a constant danger for the religion of the Israelites (cf. Nm 25; 31:16); and they were guilty by reason of their many crimes (Gn 15:16; Lv 18:25.26). This explains the severity of the treatment they received. The Hebrews were convinced that they were fighting a holy war against the enemies of Yahweh and that they were the instruments of His vengeance. Sacred writers explain this belief in the form of an order given by Yahweh to destroy the vanquished.[39] They do this all the more freely because they give little consideration to secondary causes and refer all events to God, the first cause (for example, Am 1:4; 4:7.9.10; Ex 4:11), even events that depend on human will (cf. Am 3:6; 5:27; 8:10) and fortuitous accidents (Ex 21:13). For this reason they say that God " incites " to evil (2 Sm 16:10; 24:1; 1 Sm 26:19) which He will punish

---

Yahweh (cf. Lv 27:29) and, as a consequence, withdrawn from men's use; for that reason it is destroyed. This barbarous custom is found not only in Israel, but also among the Moabites : Mesha boasts (*Mesha stone*, 1. 11.12.16.17) that, in honor of his god Chamos, he treated as *ḥerem* the Canaanite towns he had conquered. Caesar (*De bello Gall.*, VI, 17) and Diodorus (*Bibl. Histor.*, V, 27, 4) report the custom among the Celts; Paul Orosius (*Hist. adv. pag.*, V, 16, 5.6) among the Cimbrians, and perhaps Tacitus (*Ann.*, I, 61) among the Teutons. *Ḥerem* is not always applied in all its rigor (cf. Nm 31:7-53; Dt 20:13.14; Jgs 21:11); on more than one occasion the warriors divided the most precious spoils (Dt 3:6.7). On the *ḥerem*, cf. J. Döller, " Der Bann (ḥerem) im A. T. und im späteren Judentum, " *ZKTh* (1933), pp. 1-24; L. Delporte, " L'anathème de Jahwé, " *RScR* (1914), pp. 297-328; A. Fernandez, " El herem biblico, " *Bb* (1924), pp. 3-25.

[38] Yahweh is a " warrior " (Ex 15:3), " the God of the battalions of Israel " (1 Sm 17:45); the wars of Israel are " the wars of Yahweh " (Nm 21:14); it is He who wars against the enemies of Israel (Ex 17:16; 1 Sm 25:28) and conducts the campaign (1 Sm 15:2; 17:45). That is the reason why the ark, which is the symbol of His presence and His throne, accompanied the troops into combat (Nm 10:35; 1 Sm 4; 2 Sm 11:11; 15:24). He was consulted before the battle (Jgs 20:27; 1 Sm 14:37; 3 Kgs 22) and sacrifices were offered to Him (1 Sm 7:8.9; 14:34; So 1:7). This is the origin of the expression " to sanctify the combat " (Mi 3:5; Jer. 6:4; Jl 4:9), which really means to prepare for battle by religious rites, and of the other expression, " the consecrated " (Is 13:3; Jer 22:7; 51:27; So 1:7), which is used to designate combatants, who are held to certain abstinences because they are taking part in a holy war (1 Sm 21:6; 2 Sm 11:11).

[39] Cf. P. Heinisch, *Theologie*, p. 181.

nevertheless,[40] that He hardens the heart of Pharao (Ex 4:21; 7:3),[41] or that of His people (Is 6:10).[42] In Is 29:10 Yahweh punishes the people's resistance to the prophet's admonitions. The revolt of the Sichemites against Abimelech (Jgs 9:23) is the punishment of the latter's crimes (Jgs 9:24; cf. 9:5.18-20); similarly Yahweh sends a lying spirit to deceive Achab (3 Kgs 22:20-23) in order to lead him to his doom because He wishes the king to expiate Naboth's murder (3 Kgs 21), according to the sentence communicated to him by the prophet Elias (3 Kgs 21:17-19); and the bad precepts that Yahweh gives Israel for its own ruin (Ez 20:25.26) are the punishment of its incorrigible perversity.

As the God of the Covenant, Yahweh protects the right of Israel against other peoples. For this reason the victories by which they triumph are called acts of justice (literally: justices, *ṣĕdâqôth*, Jgs 5:11; cf. 1 Sm 12:7; Mi 6:5). Gideon appeals to Yahweh's judgment against the Moabites (Jgs 11:27); and David's victory over Absalom is considered to be a judgment of Yahweh who has reestablished the right of the king, dethroned by his son (2 Sm 18:31). The victory, the deliverance, the salvation of Israel are thus just as many manifestations of Yahweh's justice (Is 41:2.10; 45:8.13; 56:1, etc.), and God's justice can be placed parallel to His salvation (Is 45:8; 51:5-6.8; 56:1; Ps 51:16; 98:2), to His blessing (Ps 24:5), or to His steadfast kindness *(ḥesed)* (Ps 36:6.7.11; 103:17; 145:17). God's justice in the Old Testament is not opposed to His kindness *(ḥesed)*, His mercy or His grace; it includes these attributes. This doctrine will be taken up by St. Paul (Rom 3:22-26).

Among the prophets, however, and this is a characteristic of their teaching, Yahweh's justice shows itself not only in the restoration of Israel's rights when these are threatened by their neighbors, it also includes a moral reform that will restore justice within Israel and will re-establish it in a state according to the will of God who made the Covenant. As gifts of the new espousals Yahweh will

---

[40] In the parallel passage (1 Par 21:1) the text of 2 Sm 24:1 was corrected according to a more advanced theology: it is no longer Yahweh but Satan (no article; the term has already acquired the value of a proper name, which proves the recent date of the correction), who incites David to take the census.

[41] According to Ex 7:13 Pharao's heart was hardened or "became heavy" (7:14); according to Ex 8:11.28; 9:35: "Pharao made his heart heavy."

[42] Since Isaias urges the people to return (for example, 1:16-20) and hopes that the evils which are about to descend upon Israel will purify the people (for example, 1:24-26), it is obvious that he does not intend to say that his mission is to blind the guilty people still further (6:9.10); he means that his mission will not succeed with the great majority who will persist in their evil ways, that it will be the occasion of a still greater blindness which will make the divine punishment quite inevitable.

bring Israel justice and right, fidelity and the knowledge of Yahweh (Os 2:21), all of which Israel had lacked until then (Os 10:12; 12:7).[43] When by means of severe trials Yahweh will have purified Sion of all its impurities, that is to say, of the injustices the people had committed (Is 1:22.23), the city will become once more " the city of justice and the faithful city " (Is 1:25.26), because justice will have been restored to honor, as had once been the case (Is 1:21). The punishments, which will eliminate the guilty, will be a judgment, an act of the justice of God who will redeem Sion from its moral decline: " Sion shall be redeemed by judgment *(mišpaṭ)*, and her repentant ones by justice " (Is 1:27).[44] An analogous idea is expressed by Is 4:4 where it is proclaimed that Yahweh will wash the filth of Sion by the spirit of judgment and the spirit of destruction, that is to say, by the divine power, which, condemning the guilty, " will take away the evil from the midst of His people " (Dt 17:7; 19:19, etc.).

Since the king is the supreme judge and, therefore, the guardian of right, the ideal king of the messianic times will be invested with the spirit of Yahweh who will confer upon him understanding, counsel, strength, and the knowledge of Yahweh, that is to say, all the qualities needed for the perfect exercise of justice, by which he will establish the reign of right and peace: " He shall judge the poor with justice, and with equity decide for the meek of the land. He shall strike the ruthless[45] with the rod of His mouth, and with the breath of His lips He shall slay the wicked. Justice shall be the girdle round His loins, and faithfulness the girdle round His waist " (Is 11:2-5; cf. Jer 23:5.6). The king's collaborators in the exercise of judiciary power will also be filled with the spirit of justice, because Yahweh will be " a spirit of justice to him who sits in judgment " (Is 28:6).

In the edifice that Yahweh will build on the tried stone which He placed in Sion, all materials will be placed in straight line with law and justice: " See, I am laying a stone in Sion, a stone that has been tested, a precious cornerstone as a sure foundation. He who puts his faith in it shall not be shaken.[46] I will make of right a measuring line, of justice a level " (Is 28:16.17). To the kingdom, founded

---

[43] The words " in justice and judgment " are held by certain critics, without sufficient cause, to be a gloss.

[44] The word *wĕšâbêyâh* (= the converted) has been read *wĕšibyâh* (= his deported) by the LXX and the Syriac version; certain critics propose the reading *wĕyošĕbeyâh* (= his inhabitants). Several reject, without sufficient reason, the authenticity of this verse.

[45] Instead of *'ereṣ* (= the land), read *'arîṣ* (= the tyrant).

[46] Instead of *yâḥîs* (= will hasten), read *yâmîš* (or *yâmûš* = will yield, will totter).

on the messianic king,[47] only those will be admitted who respond to the demands of law and justice, that is to say, who themselves practise justice.

The prophet of Is 61:1-11, like the messianic king, has been entrusted with the mission to vindicate the right of the oppressed, to free the captives, to console the afflicted, and to perform all these things so well that those who benefit from his acts will be called " oaks of justice " (61:3), that is to say, they will enjoy prosperity ensuring their social and individual integrity (cf. Is 60:18.21), for Yahweh loves justice and hates deception and gives to each one what is his due (61:8).

In messianic times, the Spirit, flowing down from heavenly heights, will transform world and men : the desert will become an orchard and the orchard be regarded as a forest; in the desert where force was supreme, right *(mišpaṭ)* will abide; in cultivated regions where injustice reigned, justice will dwell; peace will be the work of justice (Is 32:15-17; cf. 60:17.21).

According to the old concept, divine justice is exercised principally on behalf of the people, and divine sanction affects the whole people, the whole family (Nm 16:30; Jos 7:24) down to the remote descendants of the guilty ones (Ex 20:5; 34:7; Nm 14:18; 2 Sm 21:6; 3 Kgs 14:10). Even in pre-exilic prophets punishments are mostly collective (Am 7:17; 8:10; 9:1-4; Os 1:4; 7:12; Is 14:21; Mi 6:1-5; Jer 5:9; 11:22; 29:32). The idea that children expiate the crimes of their parents was so deeply rooted that it had taken the form of a proverb : " The fathers ate unripe grapes, and the children's teeth are set on edge " (Jer 31:29; Ez 18:2). This idea is explained by the strict solidarity that united all the members of the family, the clan, the tribe. All men looked on themselves as " the bones and the flesh " of their kinsfolk and their brothers (Jgs 9:2.3; 2 Sm 5:1); they believed that they formed an organic totality with their ancestors and while this cohesion insured the salvation and prosperity of each individual, it also brought about the destruction of all in the event of misfortune. For this reason it was believed to be perfectly natural that the fault of a few, or even of an individual, would result in the punishment of the whole group.

Jeremias (31:30) was the first to react against this opinion. He proclaimed that at the time of the future restoration " everyone shall die for his own iniquity : the teeth of him who eats the unripe grapes shall be set on edge. " Although he was convinced that Yahweh

---

[47] Cf. P. Volz, *in h.l.;* cf. Is 7:14; 9:5.6; 11:1-8.

"probes the mind and tests the heart, to reward everyone according to his ways and according to the merit of his deeds" (Jer 17:10), he admits that there is still collective retribution in the present: Yahweh repays the father's guilt, even into the lap of their children" (Jer 32:18; cf. 2:5-9; 11:22; 29:32).[48] Ezechiel (18) definitively and absolutely rejects the popular saying: "There shall no longer be anyone among you who will repeat this proverb in Israel. For all lives are mine: the life of the father is like the life of the son, both are mine. Only the one who sins shall die" (18:3.4).

In Dt 24:16 this principle is established as a rule of criminal law.

Besides this school of thought, which admits that divine justice is exercised on behalf or against the whole group, there exists another which sees in Yahweh the just judge of individuals. In fact, since Yahweh is the head of the tribe, He is the one who looks after the rights of each of its members. Even in the remote past appeal was made to His judgment to settle private differences (Gn 16:5; 1 Sm 24:13; Ex 18:15; 22:7.8), because He was believed to be an equitable and incorrupt judge (Dt 10:17). Joseph's whole story shows how Yahweh's justice looks after the cause of the persecuted just. In many psalms the poor and the oppressed entrust the defense of their cause and of their rights to Yahweh (Ps 9:5; 35:23.24; 43:1; 76:10; 94:2; 129:4; 143:1.3.11). Some psalms go so far as to invoke divine justice to obtain the pardon of their faults (Ps 51:16; 143:1.2). The repentant sinner, indeed, who acknowledges his fault and submits it to Yahweh's just judgment, knows that he can count henceforth not only on the pardon, but on the protection of his God who will undertake his defense and the establishment of his rights (Mi 7:9). In delivering the repentant sinner from the evils that are the consequence of his faults and in restoring his happiness, Yahweh manifests His justice (Mi 7:9; cf. Is 41:10; 45:8.13; Ps 98:2). So true is it that Yahweh gives to each one what is his due, to the just good things, to the wicked bad things, that He is said to apply the law of talion to each one: "Toward the faithful *(ḥasid)* You are faithful, toward the wholehearted You are wholehearted, toward the sincere You are sincere, but toward the crooked You are astute" (Ps 18:26.27).

Yahweh "scorns the scorner,[49] but to the humble He shows

---

[48] The authenticity of this passage is much contested. A. Condamin (*Le livre de Jérémie*, Paris 1920, p. 249) and F. Nötscher (*Das Buch Jeremias*, Bonn 1934, p. 241) seem very hesitant. Whatever be the truth, it is manifest that the idea of collective retribution still haunts the prophet's mind (cf. Jer 2:5-9; 11:22; 29:32; cf. F. Nötscher, *op. cit.*, p. 233; *Die Gerechtigkeit Gottes*, p. 75).

[49] In the sapiential books "scorners" who scorn God and men (Prv 1:26) are the worst of all the wicked; they are the proud, the arrogant (Prv 21:24) who sow

kindness" (Prv 3:34; Ps 37:13; cf. Prv 1:26).[50] In the Old Testament (for example, Is 3:10.11),[51] especially in the sapiential books, adversity is the normal sanction for sin (Prv 1:18.19; 2:18.19.22; 5:22.23; 6:11.15; 15:27.28; Jb 4:6-9; 5:3-5.12-15; 11:4-12; Ps 1:4-5, etc.) and prosperity is the reward of virtue (Ps 1:1-3; 15:2-5; Prv 3:13-18; 12:7; Jb 8:20-22, etc.). Experience proves only too often that the reality does not correspond to the theory, and more than one wise man since the days of Jeremias (12:1.2; 15:15-18) has asked himself in anguish "why does the way of the wicked prosper," while the just man is overwhelmed by misfortunes (Ps 73:2-9.13.14). This painful problem is the subject of the whole book of Job who reacts against the popular opinion which held that adversity is the sanction for faults. Although no fully satisfactory solution appears in the Old Testament before the book of Wisdom, no one seriously held doubts about Yahweh's justice (cf. Ps 73:18-28; Jb 19:25-29; 31:35-37; 40:8; 42:3).[52]

§ 9. *The sentiments of God*

The Old Testament attributes man's sentiments to God, sentiments that flow from the divine attributes, especially love, repentance, jealousy, anger, hatred. Love is the manifestation of goodness, repentance of mercy, jealousy of the personality and unicity of God; anger and hatred are associated with divine holiness, which is, as we have seen, less an attribute than the constitutive element of the divinity.

1. *The love of God.* — The Hebrew uses several different words to express love or benevolence: *'âhâb* (*'âhăbâh* = love), "to love," a verb which can have for object a person but also a material thing (for example, Gn 27:4.9.14; Os 3:1) of either the moral or spiritual order, such as justice (Ps 45:8), good or evil (Am 5:15; Ps 52:5). It may designate sexual love (Os 3:1; Ez 16:33.36.37), conjugal love

---

discord and hatred (Prv 22:10; 29:8), who seize those who reprove them (Prv 9:7.8; 13:1; 15:2); they are the most obstinate adversaries of the wise men.

[50] The same idea is found in the prophets and is applied to the people: because Israel has turned away from its God, Yahweh turns away from Israel (Os 4:6; Jer 5:19; 16:10-13).

[51] These two verses are a gloss and interrupt the text.

[52] The last words of Job (31:31-37) are an appeal to the judgment of God: Job brags of daring to carry upon his shoulder the scroll that contains all the accusations of his opponents and of daring to appear before God, with head erect, in the attitude of one who is innocent and not guilty. He has not lost, therefore, his trust in the justice of the supreme Judge, whose judgment he accepts.

(1 Sm 1:5), paternal love (Gn 25:28; 44:20), or friendship (1 Sm 16:21; 18:1.3), love of neighbor (Lv 19:18.34) or love of God (Dt 5:10). Fairly frequently it signifies a preference (1 Sm 1:5; Dt 21:15, etc.). *Dâbaq* signifies attachment (Gn 2:24; 34:3; Dt 10:20); *ḥâšaq* (Gn 34:8; Dt 7:7; 10:15), *ḥâpeṣ* (Gn 34:19) and *râṣâh* (Gn 33:10; 2 Sm 24:23) signify "to take pleasure in," "to be pleased with"; *riḥâm*, to love or to have pity; *ḥûs* and *ḥâmal*, to have compassion; *ḥânan*, to do a favor, or to show one's favor (*ḥen* = grace, favor). Finally the word *ḥesed* expresses kindness or helpful fidelity. [1]

Of all these terms expressing love, benevolence, or mercy, very few are applied to God in the older texts (Gn 33:5.11; Nm 6:25; perhaps Ex 22:26; 34:6). God's love, His condescension, His mercy, nevertheless, manifest themselves already in the old traditions enshrined in Genesis, for example toward the first man (Gn 2:8; 3:11), toward Noe and his family (Gn 7:1.16), toward the patriarchs (Gn 12:2.3; 15:1-18; 33:5.11, etc.). And certain old theophoric names express or suppose God's love toward man, such as *'El-yâdâ'* (= God knows, 2 Sm 5:16), *'El-ḥânân* (= God shows favor, 2 Sm 21:19) names used in the days of David, or *'Eli-'âb* (= my God is father, Nm 1:9), a name borne by a Zabulonite chief, or *'Eli-'ezer* (= my God is help, Gn 15:2; Ex 18:4), the name of a servant of Abraham and of a son of Moses, or *Yedîdyâh* (= beloved of Yahweh, 2 Sm 12:25), the surname of Solomon.

It is, however, especially the prophets who show forth Yahweh's love toward Israel. They describe this love either: a) under the form of conjugal love, or b) under that of paternal love.

a) Osee was the first to recognize that the bond established by the covenant between Yahweh and His people is a bond of love; for this reason he describes the covenant of Sinai as a marriage of love contracted by Yahweh with Israel in the days of her youth (2:17; 9:10; 10:1; cf. 6:7; 12:10; 13:4). But in spite of all the proofs of love Israel was faithless (11:4), she has proved unfaithful to her spouse and has committed adultery with all the Baals of Canaan (2:7.8.14). Because of this Yahweh wishes to repudiate the unfaithful one (2:4) and chastise her without pity (2:8-15; 7:12; 8:13; 13:7.8), in order to bring her to repentance (5:15) and to restore her to her position as spouse and to her former happiness (2:16-25; 14:5.6). Osee explains this incomprehensible love, which persists in spite of all the infidelities of Israel and which defies all juridic norms regulating marriage, by the holiness

[1] For the exact meaning of *riḥâm, ḥûs, ḥâmal, ḥânan (ḥen)* and *ḥesed*, cf. above § 8, B, 1, pp. 62 ff.

of Yahweh (11:8.9), that is to say, by that which differentiates God from all men and from every creature: "I am God and not man, the holy one in your midst" (11:9). No one has insisted like Osee on the mysterious and irrational character of divine love. God strongly desires the good of the beloved object (2:16-25) and wishes to treat the beloved object with tenderness and gentleness (10:4; cf. 10:11; 13:4.5); but disappointed by Israel's inconstancy (6:4) and repeated infidelities (2:4.7.15; 4:1.2; 5:3.4, etc.), His love turns into the fury, as it were, of a lioness (13:7.8); His love, however, continues despite all disappointments (11:8.9) and waits only for the repentance of the unfaithful one (14:2) in order to pardon her (5:15; 14:5.6; cf. 2:16-18.21.22).

Jeremias has borrowed from Osee the figure of Yahweh's marriage with Israel to represent the covenant (2:1.2.13), and he stigmatizes Israel's infidelities to her God as adulteries and prostitutions (2:5.23-25; 3:1-4.6-11.13). The outraged husband can only repudiate His fickle spouse (3:1); His love turns into implacable hate (12:8; 13:14; 16:5; 21:7). Yahweh, nevertheless, does not deliver the object of His love to the enemies without regret, and He suffers as He watches His cherished vine, His domain, trodden underfoot by merciless strangers (12:7-12), because Israel is still, in spite of everything, His beloved one (11:15; 12:7.10) whom He loves with an eternal love (31:3). For this reason He urges her to recognize her errors and return to Him (3:12.13; 4:1), so that He may be able to pardon her, and He promises to enter into a new covenant with her, one that will bring about the inner renewal of all her sons (31:33.34).

Ezechiel describes Yahweh's love for Israel with his usual vigor and realism. Israel was an abandoned child whom Yahweh rescued out of pity and surrounded with the most attentive care; when the child grew into maidenhood, He made a covenant with her and took her for His spouse; He lavishly gave her every gift. But the young girl abused all this most shamefully and prostituted herself to every passerby, that is to say, she gave herself up to the worship of all the gods of Canaan and the neighboring nations. In return, Yahweh surrendered her to her most cruel enemies (16:1-52).[2] But since Israel's humiliation, when she was led into captivity, is a profanation of His holy name (36:21), Yahweh will deliver Israel and will conclude with her a new covenant, an eternal covenant which will bring about

[2] In chapter 23 Ezechiel resumes the same image, but this time with the two sisters, Juda and Israel.

both the restoration of the nation and the moral religious regeneration of the individuals (36:23-31). According to Ezechiel it is not out of love toward His people (cf. 36:22.32), but for the sanctification of His name [3] that Yahweh will accomplish the restoration of Israel.

In the book of consolation for Israel (Is 42:1-66:24) the figure of Yahweh's marriage recurs several times to describe the restoration of Israel: Sion was an abandoned wife (Is 49:14; 54:6; 60:15; 62:4), deprived of children (49:20; 51:18; 54:1), carried into captivity (Is 40:2; 52:2, etc.), because Yahweh had cast her off (Is 50:1). But her opprobrium, her solitude, her wretchedness and her servitude will end because He who made her is her spouse and her redeemer. He will call her back; can a woman married in her youth be repudiated? "For a brief moment I abandoned you, but with great tenderness *(raḥămîm)* I will take you back. In an outburst of wrath, for a moment I hid my face from you; but with enduring love *(ḥesed)* I take pity on you" (Is 54:7-8).

b) To the Semites the national God is not only the king but also the father of His people, that is to say, the Lord and protector: just as Chamos is the father of the Moabites (Nm 21:29; cf. Jer 2:27; Mal 2:11), so Yahweh is the father of Israel (for example Ex 4:22; Dt 14:1; 32:5; Is 1:2) because He begot her (Dt 32:18), that is to say, He created her (Dt 32:6; Ps 100:3; Is 43:1.21; 54:5), raised and nourished her (Is 1:2; Dt 8:5). This idea, however, implies rather the protection of God (Dt 1:31; 32:10-14) than His love.

The prophets stress more the love which results from the divine paternity. Osee (11:1-4) describes Yahweh as the most tender of fathers; when Israel was a child, Yahweh loved her; since Egypt He called her repeatedly, taught her to walk, took her in His arms, lavished His care; in spite of the infidelities of this ungrateful people, Yahweh drew her with human cords, with bands of love. He treated her as one treats an infant, raising her to one's cheeks, He stooped to feed her. [4] He cannot resign Himself to abandon Israel; at this thought His heart is overwhelmed, His pity is stirred; Yahweh will contain His wrath and will not destroy Ephraim again, because He is God and not man, because He is holy (Os 11:8.9).

In the words of Jeremias Yahweh laments the infidelity of His sons, to whom He wished to give a land of delights (3:19); He appeals to them most pressingly (3:14.22): because Israel is His first-born

---

[3] For the meaning of this expression, see above § 6.

[4] For the justification of this interpretation, cf. A. Van Hoonacker, *Les douze petits prophètes*, Paris 1908, pp. 105 ff.

(31:9; cf. Ex 4:22), His beloved son, His favored child. Each time He threatens, He thinks of him with love, His affections overflow, His pity awakens (31:20).

Yahweh can no more forget Sion than a mother can forget her infant: "Can a mother forget her infant, be without tenderness for the child of her womb? Even should she forget, I will never forget you" (Is 49:15).

Like Osee and Jeremias, the Deuteronomist sees in the covenant a manifestation of the love of God; it is because Yahweh has loved Israel and its ancestors, not because of its merits or number (7:7; 9:4), that He led it out of Egypt and chose it for Himself, from all the nations, as His special people, His holy people (4:37; 7:6.7; 10:14.15); it is because of His love that He protects them and gives them the land promised to their fathers (9:5-7; 23:6; 28:63), and this in spite of the wickedness of this "stiff-necked" people (9:6-29). The very law that Yahweh imposed on Israel is not the insupportable yoke of a tyrant; it is within man's reach, in his mouth and in his heart so that he may carry it out (30:11-14); it has been given to him to make him wise and intelligent (4:6), to educate him (4:36), to instruct him even as a father instructs his children (8:5); it is therefore a manifestation of God's love for His sons (14:1). For this reason the law asks man to love unreservedly and undividedly (6:5; 10:12). The love of God is, in Deuteronomy, also the foundation on which the covenant rests and which assures its continuance.

Even in the writings of the prophets, where stress is laid on the universality of the divine power, Yahweh's love toward strange peoples is rarely stated; and ordinarily it is spoken of as in the future and in terms of a restoration of the kingdom of God (so in Is 2:2-4 = Mi 4:1-4; Is 25:6-8; 19:18-25; Jer 12:15; Jon 4:11). Without doubt, the extension of divine domination over all the nations is a blessing for them; it is most often presented, however, as the triumph of Yahweh on behalf of Israel, even as the submission of the nations to the chosen people (Is 14:2; 49:22.23; 60:4.9-12; 66:12.20, etc.).

Rarer and later are the texts which extend God's love to all creatures (Ps 145:9; Sir 18:13; Wis 11:24).

Although pre-exilic texts rarely mention Yahweh's love toward individuals, it cannot be said with the Wellhausen school that this idea does not appear before Jeremias (16:19). If, indeed, the term ordinarily does not occur, old traditions connected with the patriarchs and a number of ancient theophoric names [5] show forth divine

[5] See above p. 62.

benevolence and mercy. Many of the psalmists later express their confidence in Yahweh's love and mercy (for example, Ps 25:6; 40:12; 42:9; 51:3; 69:17; 119:77), or their own love toward their God (for example Ps 18:2; 63:2; 73:25; 116:1). Few are the texts, even after the Exile, which affirm Yahweh's love toward a determined individual (Neh 13:26; Ps 127:2; Is 48:14; 3 Kgs 10:9; 2 Par 9:8); more frequent mention is made of God's love toward certain categories of persons, such as the just (Prv 15:9; cf. 3:12; Ps 146:8; Wis 3:9; 7:14; Sir 4:10; 18:14), the pure of heart (Prv 22:11, LXX), and strangers who have settled as clients on Israel's soil (Dt 10:18; Ps 146:8).

2. *The repentance of God.* — The verb *niḥam* that is ordinarily translated by "to repent," can mean "to pity" (for example Jgs 21:6.15; Ps 90:13), "to allow oneself to be swayed" (Jgs 2:18; Am 7:3.6), to change from anger to mercy or inversely (Jer 18:8.10), or, in order to use a biblical expression: "to repent of evil" decided upon (Ex 32:12.14; Jer 18:8.10; 26:3.13.19; 42:10), to regret (Gn 6:6; 1 Sm 15:11), to repent (Jer 31:19; 1 Sm 15:29), to console oneself (Jer 31:15), in *Piel*, to console (Is 12:1; 49:13; 51:3.12; 52:9, etc.; Jer 31:13). In most instances, with the exception of those where the meaning of "to regret," "to repent," or "to console oneself" is found, the verb expresses a movement of mercy.

Since the Old Testament makes use of very many anthropomorphisms, [6] it is not surprising that repentance is attributed to God, although certain texts reject this sentiment or principle as unworthy of His holiness: Yahweh "will not lie nor repent, for He is not a man that He should repent" (1 Sm 15:29; Nm 23:19); [7] for He is faithful to His promises (Ps 110:4) and to His resolutions (Is 31:2; Jer 4:28) and "His way is straight" (Ez 18:25). While 1 Sm 15:29 and Nm 23:19 appeal to what differentiates Yahweh from man, that is to say, to His holiness in order to deny that there is repentance in Him, Osee, on the contrary, explains by this same holiness the struggle that takes places in Yahweh's heart between anger and mercy. [8]

The sacred writers considered God as a personal being, an acting will. Consequently they were unable to describe His action without recourse to the sentiments connected with the human will, although they were intimately convinced of the "entirely other" character

---

[6] See above § 3.

[7] The author of 1 Sm 15:29 has obviously felt that repentance is not becoming for God; he declares, nevertheless, in the same narrative that Yahweh "repents that He made Saul king" (1 Sm 15:11). This contradiction shows how the Hebrews were incapable of explaining the mystery of the actions of the transcendent God.

[8] Cf. above § 8, A, 3.

of God who is exalted above every earthly creature. While attributing to God sentiments which in man are contradictory, they implied that God possesses attributes which seem to be irreconcilable. When Jeremias declares that God repents of the evil He intended to do (18:8.10, etc.), and on another occasion says that He does not repent (4:28), he conveys the idea that God is at once merciful and faithful to His designs; with the first affirmation Jeremias wishes to win his hearers to trust that God is kind and compassionate; with the second he wants to warn them about the gravity and seriousness of the threats of a God who carries out His designs. Similarly the author of 1 Sm 15 affirms in verse 29 that the decree of Saul's rejection — a decree expressed in verse 11 by the formula: Yahweh repents that He has chosen — is irrevocable, because Yahweh " does not repent, " that is to say, He is immutable in His designs.

3. *The jealousy of God.* — The jealousy of the gods is a theme frequently found in all mythologies. The gods, who are represented as people, react passionately against whoever tries to usurp or endanger their privileges, their sovereignty, their possessions or their loves. In this sense jealousy is a sentiment of defense of God's personality and is common to the divinities of all ancient religions. But it has been rightly said that jealousy is a trait completely characteristic of Yahweh, [9] since in the Old Testament it most frequently expresses the exclusive character of the God of Israel. While in other ancient religions the gods or the supreme god allow their followers to offer homage to several divinities, the God of Israel suffers no rival, not even a divine image, because he is " a jealous God " (Ex 20:4.5; 34:14), who claims to reserve for Himself alone the adoration and the service of the people He has made His own (Ex 19:5.6). This idea appears alone in almost all pre-exilic texts (Nm 25:11; Dt 4:24; 5:9; 6:15; 32:16.21; 3 Kgs 14:22); in Jos 24:19 jealousy is linked with holiness, and this is also the case later in Ez 5:13; 8:3.5; 16:42; 23:25 and in Ps 78:58. Similarly those who in their zeal for Yahweh reacted violently against Israel's infidelities, " are jealous on behalf of Yahweh " (Nm 25:13; 3 Kgs 19:10; 4 Kgs 10:16). [10]

---

[9] J. Hänel, *Die Religion der Heiligkeit*, Gütersloh 1931, pp. 49 ff.; pp. 196 ff. W. Eichrodt, *Theologie*, I, p. 104, n. 1. Hänel connects jealousy with holiness and coins the word *Eiferheiligkeit*, to designate this characteristic of the God of Israel. The jealousy of Yahweh is, in fact, sometimes connected with His holiness (Jos 24:19; Ez 39:25) and, especially in the prophets, with His anger, which is itself connected with His holiness. In older texts, nevertheless, God's anger is rarely brought into relation with His holiness (Jos 24:19), but usually with the exclusive character of Yahweh.

[10] Cf. F. Küchler, " Der Gedanke des Eifers Jahwes im A. T., " *ZAW* (1908), pp. 42-52.

In the prophetical books Yahweh's jealousy is rather brought into relation with His holiness. In Ez 39:25 Yahweh declares that He " will show Himself jealous for His name, " that is to say, for the holiness of His name which was profaned by Israel's defeat and servitude (cf. 36:23-28; 39:27-29). Here jealousy is the reaction of holiness: God cannot suffer to have His holy name profaned (cf. Is 48:11); He will defend it, or, according to the prophet's word (36:23; cf. 39:27), He " will sanctify it " by restoring His oppressed people.[11]

The same idea seems to be suggested by the texts of Is 9:6 and 37:32, where Yahweh guarantees the execution of His projects of messianic restoration (Is 9:1-6) and of the deliverance of Jerusalem (Is 37:30-32), by referring to His jealousy, that is to say, to the passionate ardor with which He executes His will so that nothing stands in its way: " the jealousy of Yahweh Sabaoth will do this. " Likewise in Is 63:15; Jl 2:18; Za 1:14; 8:2 divine jealousy, several times associated with His pity for Israel, is exercised on behalf of His oppressed people. In Ez 5:13; 36:5.6; 38:19; Is 42:13; 59:17; So 3:8; Ps 79:5, however, jealousy is associated with His anger or vengeance and is directed against nations hostile to Israel. In these texts, jealousy has lost almost completely its own character and becomes practically equivalent to anger (cf. Ps 37:1; Prv 23:17; 24:19).

4. *The anger of God.* — Anger is the reaction of the holy God against all that impairs His majesty or His perfection. To express this sentiment the Old Testament uses a series of terms, several of which are figurative: *ḥâron* and *hêmah* denote ardor, heat; *'âph* (literally: nose) and *rûaḥ* (breath) are taken from the effect of anger on respiration and its organ;[12] also *'ebĕrâh, za'am, za'aph* and *qeṣeph.* The anger of Yahweh is described as a violent passion which must be released in order to return to a state of calmness: " When I have wreaked My fury upon you, I will be quiet and no longer vexed " (Ez 16:42; cf. 5:13; 6:12; 7:8; 13:16; 24:13). The Hebrews, like many of the ancients,[13] attributed to the anger of Yahweh all the public and private calamities that befell them (for example Nm 11:1.33; 25:3.9; Jos 7; Jgs 2:14.20; 3:8; 2 Sm 15:26; 24:1-5) and to His benevolence their

[11] Cf. above § 6.

[12] Cf. p. 64, note 28.

[13] Mesha attributes the reverses experienced by the Moabites to the anger of their god Chamos (1. 5); the deluge is the result of the anger of the god Enlil (Gilgamesh Epic, *AOT*², pp. 178 ff.); the Babylonian penitential psalms seek to appease the wrath of the gods which manifests itself in sickness and any other misfortune (cf. P. Dhorme, *La religion assyro-babylonienne*, Paris 1910, pp. 236 ff.).

prosperity, happiness, success. For this reason misfortunes are called "wounds," that is to say, blows *(nega'* or *maggêphâh)* of God (for example, Ex 9:14; 1 Sm 6:5; 2 Sm 24:21.23; Nm 11:33; 14:37; 25:8.9; Ps 91:10; 106:29).

Divine anger is the punishment of sin, not an explosion of the bad temper of the jealousy of an arbitrary and capricious God; for Yahweh is a just God.[14] This is obvious from the evidence of almost all the texts that mention His wrath, and also from the fact that very often the release of His anger is presented as the vengeance of an injury to His majesty (Mi 5:14; Dt 32:25.41.43; Jer 11:20; 20:12; Ez 25:12-14; Lv 26:25; Nm 31:3; Is 34:8; 47:3; 61:2; Ps 94:1; 149:7; cf. Jgs 11:36; 2 Sm 22:38).[15]

In some old accounts, however, Yahweh's anger seems to flare up without reason. Certain authors believe that they find here the proof of the "demonic" character of the God of the ancient Hebrews.[16] Such is the mysterious passage of Ex 4:24-26.[17] According to this text Yahweh attacked Moses during the night, while he was travelling with his wife and his young son, and tried to kill him. Sepphora, to save her husband's life, circumcised the son and touched his feet,[18] saying: "You are a spouse of blood to me"; thus she calmed the anger of Yahweh. Setting aside some incomprehensible details the general sense of the passage seems to be this: Yahweh wanted to put Moses to death because his son (and perhaps Moses himself) was not circumcised. Sepphora saved the life of her husband, for by circumcising the son she pacified the anger of Yahweh. This eruption of Yahweh's anger, it seems, had been provoked by the transgression of a ritual precept (cf. Gn 17:10); this event is not meaningless, therefore, but wishes to stress the importance of circumcision (cf. Gn 17:14).

1 Sm 6:19 and 2 Sm 6:6.7 relate that Yahweh struck the inhabitants

---

[14] Cf. above § 8, B, 3.

[15] Cf. W. Eichrodt, *Theologie*, I, p. 133.

[16] P. Volz, *Das Dämonische in Jahve*, Göttingen 1924, followed, with certain reservations, by E. Sellin (*Theologie*, pp. 33 ff.).

[17] The text is particularly obscure, perhaps corrupt, and has given rise to very different and often fantastic interpretations. Cf. J. Hehn, "Der 'Blutsbräutigam' Ex 4:24-26," *ZAW* (1931), pp. 1-8, who corrects the MT according to the LXX; P. Heinisch (*Das Buch Exodus*, Bonn 1934, pp. 61-64) and T. Böhl (*Exodus*, Groningen 1928, pp. 107-108) who try to explain it without correcting it.

[18] It is impossible to determine with certitude to whom the possessive pronoun refers (Yahweh, Moses or the son) or to indicate the meaning of the words "his feet" (literal meaning or euphemism for the male organ). The text does not say that Sepphora "touched the feet" with the foreskin of her son, as many translators suppose.

of Beth-Semes because they looked at the ark, and He struck Oza because he touched it. These accounts emphasize the holiness of the ark which is the symbol and throne of Yahweh, the holy God, " before whom no one can stand " (1 Sm 6:20). No one profane can, without endangering his life, enter into contact, even by a simple look (Ex 19:21), with the Holy One; he must have been " sanctified " (Ex 19:10; Jos 3:5; 7:13), if he wants to be able to draw near without danger (Ex 19:22). [19] Once again Yahweh's anger is motivated by a violation of a ritual law.

The account of Jacob's struggle with the divine being who attacked him at the ford of Jabok (Gn 32:23-33) referred perhaps originally not to God *(El)*, but to a local spirit who defended the crossing of the torrent. This would explain the strange character of the episode which Osee (12:5) interprets as the struggle of Jacob with an angel.

According to 2 Sm 24:1, finally, " the anger of Yahweh was again aroused against Israel. " Here the context supplies no reason. But it seems that this expression is merely a naive way of explaining an incomprehensible case : how was David led to commit the fault that brought about the divine punishment? Granted that the Hebrews trace back to God, the first cause, all events, even those that are fortuitous and dependent on human liberty, [20] and that they believed calamities to be the result of the anger of God, it was thought that Yahweh had incited the king to take a census of the people, [21] because He wished to try Israel, or, according to the language of the times, because He was irritated against Israel. Similarly David sought to explain Saul's strange fury against him (1 Sm 26:19) and Shimei's wild hatred (2 Sm 16:10) by supposing that Yahweh had aroused them against him. In no way, however, does he doubt Yahweh's justice and goodness (2 Sm 16:12). On the contrary, he humbly submits himself to the mysterious and incomprehensible will of an almighty, wise, just and merciful God whose designs are beyond human understanding : " If Yahweh has said to him, ' Curse David! ' then who shall say : Why have you done so? " Yahweh is the master and has not to render account to any one. As the prophets will say

[19] Cf. above § 6.

[20] Cf. above § 8, B, 3.

[21] According to popular opinion every census is dangerous and culpable, because it is a lack of confidence in God : it is unbecoming to count His gifts. In the O. T. God is the author of the increase of mankind (Gn 1:28), He forms men in a mysterious way (Jb 10:8-12); a census is, as it were, a suspicious verification of His work, an act of distrust in Him; so much the more, because He promised innumerable descendants to Israel's ancestor (Gn 15:5; cf. A. Schutz, *Die Bücher Samuel*, Münster im W. 1920, II, p. 284).

later (Is 29:16; 45:9; 64:7; Jer 18:6) and the book of Job (10:9), man is in the hand of God, His creator, like clay in the hand of the potter who fashions it as he wishes; " dare the clay say to its modeler : ' What are you doing? ' (or to its maker) : ' You are unskillful ' " (Is 45:9). [22]

No one has described more vigorously than the book of Job (38-41) the mysterious and incomprehensible character of the divine anger, whose punishments fall upon the just as well as upon the wicked (9:22-24) : God is almighty and holy; His plans and His action, always wise and just, confound the human mind (42:3). Before the Most High, Job, who has criticized Him, can only bow and be silent (40:4); to annul the judgment of the Almighty, it would be necessary to be as almighty as He (40:8).

---

[22] Instead of *ûpŏʿâlĕkâ* (= thy work) and *lô* (= to him), read *lĕpoʿâlô* (to him who has done it) and *lĕkâ* (= to thee); literally " thou hast no hands. "

CHAPITRE II

GOD AND THE WORLD

§ 1. *The world according to the Old Testament*

The Old Testament has no special word for " world." It speaks of " heaven and earth " (Gn 1:1; 2:1; 2:4), of " the sky, the earth, the abyss and the world beneath the earth " (cf. Ex 20:4; Ps 135:6; Jb 11:8.9). The Hebrews represented the universe in much the same way as did the Babylonians who in turn, it seems, borrowed their concept from the Sumerians.

The heaven was to them a solid vault (Gn 1:6; Prv 8:28),[1] like a mirror of molten metal (Jb 37:18);[2] it rested on pillars (Jb 26:11), that is to say, on the mountains which at the horizon seem to support the firmament. Its task was to separate the upper waters from those of the lower abyss (Gn 1:7; Ps 104:3; 148:4) which formed a single mass in the primitive chaos (Gn 1:6). In the firmament there were vents, through which God, whenever He wished, poured water on the earth (Gn 7:11; 4 Kgs 7:2.19; Ps 78:23; cf. Jb 38:22), that is to say, life-giving rain (4 Kgs 7:2.19; Ps 78:23), and released the devastating torrents of the deluge (Gn 7:11; 8:2). Above the upper waters beams have been fixed which support " the upper chambers "[3] where Yahweh dwells (Ps 104:3; cf. Ps 29:10). Elsewhere Yahweh's dwelling is described as a tent of which heaven is the cloth that Yahweh has unfolded to dwell therein (Is 40:22; Ps 104:2; cf. Is 42:5; 44:24; 48:13; 51:13; Jb 9:8). Just as the Babylonians distinguished three (or seven) heavens, the Hebrews spoke of several heavens, without being precise about the exact number; they distinguished " the heaven " from " the heaven of heavens " (Dt 10:14; 3 Kgs 8:27; Neh 9:6), that is to say, the upper heaven (cf. Ps 148:4); later Judaism admitted three (2 Cor 12:2), and perhaps under the influence of Babylon, they

---

[1] In Hebrew *râqî'a* from the root *rq'* = to strike, to hammer, to extend by stroke with a hammer; the Greek στερέωμα and the Latin *firmamentum* suggest a solid, rigid construction.

[2] The ancients used mirrors made of polished molten metal plates (cf. Ex 38:8).

[3] The " upper chamber " is a room built on the roof. It is the master's private apartment (Jgs 3:20; 2 Sm 19:1; 4 Kgs 1:2) and sometimes set aside for distinguished guests (4 Kgs 4:10).

spoke of seven. But unlike the Babylonians who made each heaven the domain of a special god, the Old Testament proclaimed that to Yahweh " belong the heavens, even the highest heavens, as well as the earth and everything on it " (Dt 10:14).

The earth is an immense disc that rests on columns (Jb 9:6), on bases (Jb 38:4.6), or foundations (Ps 18:16; 104:5; Is 24:18; 40:21; Jer 31:37; Mi 6:2; Prv 8:29), which are the mountains (Ps 46:3); these bases are sunk deep in the waters of the lower ocean (Jb 9:6; Ps 24:2; 136:6), the abyss *(tĕhôm)* [4] which stretches beneath the earth (Gn 49:25) or the great deep (Gn 7:11) whence fountains rise (Gn 7:11; 49:25; Prv 8:28), whose waters surround the earth on all sides but are held in place by the limit imposed on them by God (Prv 8:29; Jb 38:11; Ps 104:9). Established on solid foundations, the earth is stable (Ps 24:2; 93:2; 96:10), " it shall not be moved forever " (Ps 104:5). On the other hand, according to Jb 26:7, God " suspends the earth over nothing at all. "

The sea is the stormy element that God alone can control (Ps 89:10; Jb 26:12). Yahweh has set the sandy shore as boundary for the sea (Jer 5:22) and has set limits to the waters which hinder them from trespassing on dry land (Prv 8:29; Jb 38:11; Ps 104:9); He has enclosed it with two barred doors (Jb 38:8.10) and has stationed sentinels to guard it as a redoubtable dragon (*tannîn*, Jb 7:12). [5] The sea *(yâm)*

---

[4] In Gn 1:2 the same word denotes primordial chaos where all the waters were still assembled.

[5] *Tannîn* (δράκων in LXX) is a mythological monster which is compared with Rahab (Is 51:9), sometimes with Leviathan (Is 27:1; Ps 74:13.14), the great *tannîn* (Ps 74:13), " the *tannîn* that is in the sea " (Is 27:1), " the fleeing serpent, the coiled serpent " (Is 27:1) with several heads (Ps 74:13.14). This monster originates from Phoenicia; it is described in the Ras Shamra tablets in identical terms under the name " Lotan " (cf. *Syria*, 1931, p. 357; 1934, pp. 305 ff.; Virolleaud, *La déesse Anat*, Paris 1938, p. 50; cf. R. de Vaux, *RB*, 1937, p. 545; A. Bea, *Bb*, 1938, p. 445; " Liwjatan, " *BW*, col. 961 ff.). Nabuchodonosor is compared to a dragon *(tannîn)* who has devoured everything (Jer 51:34); similarly Pharao, in Ez 29:3-6 and 32:2-6, is " like the great *tannîn* that crouches in the midst of the rivers, " " like the *tannîn* in the sea. " In Jerusalem a fountain was called " the fountain of the *tanninîm* " (Neh 2:13). In Gn 1:21 and Ps 148:7 the *tanninîm* are big fish; in Ex 7:9.10.12; Ps 91:13, they are poisonous serpents (Dt 32:33).

Rahab is another *tannîn* (Is 51:9) that has helpers (Jb 9:13) just like Tiamat (cf. the Babylonian creation poem *Enuma eliš*, IV, 107) and seems to be associated with the stormy sea. At the beginning of creation this monster has been tamed by God (Ps 89:10.11; Jb 26:12.13), but continues to be dangerous; God keeps it subject by means of a guard (Jb 7:2); He had to conquer it in the crossing of the Red Sea (Is 51:9; cf. Jb 26:12.13) and reduced it to silence (Is 30:7). In Ps 87:4 Rahab is the symbol of Egypt. Several critics consider Rahab to be the Hebrew equivalent of Tiamat (cf. R. Gunkel, *Schöpfung und Chaos*, Göttingen 1921; T. K. Cheyne, " Rahab, " *EB*, IV, col. 4006; P. Dhorme, *Le livre de Job*, Paris 1926, p. 121; J. Hempel, " Drache, " *RGG* [2], I, cols. 1996-1998, etc.); R. Dussaud (" *Les trois premiers versets de la Genèse*, " *RHR*, 1929, II, p. 140) identifies it with

is parallel with the lower abyss (*tĕhôm*, Jb 28:14; Is 51:10), in which several critics see a reminiscence of Tiamat, the Babylonian goddess who personifies the sea, who was pierced by Marduk and whose body, when cut in half, turned into the sky to hold back the upper waters [6] (cf. Gn 1:7). To the Babylonians, and especially to the Phoenicians, [7] the sea is the turbulent element which, although vanquished by God at the beginning of creation (Ps 89:10.11; 104:5-9; Jb 38:8-11), is still a dangerous threat (Jb 7:12; Hb 3:8; Nah 1:4; Ps 46:4). It can scarcely be denied that the Hebrew poets borrowed here from Babylonian and Phoenician mythologies, but they freed these myths from all polytheism because the sea, the abyss, the *tanninîm*, Rahab and Leviathan, are nothing else but Yahweh's creatures (cf. Ps 89:12; Jb 38:8-11; Ps 104:26; Gn 1:7.9) and serve only to cast a more brilliant light on His greatness and omnipotence. The struggle that ensues between these wicked monsters and Yahweh illustrates the victory of life and blessing over those who bring death and malediction. The ocean *(tĕhôm)*, Rahab, and Leviathan are beings of misfortune; by subjecting them to His law, Yahweh makes them a source of blessing and life, for from the ocean come life-giving waters : the upper ocean gives us rain and dew, the lower ocean gives us springs and rivers. Thus the much-feared *tĕhôm* is placed at the service of man whom it had once threatened to destroy, and it is now possible to speak of " blessings from the skies above " and " blessings from the abyss beneath " (Gn 49:25; Dt 33:13). [8]

Beneath the land of the living, finally, there is " the nether world " (Jon 2:7; 1 Sm 28:13; Is 26:19), where the dead dwell. The Hebrews usually refer to this region as Sheol *(šĕ'ôl)* (for example, Gn 37:35; 42:38; 44:29.31; Nm 16:30.33). He who descends to that place never returns (Jb 7:9) : it is a place of darkness (Jb 10:20.21; 38:17; Ps 88:7.13) and dust (Is 26:19; 29:4; Jb 17:16). It is described as a house, the house of assembly for everyone alive (Jb 30:23), it is closed by doors (Jb 38:17) and bars (Jon 2:7). The Hebrew idea

---

Apsou (the ocean of sweet water) who was cast into a slumber by Ea's incantations (*Enuma eliš*, I, 60-69, on P. Dhorme, *Choix de textes religieux assyro-babyloniens*, Paris 1907, pp. 11-13).

[6] *Enuma eliš*, IV, pp. 93-140; Dhorme, *op. cit.*, pp. 53-57.

[7] Cf. *Syria* (1935), pp. 29-45; A. Lods (" Les poèmes de Ras Shamra et l'Ancien Testament, " *RHPhR*, 1936, pp. 113-115), considers the struggle of Yahweh with the sea and marine monsters to be an echo of Phoenician mythology, especially of the revolt of a god called *Zbl ym* (he who dwells in the sea) and *špṭ nhr* (the Suffete of the river) against Baal. The struggle ends in the victory of Baal who hurls his chariot against that of his adversary, " and the sea subsides and leaves the earth... Baal strikes(?) the sea and restores it to its place; he overcomes the Suffete of the river " (III *ABA*, 1, 23-27; *Syria* (1935), pp. 29-45).

[8] J. Pedersen, *Israel*, I, II, Oxford 1926, pp. 472 ff.

of Sheol resembles that of the Babylonians [9] and other ancient peoples. But the abode of the dead was for the Babylonians the kingdom of Nergal and of the goddess Ereškigal, while the Hebrews believed it to be subject to Yahweh (Am 9:2; Ps 139:8; Jb 26:6) just as much as the land of the living. [10]

§ 2. *God, the Author of the World*

M. J. Lagrange, "Hexaméron," *RB* (1896), pp. 381-407; V. Zapletal, *Der Schöpfungsbericht der Genesis* [2], Regensburg 1911; A. Kirchner, "Die babylonische Kosmogonie und der biblische Schöpfungsbericht," (*ATA*, III, 1), Münster 1911; F. Ceuppens, *De historia primaeva*, Rome 1934; H. Gunkel, *Schöpfung und Chaos in Urzeit und Endzeit* [2], Göttingen 1921; commentaries to *Genesis* by F. von Hummelauer (1895), P. Heinisch (1930), H. L. Strack (1905), S. Driver (1904), A. Dillmann (1892), H. Holzinger (1898), H. Gunkel (1917), O. Procksch (1913), J. Skinner (1916), F. Böhl (1925); R. Dussaud, "Les trois premiers versets de la Genèse," *RHR* (1929), II, pp. 140 ff.; G. Lambert, "La création dans la Bible," *NRTh* (1935), pp. 252 ff.

1. *The verbs denoting creative action.* — The Old Testament makes use of several verbs in order to state that God is the author of the world: *qânâh* (= to prepare, Gn 14:19.22; Ps 139:13, of the human body), *kônên* (= to strengthen, to establish firmly, Is 45:18; Ps 119:90), *yâṣar* (= to fashion, Gn 2:8; Is 45:18), *bânâh* (= to construct, Am 9:6), *yâsad* (= to found, Ps 24:2; Am 9:6), *hôlîd* (= to engender, Jb 38:28; Ps 90:2), *'âśâh* (= to make, Gn 1:7; 2:2; 6:6), lastly *bârâ'* (= to create, Gn 1:1). Several of these verbs describe God's creative action in a poetic way, as the work of an artisan or an architect, even that of a father; some texts even go so far as to speak of the fingers, hands or palm of the divine worker (Is 40:12; 45:12; 48:13; Ps 8:4.7; 19:2). These are anthropomorphisms like many others found in the Old Testament; they are to be explained in the same way, [1] although they may perhaps come from mythological accounts of which there are other traces in the Bible. On the other hand, the verb *bârâ'* in the *Qal* and *Niphal* forms is used only to denote God's action in the production of an object or a prodigy (Ex 34:10; Is 48:7; Jer 31:22; Ps 51:12).

---

[9] Cf. P. Dhorme, "Le séjour des morts chez les Babyloniens et les Hébreux," *RB* (1907), pp. 60 ff.

[10] Ps 88:6, however, declares that Yahweh is no longer mindful of the dead, for they are taken out of His hand, that is to say, withdrawn from His protection (cf. vv. 12 and 13). It is true that those who dwell in "the land of forgetfulness" (v. 13) no longer praise Yahweh (v. 12; cf. Ps 6:6; 115:17; Is 38:18.19). On the fate of man after death, see below II, I, § 7, 3.

[1] See above I, § 3.

2. *The antiquity of the idea.* — The idea of the creation of the world by God is surely much older in Israel than some critics think.[2] In fact, this idea is found from very early times among neighboring peoples, the Sumerians, Babylonians, Egyptians and Phoenicians with whom Israel was in contact at all times. It is attested, at least implicitly, in the oldest poems that we possess (Jos 10:13; Jgs 5:20; Gn 49:25; Ex 15:8.11; Dt 33:14; Ps 29), because Yahweh figures in them as the master of the elements of nature. According to Gn 14:19.22, El Elyon (the Most High God) was recognized as the Creator of heaven and earth in the days of Abraham.[3]

3. *Creation according to Gn* 2. — The oldest text that shows forth God as the Creator is Gn 2:4 b-22. It places greater emphasis on the creation of man than on the creation of the world; reference to the latter is made in a subordinate clause: " when Yahweh Elohim made the earth and the heavens there was not yet any field shrub on the earth " (Gn 2:4 b-5). Yahweh fashioned man out of the dust of the ground and breathed into him the breath of life; then He planted the garden of Eden, and placed man there to cultivate and keep it. Lest man be alone, Yahweh formed animals out of ground; but when man found no helper like himself and was in need of it, Yahweh formed the woman out of man's rib and brought her to him. The whole account centers about the creation of the man and the woman, whose fault he wishes to relate, for it was the origin of all the evils which mankind suffers (Gn 3). But in spite of the anthropomorphisms and naïveté of this old account, Yahweh appears there as the only author of the earth and the heaven and of all that lives on the earth, plants, animals and man, for whom all else was made.

4. *Creation according to prophets and poets.* — Prophets and poets take pleasure in celebrating the only God, creator of the universe and all it contains. Expressing themselves like poets, they like concrete terms and highly colored images that speak to the imagination, and which are often borrowed from old Babylonian and Phoenician myths, preserved in Israel's popular tradition and language. Yahweh is " He who formed the mountains,[4] and created the wind...who made the dawn and the darkness, who strides upon the heights of

---

[2] B. Stade, *Biblische Theologie*, pp. 92 ff.; 238 ff., who claims that it appeared only in the 8th century. On the contrary, H. Gunkel (*Die Genesis*, 1917, p. 119) rightly admits that it belongs to the oldest part of Israelite tradition.

[3] The account is of a much later date but has preserved many ancient characteristics. What we know about El, Elyôn and the God of heaven, no longer allows us to reject the notice of Gn 14:19.22 as an obvious anachronism (cf. I, § 2).

[4] LXX read *hâraʿam* (" the thunder ") instead of *hârîm* (mountains).

the earth, [5] Yahweh, the God of hosts is His name" (Am 4:13; cf. also 5:8; 9:6; Is 40:12.25 ff.; 44:23; 45:18). He shuts in the sea, like some awesome monster (Jb 7:12; Hb 3:8), by the sands of the shore (Jer 5:22) or by limits (Prv 8:29; Jb 38:11; Ps 104:9); "He shut within doors the sea, when it burst forth from the womb; He made the clouds its garment and thick darkness its swaddling bands; He set limits for it, [6] and fastened the bar of its door, and said: Thus far you shall come but no farther" (Jb 38:8-11). Here the sea is represented as a new-born child, coming forth from the womb of the earth (or from the abyss?), which Yahweh swaddles and subordinates from the moment of its birth. On other occasions He threatens it (Na 1:4; Ps 18:16; 104:7; 106:9), grows angry with it, fights against it, as a warrior mounted on His chariot (Hb 3:8). "He has marked out a circle on the surface of the deep as the boundary of light and darkness. The pillars of the heavens tremble and are stunned at His thunderous rebuke; by His power He stirs up the sea, and by His might He crushes Rahab. His wind clears the heavens, and His hand pierces the fleeing serpent" (Jb 26:10-13). [7] The parallelism between the sea and Rahab proves, if not the identity of the sea with the mythological monster, at least the close relationship that unites one with the other (cf. Is 51:9). [8] Yahweh's victory over Rahab and the sea is also recalled in Ps 89:10.11, in connection with the creation of the world (Ps 89:12.13): "You rule over the raging sea, when its waves rise you still them. You have crushed Rahab like one who is slain; with Your powerful arm You have scattered Your enemies"; these enemies seem to be Rahab and her helpers (Jb 9:13). All these poetic passages describe the creation of the ocean as Yahweh's victory over the sea and a sea monster; they recall the Phoenician myth of a god called "the Suffete of the river" and "He who dwells in the sea," who has revolted against Baal and his victory. Baal hurls his chariot against his adversary "and the sea grows calm; it moves back from the land.... Baal strikes (?) the sea and restores it to its place; he overcomes the Suffete of the river" (cf. Hb 3:8). [9]

[5] This recalls the Babylonian reliefs that represent the solar god walking on the summits of the mountains (*AOB* [2], n. 319, 320).

[6] Instead of *wâ'ešbor* (I broke), read *wâ'ešît* (LXX = I shall place); and *ḥuqqô* (= its limit), instead of *ḥuqqî* (= my limit).

[7] For the justification of the corrections and of the translation, cf. P. Dhorme, *Le livre de Job*, Paris 1926, pp. 341-343.

[8] Is 51:9: "Was it not you who cut Rahab in pieces, you who pierced the *tannîn*? Was it not you who dried up the sea, the waters of the great deep, who made the depths of the sea into a way for the redeemed to pass over?" The reference here is to Yahweh's victory at the crossing of the Red Sea.

[9] Cf. the poem entitled "The revolt of Kôšer against Baal" (*Syria*, 1935, pp. 29-45), cited by A. Lods "Les poèmes de Ras Shamra et l'A. T.," *RHPhR*, 1936, pp. 113-

Other critics see here reminiscences of the Babylonian poem of creation which describes Marduk's victory over Tiamat, that is to say, the sea.[10] It will be noticed that later and profoundly monotheistic authors have used these old mythological traditions of neighboring peoples to exalt the power and grandeur of the only God, creator of the universe. But it is probable that these myths had been circulating in the popular religion of Israel several centuries earlier.

5. *Creation according to Gn 1.* — The author of Gn 1 has also known these traditions, but he modified them profoundly in order to stress the omnipotence of Elohim, the creator of heaven and earth. The account opens with a short phrase which has the value of a title, summing up the whole section: "In the beginning God created the heavens and the earth" (1:1).[11] The word *běrê'šît* is in "the absolute state"[12] and expresses the beginning in time of all things.[13] In the beginning of all things, Elohim, that is to say, the God in whom is concentrated all that is divine,[14] created "the heavens and the earth," that is to say, the organized world (cf. Gn 2:1.4; 14:19.22), not the chaos which is called "the land," the *těhôm* or "the waters" (Gn 1:2). The verb *bârâ'* signifies the action by which God produces something new or prodigious, and the *Qal* and *Niphal* form is used solely for God's productive action; but by itself it does not indicate a creation *ex nihilo*, because it may be parallel to *'aśâh* (to make, Gn 1:26.27), to *yâṣar* (to model, Am 4:13; Ez 43:1.7, etc.), and to *hoṣî'* (to bring out, Is 40:26).[15] The idea of creation *ex nihilo*, nevertheless, seems here to be implicitly contained in the account, since God is represented as the author, the supreme and sole Lord of the whole world; if then everything depends on the one God, it is probable that the chaos, of which there is question in verse 2, is no exception.

---

115), W. F. Albright, "The Psalm of Habakkuk," *Studies in O. T. Prophecy*, London 1950, pp. 1 ff.

[10] Cf. p. 87, note 5.

[11] It is possible, grammatically, to interpret the word *běrê'šît* as in the construct state and to translate: "In the beginning when God created heaven and earth, the earth was empty and without shape" (Skinner, *in h.l.*), or, to consider verse 2 as a parenthesis: "In the beginning, when God created heaven and earth... God said" (cf. Gn 2:4 b.5; *Enuma eliš*, I, 1; Ezr 6:1-6) (Dillmann, Holzinger, Loisy, etc.). But this construction is less natural (Gunkel, *in h.l.;* Wellhausen, *Prolegomena*, p. 141, n. 1; Driver, *in h.l.;* Procksch, *in h.l.;* Eichrodt, II, p. 5; Ceuppens, *De historia primaeva*, pp. 5 ff.; and all Catholic commentators). All ancient versions translated: "In the beginning God created heaven and earth."

[12] It is written with the article in the *Hexapla :* βαρησήθ (Field, *Origenis Hexaplorum quae supersunt*, I, p. 7).

[13] *Běrê'šît* has a temporal meaning as, in Dt 11:12; Jer 26:1; 27:1 and is the opposite to "the end of days" (cf. Dt 11:2; Is 41:22; 46:10; cf. Procksch, *in h.l.*).

[14] Cf. above I, §2, 4.

[15] Cf. P. Humbert, "Emploi et portée du verbe bârâ (créer) dans l'Ancien Testament," *ThZ*, 3 (1947), pp. 401 ff.

The idea of primitive chaos was borrowed from the cosmogonies where chaos existed before all beings, even before the gods; but our author, who has arranged his account with such obvious logic, would not have kept the idea if he had thought of primordial chaos as of something independent of God.

Creation *ex nihilo* is expressed formally only in a recent Greek text (2 Mc 7:28): " Look up at the heaven and earth, and see all that is in them, and perceive that God did not make them out of things that existed " (οὐκ ἐξ ὄντων ἐποίησεν αὐτὰ ὁ θεός). [16]

Some authors [17] hold that the book of *Wisdom* (11:17), under the influence of Greek philosophy, adopted the idea of matter existing before the creation of the world, when it speaks of the almighty hand of God that created the universe from formless matter (ἐξ ἀμόρφου ὕλης). The expression, no doubt, is borrowed from Greek philosophy, [18] but this does not prove that the author also borrowed at the same time the idea of eternal matter, [19] since he declared earlier (1:14) that " God created all things that they might have being " (ἔκτισε τὰ πάντα εἰς τὸ εἶναι), and affirms (11:25) that no being would subsist if God did not will it, and would not continue in existence if it had not been called into existence by Him. It may be, therefore, that he simply wished to use a more philosophic term to express Gn 1:2 (the earth was *tohû wâbohû*) which the LXX had translated by ἀόρατος καὶ ἀκατασκεύαστος, and to designate not *creatio prima* but *creatio secunda*, that is to say, the creation by which God brought order into the chaos and formed of it the different parts of the organized world, of the κόσμος. [20]

The author of Gn 1 wishes to recommend the sabbath rest by referring to the example of God who made the world and all it contains in six days and ceased to work on the seventh day (Gn 2:2.3;

---

[16] The Vulgate, the Syriac version and some Greek manuscripts read: ἐξ οὐκ ὄντων " out of nothing. " This reading is preferred by H. Bévenot (*Die beiden Makkabäerbücher*, Bonn 1931, p. 205). The editions of the LXX by Swete and Rahlfs give only the reading οὐκ ἐξ ὄντων which is that of A. Kampfhausen (Kautzsch, *Die Apokryphen und Pseudoepigraphen des A. T.* [2], I, p. 100) who translates " that these things have been made by God from those which were not "; J. Moffatt (Charles, *The Apocrypha and Pseudepigrapha of the O. T.*, I, p. 141) translates as we do; Abel *(in h.l.)* : " made them out of nothing. "

[17] For example, G. L. Grimm, *Kurzgefasstes exegetisches Handbuch zu den Apocryphen des A. T.*, VI, Leipzig 1860, pp. 211 ff.

[18] Plat., *Tim.*, 51 a.

[19] Philo admits this (*Cher.*, 35); but elsewhere he retains the Jewish doctrine of creation *ex nihilo* (*Somn.*, I, 13; *Moïs.*, II, 8).

[20] Cf. P. Heinisch, *Das Buch der Weisheit*, Münster im W. 1912, p. 227; A. T. S. Goodrick, *The Book of Wisdom*, London 1913, p. 248; J. A. F. Gregg, *The Wisdom of Solomon*, Cambridge 1922, p. 110; J. Fichtner, *Das Buch der Weisheit*, Tübingen 1938, p. 45.

cf. Ex 20:11; 31:17). Having six working days at his disposition, he assigns to each of them one of the principal works of God:[21] on the first day, God made light; on the second day, the firmament that separates the upper waters from the lower waters; on the third, the firm earth and the plants. Thus in the course of the first three days are produced the light, the precondition of every activity and life, and the regions that are to be filled during the next three days. On the fourth day, God made the stars that move in the sky; on the fifth, the fish and birds which live respectively in the water and in the air; on the sixth, animals and men who are to populate the earth. Man is placed at the end of the divine work, because he is its summit, since he is made to God's image, and he is the king of all living creatures (Gn 1:26.28), who were made for him (cf. Is 45:18; Ps 8:4-9). What God made "is good" (Gn 1:4.10.12.18.25), and the total work is "very good" (Gn 1:31), that is to say, in conformity with the thought and will of its author. God can rejoice in His works (Ps 104:31) and His works proclaim His glory (Ps 19:1-5; cf. 8:2.10).

The whole account highlights the omnipotence and wisdom of the one God, who existed "in the beginning" of all things and who by a single word created each one of them.[22] God said: "Let there be light" and there was light (1:3.6.9.11.14.20.24); "He spoke, and it came to be; He commanded and it stood forth" (Ps 33:9); God has only to say a word in order that creatures exist instantly: "By the word of Yahweh the heavens were made, and by the breath of His mouth all their hosts" (Ps 33:6; Sir 42:15; Wis 9:1); for the efficacy of His word is not to be resisted and is irrevocably fulfilled (Is 55:10.11; Wis 18:14-16).

The wisdom of God appears no less clearly in the ordered plan of all His work: plants are provided with seeds, animals are given fecundity to assure their perpetuity, and all is disposed for the sake of man to whom is given dominion over all living creatures (1:28). Yahweh, "who created the heavens, He is God, who formed the earth, and made it and established it; He did not create it to be a waste, He formed it to be lived in" (Is 45:18). This wisdom manifested by God in the creation of the world was admirably celebrated by

---

[21] It seems that the number of divine works (eight or nine depending on whether the fish and birds are considered as one work or two) was controlled by tradition, since it does not correspond to the number of working days which the author wished to retain.

[22] On the divine word, see below III, § 8.

the prophets (Is 40:28; 45:18; Jer 10:12), the poets (Ps 24; 8; 104; 136:5; Jb 26:12; 28:23.27; 38:36.37), and the wise men (Prv 3:19.20; Sir 1:10; Wis 7:24; 9:1.2; 14:4), who have made wisdom the counselor of God and His helper in the work of creation (Prv 8:22-31; Sir 24:3; Wis 8:6).

6. *The cosmogonies of the ancient East and the Old Testament.* — All the ancient peoples with whom Israel was in communication attributed the origin of the world to their gods. But, while all the cosmogonies of the ancient East are at the same time theogonies, Israel always considered its God as a personal being, independent of the elements of nature, and their absolute master, because He is their author and, therefore, existed before them. This doctrine, on which all the traditions collected in the Old Testament agree, essentially differentiates the Hebrew conception of the origin of the world from all the conceptions of neighboring peoples, whatever may be the resemblances which unite them and which are only to be explained as the direct or indirect borrowings made by Israel from the Egyptian, Sumerian-Babylonian and Phoenician cosmogonies.

Among the Egyptian cosmogonies, the one which was popular among the people of Hierapolis considered Atum to be the ancestor of the gods, who drew from himself a first divine couple, Shu (the air) and Tefnet (the void); from this first couple a second one was born, Geb (the earth) and Nut (the sky), who held themselves close together but who were separated by Shu (the air), who slipped between them and held Nut raised above Geb (the earth).

The priests of Hierapolis imagined a more learned and better ordered theory: in the beginning there existed a water, where floated the inert germs *(nenu)* of all being; it was called " the water born of Nun, " in which were found all the characteristics of the god Nun, but which was in essence unorganized chaos. In Nun lived a still undefined spirit (Tun or Atum), who bore within him the sum of future existences. Atum wished " to found in his heart (mind) all that exists " and, by an effort of his will, raised himself above the water (Nun). Henceforth the sun and light existed, and Atum, divided in two, now exteriorized outside of the primordial water, took the name of Ra who created the other gods. According to another explanation, the gods were the physical development of Atum-Ra, the members of the demiurge: " the sum of existence and of creatures, that is his body. " According to other texts creation was realized when the mouth of the demiurge uttered the names of all things. The papyrus of Mesnim makes him say: " I created all the forms with what came forth from my mouth (that is to say, by my word), when there was neither heaven nor earth." [23]

Several Babylonian cosmogonies [24] are known. The most extensive is the poem of creation *(Enuma eliš)*, which probably dates from the beginning of the second millenium B. C., but depends on much earlier Sumerian traditions. This poem opens with a description of primordial chaos formed by the waters of Apsu (the ocean of fresh water) and of Tiamat (the sea) who existed before all the gods. "When the heavens above were not named, and the earth below had no name, [25] from the primordial ocean, their father, and from the stormy Tiamat, their mother, the waters mingled and became one. No reed hut had been matted, no marsh land had appeared. When none of the gods had been brought into being, when none had been called by name, when no destiny had yet been determined, then it was that the gods were created.... " [26] Tiamat, annoyed by the gods, plotted their destruction. She was aided by her husband Apsu. But he was overcome, put in chains, and finally killed by the wise Ea. In her anger Tiamat created a series of redoubtable monsters to engage in a struggle against the gods who delegated Marduk (the chief god of Babylon) to fight against her. Marduk caught his adversary in a net, pierced her and after having stabbed the monsters, her auxiliaries, cut her body in two: "Half of her he set up and ceiled it as sky, he drew the bolt, he posted guards, he enjoined them to allow not her waters to escape." Thus was created the firmament which supports the upper waters. Then Marduk fixed the dimensions of the ocean (Apsu), made the earth, the stars that determine the sacred seasons and years, and lastly man, formed from the blood of a god who had been put to death, and created to worship the gods.

According to Philo of Byblos, [27] who claimed to reproduce the facts given by Sanchoniathon, [28] the Phoenicians explained the origin of the world as the immanent development of matter and of force

---

[23] According to A. Moret, *Le Nil et la civilisation égyptienne*, Paris 1926, pp. 430-437; cf. *id.*, *Mystères égyptiens*, Paris 1922, pp. 105 ff.; L. Dürr, *Die Wertung des göttlichen Wortes im A. T. und im alten Orient*, Leipzig 1938, pp. 22 ff.

[24] The texts were assembled by H. Gressmann (*AOT* [2], pp. 108-138) and less completely by P. Dhorme (*Choix de textes religieux assyro-babyloniens*, Paris 1907, pp. 1-97); cf. also J. Plessis, "Babylone et la Bible," *DBS*, I, cols. 713-737.

[25] What has no name has no existence, according to the ancient idea.

[26] Cf. translation by Dhorme (*Choix de textes*, pp. 3-5); ANET, pp. 61 ff.

[27] Cited by Eusebius (*Praep. ev.*, I, 10).

[28] Several critics consider Philo of Byblos as a forger who attributed to a very old Phoenician writer (whom he had invented), named Sanchoniathon, the euhemeristic theories which he defends (cf. *ERS* [2], pp. 396 ff., where the principal bibliography is given). Others (Renan, Movers, F. Lenormant) admit, on the contrary, that Philo drew his information from an old Phoenician source, but that he combined them with Greek elements and interpreted them according to his own

contained in primordial chaos. Thus they were not thinking of creation. In the beginning, only wind and darkness existed, out of which Môt was formed, who was of clay, according to some, and a mixture of aqueous substances, according to others. Môt, who had taken the form of an egg, was the origin of all things, of sun, moon, stars, plants, animals and men. The gods are not mentioned because Philo did not acknowledge their existence; but it is probable that they were believed to have issued from Môt, as was held in the other cosmogonies of the Ancient East.

The resemblances that exist between the narration of Gn 1 and the traditions of peoples who were Israel's neighbors are obvious: at the origin of the world they all mention in particular the watery chaos whose elements, when separated, formed the organized universe. Egypt knew the separation of heaven and earth and the creation by the word of the supreme god. The relations between Gn 1 and the Babylonian cosmogony are still closer: primitive chaos is called *tĕhôm* (Gn 1:2), which recalls the name of Tiamat *(Tiamatu)*; the firmament is formed by the separation of the lower and upper waters, just as a half of Tiamat's body, placed in the sky, constituted the upper ocean; then were formed the earth, the stars, the signs of times (Gn 1:14), animals, and lastly man. Finally, according to Gn 1:2, chaos is a watery mass over which darkness extended and where the spirit *(ruaḥ)* of God hovered, all of which recalls the Phoenician cosmogony. Some writers, translating the verb *mĕraḥephet* by "he was incubating," saw in this a reminiscence of the Phoenician primordial egg. But this translation is hardly probable. The *ruaḥ* of God seems to denote the breath of God, which is about to enter into action by the word (verses 3.5, etc.) and which hovered, like the wind (cf. 2 Sm 22:11), like a bird that beats its wings (Dt 32:11), over the waters. [29]

The resemblances that exist between the biblical cosmogonies and those of neighboring peoples should not make us forget the essential differences that separate them: in the Old Testament, the author of the world is a personal God, unique, totally independent of the universe; in all the cosmogonies of the ancient East, the gods, who often fight among themselves, have come from chaos, because they

opinions. O. Eissfeldt (*Ras Schamra und Sanchunjaton*, Halle 1939, pp. 75 ff.) seems to strike the right note by distinguishing the authentically very old Phoenician facts and the euhemeristic opinions that are Philo's own. He admits, in particular, the exactitude of the broad outlines of the cosmogony that Philo says was that of the Phoenicians.

[29] For the justification of this interpretation, cf. our article, "L'esprit de Jahvé, source de vie dans l'A. T.," *RB* (1935), pp. 489-491.

are only personified and divinized forces of nature. The God of Israel is prior to all other beings, consequently prior to chaos, and has neither beginning nor end; among the neighboring peoples, the gods are subsequent to chaos which existed independently of them, and the triumph of some gods involves the death of others. The obvious superiority of the Israelite doctrine over that held by theologians of peoples who were older and much more advanced in arts and knowledge, is not to be explained merely by the genius of Israel, whose intellectual as well as material civilization has always been a derivative of the civilization of its powerful neighbors. It can only be explained by the revelation that God entrusted to His chosen people.

This doctrine is clothed in a form borrowed from the ideas of those days about the physical constitution of the world, and from traditions popular in Israel probably since the occupation of Canaan. In that country, so close to Phoenicia and subject to the political and religious influence of Babylon and later of Egypt, Phoenician, Babylonian and Egyptian myths, describing the origin of the world, must have been known since the time before the Israelite conquest. [30] It is very probable that the Hebrews learned them from the Canaanites, and they gradually became part of the ideas and language of the people. [31] The sacred authors have kept the elements of these traditions which, while foreign in origin, had taken root in Israel; but they had cleansed away every trace of polytheism and transformed them so that they might serve to glorify the one God.

§ 3. *The conservation of the world*

The world and all it contains owe not only their origin to God, but also their permanence in being (Wis 11:25). Nothing could be more opposed to the doctrine of the Old Testament and to the thought of the author of Gn 2:2.3 than to interpret, in an absolute sense, the cessation of the Creator's work on the seventh day, as if thereafter God no longer intervened on behalf of His creatures and their activity. The anthropomorphic expression of Gn 2:2.3 has been made necessary by the purpose of the account, which seeks to justify the obligation of the sabbath rest by referring to the example of the Creator who, after having worked for six days in order

[30] Among the Tell-el-Amarna letters, originating from Palestine and Syria, have been found Babylonian mythological texts which served as models for the apprentice-scribes of Canaan and probably of Egypt.

[31] Cf. V. Zapletal, *Der Schöpfungsbericht*, pp. 129-132, who notes, quite correctly, that a direct dependence on the Babylonian tradition is hardly probable, since, in addition to Babylonian elements, Israel also retained elements coming from Phoenicia and Egypt.

to create and organize " the heavens and the earth and all their hosts, " rested on the seventh day. But this rest is no more final and permanent than the one imposed on man.

On the contrary, it is God who intervenes directly in all the phenomena of nature: He gives or withholds the rain (Am 4:7; Ps 104:13; 147:8), makes springs and rivers flow (Ps 104:10; 107:35) or dries them up (Ps 107:33), ripens rich harvests (Os 2:10; Gn 26:12; 27:28; 49:25) or hinders their growth (Am 4:6.9), makes man and beast fertile or sterile (Gn 21:1.2; 29:31; 30:2; 49:25; 1 Sm 1:5.11.20), gives food (Ps 104:14.15; 147:8.9; 145:15.16; Jb 38:39-41), forms children in their mother's womb (Ps 139:13; Jb 10:8-12; 31:15), brings them to birth (Ps 22:10) and death (Ps 90:3; 104:29; Jb 34:14.15), gives them the breath of life (Is 42:5; Jb 27:3; 33:4) or takes it from them (Ps 104:29; Jb 34:14.15). It is Yahweh who covers rivers with ice (Ps 147:18; Jb 37:10), who makes the earth tremble (Ps 18:16; Na 1:5; Jb 9:6), the thunder roar (Ps 18:14; 29:3.4), the lightning flash (Ps 144:6), the volcano smoke (Ps 104:32; 144:5), the dawn rise (Am 5:8), and darkness spread (Am 5:8; Ps 104:20). It is He who makes the stars move in order (Is 40:26; Jb 9:7.9; Ps 147:4) and who ensures the regular succession of day and night and seasons (Gn 8:22).

This regularity of natural phenomena, which we explain by the laws of nature, is in the Old Testament related to time. Yahweh does each thing in its time: He gives rain in its time (Jer 5:24; Lv 26:4) so that the earth can produce its harvests (Lv 26:4; Dt 11:14; 28:12). The trees bear their fruit, under God's direction, in due season (Ps 1:3). To all, men and beasts, God gives food in due time (Ps 145:15). He determines the time when the hinds calve (Jb 39:1); He makes the constellations rise in their season (Jb 38:32) and holds in His hand the time of the devout man (Ps 31:16). Migrating birds know their time (Jer 8:7). For everything there is a time set by God (Eccl 3:1.17).[1]

When the Old Testament mentions the laws to which natural phenomena are subject, the reference is to laws imposed from without by God, not to internal laws resulting from the nature of things and the play of secondary causes. In this sense Jeremias speaks of the laws *(ḥuqqôt)* of the harvest (5:24), and of the stars (31:35.36), of the heavens and of the earth (33:25), and the poets speak of the limit *(ḥoq)* which God set for the sea (Prv 8:29; Jb 38:11),[2] of the law given to the

---

[1] L. Köhler, *Theologie*, p. 74.

[2] The word designates here, it seems, rather a material limit (cf. Ps 104:9: " a circle "; Jer 5:22: " the sand ").

rain (Jb 28:26), to the stars (Ps 148:6), to the sky (Jb 38:33). These laws designate the orders which express Yahweh's constant will, as is shown by the parallelism of the word " law " with " His covenant " (*bĕrît*, Jer 33:25), that is to say, with the pact concluded by God with day and night (cf. Jer 33:20; Os 2:20), a pact that guarantees the solidity of that pact which unites Him with the house of David and Jacob. Let the sun, the moon, the stars, the heavens praise Yahweh " for He commanded, and they were created, He established them forever; He fixed their limit *(ḥoq)* which they cannot transgress (Ps 148:5.6).

Similarly fertility, which assures the perpetuity of vegetable, animal and human species (Gn 1:11.22.28), as well as the regularity of the courses of the sun and the moon, which determines the seasons, the days, and the years (Gn 1:14), are due to the explicit commandments of the Creator; and when the order thus established was troubled by the deluge, it was restored by God's explicit promise (Gn 8:22).

Certain texts seem to foresee the end of the created world, but it may be questioned whether they announce it as a definite fact; for they may intend merely to oppose with vigor the perishable and changing character of creatures to the immutability of God and the perennial nature of the salvation which He will effect: " The heavens shall vanish like smoke, and the earth shall be worn away like a garment, and the inhabitants thereof shall perish like flies. But My salvation shall remain forever, and My justice shall never fail " (Is 51:6). " Of old You established the earth, and the heavens are the work of Your hands. They shall perish, but You will remain, though all of them will grow old like a garment. You change them like a garment, and they are changed: But You are the same, and Your years have no end " (Ps 102:27.28). And when Is 65:17; 66:22, in his description of eschatological salvation, announces that Yahweh will create new heavens and a new earth, he is thinking less, it seems, of the end of this world, than of its radical transformation which will make it into a place of delights and of peace, exempt forever from the miseries of the present century (cf. Is 11:6-9; 65:18-25). This idea will be taken up in the New Testament (2 Pt 3:13; Ap 21:1), where greater stress will be laid on the end of the present world (2 Pt 3:7).

§ 4. *The government of the world*

Divine Providence

The action of God in the physical and human world is neither arbitrary nor disordered; it is exercised according to a plan and is directed toward a determined goal, as we have seen. God made the elements subject to His laws, which assure the regularity and constancy of natural phenomena and bring about each thing in its proper time. He also directs human events, and as a result, history and each man in particular. It is indeed in the conduct of peoples, particularly of Israel, and of individuals that the Hebrews saw divine providence especially manifest.

Although the Old Testament has no Hebrew word to designate divine providence,[1] the idea occurs frequently; one speaks of the thoughts of God (Is 55:8.9; Ps 33:11), of His designs or His counsels (Is 5:19; 14:26; 19:17; 28:29; Ps 33:11; Jb 38:2; 42:3, etc.).

Even in the earliest accounts, the liberation of the Israelite tribes from Egyptian oppression, the crossing of the Red Sea, the wanderings in the desert under the guidance and constant protection of Yahweh, the making of the covenant, followed by the conquest of the land promised to their forefathers (Gn 15:7; 17:8) — all these are considered to be manifestations of divine providence. This theme is frequently taken up (for example, Ps 78; 105; 106; Jos 24; Neh 9; Jgs 5). They like to recall Yahweh's guidance of Israel, and the fact that He has led and still leads His people just as a shepherd leads his flock (for example, Gn 49:24; Os 4:16; Ex 15:13; Dt 4:27; Is 40:11; 49:10; 63:11-14; Jer 31:10; Mi 2:12; 7:14; Ps 48:15; 78:52; 77:21).

The whole deuteronomistic historiography is dominated by the idea of divine providence guiding Israel: it is God who directs all the political and military events of the history of Israel, in such a way that they are the just sanction of the fidelity or infidelity of the people to the stipulations of the covenant which unites the people with Yahweh (for example, Jgs 2:11-15; 3:7.8.12; 4:1; 1 Sm 7; 3 Kgs 13:33.34; 14:22-24; 15:1-4, etc.).

The prophets show that God's providence extends to every nation (Am 1:2-2:3; 9:7); Yahweh makes use of the most powerful empires to execute His plans (Is 7:18; 10:5-14; 13; 41:25; 43:14; 45:1-4

---

[1] In Job 10:12, the word *pĕqudâh,* which denotes attentive care or solicitude, comes close to the meaning of providence; the book of Wisdom uses the word προνοία (14:13; 17:2) to express this concept.

Jer 25:9; 27:6; Ez 6:3; 16:37; 23:22), even against their own will (Is 10:15.16; 29:15.16); for they are destined to constitute God's universal kingdom (Is 2:2-4; cf. 10:12; 14:26; 18:7). If in the book of Daniel (2:31-45; 7; 8) and the Jewish Apocalypses the oriental doctrine of the different ages of the world was adopted, it was profoundly modified by the belief in divine providence. In fact the cycle of successive ages was not meant to recommence after the golden age; it terminates in the definitive establishment of the eternal kingdom of God. [2]

God has established in advance the plans which will be fulfilled in their own time: " Have you not heard that I have determined it long ago? From days of old I have planned it, and now I bring it to pass " (4 Kgs 19:25). " I am God, and there is none like Me, from the beginning I declare the end, and in advance things not yet done " (Is 46:9-10; cf. 42:9; 44:7; 45:21). He predestines, prepares, and guides those who have a particularly important message to fulfill (Jer 1:5; Is 45:1-4; 49.1.2.5). Thus all is foreseen by God and determined in its time; and it is He who brings about events in their time (Is 60:22). There is a time for vengeance (Jer 51:6), a time for distress (Is 33:2), a time for misfortune (Am 5:13), for visitation (Jer 8:12), for terror (Ez 35:5), for cure (Jer 8:15; 14:19), for final chastisement (Ez 21:30), for the judgment of the nations (Ez 30:3), a time of salvation and of grace (Is 49:8). [3]

Divine providence operates, too, in favor of individuals. In the older accounts, no doubt, this providence is less apparent than that which deals with a people or a tribe, because in early days the feeling of solidarity that united members of a social group was stronger than that concerning the interests of the individual. [4] But it cannot be said that the idea was unknown before the prophetic period, [5] since certain narratives and some personal names prior to the prophets already attest it, for example the name of Saul's son *Jonathan* (= Yahweh has given), and *Yĕhôyâda'* (= Yahweh knows, 2 Sm 8:18) in the time of David. Likewise the traditions connected with Noe (Gn 6:8; 7:1.16, etc.), with Abraham (Gn 16; 20), with Isaac (Gn 24), and especially with Joseph (Gn 37:39-50) clearly prove it: in all his adventures Joseph sees the hand of God. When he reveals himself to his brothers, he declares to them: " Do not be distressed nor angry with yourselves that you sold me (to be brought) here: for God sent

---

[2] Cf. W. Eichrodt, *Theologie*, II, p. 90.
[3] Cf. L. Köhler, *Theologie*, p. 75.
[4] Cf. above I, § 8 B, 3, p. 73.
[5] R. Smend, p. 103; B. Stade, *Theologie*, p. 194.

me before you to save life. For the famine has been in the land these two years, and there are yet five years, in which there will be neither plowing nor reaping. And God sent me before you to preserve for you survivors and to deliver you. So it was not you who sent me here, but God; and He has made me a father to Pharao, lord of all his house, and ruler over all the land of Egypt" (Gn 45:5-8). God makes even men's faults serve His plans: "You meant evil against me; but God turned it into good, to bring it about that many people should be kept alive, as they are today" (Gn 50:20).

Nevertheless it was under the influence of the prophets that this doctrine developed and deeply penetrated the teaching of the wise men and the poetry of the psalmists. "In his mind a man plans his course, but the Lord directs his steps" (Prv 16:9; cf: 16:1; 19:21; 20:24; Jb 5:19-27; 14:5). A psalmist gives thanks to God because God guided him and assured him a privileged fate (Ps 16:5-8), another exhorts in these terms: "Commit your way to the Lord, trust in Him, and He will act. And He will make your vindication dawn like the light, and your right like the noonday" (Ps 37:5-6). "The steps of a man are made firm by the Lord, and He approves his way" (Ps 37:23; cf. Ps 5:9; 23; 27:10; 73:23.24; 139:16, etc.). The Hebrew is so convinced of God's intervention in every event that he attributes even misfortunes to Him: "Does evil befall a city, unless the Lord has done it?" (Am 3:6). "I form the light, and create the darkness; I make well-being and create woe" (Is 45:7; cf. 54:16; Lam 3:38; Eccl 7:14). It is God who presents the victim to the hand of the involuntary murderer (Ex 21:13). What we call chance, the Hebrew calls "an encounter" (*miqĕreh*, 1 Sm 6:9; Ru 2:3), because he sees in it an event brought about by God (Ru 2:20). That is why he believes the results obtained by casting lots to be a decision of Yahweh (1 Sm 10:19-21; 14:38-42; Jos 7:12-18; Jon 1:7): "Lots are cast into the lap, but its decision depends entirely on the Lord" (Prv 16:33).

The problem of reconciliation between evil and divine providence is solved in different ways in the Old Testament; but recourse is never had to the hypothesis of dualism which explains the origin of evil by the existence of an evil principle, hostile to the good God, the principle of good. Israel knew of but one God, author of good and evil.

With regard to physical evils, the oldest and most widely held solution is that these evils are the punishment of sin. This idea is found in almost all the books of the Old Testament. As early as in Gn 3:16-19, the ills which men suffer, especially death, are presented as the punishment of the fault of the first human couple. The catastrophe which destroyed the cities of Sodom and Gomorrah is the sanction for the crimes of their inhabitants (Gn 18:20). The tribulations that befall Joseph's brothers are the expiation for their attempt upon Joseph's life. This doctrine is the basis of the prophets' pleas for conversion: happiness is brought about by conversion, while continual wrong-doing increases misfortunes (for example, Is 1: 18-20; 4:2-6; 44:22; 45:22; Jer 3:14.15; 4:1-21; 3 Kgs 8:33-40); it is the foundation for the teaching of the wise men (for example, Ps 1:4-6; 112:10; Prv 11:3.5.6; 12:6.13.14; the discourses of Job's friends; Sir 5:1-15; 10:12-17; 11:14-17; 39:28-31).

Another solution sees in misfortune a trial intended to purify Israel (Is 1:25.26; 4:4; 48:10; Am 9:9.10, etc.), or to lead to conversion (Is 1:5-8). Tribulations test fidelity: "And you shall remember all the way which the Lord has led you for forty years in the desert, to humble and to test you, so that may be made manifest what was in your heart, whether you would keep His commandments or not" (Dt 8:2). God allows Satan to overwhelm Job with evils in order to test him and to show His servant's fidelity (Jb 1; 2). He chastises man to instruct and correct him (Jb 5:17-19; Prv 3:11.12; Ps 94:12), to convert him and make him happy (Jb 33:19-22.25-28; 36:7-11; cf. 2 Mc 6:17; 8:18.32.33; Wis 11:10; 12:20), and to purify the just (Wis 3:6).

A third solution presents the sufferings of the just as the expiation of the faults of others: the Servant of Yahweh is charged with misfortunes which are the consequences of the sins of His people; innocent, He expiates the sins of the guilty: "Surely he has borne our infirmities and carried our sorrows.... he was wounded for our transgressions, he was bruised for our iniquities. The chastisement that made us whole was upon him, and by his bruises we are healed. We all, like sheep, have gone astray; every one has turned to his own way; and the Lord has laid on him the iniquity of us all" (Is 53:4-6). He offers His life as an expiatory sacrifice for sin (Is 53:10). This idea of vicarious expiation rests on the realization of solidarity, that unites the members of the same tribe, as well as on that of expiatory sacrifice (*'ašam*), in which the victim is offered instead of the offerer.

The last solution, finally, defers the compensation for present evils until the future. This idea appears in the messianic hope that looks to the future for the restoration of the oppressed people. This restoration, it was believed, would put an end to Israel's present sufferings and would bring a future of unmixed happiness. This solution, without doubt, applies only to the nation and not to individuals. However, when this solution was joined to the idea of the resurrection of the just (Dn 12:2.3; 2 Mc 7:9.11.14.23), it was believed that the just would share in the blessings of the final kingdom of God, in compensation for the sufferings of the present life.

Had the author of Psalm 73, who examined the problem, discovered a more complete solution, since he hopes that God, who does not abandon him and guides him with His counsels, " will receive " him later into His glory (v. 24; cf. Ps 49:16)? [6] He wishes to rely only on God: " Whom have I in heaven but You? And there is nothing upon earth that I desire besides You. My flesh and my heart may fail, but God is the rock of my heart and my portion forever " (vv. 25.26). He has confidence that he is near God in whom he finds his refuge (v. 28; cf. Ps 16:11). Finally, in the Greek book of Wisdom (3:1-9; 5:15.16), there is clearly expressed the idea of blessed immortality, which will be the definitive compensation for the evils the just man has suffered in this life as well as the reward for his fidelity to his God.

At all times moral evil has been judged incompatible with the just and holy God. It is the work of man whose liberty is loudly affirmed (Dt 11:26-28; 30:15-20; Jer 21:8; Sir 15:14-17), and is everywhere taken for granted. Sir 15:11-20 sums up Israel's thought: " Say not: It was God's doing that I fell away; for what He hates He does not do [7]... Yahweh hates evil... If you will, you can keep the commandments.... No man does He command to sin. " On the other hand, the Old Testament affirms no less clearly that Yahweh is the supreme master of the human will: " Like the clay in the potter's hand, so are you in My hand " (Jer 18:6). " Like a stream is the king's heart in the hand of Yahweh; wherever it pleases Him, He directs it " (Prv 21:1; cf. Ps 33:15; Za 12:1). But no attempt has been made to explain how God's almighty action on man is reconciled with the latter's liberty and responsibility. Yet it was recognized that God can make men's faults serve His plans (Gn 50:20; cf. 45:5-8).

In many passages, on the contrary, human liberty appears to be sacrificed: God, it is said, hardens Pharao's heart (Ex 4:21; 7:3), or He hardens the heart of His people (Is 6:10); He pours on them a spirit of lethargy and blinds them (Is 29:10); He excites them to evil (1 Sm 26:19; 2 Sm 16:10; 24:1); He sends an evil spirit who provokes the Sichemites to revolt against Abimelech (Jgs 9:23), and a lying spirit to deceive Achab (3 Kgs 22:20-23). To explain these

---

[6] Unfortunately this interpretation is doubtful, cf. Part II, II, § 3, c.

[7] According to the Hebrew and Syriac text.

expressions, it must be remembered that the Hebrews hardly considered secondary causes and referred all events, even those that were fortuitous (Ex 21:13) or depended on man's will (Am 3:6; 5:27; 8:10) to God, the first cause. They did not distinguish, furthermore, between what God wills and what He permits. Most of the cases mentioned here, by the way, with the exception of 1 Sm 26:19; 2 Sm 16:10; 24:1,[8] deal with divine punishments, as the context indicates.

§ 5. *The miracle*

A miracle is ordinarily defined as a fact produced by God's immediate intervention, outside the ordinary course of the natural order. A miracle is a departure, through God's act, from what we call the laws of nature, that is to say, from the constancy of natural phenomena which results from nature and the sum of the active and passive faculties of each created being.

The Hebrews had a much wider and far more vague idea of a miracle because they attributed all natural phenomena to God's action and explained their regularity by God's will alone.[1] Everything in nature and every event which seemed to them admirable, mysterious, striking, startling, terrifying, and which consequently became for them a special manifestation of God's power, was in their eyes a mighty act *(gĕbûrâh)*, a powerful act (δύναμις, for example, Dt 3:24; Ps 20:7; 106:2), a great thing (*gĕdôlâh*, for example, 4 Kgs 8:4; Ps 71:19; 136:4;Jb 5:9; 9:10; 37:5), a marvelous or startling thing (*pele'*, *niflâ'âh*, for example, Ex 15:11; 34:10; Ps 71:17; Jb 5:9; 9:10; 37:5), a work (*'ălîlâh*, *ma'ălâl*, *ma'ăśeh*, for example, Ps 77:12 ff.; 86:8; Is 12:4), a terrifying thing (*nôrâ'*, for example, Ex 34:10; 2 Sm 7:23), finally a prodigy (*môphêt*, for example, Ex 7:3; Dt 4:34; 6:22; Ps 78:43; 105:5), or a sign (*'ôt*, for example, Ex 7:3; Dt 4:34; 6:22; 7:19, etc.). It will be observed that several of these words apply as well to prodigies, such as those that characterized the Exodus, as to marvels of nature such as rain or thunder (for example, Ps 136:4; Jb 5:9; 9:10; 37:5.14-16).

Because Yahweh produces all natural phenomena and historical events, the difference between the natural and the supernatural does not exist in the eyes of the Hebrews. God's power has no limits; to Him nothing is impossible (Gn 18:14; Jer 32:27); He does whatever

[8] On these passages, see above p. 83 ff.
[1] Cf. above, Chapter II, § 3, pp. 99 ff.

He wishes (Ps 115:3; 135:6) and, therefore, He can act as easily in an extraordinary as in an ordinary manner. Nevertheless, the extraordinary character of the divine intervention impresses the Hebrews less (Jos 10:14; 1 Sm 3:11; 4 Kgs 21:12; Jer 19:3) than the finality and the benevolence which that intervention manifests on the part of Yahweh (Ps 106:7).[2] This is the reason why prodigies are often called signs and why the words *'ôt* (sign), *môphêt* (prodigy) or *niflâ'âh* are very often combined (for example Ex 7:3; Dt 4:34; 6:22; 7:19; 26:8; 29:2; 34:11; Jer 32:20 ff.; Ps 78:43; 105:43; 1 Par 16:12). Yahweh's startling interventions in nature and history manifest His glory; they are the revelation of the holy and almighty God.[3] Miracles serve in certain cases to accredit the prophets in the eyes of their contemporaries: to prove the divine origin of his oracles, Isaias offers king Achab " a sign in the depths of Sheol or in the heights of heaven " (Is 7:11), or makes the shadow on the sundial turn back (Is 38:7.11) at the request of Ezechias. It is known, however, that sorcerers can work wonders similar to those the men of Elohim work (Ex 7:12:22; 8:3), and the book of Deuteronomy (13:2-4) warns against prophets or dreamers who will promise and perform a prodigy to draw men to the worship of other gods. In such a case it is Yahweh Himself who is testing the fidelity of His people. From this last text, it is clear that a miracle in itself is not considered as a sign which proves the divine mission of a prophet; it serves as a valid testimony only if it corresponds to Yahweh's known nature. That is the reason why in many cases the miracle is related to the holiness, which is, so to speak, the very essence of Yahweh (1 Sm 6:20; 2 Sm 6:6.7; Ex 15:11; Ps 77:14; Lv 10:1 ff.).[4]

§ 6. *Angels and devils*

L. Hackspill, " L'angélologie juive à l'époque néotestamentaire, " *RB* (1902), pp. 527-550; J. B. Frey, " L'angélologie juive au temps de Jésus-Christ, " *RScPT* (1911), pp. 75-110; L. Dürr, " Ezechiels Vision von der Erscheinung Gottes im Lichte der vorderasiatischen Altertumskunde " (*ATA*, IX, 1), Münster im W. 1917; P. Dhorme and L. H. Vincent, " Les Chérubins, " *RB* (1926), pp. 328-358; 481-495; M. J. Lagrange, " L'ange de Jahvé, " *RB* (1903), pp. 212-223; J. Touzard, " Ange de Yahweh, " *DBS*, I, cols. 242-263; W. Grossouw, " Engel, Engel van Yahweh ", *BW;* J. Rybinski, *Der Mal'akh Jahwe*, Paderborn 1930; F. Stier, " Gott und sein Engel im A. T. " (*ATA*, XII, 2), Münster im W. 1934; B. Stein, " Der Engel des Auszugs, " *Bb* (1939), pp. 286-307; A. Kohut, *Ueber jüdische Angelologie und Daemonologie in ihrer Abhängigkeit vom Parsismus* (*Abhandlungen f. d. Kunde*

[2] In this verse " the prodigies " accomplished by Yahweh in order to save His people are a parallel expression to " the multitude of His favors " *(ḥesed)*.
[3] Cf. below III, § 10.
[4] Cf. W. Eichrodt, *Theologie*, II, p. 85.

des Morgenlandes, IV, 3), Leipzig 1866; A. B. Davidson, "Angel," *HDB*, I, pp. 93-97; G. B. Gray, "Angel," *EB*, I, cols. 165-170; W. Bousset-H. Gressmann, *Die Religion des Judentums* [3], pp. 320-342; W. Grundmann-G. von Rad-G. Kittel, "Angelos," *ThW*, I, pp. 72-81; J. Weiss, "Dämonen-Dämonische," *PRE* [3], IV, pp. 408-419; A. Wünsche, "Teufel," *PRE* [3], XIX, pp. 564-574; O. C. Whitehouse, "Demon," *HDB*, I, pp. 590-594; *id.*, "Satan," *HDB*, IV, pp. 407-412; G. B. Gray, "Satan", *EB*, IV, cols. 4296-4300; H. Duhm, *Die bösen Geister im A. T.*, Tübingen 1904; J. Tamborino, *De antiquorum daemonismo*, Giessen 1909; A. Jirku, *Die Dämonen und ihre Abwehr im A. T.*, Leipzig 1912; T. Canaan, *Dämonenglaube im Lande der Bibel*, Leipzig 1929; S. Smit, *De Daemoniacis in Historia Evangelica*, Rome 1913; H. Kaupel, *Die Dämonen im A. T.*, Augsburg 1930; W. Foerster, *Daimon;* W. Foerster-G. von Rad, "Diaballô," *ThW*, IV, pp. 1-16; 69-78.

A. Angels

1. *The angels' names.* — The Old Testament knows heavenly beings who bear several different names : sons of God (*bĕnêy, 'ĕlôhîm*, Jb 1:6; 2:1; 38:7; *bĕnêy 'êlîm*, Ps 29:1; 89:7), that is to say, beings who belong to the divine world, [1] saints (Ps 89:6.8; Jb 5:1; 15:15; Za 14:5; Dn 4:14), sons of the Most High (Ps 82:6), the mighty ones (*'abbîrîm*, Ps 78:25), those on high (*râmîm*, Jb 21:22), warriors (*gibbôrîm*, Ps 103:20; Jl 4:11), sentinels (Dn 4:10.14.20). Their most frequently used name, *mal'âk*, expresses their function as messengers, [2] which the LXX justly translated ἄγγελος (messenger). This term passed into Latin (*angelus*) and modern languages (angel, *ange*, *angelo*, *ángel*, *Engel*). Taken as a group they are called the army of Yahweh (Jos 6:14; 3 Kgs 22:19; 2 Par 18:18; Ps 148:2), the encampment of God (Gn 32:2.3), the assembly of God (Ps 82:1) or the saints (Ps 89:6.8). The Cherubim (Gn 3:24) and the Seraphim (Is 6:2-6) also belong to the heavenly world.

2. *Before the Exile.* — a) *Groups of angels.* In the texts prior to the Exile, angels are rarely mentioned and usually in groups : in Gn 32:2.3 they appear in great numbers to Jacob who calls them "the encampment of God." In a dream Jacob saw angels ascending and descending a ladder which reached to heaven (Gn 28:12); two angels presented themselves to Lot to warn him to leave Sodom (Gn 19:1). Josue met a man who told him that he was the chief of Yahweh's army (Jos 6:14). Micheas sees Yahweh enthroned in the midst of

---

[1] The word son is not used here in the proper sense; it simply expresses membership in a specified class, as in the expressions "sons of prophets," "sons of perfumers" (Neh 3:8), or "sons of the poor" (Ps 72:4), where prophets, perfumers and the poor are meant.

[2] It is often used to designate a human messenger sent by a man (for example, Gn 32:4; Nm 20:14; 21:21; Jgs 9:31;) rarely a human messenger sent by God (prophet : Ag 1:13; Is 44:26; 2 Par 36:15; priest : Mal 2:7; Eccl. 5:5).

the heavenly army, whence a spirit[3] is sent to deceive Achab (3 Kgs 22:19-23). Isaias (6:2-4) sees the throne of God surrounded by Seraphim who acclaim His holiness. In the prologue to the book of Job (1:6 ff.), Yahweh holds court with the sons of God;[4] finally, in Gn 6:1-4, mention is made of the sons of God uniting with the daughters of men whence sprang a race of giants.[5]

Apart from the old fragment of Gn 6:1-4 the meaning of which is extremely obscure, the angels, mentioned in groups, appear like the court or army of Yahweh whence certain members are occasionally detached to perform special missions (Gn 19:1 ff.; Jos 6:14; 3 Kgs 22:19-23). The role attributed to them is rather hidden; and not one of them seems to have a function which would place him on a pedestal, with the exception of " the chief of the army of Yahweh " (Jos 6:14), a position explainable by the very nature of things, since every army supposes a commander.

b) *The Angel of Yahweh.* There is a heavenly personage, on the other hand, who frequently appears and whose work as divine messenger is clearly determined: it is the angel of God *(mal'ak 'élôhîm* or *hâ'élôhîm)* or the angel of Yahweh *(mal'ak Yahweh).*[6] He is sent

---

[3] This is the only Hebrew text of the O. T. in which a heavenly being is called a spirit *(hârûaḥ)* without any qualification. Ps 104:4 should be translated: He made the winds *(rûḥôt)* His messengers. The evil spirit coming from Yahweh seems to denote an individual spirit in Jgs 9:23; 1 Sm 16:14 b.15.16; 18:10-11; 19:9 (cf. P. van Imschoot, " L'action de l'esprit de Jahvé dans l'A. T., " *RScPT*, 1934, pp. 559 ff.).

[4] The prologue of Job is probably prior to the Exile.

[5] Jewish tradition (LXX; Hen. 6-11; Jubil. 5:1-6; Test. Rub. 5;6.7; Test. Nepht. 3:5; Philo, De Gig.; Flav. Jos., Ant. I, 3.1) and the early Fathers (Justin, Athenagoras, Clement of Alexandria, Irenaeus, Tertullian, Cyprian, Ambrose, Lactantius, Commodius, Eusebius of Caesarea, Clementine Homilies), perhaps Jude 6-8 and 2 Pt 2:4 (cf. J. Chaine, *Les épîtres catholiques*, Paris 1940, *in. h.l.*) and all non-Catholic critics interpret the *běněy hâ'élôhîm* of Gn 6:1-4 according to the ordinary meaning of the expression in the Hebrew Bible (Jb 1:6; 2:1; 38:7; Ps 29:1; 89:7), that is to say, as angels. Most Catholics, following the example of several Fathers (John Chrysostom, Cyril of Alexandria, Theodoret, Augustine, Jerome), read the passage to mean that the sons of Seth united with the daughters of Cain, or men and women (Closen), since angels were held to be spiritual beings as the Fourth Lateran Council affirms (Denzinger, *Enchiridion*, n. 428). It may be asked if this was the opinion of the author of the old account which is obviously a handed-down story (cf. C. Robert, " Les fils de Dieu et les filles des hommes, " *RB*, 1895, pp. 340-374; 525-552; H. Junker, *Die biblische Urgeschichte*, Bonn 1932; *id.*, " Zur Erklärung von Gen 6:1-4, " *Bb*, 1935, pp. 205-212; P. Joüon, " Les unions entre les Fils de Dieu et les Filles des hommes, " *RScR*, 1939, pp. 108-112; G. E. Closen, *Die Sünde der Söhne Gottes. Ein Beitrag zur Theologie der Genesis*, Rome 1937; G. Philips, " De spiritualitate Angelorum et matrimonio ' Filiorum Dei, ' " *Revue Ecclésiastique de Liège*, 31 (1940), pp. 290-300; " Zonen Gods, " *BW*).

[6] The two expressions are synonymous. The translation is usually given as " the angel " of God or of Yahweh, as if it would concern a personage unique in its kind. Yet it is not clear that reference is always made to the same angel; and grammatically it is possible to translate: " an angel " of God or of Yahweh (cf. F. Stier, *Gott und sein Engel*, pp. 60 ff.).

by Yahweh to protect Israel during the crossing of the Red Sea (Ex 14:19), to lead them in their wanderings (Ex 23:20; Nm 20:16), to strike their enemies (4 Kgs 19:35); he protects Abraham's servant (Gn 24:7) and Jacob (Gn 49:16); he stops Balaam (Nm 22:22) and frequently transmits messages and divine orders (Gn 16:7-11; 22:11.15; 31:11; Jgs 2:1-4; 6:11-24; 13:3-23; 4 Kgs 1:3.15). It is not certain, nor even probable, that the expression *mal'ak Yahweh* always denotes the same person; but he always reveals himself to be a benevolent messenger on whose help man can rely (1 Sm 29:9), and whose prudence and wisdom are greater than man's (2 Sm 14:17.20). He represents Yahweh Himself and appears or intervenes in favor of His people or of some of His faithful ones. In only one case (2 Sm 24:16 = 1 Par 21:16), at least according to the present text,[7] is he attacks Israel; but it is to punish the people for their faults (cf. Ex 23:21; 32:34).

In several texts (Gn 16:10 ff.; 21:17 ff.; 22:11 ff.; Ex 3:2 ff.; Jgs 2:1 ff.; 6:11 ff.; 13:3 ff.), the angel of Yahweh or of God speaks or acts as if he were God Himself, although he appears as distinct from Yahweh. Thus the angel of Yahweh declares to Agar that she will have a son and through the son many descendants "because Yahweh has heard your humiliation." "And Agar named Yahweh who spoke to her : *'Attâh-'êl-rô'î*" (Gn 16:7-13). The angel of God called to Agar from heaven, saying: "What is the matter, Agar? Fear not; for God has heard the boy's cry... take the boy, for I will make him a great nation" (Gn 21:17 ff.). The angel of Yahweh called Abraham from heaven, saying: "Do not lay a hand on the boy; do nothing to him. I know now that you fear God, since you have not withheld your only son from me" (Gn 22:11-12; cf. also 22:14-18). The angel of God spoke to Jacob in a dream, saying: "I am the God of Bethel, where you anointed the memorial pillar and made a vow to Me" (Gn 31:11-13). It is the angel of Yahweh who appears in fire flaming out of a bush; but it is Yahweh who speaks to Moses (Ex 3:2.5). The angel of Yahweh addresses the Israelites with these words: "It was I who brought you up from Egypt" (Jgs 2:1-4). Appearing to Gedeon he said: "Yahweh is with you"; and it is Yahweh who promises him victory and a sign;[8] but it is the

[7] The text of 2 Sm 24:15-17 does not seem to be in the right order; verse 17 probably should follow verse 15.

[8] The LXX, in verses 14 and 16 of Jgs 6:11 ff., have "the angel of the Lord" instead of "the angel of Yahweh." Several authors (Lagrange, Zapletal, Kittel, Burney) suppose that primitively the text mentioned only Yahweh and that "the angel of Yahweh" or of God (verse 20) was introduced into the Massoretic Text and in a more logical way by the LXX.

angel of Yahweh who performed the sign. Whereupon Gedeon cried: "Woe to me, for I have seen the angel of Yahweh," just as if he had seen Yahweh Himself (Jgs 6:11-24). Likewise Manoe, when he recognized the angel of Yahweh in the man who had spoken to him and to his wife, said: "We shall die because we have seen God" (Jgs 13:2-22). Osee (12:4.5) also identifies the angel against whom Jacob struggled (Gn 32:25-31) with Elohim.

To these texts may be added Ex 23:20-22: "See, I will send My angel [9] before you, to guard you on the way and bring you to the place I have prepared. Be attentive to him, and heed his voice. Do not rebel against him, for he will not forgive your sin. My name resides in him. But if you heed his voice, and carry out all I tell you, I will be an enemy to your enemies." This angel is a messenger of Yahweh (v. 23). Since the name is, so to speak, a double of the person (cf. Ex 20:24; Jer 14:9), this angel, in whom the name of Yahweh resides, exercises over the people an authority similar to that of Yahweh: his orders are those of Yahweh; his voice is that of Yahweh.

Yet the distinction between Yahweh and His angel seems more pronounced in other texts, for example in Gn 24:7: "He Himself (that is to say, Yahweh) will send His angel before you," in 2 Sm 24:16: "Yahweh said to the angel who slew the people," in Nm 22:31: "Yahweh opened Balaam's eyes and Balaam saw the angel of Yahweh," and in Nm 20:16: "Yahweh sent an angel who led us out of Egypt."

After the affair of the golden calf, an angel is mentioned (Ex 32:34; 33:2) whom Yahweh will send to lead the people into the land of Canaan. In the present text, [10] this angel is clearly distinguished from Yahweh and is inferior to Him, since (Ex 33:2) he must take the place of Yahweh who, in order to punish Israel for its rebellion, refuses henceforth to lead His people personally. After having given Moses the order to go up to the land promised to his ancestors, Yahweh adds (33:2-3): "I will send an angel before you, and he will drive out the Canaanites... [11] but I myself will not go up with you, because you are a stiff-necked people, otherwise I might exterminate you

---

[9] Some Hebrew manuscripts, the LXX and the Vulgate read: "my angel" as in verse 23.

[10] This whole section (Ex 32 and 33) is obviously composite; but it is very difficult to distinguish the different traditions that are there amalgamated. Several authors (Driver, Heinisch) consider 32:34 and 33:2 as glosses inserted later. Others attribute 32:34 to E, and Ex 23:20 as well as 33:1-3 to J. Eissfeldt (*Hexateuch-Synopse*, Leipzig 1922, p. 156) attributes 32:34 to E, 33:1-3a to J, 33:3b-4 to L (lay source).

[11] The LXX and the Syriac read: "He will cast out."

on the way." Here we have a conception different from that which appears in Ex 23:20 and especially in Jgs 2:1-4, etc., since the angel, sent to guide Israel, is a substitute for the holy God whose personal presence would be a permanent danger for a rebellious people.

The same antithesis between Yahweh and His angel is found in the reading of the LXX in Is 63:9 where an allusion is made to Ex 33:14: "And He was to them a savior in all their difficulties. It was not a messenger, not an angel, but His face that saved them," [12] that is to say, He Himself, Yahweh in person. [13] The whole verse insists on the love of Yahweh, who saves and leads His people. Here the prophet follows the tradition reported by Ex 33:12-15, where Moses, anxious to know the name of him whom Yahweh will send to lead His people asks Yahweh and He answers: "My face will go with you and I will give you rest," that is to say, I shall go in person. [14]

To explain all these facts, several theories have been elaborated. The first considers the angel of Yahweh as a messenger really distinct from God. [15] It is based on the meaning of the word *mal'âk* (= messenger); now the messenger is necessarily distinct from the one who sends him. This distinction is clearly affirmed in several texts (Gn 24:7; Nm 23:31; Ex 33:1-3; Is 63:9, LXX; 2 Sm 24:16). But how to explain, according to this hypothesis, the identification, frequently implied or stated, between Yahweh and His angel? [16]

---

[12] The MT reads: "In all their troubles, he was not troubled, and the angle of His face saved them." Almost all modern critics prefer, with good reason, the reading of the LXX who connect the first words with the preceding verb and read *sîr* (= messenger) instead of *sâr* (he was troubled) and *mal'âk* instead of the construct state. The angel of His face is never mentioned in the O. T.; he appears in the Apocrypha (Jubil. 1:27.29; Test. Lev. 3:18; Test. Jud. 25). It is very probable that the Massoretic reading was influenced by the later angelology of the Jews. The reading of the LXX alone respects the parallelism of the passage.

[13] "His face" means "in person, Himself," as in Ex 33:14.15; Dt 4:37 (cf. F. Nötscher, *Das Angesicht Gottes schauen*, Würzburg 1924, pp. 47 ff.). The expression *penew* is parallel to *hû'* (= himself).

[14] If it is admitted with Driver and Heinisch that the passage Ex 35:12-15 is the conclusion of 33:1-3, it must also be admitted that the words "and I will send an angel before you, and I will drive out the Canaanite, the Amorrite, the Hittite, the Pherezite, the Hevite, the Jebusite" are a gloss. If Yahweh had just announced that He would send an angel to be their guide, Moses would not have asked the name of him who would be sent, because in ancient times proper names were not given to angels. Heinisch and Driver admit that at the intercession of Moses, Yahweh allowed Himself to be influenced and He withdrew His threat that He would no longer accompany His people in person (verse 3).

[15] Following St. Augustine and St. Thomas, for example Rybinsky, *Der Mal'akh Jahwe*; Stier, *Gott und sein Engel*, and others.

[16] Stier (*op. cit.*, pp. 9 ff.) explains this apparent identification by "the style of the messenger." This remark is correct. In fact the Hebrews (and the Babylonians) are accustomed to put in direct discourse, on the lips of the messenger, the words that were to be delivered on behalf of the one sending the message; thus the

As for the texts alleged to support this theory, they are less convincing than they seem; Gn 24:7 simply affirms that Yahweh will send an angel, His messenger; but is this angel the one designated elsewhere as *mal'ak Yahweh?* In Nm 20:16, Ex 33:1-3 and Is 63:9 there is mention made of an angel, but this angel is not necessarily the same one who appears in the passages of Ex 23:20 ff. and 14:19 which belong to a different source. 2 Sm 24:16 distinguishes the destroying angel from Yahweh; in the present text and in 1 Par 21:16 which is derived from it, the destroying angel seems to be identified with the angel of Yahweh; but the text is now probably not in order. Primitively the angel of Yahweh intervened only in the account of the foundation of the altar on Orna's threshing floor, [17] and the destroying angel in the account of the punishment of David's fault. The only text, therefore, that remains to support the theory is Nm 22:31; and again in verse 35, the angel of Yahweh, as if he were God, addresses Balaam : " Speak only the word which I bid you. "

The second theory supports the identity of the angel of Yahweh with Yahweh. [18] The angel of Yahweh or of God is but the sensible manifestation of the invisible God; He is God manifesting Himself under a form perceptible to the senses. This is why in the ancient texts he expresses himself as if he were God, and those who saw him believed that they had seen God. In the beginning, the expression " the angel of Yahweh " is the product of a still primitive theological reflection, which sought to distinguish the being of God from some of His external activities, or to veil certain anthropomorphisms. In the measure that God's transcendence was more affirmed and angelology developed, the angel of Yahweh was more and more separated from Yahweh, finally becoming His high vizier. [19]

---

ambassador of Israel is asked to say to the Amorrite king : " Allow me (that is to say, Israel) to pass through your land " (Nm 21:17; cf. also Nm 22:5, Jgs 11:12; 1 Sm 6:21; 2 Sm 12:27; 4 Kgs 16:7; 19:20, etc.). In the same way the prophets often use direct discourse to convey Yahweh's oracles : " Thus speaks Yahweh : I have brought up sons " (Is 1:2 ff.). Yet there is a difference : words reported in " the style of the messenger " are usually introduced by their stereotyped formula : " N. sends to say : " or " N. sends messengers saying... " These stereotyped formulas are missing in all the passages where the angel of Yahweh appears and speaks as Yahweh. Besides, this explanation does not take into account the fact that those who see the angel of Yahweh believe that they have seen Yahweh Himself (Gn 16:13; Jgs 13:22; cf. 6:22).

[17] Cf. P. Dhorme, *Les livres de Samuel*, Paris 1910, pp. 144 ff.

[18] With important nuances, this is the opinion of R. Smend, E. Kautzsch, B. Stade, K. Marti, A. B. Davidson, B. Cray, O. Procksch, and among Catholics it is held by J. Hehn, J. Touzard, F. Nötscher, B. Stein, W. Grossouw.

[19] It is F. Stier who has coined this expression that so well characterizes the angel of Yahweh in recent books of the O. T.

Those who hold the third theory [20] are of the opinion that the angel of Yahweh (or of God) was introduced afterwards into accounts that primitively had spoken only of Yahweh or Elohim. Theophanies in the early days were described as sensible manifestations of Yahweh or Elohim. Later, it was desirable to adapt these old accounts to the exigencies of a more advanced theology, and to play down details that were not in accord with the transcendence of God. As it was no longer admitted that God showed Himself in person, the angel of Yahweh was introduced into texts that primitively spoke only of Yahweh. But these corrections were made discreetly, the texts were changed as little as possible. Out of this resulted the peculiar fact that in many passages where the angel of Yahweh appears, it is Yahweh who speaks. This hypothesis — for it is no more than a hypothesis — accounts perfectly for the curious alternation, in many texts, between Yahweh and His angel. Unfortunately it receives little support from textual criticism. Furthermore, why were similar corrections not made in the other accounts of theophanies which are to be found in Genesis and Exodus (for example, Gn 2:8 ff.; Ex 24:9-11)?

It must be noted that the angel of Yahweh is never mentioned in the prophetic books, [21] except in that of Zacharias; in post-exilic books this angel no longer plays the role he played in the earlier books. After the Exile, as a general rule, he is clearly distinguished from Yahweh; [22] he is the great vizier of God [23] or simply His messenger, the executor of one of His works.

Since Yahweh is recognized as the powerful and glorious king (Is 6:5; Ps 24:7-10), as the king of the world (Ps 29:10; 93:1-4; 95:3-5; 96:10; 97:1), having an army subject to Him (Jos 5:13-16; Gn 32:2.3; 3 Kgs 22:19; cf. Jgs 5:20) [24] and a court of heavenly beings (Is 6:1-6; 3 Kgs 22:19; Jb 1:6; 2:1; Dn 7:10), it is quite natural that He be also given a grand vizier, just as the

[20] Several modern commentators of Gn and of Jgs, G. von Rad *(op. cit.)* and Lagrange *(op. cit.)*.

[21] The expression *mal'ak Yahweh* reappears, it is true, in Ag 1:13, but designates the prophet himself as Yahweh's messenger, and in Mal 2:7 it designates the priest (cf. Eccl. 5:5); in the plural it designates the prophets in Is 44:26 and 2 Par 36:15.

[22] This distinction is even found in several old texts where the expression *mal'ak Yahweh* designates a messenger of Yahweh (for example, Gn 24:7; 48:16; Ex 23:20-23; Nm 20:16; 22:22; 4 Kgs 1:3.15; 19:35; 2 Sm 14:17.20; 1 Sm 29:9).

[23] In Babylonian and Egyptian religions the gods' court is organized on the model of the kings' court, in which the great vizier plays the first role. In Babylon it is above all Nebo, the herald of the gods, who fulfills the function of the first minister of the highest god (cf. F. Stier, *op. cit.*, pp, 134 ff.)

[24] Cf. also the old divine name *Yahweh Ṣebâ'ôth*, that is to say, Yahweh the God of the heavenly and earthly armies (cf. above I, § 2, 6).

powerful kings of Egypt and Babylon and the kings of Israel had one. [25]

Before the Exile, however, this prince of the heavely court does not play a prominent role. Jos 5:13 mentions, it is true, " the prince of Yahweh's army " who appeared to Josue; Ex 23:20-22 attributes to the angel, whom Yahweh will send to protect and guide Israel, the power to give orders to the people and to chastise them, if they were to transgress these orders; this angel, in whom the name of Yahweh resides, is God's representative; finally, according to Ex 33:1-3, an angel will take the place of Yahweh when He refuses to accompany the guilty people. If these texts would form a literary unity, one might find in them the image of the vizier of God; but since they belong to independent traditions, there is nothing in them to prove that they designate a single individual : in Jos 5:13, it is a military chief; in Ex 33:1-3, a guide; in Ex 23:20-22, the angel is God's representative and, in Yahweh's absence, wields divine power, just as a grand vizier would do.

3. *After the Exile.* — The functions of the angels are more precisely stated : Ezechiel (9:2) sees in one of his visions " a man dressed in linen, carrying a writer's case at his waist, " that is to say, an angel carrying out the functions of a scribe; he seems to be placed over six angels and charged to mark with a *taw* those whom Yahweh wishes to spare in the massacre of the inhabitants of Jerusalem (9:6).

Zacharias (1:8-17) [26] sees " a man standing among myrtle trees " who commands three horsemen, that is to say, messengers sent by God to inspect the whole earth, and later he receives their reports.

---

[25] The vizier of Egypt is well known. " Each morning he went alone to the king, made his report and received his instructions. After an interview with the head of the treasure, he had the doors of the royal house opened, that is to say, the different offices of the palace, and the official day began. Through his hands passed all the business of the land, all important documents received his seal, all officials were subject to him : justice, public works, finances and armed forces were under his control. He really governed in the name of the king and replaced him when absent. " In Israel the " head of the house " of the king plays approximately the same role (Is 22:21-22), if not in the days of David and Solomon (cf. 3 Kgs 4:6), at least later (cf. R. de Vaux, " Titres et fonctionnaires égyptiens à la cour de David et de Salomon, " *RB*, 1939, pp. 401-403). Others recognize the vizier in the *mazkir*, a person of great importance at the court of the kings of Israel (2 Sm 8:16; 20:24; 3 Kgs 4:3; 4 Kgs 18:18.37; Is 36:3.22; 1 Par 18:15; 2 Par 34:8); R. de Vaux sees in him rather the king's herald.

[26] The present text seems to have been retouched, which makes the interpretation doubtful. There seem to be good reasons for suspecting the authenticity of these words : " And the angel who spoke with me, said to me : I will show you what these are " (verse 9b). The angel who explains the visions (1:13.14; 2:2.7; 4:1.4.5, etc.) announces the answer, given by the man (verse 10) " who was standing among the myrtle trees. "

This "man" is identified (v. 11) with the angel of Yahweh who intercedes for Jerusalem and Juda (v. 12), and seems to be identical with "the angel who spoke to me" (v. 13.14) and who communicated to the prophet the words and consolations of Yahweh (v. 14) which announced the end of the divine wrath and the restoration of Jerusalem (v. 16 ff.). In the fourth vision (Za 3:1-7), the angel of Yahweh is the supreme judge, who rejects the accusation brought against the high priest Josue (v. 2),[27] who purifies him[28] and transmits to him Yahweh's word (v. 6.7), promising him the government of the temple and access to the angels who are in God's service. In these visions, Yahweh is described as the Great King, who from the interior of His palace, while remaining invisible, governs through His intermediary, the grand vizier and his officials. The angel of Yahweh, who has angels subject to his order (1:8; 2:7.8; 3:4), is the intermediary between Yahweh and creatures: he makes the angels carry out their mission of inspection and finally transmits their reports to God; he transmits to the prophet and the high priest Yahweh's words (1:14; 3:6 ff.) and intercedes for the people; he administers justice in Yahweh's name (3:1.2) and purifies the accused of his iniquity (verses 3.4). Under the orders of the angel of Yahweh, the angels here are charged with the administration of the empire of the King of the world,[29] whose transcendence is thus brought into better light.

The book of Daniel knows Israel's angelic protector, Michael (10:13.21), who is one of the first princes and, at the end of time, will defend God's people (12:1); he also names the prince, that is to say, the angel of the kingdom of Persia and of the Greeks (10:13.20). These angelic protectors of the nations (Dt 32:8, LXX; Sir 17:17) took the place of the tutelary gods, whom Yahweh had given to the *goyîm* (Dt 4:19),[30] and are like the satraps through whom Yahweh exercises His dominion over the nations. With these "princes" of the nations may be compared the "sentinels" (Dn 4:10.14.20)[31]

---

[27] Instead of Yahweh, read: the angel of Yahweh; and in verse 5, "he said" instead of "I say."

[28] The angel of Yahweh declares to Josue: "Behold I take your iniquity away from you" (verse 4); he makes him change his filthy garments which were a sign of mourning and of impurity, and clothes him with festal garments (verses 4-5).

[29] Cf. Hen. 85-90; 6:2 ff.; Jubil. 1:27 ff., where the vizier of God is called the angel of His face; Test. Dan. 5; 6; 12; Ass. Mos. 10:1 ff. (cf. F. Stier, *Gott und sein Engel*, pp. 79 ff.).

[30] For the meaning of this text, cf. p. 36.

[31] The watchers are in Hen. 12:2.3; 20:1 (cf. 39:12; 40:2; 61:12) those who do not sleep, the highest angels. Elsewhere the fallen angels are called the watchers (Hen. 10:9.15; 12:4; 13:10; 14:1.3; 16:2; Jubil. 4:22; 7:21; 8:3; 10:5; Test. Rub. 5; Test. Nepht. 3).

and the seven " eyes of Yahweh that range over the earth " (Za 4:10), which designate the angels through whom God governs the world.

Even before the Exile there was at times an angel mentioned, sent by God to protect or help this or that person (Gn 24:7.40; 48:16; 3 Kgs 19:5.7). After the Exile, the idea [32] became widespread that Yahweh confides the protection of His faithful ones to angels: " He has given His angels command about you, that they guard you in all your ways. Upon their hands they shall bear you up, lest you dash your foot against a stone " (Ps 91:11.12); " the angel of the Lord encamps around those who fear Him, and delivers them " (Ps 34:8; cf. Dn 3:49.50, V; 6:23; Jdt 13:20; Tb 5:17.22; 12:12.15); angels intercede for men before God (Jb 5:1; cf. 33:23).

Yet, certain angels can be the agents of divine chastisements: " the destroyer " killed the first-born of the Egyptians (Ex 12:23); an angel (the angel of Yahweh according to 1 Par 21:12.16.27) made 70,000 men of Israel die by the plague (2 Sm 24:15-17); the angel of Yahweh sowed death among the Assyrian troops besieging Jerusalem (4 Kgs 19:35). In the vision of Ez 9:3-11, angels carry out the death sentence pronounced by Yahweh against the guilty Israelites. A psalmist wishes that the angel of Yahweh would sweep away his adversaries just as the wind carries away the chaff from the threshing floor (Ps 35:5). There, are, therefore, " angels of misfortune " (Ps 78:49) whom God releases in His wrath against the wicked.

Just as the functions of the angels become more specific and are arranged in hierarchical order, so do their personalities receive more precise characteristics. Since Daniel, some angels in higher ranks receive proper names: *Mîkâ'êl* (= Who is like God?, Dn 10:13) is one of the first princes (10:21) or the great prince (12:1); *Gabrî'êl* (= man of God, Dn 8:16; 9:21) explains the visions to Daniel; *Râphâ'êl* (= God cures) is " one of the seven holy angels who offer the prayers of the saints and who can appear before the majesty of the Holy " (Tb 12:15, LXX). [33] The books of Henoch and IV Esdras know several other names: Uriel, Raguel, Sarakiel, Jeremiel, etc.

---

[32] In recent Judaism and in the New Testament it develops into a belief in guardian angels (Test. Jos. 6; Targ. Ps. Jon. on Gn 33:10; 48:16; Acts 12:15 ff.; Mt 18:10).

[33] Seven is a sacred number and is frequently used in connection with the angels, especially the higher angels; as early as Ez 9:2 and Za 4:10; then in Tob 12:15; Hen. 90:21.22; Test. Lev. 8; Apoc 1:4.20; 3:1; 4:5; 5:6; 8:2.6). It is possible that this usage has been influenced by that of the court of the Persian Great King, whose throne was surrounded by seven princes (Est 1:14; P. Heinisch, *Theologie*, p. 105). Several critics find in this a vestige of Persian religious doctrine that recognized seven Ameshas Spentas, " the holy immortals "; others thought of the seven planetary gods of the Babylonians. On this question cf. M.M. Schumpp,

The number of angels is incalculable : " Thousands upon thousands ministered to Him, and myriads upon myriads attended Him " (Dn 7:10; Ps 68:18). They form the court, the army (3 Kgs 22:19; Jb 1:6; 2:1; Dn 7:10), and the council (Ps 89:6) of the King of heaven (Dn 4:34); they sing His praises in heaven (Ps 29:1.2; 103:20.21; 148:1.2; Jb 38:7) and escort Him in the theophanies (Za 14:5; Ps 68:18; Dn 7:10). Although they belong to the divine world and are, for this reason, called the sons of God (Jb 1:6; 2:1; 38:7; Ps 29:1; 89:6) or of the Most High (Ps 82:6), or the saints (Ps 89:6.8; Jb 5:1, etc.), they are infinitely inferior to the holy God (Sir 42:17) who discovers faults even in them (Jb 4:18; 15:15).

4. *Nature and origin of the angels.* — The Old Testament does not speculate on the nature or origin of the angels; it is concerned solely with their function and activity. The name " messenger, " which it applies most often to them, is that of their principal function and shows their dependence on God, their inferiority in relation to Yahweh. " Even God's holy ones must fail in recounting the wonders of the Lord. God gives His hosts the strength to stand firm before His glory " (Sir 42:17 Heb.). From this close dependence on God it may be concluded that the angels are considered to be God's creatures, although no text of the Old Testament formally affirms that they were created by Him, nor at what moment. [34] Ps. 148:1-6 invites the angels and the stars to praise God, because they were created by Him : " Let them praise the name of Yahweh, because He commanded and they were created " ; the reason alleged by the psalmist seems to apply, in his mind, both to the angels and the stars. According to Jb 38:7, " the sons of God " and the stars acclaim in chorus the creation of the world by God; here they are associated with the stars, who are not gods (Dt 4:35), as the nations believed who adored them, but creatures of the one God (Gn 1:14-18; Ps 33:6; 96:6; 148:5; Is 40:26).

Since the angels and the stars are very intimately associated (Ps 148:1-5), and even compared with one another (Jb 38:7), so that the former constitute the army of Yahweh (Jos 6:14; 3 Kgs 22:19; Ps 148:2) and the latter the army of heaven (Is 40:26; 45:12; Jer 33:22; Ps 33:6; Neh 9:6), it may be asked, if from the beginning the Hebrews distinguished between them. Certain texts (Jgs 5:20 : the stars have fought for us; Is 24:21 : Yahweh punishes the heavenly army; Is 40:26 :

Das Buch Tobias, Münster im W. 1933, pp. 229 ff. who also gives the principal bibliography.

[34] According to Jubil. 21 ff. they were created on the first day; according to Slav. Hen. 29 ff. and several rabbis, on the second day of God's work.

He calls the heavenly army by name and leads them out in order) seem to allow us to suppose the contrary and to believe that these powerful beings, the stars (Jgs 5:20; Is 40:26; Dt 4:19), adored as gods by the nations, especially by the Babylonians (Dt 4:19; 17:3; 4 Kgs 17:16; 21:3.5), were debased by the Hebrew monotheists to the rank of servants and messengers (*mal'âkîm*, angels) of the one God who " makes the winds His messengers, and fire and flame His servants " (Ps 104:4). [35]

In almost every text angels are represented as men (Gn 18; 19; Jos 5:13; Jgs 13:6.10.11; Ez 9:2; Dn 9:21; 10:5; Tb 5:5 ff., etc.); they have no wings; they ascend and descend the ladder that reaches from earth to heaven (Gn 28:12); later they are described as soaring between heaven and earth (1 Par 21:16; cf. 1 Sm 24:17) and moving rapidly through the air (Dn 9:21; 14:35.38, V), perhaps by means of wings. Sometimes they seem awe-inspiring, terrifying (Jgs 13:6; Dn 8:17; 10:7), their faces are luminous, their eyes radiating light, their garments shining (Dn 10:5.6; 2 Mc 3:25.26; Mk 16:5; Acts 1:10; 6:15; 10:30); sometimes it seems that they are beings of fire (4 Kgs 2:11; 6:17; Dn 10:6).

The oldest accounts show the angels taking part in meals (Gn 18:19; cf. Ps 78:25); but already Jgs 13:15.16 suggests that they do not eat. Later (Tb 12:19) it is said that they seem to eat human food, but in reality would consume an invisible nourishment; this supposes that, unlike men, they have no bodies. Although Judaism admitted that " the sons of God " had united with women and begotten giants (Gn 6:1-4), [36] it also held the angels to be spiritual beings : God had said to the fallen angels : " But you were formerly spiritual, living the eternal life, and immortal for all generations of the world. And therefore I have not appointed wives for you, for the abode of spiritual beings of heaven is in heaven " (Hen 15:6.7; cf. Mk 12:25).

5. *The Cherubim.* — The English term represents, by way of the Latin *(cherubim)*, the Hebrew plural *(kĕrûbîm)* of the word *kĕrûb*, which seems to have been taken from the Akkadian verb *karâbu* (= to bless). This verb is used, like the Hebrew *bârâk*, with God as subject or as object. In idiographic writing it is represented by a sign composed of a hand to the mouth, which is the classic sign of blessing or of prayer [37] in Babylon. The present participle of the verb *karâbu* is *kârîbu* (fem. *kâribatu)* which denotes " one who prays, "

[35] Cf. W. Eichrodt, *Theologie*, II, p. 104.

[36] Cf. above, p. 109, n. 5.

[37] Cf. the Latin *adorare*, which is composed of *ad* + *os*.

the faithful who adores the divinity, sometimes the loyal subject who pays homage to the king, but it can also denote the god (or goddess) who intercedes, who is often represented in Akkadian reliefs[38] and whose images are meant to pray for the absent. The *kâribu* (one who prays) or *karûbû* (one who eminently prays) is a divine being who belongs to the same category as the *lamasu* (fem. *lamastu*), that is to say, the winged bull (or an animal of the feminine sex) that guarded the entrances to the temple and royal palaces.

In the old account of Gn 3:24, Cherubim with a sword of jagged flames are stationed by Yahweh to prevent man from approaching the tree of life (cf. Ez 28:14.16). No description of the Cherubim is given, but very likely they should be visualized in human form just like the most ancient Babylonian *kâribi.* With the "sword of jagged flames" they correspond exactly to the *kâribu* and *lamasu* who guarded the entrances to the Akkadian temples. Mention must also be made of the two winged Cherubim, made of gilded olive wood, who with their outstretched wings formed a kind of shelter for the ark of Yahweh in the Holy of Holies of Solomon's temple (3 Kgs 6: 23-28; 2 Par 3:10-13), and of the Cherubim of chiseled gold with opened wings who were placed on "the propitiatory," that is to say, the cover of the holy ark (Ex 25:17-22; 37:6-9). These Cherubim, who were probably human figures fitted with Egyptian-style wings,[39] seem to be the guardians of the symbol of Yahweh's presence, who, according to Ex 25:22; Nm 7:89 spoke to Moses "from the midst of the two Cherubim who are on the ark of the testimony." But the expression "Yahweh who is enthroned over the Cherubim" (1 Sm 4:4; 2 Sm 6:2; 4 Kgs 19:15 = Is 37:16; Ps 80:2; 99:1; Dn 3:55) suggests the image of winged animals who serve as a throne[40] or as "mounts"[41] for Yahweh, who is described elsewhere as "mounted on a Cherubim" and flying on the wings of the wind (Ps 18:11 = 2 Sm 21:11; cf. Is 19:1; Ps 104:3).[42]

[38] Cf. *RB*, 1926, pl. VIII, figs. 3, 4 and 5. Our treatment of the Cherubim is borrowed from this brilliant and solid monograph, whose every statement is supported by texts and archaeological documents.

[39] Cf. *RB*, 1926, p. 487, fig. 5; p. 488, fig. 6; and p. 485, fig. 4.

[40] Cf. the seat supported by animals with human faces of Sendjirli, fig. 6, in M. Dibelius, *Die Lade Jahves*, Göttingen 1906, p. 81 and the design on ivory coming from Megiddo (1200 B.C.) in G. L. Wright – F. V. Filson, *The Westminster Historical Atlas to the Bible*, 1946, p. 45.

[41] Cf. the relief of Maltai (fig. 5, Dibelius, *op. cit.*, p. 80) where the gods are carried by strange beasts, some of which are winged.

[42] Is 19:1 "mounted" *(rkb)* on a light cloud (cf. Ps 104:3) recalls the messenger of Alyan "straddling *(rkb)* the clouds" in the Ras Shamra texts (II, *AB*, III, 11; V, 122, etc., cf. J. W. Jack, *The Ras Shamra Tablets*, Edinburgh 1935, p. 48). S. Mowinkel, "Drive and Ride in the O. T.," *VT* 1962, pp. 288 ff.

According to Ex 26:1.31; 36:8.35, figures of Cherubim were woven into the curtains and the veil of the tabernacle; and according to 3 Kgs 6:29, sculptured and gilded Cherubim decorated the cedar paneling and the doors of Solomon's temple (3 Kgs 6:32.35); they alternated with palm trees, or more probably faced each other around a palm tree in continuous friezes between garlands of flowers.[43] Perhaps they had human form (cf. Ez 28:14.16) as did the figures that decorated the movable basins of the temple (3 Kgs 7:29); however, they might have had the form of lions or winged bulls with human face, as suggested by a relief (11th or 10th century) discovered in a royal cave in Jerusalem.[44]

In Ezechiel's visions (1:4 ff.; 9:3; 10; 11:22) Cherubim form the movable throne or chariot on which the glory of the Lord descends from heaven and returns thereto. They " have human appearance " (1:5), yet each one has four faces : the face of a man, of a lion, of a bull, and of an eagle (1:10), four wings and human hands under the wings, four straight legs with bulls' hooves; their brilliance is as the lightning (1:13) and their spirit moves the wheels in relation to their own movement (1:15-21). It is difficult to imagine exactly this mysterious chariot of the divine glory; but the Cherubim are here certainly composed beings, having members of different animals, of which there are many examples in Assyro-Babylonian sculpture.[45]

It is undeniable that Israel borrowed the word and the plastic form from Babylon; however, it transformed the concepts : for the Babylonian *kâribi* and others are second class masculine and feminine divinities, while the Cherubim are sexless ministers of the one God whose invisible presence they manifest and whose action they symbolize. Maybe they are only poetical images, as in Ps 18:11 = 2 Sm 21:11 and in the visions of Ezechiel, or symbols, destined to show the transcendence and omnipotence of Yahweh.

6. *The Seraphim* (Hebr. *šĕrâphîm*) are mentioned only once in the Old Testament (Is 6:2-6). Several authors derive the word from the verb *śâraph* (to burn); others thought of an Egyptian word *seref*, that denotes winged griffins, guarding the entrance to Beni Hassan's tomb; others have recourse to an Arabic verb meaning " to be noble. " The word *śârâph* is used as an adjective with *nâḥâš* (serpent), to denote the fiery serpents who attacked the Israelites in the desert (Nm 21:6-9; Dt 8:15) and seem to have been called fiery because of

[43] As in the Syro-Hittite and Mesopotamian relief friezes on the walls of Assyrian palaces.
[44] Cf. *RB*, 1926, fig. 7, p. 489.
[45] Cf. the hybrid dragons, bulls or winged lions with human faces, two-headed genii, etc., *RB*, 1926, fig. 8 and 9, p. 492; fig. 7, p. 489; pl. IX, fig. 1-4.

the burning pain of their bite. The brazen serpent is also called *śârâph* in Nm 21:8; finally Is 14:29 and 30:6 mention a flying serpent (*śârâph mĕʿôphêh*), which is a creation of popular imagination.

The Seraphim of Is 6:2-6 are heavenly beings who surround Yahweh's throne (cf. 3 Kgs 22:19) and proclaim His holiness in alternating choirs. Their principal function, therefore, is to praise the holy God; but they are also charged to remove the profane and to purify those who are allowed to draw near to Yahweh (Is 6:6). Out of reverential fear of the holy God, they will veil their faces and their feet with their wings. At the sound of their voices the threshholds of the temple are shaken. The smoke that fills the sanctuary seems to be the effect of their breath, which would suppose that they are of a fiery nature, as their name probably indicates, as does the fact that it is with fire that they purify the profane. They have hands, feet, a human voice, although they have three pairs of wings: with one pair, they veil their face, with another they cover their body and their feet, with a third they fly. Several authors conclude from their name, which can also mean a serpent, that they have the body of a serpent and are composed beings, like Ezechiel's Cherubim. This is not necessarily the case, since the word *śârâph* (meaning burning) may have been given to serpents only because of the burning pain of their bite. There is no reason to believe, as some affirm, that the Seraphim were the guardians of the temple's threshhold.

B. Demons, Satan

1. *Demons.* — The books of the Old Testament prior to the Exile rarely mention demons. Obviously they played only a minor role in the religion of ancient Israel, at least in the official religion and in the religious life of Yahweh's faithful ones. This phenomenon is all the more remarkable in that it constitutes an exception among the religion of the peoples of the ancient East, such as the Assyro-Babylonians and the Egyptians, whose demonology was highly developed and whose liturgy abounded in exorcisms.[46] This is a consequence of Israelite monotheism; since it recognized only one God, the author of misfortune as well as of fortune (Am 3:6; 4:6.7.9.10; Is 45:7; Lam 3:37.38; Jb 9:24), one never thought of explaining the origin of evils by the action of demons.

Yet it seems that the ancestors of the Hebrews feared more the

[46] Cf. for example P. Dhorme, *La religion Assyro-Babylonienne*², Paris 1910; *Les religions de Babylonie et d'Assyrie*, Paris 1949; G. Furlani, *La religione Babilonese-Assira*, 2 vols., Bologna 1928; A. Erman, *Die Religion der Aegypter*, Berlin 1934.

malevolent action of demons. This fear probably accounts for the origin of certain interdicts and ritual prescriptions which have been preserved in the Law but which have been transformed, for example the prohibitions concerning the use of certain foods (Lv 11), relations with pregnant (Lv 12) or menstruating women (Lv 15:19-30),[47] the order to attach little bells to the sacerdotal garments of the high priest (Ex 28:33-35).[48]

No doubt in the lower classes of Israelite society there were always people haunted by the power of demons, who practiced magic, divination and necromancy. The first book of Samuel (28) describes in detail a scene of this kind, the summoning of the spirit of Samuel. The dead who "rises from the earth" is there called an elohim (28:13), as perhaps in Is 8:19.[49] The spirits of the dead, according to a fairly large number of exegetes, were also designated by the name *'obôt*, which recurs frequently in the texts where there is question of divination and magic (Lv 19:31; 20:6.27; Dt 18:11; 1 Sm 28:7.9; 4 Kgs 21:6; 23:24; Is 8:19; 19:3; 29:4); but this interpretation is disputed.[50] These practices have been repeatedly forbidden by the Law (Lv 19:31; 20:6.27; Dt 18:10.11) and by the kings (1 Sm 28:9; 4 Kgs 23:24), and have been reproved by the prophets (1 Sm 28:9; Is 8:19) with the result that they were forced into the background, and it may be said that there was neither magic nor divination in Israel (Nm 23:23).[51] Consequently the number of demons that found place in the Old Testament is extremely small.

Is the *'ălûqâh* (Prv 30:15), a feminine vampire, as it is believed?[52] Are the *'iyyîm* (Is 13:22; 34:14; Jer 50:39) and the *ṣiyyîm* (Is 13:21;

---

[47] Cf. below; the pure and the impure, part II, II, B.

[48] The sound of the little metal bells had to be heard when the high priest entered and left the sanctuary "lest he die" (Ex 28:35). The ancients believed in the efficacy of sound, especially when produced by a metal object, to drive demons away (cf. P. Heinisch, *Das Buch Exodus*, p. 217). Most commentators interpret the little bells in this way; but may we suppose that Yahweh's sanctuary was haunted by demons? Cf. above, p. 42, n. 2.

[49] If in Is 8:19 the words "should not a people inquire of their gods, apply to the dead on behalf of the living?" are part of the people's discourse, reproved by the prophet, then the gods *(elohim)* being parallel with the dead seem to designate the spirits of the deceased (cf. Marti, Condamin, Fischer, *in h.l.*); Duhm, Procksch, Feldmann *(in h.l.)* consider them to be the answer of the prophet and translate: "Does not a people inquire of his God? Does it consult the dead on behalf of the living?"

[50] Jirku, *Die Dämonen*, pp. 5 ff.; H. Schmidt, *ZAW*, 1923, pp. 253 ff.

[51] This is not favorable to S. Mowinckel's thesis (*Psalmenstudien*, I, Kristiania 1921); he sees in many psalms cultic lamentations which are part of incantation rites against the evil work of sorcerers. This hypothesis, presented with power and erudition, is far from being proved (cf. the account of E. Podechard, *RB*, 1923, pp. 141-145).

[52] A. Jirku, *op. cit.*, pp. 55 ff.; J. Wellhausen, *Reste arabischen Heidentums*, Berlin 1897, pp. 149 ff.; W. Oesterley, *The Book of Proverbs*, London 1929, p. 275.

23:13; 34:14; Jer 50:39; Ps 74:14) demons who haunt ruins and desert places? [53] The meaning of the first word is doubtful (bloodsucker?), the second is generally translated by jackal, and the third by wildcats.

It is very probable that the evil spirit, sent by God or coming from Yahweh, is a demon who provokes the revolt of the Sichemites against Abimelech (Jgs 9:23) and Saul's crisis of melancholic anger (1 Sm 16:14 ff.; 18:10.11; 19:9.10). [54] But it will be observed that he is entirely subject to Yahweh and acts only to carry out the punishments decreed by God.

2. *Azazel.* — The ritual of the day of expiation (Lv 16), at any rate, has preserved the name of a demon, Azazel, who is believed to dwell in the desert (Lv 16:22) and seems to have been associated with sin, since to him was sent the goat laden with the sins of Israel (Lv 16:21). This goat was not offered in sacrifice to Azazel, but was sent to him (Lv 16:10.21) and was meant to carry away the people's sins (Lv 16:21), [55] as the living bird carries away the leper's impurity in the rite of purification of Lv 14:4-7. The meaning of *'Aza'zêl*, the character and appearance attributed to this demon are uncertain. [56] In later Judaism, he became one of the leaders of the fallen angels (Hen 6:7; 8:1; 9:6, etc.) and had to be chained by Raphael in the desert of Dudael until the day of judgment, when he will be cast into the fire (Hen 10:4 ff.).

3. The *śĕ'îrîm* and the *šêdîm.* — The book of Isaias (13:21; 34:14) mentions in poetical descriptions demons who, according to popular belief (Lv 16:22; Bar 4:33; Tb 8:3; Mt 12:43), haunt desert places and ruins: the *śĕ'îrîm* which are represented as goats, [57] and Lilith (Is 34:14) who is in Babylon a feminine demon *(lilîtu)*. Lv 17:7 forbids the offering of sacrifices, which would be idolatry, to the *śĕ'îrîm*. This implies that at a certain period the Israelites worshipped

---

[53] A. Jirku, *op. cit.*, pp. 36 ff.

[54] Cf. P. van Imschoot, "L'action de l'esprit de Jahvé dans l'A. T.," *RScPT*, 1934, pp. 559 ff.; Förster, "Daimon," *ThW*, II, pp. 11 ff.

[55] Analogous purification rites are reported by S. Landersdorfer ("Studien zum biblischen Versöhnungstag," *ATA*, X, 1, Münster 1927, pp. 23 ff.) and by Gustavs ("Kultische Symbolik bei den Hethitern," *ZAW*, 1923, pp. 139 ff.).

[56] Some authors explain it by the verb *'âzal* which means to put at a distance; Azazel, then, would be one who puts sins at a distance (B. Baentsch, *in h.l.*); but this etymology is doubtful. Jirku (*op. cit.*, p. 34) suspects that the primitive name *'Azaz'êl* (= God is strong) was deliberately disfigured by the Massoretes; cf. other explanations suggested in the *Yoma* edition of S. Meinhold, p. 17, n. 1.

[57] The word *śâ'îr*, literally: hairy, often designates the male goat, for example Lev 4:23.24.28; 16:5-27.

them; this appears to be confirmed by 2 Par 11:15 for Roboam's reign. Yet one may question, if in these last two texts reference is really made to sacrifices offered to demons. In fact the Jews were quick to call the gods of other nations demons; and the sacrifices offered to these gods they called oblations made to demons (Ps 96:5, LXX; Bar 4:7; 1 Cor 10:20).

The same question is raised even more insistently in connection with the *šêdîm* (LXX and V: demons) who, according to Dt 32:7 and Ps 106:37, were worshipped by the Israelites. These *šêdîm* who " are not God " (Dt 32:17) are considered to be similar to foreign gods (Ps 106:36.37), and seem to be the Babylonian *šêdu*, bull-gods, sometimes benevolent, sometimes evil. Did Hebrew writers reduce the Babylonian *šêdu* to the rank of devils?

This was the opinion of the Greek translators of the Bible; they readily translated by δαιμόνια, malevolent spirits, Hebrew terms that had no pejorative sense: *śĕʿîrîm* in Is 13:21; 34:14, who in other passages (Lv 17:7; 2 Par 11:15) are interpreted as μάταια (vain things) and εἴδωλα (idols); *šêdîm* (Dt 32:17; Ps 106:17), *ṣiyyîm* (Is 34:14), who are sometimes turned into sirens (Is 34:13; 43:20; Jb 30:29), and into ostriches (Is 13:21; Mi 1:8; Jer 50:39, LXX; 27:39). In a similar way they interpreted Ps 96:5: " all the gods of the nations are things of nought " *('ělilîm)* by " they are δαιμόνια. " They made a demon out of the god Gad (Is 65:3) by adding to the Hebrew text " (they sacrifice) to demons that do not exist "; in Ps 91:6 " the pestilence that roams at noonday " becomes " the noonday devil. " [58] Bar 4:7 finally condemns idolatry practiced by Israel in these words: " For you provoked your Maker with sacrifices to demons, to no-gods. " From these texts it may be seen that at the time the Hebrew Old Testament was being translated, demonology had developed among Alexandrian Jews, under the influence, without doubt, of popular Greek demonology, and that Israelite monotheism reacted against Graeco-Roman polytheism by reducing the gods of the Gentiles to the rank of demons (cf. 1 Cor 10:20).

4. *Asmodeus.* — The popular tale of the book of Tobias places before our eyes a malevolent demon, Asmodeus, who put to death one after the other of the seven husbands of Sara, Raguel's daughter, on the very day of their marriage (3:8). He was said to be in love with the young girl (6:15, LXX B), and it was believed that he exercised his power over those who allowed themselves to be dominated by the

[58] S. Landersdorfer (" Daemonium meridianum, " *BZ*, 1929, p. 294) believes that the reference in the Hebrew text was to a demon.

sexual instinct (6:6.17); this seems to indicate that he was a demon of lewdness. On the advice of the angel Raphael, Tobias drove the demon away by burning the heart and liver of a fish he had caught in the Tigris. Asmodeus fled to Upper-Egypt and was chained there by Raphael (8:2.3). Almost all critics agree in recognizing in Asmodeus the demon Aešma daêva, who in the Persian religion is the demon of anger, the second in rank after Angra Mainyu. The method chosen by the angel to chase the demon (Tb 6:8; 8:3) is commonly used in ancient magic, for example in Assyro-Babylonia where fumigations often accompany the formulas of incantation in ceremonies of exorcisms.[59] We have here an adaptation to popular usages and beliefs that had developed among the Jews,[60] probably under Persian influence. The sacred writer, however, refers in the end to God the efficacy of all the remedies revealed by the angel Raphael for the cure of Tobias and the expulsion of the demon, because the angel explains that he was sent by God to cure Tobias and to deliver Sara from the demon (Tb 12:14) and includes these happy events among the works of God and the benefits due to His mercy (Tb 12:6.7).

5. *The serpent.* — In the very old account of the temptation in the garden of Eden, the serpent has a strongly marked demonic character. Yet he is, in the author's eyes, a true animal, no doubt more cunning than the other "beasts of the field" (Gn 3:1), but belonging to the same group of living creatures created by Yahweh (Gn 2:19); he is "cursed among the domestic animals and all the beasts of the field" (Gn 3:14). He is neither a pure symbol, nor a mask, nor an appearance under which is hidden a demon, since Yahweh curses him and condemns him to walk henceforth on his belly and to eat dust all the days of his life (Gn 3:14).[61] The punishment is inflicted on the serpent himself, not to another being hidden in him, and Yahweh punishes not a pure symbol, not a mask, nor a mere appearance, but a real animal.

---

[59] Fumigations were still used in recent Judaism for the expulsion of demons, for example Pesiq. 40 a; Flav. Jos., Ant. VIII, 2-5; Bell. Jud. VII, 6, 3; numerous Babylonian examples are to be found in H. Zimmer, *Die Beschwörungstafeln Surpu*, Leipzig 1901.

[60] Cf. M. Schumpp, *Das Buch Tobias*, Münster im W. 1933, p. 170.

[61] The ancients believed that serpents ate dust (Mi 7:17). To lick the dust, is an often repeated phrase (Is 49:23; Mi 7:17; Ps 72:9 and the Amarna letters 100, 36); it means to be humbled or to humble one's self, when it is applied to men. Dust is the food of infernal beings and of the dead (*Descente d'Ištar*, V, 5) according to Babylonian beliefs. To walk on one's belly seems abnormal, that is why it is interpreted as a divine punishment. Did they believe that before this punishment the serpent had paws or walked erect, as some Babylonian reliefs represent him (*AOB*, n. 603)? Popular belief recognized also flying serpents (Is 14:29; 30:6).

Yet he is not an animal like all others, since he is able to speak (cf. Nm 22:28-30), he is intelligent, he possesses knowledge superior even to that of man. In fact he knows the secret of the tree of good and evil which man does not know (Gn 3:5). Nor is he merely an animal who can talk, such as are to be found in all popular fables, since the author of the tale who has so clearly marked man's superiority over all " the beasts of the field " (Gn 2:19.20) would not attribute to one of them knowledge that man does not possess. Moreover, what makes the serpent " more cunning than all the beasts of the field " (Gn 3:1) is not the gift of speech but the knowledge of Yahweh's secret about the tree of good and evil. [62] So it must be admitted that the serpent is one of several demonic animals known in the ancient East, [63] a mythological monster hostile to God like the Leviathan, a seven-headed serpent (Is 27:1; Ps 74.13.14; Jb 3:8), and Rahab (Is 51:9.10; Ps 89:10-12; Jb 7:12; 9:13; 26:12.13). This demonic animal is maliciously disposed toward man, since he knowingly deceives man and urges him to disobey Yahweh (3:5.13), and toward God whom he accuses of jealousy and lying (3:4.5). He appears, therefore, as an adversary of Yahweh and of man, whom he leads into temptation.

When these characteristics were later crystallized in the person of Satan, the book of Wisdom (2:24) and the New Testament (Jn 8:44; Ap 12:9; 20:22) will explain that the serpent is the devil (διάβολος = satan). [64]

6. *Satan.* — Satan is in Hebrew *(śâtân)* a common noun; it denotes an adversary either in battle (for example, 1 Sm 29:4), or, on any other occasion, an opponent (for example 2 Sm 19:23), but especially in a lawsuit (Ps 109:6; Za 3:1): the satan is the accuser before the

---

[62] T. Vriezen, *Onderzoek naar de Paradijsvoorstelling by de oude Semietische Volken* Wageningen 1937, p. 173. M. A. Van den Oudenryn (*De Zonde in den Tuin*, Roermond 1939, pp. 87 ff.) admits that the serpent is a real animal, but was possessed by a demon. This distinction between the serpent and the demon is no way indicated in the text of Gn 3; if the serpent is only the unconscious instrument of a demon, why is he punished?

[63] In Babylonian mythology there is a serpent among " the seven " redoutable demons, and there are several serpents among the helpers of Tiamat (*Enuma eliš*, I, 131-139; IV, 104. 129); there are also many reliefs representing a god fighting a serpent (*AOB*, fig. 374, 380, 397, 400). On the serpent in ancient mythologies, cf. J. Coppens, *La connaissance du bien et du mal et le péché du Paradis. Contribution à l'interprétation de Gen II-III*, Paris 1948, pp. 92-98, with a very complete bibliography.

[64] Cf. A. Van Hoonacker, " The Literary Origin of the Narration of the Fall, " *Expositor*, VIII, 1916, pp. 480-498; J. Hehn, " Zur Paradiesschlange, " *Festschrift für S. Merkle*, Düsseldorf 1922; S. Landersdorfer, " Der Sündenfall, " *ThG*, 1922, pp. 38-60; L. Dürr, *Ursprung und Aufbau der israelitischjüdischen Heilandserwartung*, Berlin 1925, pp. 69-73; W. Eichrodt, *Theologie*, II, p. 110.

tribunal, he who "recalls the fault" (cf. Gn 41:9; 3 Kgs 17:18). The word expresses a hostile disposition rather than a habitual function: one becomes another's satan when one opposes him; thus the angel of Yahweh becomes Balaam's satan when he stations himself in the road to hinder the diviner from passing (Nm 22:22).

The LXX translated the world satan by διάβολος which in Greek signifies calumniator; but they use it in the sense of adversary or accuser, according to the meaning of the Hebrew (for example, Ps 109:6; Est 7:4; 8:1). The word was taken into Latin *(diabolus)*, whence it passed into modern languages (devil, *diable*, *diavolo*, *duivel*, *Teufel*) with the special meaning which Satan and διάβολος acquired when they became the name of the wicked spirit, hostile to God and man.

If the prologue of the book of Job (1:6-12; 2:1-7) is prior to the Exile, it is the oldest text in which the term satan is applied to a superhuman being. "The satan" (Hebr. *hassâtân*, with the article) appeared at Yahweh's court with the "sons of God," that is to say, the angels. He is not yet a wicked spirit, but seems to be one of the "sons of God," since, like them, he has free access and the right to speak at the court of the heavenly King. [65] His task is to go through the world and to inspect the conduct of men of which he is, at the heavenly court, the accuser (the satan). When Yahweh asks him if he has noticed the piety of His servant Job, he laughs. He does not believe in the soundness of a virtue motivated by advantages and proposes to Yahweh to test Job by depriving him of all the possessions with which Yahweh had blessed His servant, and by striking his flesh with a frightful plague. Yahweh consents under the condition that the life of Job be spared. The satan has no power by himself; he is only the executor of the divine will (Jb 1:11; 2:5), and his power

---

[65] In a similar way, in the vision of Micheas (3 Kgs 22:19-23), a spirit, who belongs to the army of Yahweh, takes part in the deliberation, which is presided by Yahweh, and proposes the means looked for by Yahweh to entice Achab: "I will go forth, and will be a lying spirit in the mouth of all his prophets," who promise victory against the Syrians. This spirit presents himself as the executor of the will of Yahweh, who has decided to deceive Achab in order to lead him to ruin, by engaging him into a war against the Syrians (22:20). It is Yahweh who takes the initiative of deceiving Achab. The spirit is not a perverse being; if he proposes to present himself as "a lying spirit," it is only to execute the decision taken by God, to whom, according to the old conception which does not distinguish what God permits from what He wills, one attributes all good and evil events (Am 3:8; Is 45:7; Jb 9:24; Lam 3:8; cf. pp. 70, 71). One does not yet fear to say that Yahweh will deceive Achab (22:20), in order to punish him for his crimes; but, whereas in other texts (for example, 2 Sm 16:10; 24:1 ff.) it is frankly said that He incites to evil (cf. p. 84), here already the execution of the project to deceive Achab is entrusted to an intermediary being. Later on the plan as well as the execution of evil (1 Par 21:1) will be attributed to an essentially perverse being, to Satan.

is limited by the orders of Yahweh (Jb 1:12; 2:6). With God's permission he tempts Job in the sense that he puts his virtue to the test; but he does not intend to seduce him, to push him directly to sin. The satan, however, who disposes of the most terrible sickness and calamities, has already in himself some of those alluring traits which will make him later a perverse and formidable being. [66]

In his fourth vision Zacharias (3:1-7) sees a scene of judgment: The high priest stands before the angel of Yahweh as before his judge; to the right of the priest stands " the satan " (Hebr. *hassâtân*), that is to say, the accuser, who turns against him (Hebr. *lĕśitnô*, to oppose him). But the angel of Yahweh [67] takes up the defense of the high priest and says to satan: " May Yahweh rebuke you, Satan, He who has chosen Jerusalem. " Here satan is the accuser who pronounces the indictment before the tribunal. [68] Nothing indicates animosity of any kind on the part of satan against God, not even against the high priest; for, if he opposes him, it is only because the priest is really guilty (v. 4). The angel of Yahweh, without doubt, wishes that Yahweh should rebuke the accuser; but he wishes it because the accusation that had been made against the guilty high priest, injures Jerusalem, which Yahweh had chosen. And it is for the sake of Jerusalem that Yahweh pardons the high priest who is consequently purified of his iniquity and restored to his former dignity (vv. 3-5).

In the third century, the author of Paralip (1, 21:1), taking up the account of 2 Sm 24:1 ff., corrects the text of 2 Sm 24:1: " Again the anger of Yahweh was kindled against Israel, and He incited David against them, saying: ' Go, number Israel and Juda. ' " Unable, however, to admit any longer that God incites to commit a fault which He will punish, the author of 1 Par 21:1 ff. suppresses the mention of the anger of Yahweh and attributes the suggestion of a census of Israel to Satan; he writes: " Satan (Hebr. *śâtân*, without article) stood up against Israel and incited David to number Israel. So David said to Joab and to the commanders of the army: ' Go, number Israel.... ' " The author retained the classic expression which designates the attitude of an accuser (*'âmâd 'al*, to stand up against, cf. Ps 109:6; Za 3:1); but he understands the term Satan as a proper

[66] Cf. Von Rad, *ThW*, II, p. 72.

[67] The text has: Yahweh says; but it must be read: the angel of Yahweh says.

[68] In the actual text the object of the indictment is not mentioned. Kurt Galling, *ZMR*, 46 (1931), p. 200, followed by T. Robinson-F. Horst (*Die Zwölf Kleinen Propheten*, Tübingen 1938, p. 218) supposes that the accusation was indicated in verse 2; he changes the reading: " And Satan said: May Yahweh rebuke you (priest), may Yahweh who has chosen Jerusalem rebuke you. "

name and the accuser as a seducer, who allures to sin. This is quite a way from the time of Zacharias and the book of Job. The accuser (the satan) who was a celestial being and had been admitted to the court of Yahweh, who was a functionary of the divine tribunal, has become a being hostile to God, and a seducer of men; and the term which designated any enemy has become the proper name of this perverse spirit.

In Sirach 21:27: "When a godless man curses the satan (τὸν σατανᾶν), he really curses himself," the Greek translator saw Satan; but it is probable that Sirach wrote *hassâtân* and, according to the meaning of the Hebrew term, thought of a human adversary. This sentence, as a matter of fact, is parallel with the following: "The slanderer besmirches himself," and signifies that the curse pronounced against an adversary falls back on him who pronounces it.

The book of Wisdom (2:24; cf. also Apoc. Bar. 4:8; Apoc: Mos. 16; Vit. Adam 12) recognized for the first time Satan (διάβολος, without the article, as in 1 Pt 5:8; Acts 13:10) in the serpent of Gn 3: "By the envy of Satan (διαβόλου) death entered the world, and they who are in his possession (Satan's) experience it." Here the tempter of 1 Par 21:1 is identified with the serpent which seduced the first man. He is an envious being, who bears a grudge against man because of the immortality and the happiness to which man had been destined (2:23) [69]; he urges him to disobey God, in order to deprive him of the immortality for which God had created him (2:23), [70] and thus he thwarts the plans of God.

In Wisdom 2:24 appear the principal traits which the figure of Satan assumes in Judaism, where he is the one who seeks to destroy the relation between God and men, and in particular between God and Israel, either by alluring men to sin, or by accusing them before God, or by thwarting the salvific plan of God. [71]

---

[69] According to the *Life of Adam and Eve* (12-16) Satan envied man, because he had been driven from heaven for having refused to pay homage to man, created according to the image of God; according to *Sanhedrin* 59 b, because the angels served him; according to *Slav. Hen.* 31:6 (recension A), because man had received domination over the whole creation (cf. Gn 1:28).

[70] Cf. Sir 25:23: "In woman was sin's beginning, and because of her we all die"; Rom 5:12; 6:23; Jn 8:44. The allusion to Gn 2:17; 3:19, where death is the punishment of the disobedience of the first man, seems evident. It is not very probable that the author of Wis 2:24 thinks of the death of Abel, which was the consequence of the irritation or of the jealousy of Cain (Gn 4:5), not of the envy of Satan. If the author had wished to designate Cain as the adversary of Abel, he would have written τοῦ διαβόλου; this term is always used by the Greek version in passages, where there is question of Satan (Jb 1:6.12; 2:1; 1 Par 21:1; Za 3:1).

[71] Förster, *ThW*, II, p. 75.

7. *Origin of demons.* — The Old Testament did not inquire about the origin of Satan. [72] It is only in the Jewish Apocrypha that an explanation has been attempted, by making out of Satan a fallen angel. Most frequently one discovers the fall of the angels in the narrative of Gen 6:1-4 (Hen 6-11; Jub 5:1-6; Test. Rub. 5:6-9; Test. Nepht. 3:5; Philo, De Gig.; Flav. Jos., Ant. I, 3.1); Satan is the chief of the angels who allowed themselves to be seduced by the daughters of men (Hen 6:3, where he is called Semaya), and who for that fault have been driven from heaven to the earth, where they await the final judgment to be thrown into the fire (Apoc. Esdr. 4:33; Vit. Adam 39; Test. Jud. 25:3). The *Life of Adam and Eve* (Vit. Adam 12-16) indicates another occasion: Satan refused to render homage to Adam, created according to the image of God and, menaced by God, revolted openly against Him in his pride; it is for this reason that God drove him from heaven down to earth together with the angels who had followed him in his rebellion.

For a long time it has been noticed that demonology, angelology, and the doctrine of Satan began to be developed in Israel from the moment the people of Yahweh entered into contact with the Persian religion. Most of the critics deduced from this fact, which is undeniable, that this development is due to the influence of that religion, in which an important role is held by beings intermediary between the supreme God, Ahura Mazda, and the created world, as well as by demons, auxiliaries of the principle of physical and moral evil, Angra Mainyu (Ahriman). Reading certain explanations one might believe that the Jews simply borrowed from Persia the doctrine on angels, demons and Satan; Satan would be derived from the demon-serpent, Azhi Dahaca, one of the principal auxiliaries of Angra Mainyu, who deprived the first man of his glory.

This opinion presented in such a form is, to say the least, exaggerated. Well before every contact with Persia, the Old Testament knew of angels and of demons. One cannot say, therefore, that the belief in angels and demons was borrowed from the Persian religion.

The Israelite angelology was perhaps formed in the beginning as

---

[72] Several Fathers understood of Satan what had been said in Is 14:12 about the king of Babylon, whom the prophet reproaches for trying to make himself equal to God and for presuming to ascend to heaven, above the heights of the clouds. The prophet announces to him the chastisement for his pride with these words: "How are you fallen from heaven, O bright star, son of dawn!" The Vulgate already believed to find Satan in "the bright star" and translated it by "Lucifer," which afterwards became one of the names of the prince of demons. Neither in Is 14:12 nor in Ez 28:16.17 is there question of the fall of an angel, but rather of the fall of the king of Babylon and of the king of Tyrus.

a reaction against the worship of stars,[73] and was developed in proportion as the transcendence of Yahweh affirmed itself more and more; it is not necessary to call for foreign influences in order to explain this development, at least inasmuch as it appears in the sacred books; but one must not exclude every foreign influence, in particular that from Persia, on later Jewish angelology which is that of the Apocrypha and the Rabbis.

As for the belief in demons, it is prior to the religion of Yahweh itself and has maintained itself, without doubt, in all epochs of popular religiosity.[74] But in the official religion this belief has been repressed and contained by the monotheistic doctrine which attributed to Yahweh the causality of good and evil. The development of demonology, which we notice toward the end of the period preceding the Christian era and in the beginning of the latter, is a reviviscence of the old popular belief, the true cause of which can be found in the internal evolution of the Israelite doctrine: the more the transcendence, the holiness and the perfection of God were affirmed, the more the need was felt to admit intermediary beings between the holy God and the terrestrial world, in particular evil beings, in whom one could find the cause of physical and moral evil which one no longer attributed directly to Yahweh. It is possible, nevertheless, even probable, that this development has been favored by the more frequent and intimate contacts of Israel with the Greek and Persian milieu. Certain names (for example, Asmodeus), the specialization of the activity of demons, the organization of evil spirits into a kingdom, subject to a chief, called Satan, Mastema, Belial or Sammael, are perhaps developments due to Persian influence; but with regard to the whole doctrine, these are accessory elements all of which have been adopted to Israelite monotheism.[75]

In Parseeism, indeed, demonology is a consequence of metaphysical dualism which is at the base of that whole doctrine: Angra Mainyu, the principle of evil, is independent of Ahura Mazda, who is the principle of good. The former is the author of physical as well as moral evils and exercises his power over the godless and the demons; the latter is the author of all good; eventually he will overcome the principle of evil, and his victory will assure the renovation of the world. The Old Testament, on the contrary, as well as later Judaism and the New Testament, admitted only one first principle, author

[73] Cf. above pp. 118 ff.
[74] Cf. above p. 122.
[75] Cf. the balanced conclusion of W. F. Albright, *From the Stone Age to Christianity*, Baltimore 1946, pp. 278 ff.

of the entire created world; the demons and Satan in their existence and action depend on the one God. The dualism, therefore, which had been introduced by the development of the doctrine on Satan, " the prince of the world " (Jn 12:31; 14:30; 16:11) or even " the god of this world " (2 Cor 4:4; cf. Eph 2:2), remained purely moral and religious. This is an essential difference, which we must take into account when examining possible relations between Parseeism, Judaism and Christianity.

CHAPTER III

REVELATION

§ 1. *The concept of revelation*

E. König, *Der Offenbarungsbegriff des A. T.*, 2 vols., Leipzig 1882; H. Niebecker, *Wesen und Wirklichkeit der übernatürlichen Offenbarung*, Freiburg im B. 1940. P. Benoit, " Révélation et inspiration, " *RB* 1963, pp. 321 ff.

Although the Old Testament has no technical term to designate revelation, and marks no distinction between natural and supernatural revelation, the idea that God made Himself known by a special intervention on His part is attested very frequently and has been from early times. It may be said that prior to the book of Wisdom (13:1-9) the idea of man knowing God by reasoning has not been expressed. If man knows God, it is because God has manifested Himself to him : the origin of this knowledge is always due to an initiative of God.

Several different verbs are used to express this idea, especially *râ'âh* (= to see), *yâda'* (= to know), *gâlâh* (= to discover); there is the passive form : *nir'âh :* he has been seen, he made himself seen, he appeared (for example, Gn 12:7; 17:1; 48:3; Ex 3:16), the *Hiphîl* form : he made see (*her'âh*, for example, Ex 25:9; 27:8; Am 7:1.4, etc.); *nôda' :* he has been known, he has made himself known (for example Ex 6:3 : " I appeared [*wâ'êr'âh*] to Abraham, to Isaac, and to Jacob as El Sadday, but by my name of Yahweh I did not make myself known [*nôda'tî*] to them "; Is 19:21; Ez 20:5), which is likewise used in the *Hiphîl* form (*hôdî'a* = he has made himself known, for example, Ex 33:13; 1 Sm 16:3), *niglâh*, he has discovered himself, revealed himself (Gn 35:7; 1 Sm 2:27; 3:21). All these verbs signify that God made known that which man ignored, He revealed that which had been veiled (cf. Dt 29:28). Finally one designates very frequently the communications, which Yahweh makes, with the verbs " to speak " *(dibbêr)* and " to say " *('âmâr)* (for example, Ex 20:1; Am 2:4.6; 3:12, etc.), to which correspond these terms which express the perception of the divine word : *šâma'*, to hear, *râ'âh* and *ḥâzâh*, to see, *yâda'*, to know.

The means by which, according to the Old Testament, God revealed Himself or made known His plans and His will, are diverse :

theophanies, angels, oracles, dreams, prophets, spirit, word, divine works are again and again mentioned, without speaking of His acts in the history of Israel. But, in proportion to their age and their milieu of origin, these texts describe sometimes such means, sometimes others, so that we ascertain a certain evolution of the belief by the means which God used to reveal Himself, although the idea itself of revelation has hardly changed in the course of the centuries.

§ 2. *Theophanies*

J. Hänel, *Das Erkennen Gottes bei den Schriftpropheten*, Stuttgart 1923; F. Nötscher, *Das Angesicht Gottes schauen*, Würzburg 1924.

The term signifies "apparition of God," but is used to designate a manifestation of God perceptible by the senses, be it under a human form, or in some grandiose and terrifying phenomena of nature.

Although from long ago it had been believed and professed that man cannot see God and live (Gn 32:31; Ex 24:10.11; 33:20; Jgs 6:22; 13:22; Is 6:4; cf. Ex 3:6; 20:19; Dt 4:33; 3 Kgs 19:13), the tradition has conserved some old accounts of visible manifestations of God. Yahweh appeared under human form to Abraham near the terebinths of Mamre (Gn 18), and probably on several other occasions (Gn 12:7; 15:18; 17:1), to Isaac (Gn 26:2), and to Jacob (Gn 32:25-31; 35:9). Similarly it is certainly under human form that Yahweh is presented as speaking and acting familiarly with Adam and Eve in the garden of Eden (Gn 3:8-24) and with Noe (Gn 6:13; 7:16), although no verb signifying a real apparition is used in these passages.

If, as it is probable, the angel of Yahweh is only a sensible manifestation of Yahweh Himself, we must group, without doubt, the apparitions of that mysterious being with the theophanies. In two cases, the angel of Yahweh [1] is described as a man (Jgs 6:11 ff.; 13:3 ff.; Gn 18; 19; Jos 5:13). It is probable that he must be conceived in the same way in other accounts, where Yahweh and His angel are identified (Gn 16:10 ff.; 21:17 ff.; 31:11-13; Nm 22:31-35; Jgs 2:1-4). Already in these passages Yahweh no longer appears in person, but manifests Himself under a sensible form which is called His angel; there is here an effort to present the sensible apparitions of God in a less anthropomorphic manner.

The traditions which report the theophanies of Sinai are divergent: according to Ex 33:20-23 Moses could not see the face of Yahweh,

[1] Cf. above II, § 6, A, 2 b.

because " man cannot see God and live "; this is why Yahweh covered His face with His hand, until His glory had passed, so that Moses saw only Yahweh's back. In the first theophany (Ex 3:1 ff.), although it is said that the angel of Yahweh appeared to him (v. 2; cf. 3:16; 4:5 : Yahweh appeared), it seems that Moses saw only the flame which burned without consuming the bush. [2] And according to Ex 3:6, which probably belongs to a different source, Moses hides his face when God speaks to him. The most ancient traditions underline, therefore, the holiness of Yahweh, with whom no man, without danger, may enter into contact, not even by sight.

Similarly the order to purify the people (Ex 19:10; cf. Nm 11:18; Jos 3:5; 7:13) and to keep them away from the holy mountain, under pain of death (Ex 19:12.13.21-24; 34:3), sheds vivid light on the holiness of God whose words the people do not dare to hear directly, out of fear of death (Ex 20:19; cf. Dt 5:22). Finally, when Yahweh comes down to the mountain in the midst of fire, smoke, lightnings, earthquakes (Ex 19:18), with peals of thunder and trumpet blasts, wrapped in clouds (Ex 19:16; 20:18), the people perceived only those terrifying phenomena which accompanied the theophany.

Other traditions, on the contrary, admit that Moses, Aaron, Nadab, Abiu and seventy elders " saw God, " without being struck down by death, and on the holy mountain partook of a sacred meal sealing the covenant (Ex 24:9-11), or at least, that Moses saw the figure of Yahweh who spoke to him mouth to mouth (Nm 12:8; Ex 33:11), in contrast with the prophets, to whom God manifested Himself only in visions and in dreams (Nm 12:6-8; Dt 34:10). Similarly, according to Dt 4:12.15, the people heard the words which Yahweh spoke to them from the midst of the fire, but saw no figure, and Yahweh " spoke with them face to face on the mountain " (Dt 5:4), that is to say, without interpreter, or spoke to them from the height of heaven (Ex 20:22). It is even said (Nm 14:14) that Yahweh is in the midst of His people and appears *(nir'êh)* " eye to eye, " that is to say, directly, without intermediary. Without doubt, the expressions to speak " face to face " or " mouth to mouth " and to appear " eye to eye, " do not necessarily imply a corporal vision; they designate rather an immediate perception, [3] but it remains, nevertheless, that these texts attribute to the people a direct perception of the divine word

[2] The verb *nir'âh*, to be seen, to appear, is often used in a diminished sense, which by no means signifies a corporal vision; thus in the passages where Yahweh " appears " in a cloud (Lev 16:2) or in the sanctuary (Lev 9:6.23; Num 16:19), cf. F. Nötscher, *Das Angesicht Gottes schauen*, pp. 24, 31.

[3] Cf. F. Nötscher, *op. cit.*, p. 23.

and of God's presence, which is not implied in the accounts of Ex 19:12-24; 20:19; 33:20-23; 34:3.

At first sight one might be tempted to consider the traditions of the second group as the most ancient, because they admit theophanies in which the person or the voice of God are perceived by the senses. But it is Deuteronomy, which underlines the fact that the people heard the words of Yahweh; the passage of Nm 12:6-8, which attributes to Moses, in order to put him above the prophets, the privilege of having seen the figure of God, seems to be rather recent; this is certain for the remarkable finale of Dt 34:10 which derives from Nm 12:6-8; the text of Nm 14:14 seems to be a gloss. [4] The account of Ex 24:9-11, finally, will perhaps glorify the first high priest, the elders and the priesthood by associating them with the conclusion of the covenant; [5] this would be an indication for a rather recent date.

Be that as it may, no account describes the figure of Yahweh; mention is made only of " the figure *(temûnâh)* of Yahweh " (Nm 12:8) without giving any details about it or of His entourage. Thus Ex 24:9-11 describes only the sapphire tilework, as clear as the sky, on which the God of Israel was standing. In the theophany accorded to Elias (3 Kgs 19:9 ff.) Yahweh announces that He will pass before the prophet (v. 11); but Elias sees no figure; hearing the murmur of a gentle breeze which revealed to him the presence of God, he wraps his face in his mantle and perceives the words pronounced by God. Similarly Isaias (6:1 ff.), who sees the Lord seated on His throne, says nothing of His aspect, but speaks only of the train of His garment, of the Seraphim who surround Him, and of the smoke that filled the temple. Ezechiel (1:4-2:9) who expatiates gladly on the light, the fire, the Cherubim, the chariot, the firmament, the throne of Yahweh, speaks only hesitatingly of the human figure which apparently was seated on the throne. [6] Only Daniel (7:9.10) describes God as the " Ancient One, " clothed in white, seated on a throne of fire. Let us also remember that in the cases of Isaias, Ezechiel and Daniel we deal with visions, not with theophanies.

All traditions relative to the revelation of Sinai report grandiose and terrifying phenomena in which Yahweh manifested Himself to the people : they mention peals of thunder, lightnings, flames, smoke, dense clouds, trumpet blasts (Ex 19:16; 20:18), earthquake, fire, smoke

---

[4] A. H. MacNeile, *The Book of Numbers*, Cambridge 1911, *in h.l.*

[5] P. Heinisch (*Das Buch Exodus*, Bonn 1934, p. 159) attributes this passage to a later redactor *(Bearbeiter)*. Among the critics, some attribute it to J, others to E or to E'; Eissfeldt to L (*Hexateuchsynopse*, p. 152). G. Gressmann considers it to be very old (*Mose und seine Zeit*, Göttingen 1913, p. 182).

[6] Cf. I, § 7, pp. 49 ff.

(Ex 19.18), a cloud and the glory of Yahweh that covered the mountain as if with fire (Ex 24:16.17).

The cloud plays a very important role, in the accounts of the book of Exodus, as a sensible manifestation of the presence of Yahweh. Under the form of a column of cloud in the daytime and as a column of fire at night, the cloud serves as guide for the Israelite tribes in their peregrinations (Ex 13:21.22; 14:19.24, J; Nm 14:14; Dt 1:33; cf. Neh 9:12.19; Ps 78:14). Or it appears at certain moments, standing at the entrance to the sacred tent, when Moses entered there to receive communications from God (Ex 33:9.10; Nm 11:25; 12:5, E; Dt 31:15; Ps 99:7). At the inauguration of the meeting tent and of the temple, the cloud covered the tent and the temple, while the glory of God filled the dwelling, hindering Moses from entering (Ex 40:34.35, P; 3 Kgs 8:10.11). According to other texts, whenever the cloud reposed on the tent, the tribes remained in their place; whenever " the cloud rose from the dwelling " they set out on their journey. In the daytime the cloud was nebulous, whereas at night it took on the appearance of fire (Ex 40:34-38, P; Nm 9:15-22; 10:11.12). The cloud, therefore, is the symbol of Yahweh guiding His people, speaking to them, or protecting them.

As it was believed that in the beginnings of Israel Yahweh had appeared in the desert, and in particular on Mount Sinai, so they hoped that He would manifest Himself anew at the end of times in favor of His people. And the future restoration of Israel as well as the final judgment of the nations are often described by the prophets as the renewal of theophanies to which the chosen people owed its formation (Is 4:5.6, cf. Ex 40:34-38; Is 24:21-23, cf. Ex 24:9-11; Is 30:27, cf. Ex 19:16; Is 40:5, cf. Ex 24:16.17; Is 52:8.12, cf. Ex 24:9-11; 13:21.22; Jer 31:1-3; cf. Nm 14:14).

§ 3. *The angels*

God frequently makes known His orders or plans, not by appearing in person, but by sending an intermediary, a messenger charged with transmitting divine communications to men: this messenger is called the angel of Yahweh or simply an angel. Still it seems necessary to make a distinction between the angel of Yahweh or of God, who is to be identified with God Himself (Gn 16:10 ff.; 21:17 ff.; 22:11 ff.; 31:11 ff.; Ex 3:2 ff.; Jgs 2:1 ff.; 6:11 ff.; 13:3 ff.;

perhaps Ex 23:20-22) and the angel of Yahweh who is distinct from Yahweh.[1] When he is to be identified with Yahweh, we are dealing with a theophany. Here we shall consider only cases where the divine messenger is clearly distinct from the one who sends him.

Of the "three men" who appeared to Abraham (Gn 18), two are quite clearly angels distinct from Yahweh; they warned Lot of the danger of being in Sodom (Gn 19). This is also true of the angel whom God promised would assist Abraham's servant (Gn 24:7.40; cf. 48:16), or His people (Nm 20:16; Ex 32:34; 33:2; cf. Is 63:9, LXX; Jos 5:13), of the angels who would protect the just (3 Kgs 19:5.7; Ps 34:8; 91:11.12; Dan 6:23; Jdt 13:20; Tb 5:17-22; 12:12.15) and of the angel of Yahweh who played the role of the great vizier of the heavenly King (Ez 9:2; Za 1:8 ff.; 3:1 ff.).

In pre-exilic texts angels rarely intervened as messengers bringing communications from God to the prophets (3 Kgs 13:18); however, in later times this role is frequently attributed to them (Za 1:9; 2:3; 3:6; 4:1 ff.; Dan 14:33 ff., Vulg.). In the Greek Apocalypse of Baruch, an angel led the seer through the heaven and revealed divine secrets to him (1:8, etc.); on many occasions it was an angel who explained to the prophet the meaning of his visions (Dn 8:18; 9:21; 10:18; Hen 14:25; 15:1 ff.; 60:4 ff.; Jubil. 1:27 ff.; 32:21 ff.; Slav. Hen. 22:11 ff., etc.).

§ 4. *Oracles*

J. Döller, *Die Wahrsagerei im A. T.*, Münster 1923; F. Küchler, *Das priesterliche Orakel in Israel und Juda* (*Festschrift Baudissin*, Giessen 1918, pp. 285-301); R. Press, "Das Ordal im A. T.," *ZAW*, 1933, pp. 227-231; J. Begrich, "Das priesterliche Heilsorakel," *ZAW*, 1934, pp. 81-92; E. Sellin, "Efod und Terafim," *JPOS*, 1934, pp. 185 ff.; *id.*, *ZAW*, 1937, pp. 296-298; K. Budde, "Ephod und Lade," *ZAW*, 1921, p. 142; G. Hoffmann-A. Gressmann, "Teraphim," *ZAW*, 1922, pp. 25-136; H. Thiersch, *Ependytes und Ephod*, Stuttgart 1936; Cf. R. de Vaux, *RB*, pp. 296-298; H. G. May, "Ephod and Ariel," *AJSL*, 1939, pp. 44-69; N. Greitemann, "Efod," *BW*, cols. 348-349; A. R. G. Kennedy, "Urim and Thummim," *HDB*, IV, pp. 838-841; G. F. Moore, "Urim and Thummim," *EB*, IV, cols. 5235-5237; *id.*, "Ephod," *EB*, II, cols. 1306-1309; *id.*, "Teraphim," *EBm*, IV, cols. 4974 ff.; J. Morgenstern, *The Ark, the Ephod and the Tent of Meeting*, Cincinnati 1946.

1. *Oracles and divination.* — Like all peoples of antiquity, the Hebrews were always trying to discover future events, the result of an enterprise or some secret things by questioning God. Two verbs are often used to express the asking of a question of Yahweh: *šā'al*, to question

[1] Cf. above II, § 6, A, 2 b.

(Nm 27:21; Jgs 1:1; 20:18.23.27; 1 Sm 10:22; 14:37; 22:10.13.15; 23:9-12; 28:6; 30:8; 2 Sm 2:1; 5:19.23; Os 4:12; Ag 2:11) and *dâraš*, to seek, to consult (Gn 25:22; Ex 18:15; 1 Sm 9:9; 4 Kgs 22:18; Ps 34:5, etc.). Many and varied are the ways of obtaining an oracle, that is to say, an answer from God. But those who try to wrest a secret from the divinity, those who consult the dead (1 Sm 28:3.9) or other gods than Yahweh (4 Kgs 1:2-3), are reproved and condemned: divination (*qâsâm*, *niḥâš*, *'ônên*, the use of the *'ôb* and *tĕrâphîm*), necromancy and magic were severely forbidden by the law (Ex 22:17; Lev 19:26.31; 20:27; Dt 18:10.11), condemned by the prophets (1 Sam 15:23; Os 4:12; Is 8:19; Mi 5:11; Jer 27:9; 29:8; Ez 13:18-20), and prohibited by certain kings (1 Sm 28:3.9; 4 Kgs 23:24); all practice of magic was censured as a Canaanite custom which was an abomination to Yahweh (Dt 18:9-14).

Therefore the Old Testament makes a very sharp distinction between legitimate prophecies, either cultic or private, and the cultic prophecies of neighboring peoples and popular divination. Magic is always at the root of popular divination. Much of the cult of the ancient East was magic, or at least was tainted with magic. The diviner pronounced his oracle by his own power, by his higher intuition, by his art, or by the use of objects or rites which men held to be infallible in themselves or capable of constraining gods or demons; when questioned he is always in a position to give an answer. On the contrary the Israelite priest and prophet knew that no oracle could be obtained unless Yahweh consented. The Hebrew knew that he depended on His God; when he questioned Him, he awaited an answer from His goodness and kindness; he did not try to wrest it from Him; he asked for it (1 Sm 14:36-42; Gn 24:12-14; Jer 42:4), for Yahweh does not allow Himself to be constrained and is able to refuse to answer (1 Sm 14:36.37; 28:6; 4 Kgs 4:27; Ez 20:3). The prophets especially express this sentiment, for example, when they compare themselves to watchmen (Is 21:6.8), on the look-out for God's word (Ez 3:16.17; 33:7; Hb 2:1), or when they pray to obtain it (Jer 42:4), and declare that Yahweh wakens their ears (Is 50:4; cf. 5:9; 1 Sm 9:15; 2 Sm 7:27). We shall have more to say about this later.

2. *Sacerdotal oracle.* [1] — The sacerdotal oracle is pronounced by a priest and is one of the oldest forms. To pronounce an oracle is one of the priest's principal functions (Dt 33:8): just as counseling

---

[1] A. R. Johnson, *The Cultic Prophet in Ancient Israel*, 1944; A. Haldar, *Associations of the Cult Prophets, among the Ancient Semites*, 1945, cited by J. Pedersen, *Studies in O. T. Prophecy*, 1950, p. 130; G. Ostborn, *Tôrâ in the O. T.*, cited by N. W. Porteous, *Studies in O. T. Prophecy*, p. 148, n. 1.

is the specific work of the wise man, preaching that of the prophet, and making decisions *(tôrâh)* that of the priest (Jer 18:18; cf. Dt 33:10). Whether the word *tôrâh* is to be explained by the root *yârâh*, to cast, understood in the sense of "to cast lots," that is to say, to decide by lot (cf. Jos 18:6), [2] or by the root *yârâh* (*Hiph. hôrâh;* cf. Ex 24:12) to teach, [3] or by the Babylonian word *tertu*, revelation, presage, [4] it designates in any case an authoritative decision settling a doubtful case (cf. Ag 2:11-13; Jer 2:8).

Moses had earlier issued oracles to those "who were seeking Yahweh" in "the meeting tent" (Ex 33:7-11), that is to say in the sanctuary, where Yahweh met Moses and spoke to him; He settled the differences of those who came "to consult God," and "made known God's decrees and decisions" (*tôratâyw*, Ex 18:15.16). Likewise, according to Dt 17:8-12, serious lawsuits had to be taken to the sanctuary before the levitical priests, whose sentence had to be accepted without qualification under pain of death.

Beginning with the period of the Judges there are many examples of oracles given by priests (Jgs 18:5.6). Although the priest is not mentioned in Jgs 1:1; 20:18.23.27, it is certain that cultic oracles are meant, because they were obtained at Bethel, the center of the ancient cult, before Yahweh (20:18.26); a glossator even believed that the cultic acts, the sacrifices, and the oracles that took place at Bethel were justified because of the presence of the Lord's ark of the covenant and Pinhas, Aaron's grandson. On many occasions Saul and David consulted God through the mediation of the priest (1 Sm 14:18.37; 22:10; 23:2.9-12; 28:6; 30:7.8); in some cases (2 Sm 2:1; 5:19.23; 21:1) the text alludes simply to a consulting of Yahweh without any further details; but it is probable that a sacerdotal oracle is meant. [5]

The priest questioned Yahweh by the *'ûrîm* and the *tummîm* (Dt 33:8; cf. Esd 2:63), objects which are connected with the *'êphôd.* The meaning of these words, the nature, form and use of these objects are not known. [6] Sometimes the *'ûrîm* is named alone (Nm 27:21;

---

[2] J. Wellhausen, *Reste Arabischen Heidentums* [2], Berlin 1927, p. 143.

[3] W. Baudissin, *Kyrios*, III, p. 436, n. 2; L. Köhler, *Lexikon*, p. 1023.

[4] P. Dhorme, *La religion Assyro-Babylonienne* [2], Paris 1910, p. 298.

[5] The priest, the giver of oracles, may be compared to "the respondent," that is to say, to the cult prophet who gives oracles in the name of the gods Adad of Kallassu and Adad of Alep to the Babylonian king Zimri-Lim, according to a Mari tablet, edited by G. Dossin and commented on by A. Lods, *Studies in Old Testament Prophecy*, Edinburgh 1950, pp. 103-110. The text of this oracle closely resembles several biblical oracles (for example, 1 Sm 12:13-15; 13:7-15; 28:18; 2 Sm 3:9.10.18; 5:2; 7:14-16.18-29, etc.).

[6] The LXX translated *'ûrîm* by δήλωσις, δῆλοι, *tummîm* by ἀλήθεια, ὁσιότης; they were thinking of the root *'ôr*, meaning to become clear, luminous, and *tmm*, meaning

1 Sm 28:6); this is perhaps merely an abbreviation. According to Dt 33:8 oracles by *'ûrîm* and *tummîm* could be given only by Levi and his descendants, that is to say, by priests; according to Ex 28:30; Lv 8:8; Nm 27:21, these objects were kept in the container affixed to the *'êphôd* which rested on the high priest's chest.

The text of 1 Sm 14:41, preserved in the LXX version, in the Old Latin and in the Vulgate versions, [7] indicates that this mode of consulting Yahweh was by alternative. If the *'ûrîm* was drawn, it meant a certain solution; if the *tummîm* was drawn, it meant the opposite. Usually the question was phrased in such a way that the answer could be given by yes or no. [8] Therefore critics have concluded that the *'ûrîm* and the *tummîm* were two little sticks, or little pebbles of different color, or marked with different signs, perhaps a *tau* for the *tummîm*, or an *aleph* for *'ûrîm*, and that this method of questioning God belonged to the category of oracles by lot, which were widely used by many ancient peoples, for example Arabs, Babylonians, Hebrews. In Israel the sacred lot served to make known Yahweh's decisions (1 Sm 10:19-21; Prv 16:32; Acts 1:26), to disclose a culprit (Jos 7:12-18; 1 Sm 14:38-42; Jon 1:7), to allot parts (Jos 18:1-20; 19). Divination by arrows (Ez 21:26.27) and perhaps by " the wood " (Os 4:12) [9] seem to belong to the same category. Consulting Yahweh by *'ûrîm* and *tummîm* is no longer mentioned after the age of David. Ezr 2:63 (=Neh 7:65) shows that this method was no longer the custom after the exile.

The ephod *('êphôd)* is no less mysterious [10] than the *'ûrîm* and the

---

to be perfect, pure. The Vulgate translates *'ûrîm* by *doctrina, demonstratio, ostensio, doctus,* and *tummîm* by *veritas, perfectio, sanctitas, perfectus, eruditus.* No etymology satisfies.

[7] " If this guilt is in me or in Jonathan, my son, O Yahweh, God of Israel, give *'ûrîm*; but if this guilt is in Your people Israel, give *tummîm.* "

[8] However some questions required an answer that was neither yes nor no; for example 2 Sm 2:1; 5:23.24. This supposes that in these cases another method was applied.

[9] Os 4:12 : " My people consult their block of wood, and their staff gives them oracles, " may mean an oracle by lot in which little sticks were used, if the accent is placed on " staff, " to which " wood " would be parallel; but it could also mean an oracle by a sacred tree, as in 2 Sm 5:24 (cf. the oak of the diviners, Jgs 9:37; the terebinth of the seer — More, Dt 11:30; Gn 12:6), if the accent is placed on wood, understood in the sense of tree; the staff might denote a rod that would give a divine answer by flowering (Nm 17:16-24).

[10] The meaning and etymology of this word are not known; the LXX usually translate ἐπωμίς or keep the word (ἐφοῦδ); the Vulgate calls it *superhumerale.* It seems that a distinction should be made between the linen ephod *('êphôd bad)* with which one girded *(hâgar)* oneself for the sacred service (1 Sm 2:18; 2 Sm 6:14) and which seems to have been a fairly short loin cloth (cf. 2 Sm 6:20), from the ephod of the high priest (Ex 28:6-12; 39:2-7), which was apparently a kind of scapular made of some precious fabric to which was affixed the case containing the *'ûrîm* and *tummîm* (Ex 28:30; Lv 8:8). On several occasions mention is made of an ephod which was carried by a priest as a transportable object, not worn as a garment

tummîm with which it is associated in certain texts (Ex 28:30; Lv 8:8). The relationship of these objects is difficult to discover. All that can safely be said is that they were used to obtain answers from God (1 Sm 14:18, LXX; 23:9-12; 30:7-8), and that they were the oracle objects characteristic of priests (Dt 33:8; 1 Sm 22:18, where priests are said to be " men who wear the ephod "; cf. 1 Sm 23:6; 3 Kgs 2:26). [11] Further than that, nothing is known about the nature, the form and the handling of the oracle ephod. The solid ephod (statue?) and the oracle ephod are mentioned only from the time of the Judges; they are part of the official cult because the ephod is preserved in the temple of Nob (1 Sm 21:10), and the oracle ephod, if it is to be distinguished from the precedent, is in the hands of the official priest. Osee (3:4) included it among the cult objects that the people considered indispensable.

The *těrâphîm* [12] (considered as a singular or a plural noun) are associated in several places with the ephod (Jgs 17:5; 18:14-20; Os 3:4) and are also cult objects used in securing oracles (Ez 21:26; Za 10:2). They are to be found in some local sanctuaries (Jgs 17:5; 18:14-20), in the national cult (Os 3:4), and in private homes (Gn 31:19; 1 Sm 19:13). In fact Laban called them his gods (Gn 31:30.32) and it may be concluded from 1 Sm 19:13-16 that they were probably statues in human form. [13] It is not known how oracles were given by the teraphim. In several texts they are condemned as cult objects of foreign origin (Gn 35:2-4) or tainted with superstition (1 Sm 15:23; Za 10:2; 4 Kgs 23:24). They were excluded from official worship at the time of the deuteronomic reform (4 Kgs 23:24; cf. Dt 18:10.11), yet they did not disappear from popular religion (Za 10:2).

(1 Sm 22:18, where the verb *nâšâ'* is used; *bad* is a gloss, cf. LXX, B; 23:6.9; 14:3.18, LXX). This ephod was used in giving oracles (1 Sm 14:18, LXX; 23:9-12; 30:7-8) and is sometimes associated with the *těrâphîm*, which were also divining instruments (Jgs 17:5; 18:14; Os 3:4; cf. Ez 21:26; Za 10:2). In a Ras Shamra text (Syria 1934, p. 303), *těrâphîm* and *'êphôd* are the price of victory over Lotan (Leviathan); but the nature of these objects is not made very clear. What is the relation between the ephod used in giving oracles and the ephod worn as a garment? Is the oracle ephod identical with the solid ephod referred to in Jgs 8:26.27; 17:4.5; 18:14-20; 1 Sm 21:10? Is it a statue, sometimes in precious metal (Jgs 8:27; perhaps Jgs 17:5), or a box, or something else? Hypotheses are numerous and debatable.

[11] In 3 Kgs 2:26 the MT has : " You bore the ark of Lord Yahweh before David "; but it is probable that *'ârôn* was substituted for *'êphôd*, as in 1 Sm 14:18; Abiathar carried the *'êphôd* before David (1 Sm 23:6.9; 30:7), not the ark.

[12] The plural form is no proof that there were several objects. It might be a plural of intensity like Elohim, or a nominative singular with mimation.

[13] H. Gressmann *(loc. cit.)* and others speak of a mask used in giving oracles; W. Emery Barnes (*JTS*, 1929, p. 178) thinks of fetishes, divinities or tutelary deities meant to protect the house; they were placed near the sick bed to drive away demons and spells.

It is probable that the priests gave their oracles at the time of the sacrifices which devout Israelites in their troubles offered in the temple. A psalmist (Ps 5:4), at grips with a treacherous and fierce foe, seems to allude to this custom: "To You, I pray, O Lord, at dawn You hear my voice; at dawn I bring my plea expectantly before You." At the hour of the morning sacrifice, the psalmist goes to the temple (v. 8) and there makes his offerings; there he waits until the priest gives him Yahweh's answer.[14] Some liturgical psalms seem to have preserved examples of oracles obtained in the temple (Ps 20:7; 21:9-13; 60:8-10; 75:3.4.10).

We do not know how the priest discovered the divine answer when offering sacrifice; but it is certain that from signs which are not known to us it was believed that it was possible to learn whether or not the sacrifice was pleasing to Yahweh (Gn 4:3-5). Did the priest deduce God's answer from certain omens (Nm 24:1; Gn 15:11), from the behavior of the animal offered in sacrifice, or from an examination of the liver, as was done in Babylon and elsewhere? We do not know. Only once in the Old Testament is mention made of an examination of the liver (Ez 21:26); and this process is attributed to the Babylonian king. Hepatoscopy was widespread in ancient religions, as can be seen from the fact that texts and facsimiles of livers which were used in the education of Babylonian, Hittite and Etruscan diviners have been discovered in those regions.[15]

3. *Private foretelling*, that is to say, foretelling that is independent of public worship, includes the interpretation of dreams, the interrogation of Yahweh through the services of a prophet or seer; of this we will speak later. Here we will content ourselves with the mention of certain practices which are based on a profound faith in God's providence, and other practices which, on the contrary, are part of popular divination.

To the first category belongs the method that specifies in advance some definite sign, which, if it takes place, is considered to be Yahweh's answer: thus Abraham's servant asks Yahweh to show by a sign, which he describes, which young girl is destined to become the wife of his master's son. The sign he had selected was that the young girl would

---

[14] The verb *'ârak* is often used in reference to the preparation of a sacrifice (for example, Gn 22:9; 3 Kgs 18:33; Lv 1:7.8.12) and the verb *ṣippâh* is used in reference to the prophet awaiting the divine word (cf. Ez 3:17; 33:2.6.7; Mi 7:4; Is 21:6 ff.; cf. F. Küchler, *loc. cit.*, p. 295). The same author also calls attention to the sacrifices which were prepared for the oracles of Balaam (Nm 23:1-5.14-16.29.30), who was seeking an omen (Nm 24:1).

[15] See figures 108, 109 and 110 in A. Jeremias, *Handbuch der altorientalischen Geisteskultur*, Leipzig 1913, pp. 144 ff.

give him a drink of water and then would give water to his camels This she did and revealed Yahweh's choice (Gn 24:12-27; cf. 24:27; 50:51). In the same way Jonathan specified the sign by which he would know whether Yahweh would grant him a victory over the Philistines : he decided that if the Philistine guard, when seeing them, invited his servant and himself to advance toward them, Yahweh would make him victorious; but if the guard ordered the two men to halt, then the Israelites would be defeated. When the first hypothesis was fulfilled, Jonathan, followed by his servant, attacked them and slaughtered many in the enemy's camp (1 Sm 14:8-15). Sometimes a chance happening was interpreted as a sign from Yahweh (1 Sm 24:1-5; 25:18-32; 26:2-8), because they felt that nothing takes place unless Yahweh has so willed and arranged (Am 3:6; Gn 27:20; 42:28; Ex 21:13).

Another form of popular divination consisted in obtaining oracles from trees, especially from sacred trees, whose murmuring was interpreted as a divine response (2 Sm 5:24), or whose deep shadows served as a dwelling for a seer who uttered oracles, for example the terebinth of More, near Sichem (Gn 12:6; Dt 11:30), and the oak of the diviners (Jgs 9:37) in the same locality. Worship given these sacred trees was condemned by the prophets (Is 1:29 and perhaps Os 4:12). [16]

Necromancy was practiced in every period of the history of Israel (Is 8:19; 65:4; 4 Kgs 21:6). A vivid description of one such scene is given in 1 Sm 28. It was also popular in Egypt (Is 19:3) and in Canaan (Dt 18:9 ff.), although it was contrary to the law (Lv 19:31; Dt 18:11); it was forbidden by some kings (1 Sm 28:3.9; 4 Kgs 23:24), and reproved by the prophets (Is 8:19).

Finally, in Egypt, Babylon and Assyria a cup was used to draw oracles. This mode of divination was known in Israel (Gn 44:5); but there is no evidence that it was commonly used there. Twigs or small pieces of metal were dropped into a cup filled with water, their position in the cup provided an omen; or else a few drops of oil were poured in the water and their circumvolutions were believed to reveal the future or secret things.

[16] Cf. the footnote 10 in this section : on the etymology of the word ephod.

§ 5. *Dreams*

Von Orelli, " Träume bei den Hebräern, " *PRE*, XX, pp. 13-15; F. B. Jevons, " Dream, " *HDB*, I, pp. 622 ff.; " Dreams and Sleep, " *ERE*, V, pp. 28-40.

Dreams are usually purely psychophysiological phenomena, but they may be produced by God's special intervention on man's sense faculties. The ancients and peoples of inferior culture do not usually make this distinction (cf. however Sir 34:5-7), look on dreams as revelations of the future or of hidden things and as real events in which the soul of a sleeping man comes in contact with the world of gods or demons, or perceives realities which escape a man awake. Like most of the ancient people, the Hebrews admitted that in dreams God communicated to His servants a knowledge of the future (Gn 37:5-10; 40; 41; Jgs 7:13.14; 1 Sm 28:6.15; Dn 2:1; 4:2; Est 10:5; 11:5-12, Vulg.), or warnings (Gn 20:3; 31:11-13.24; Jb 7:14; 33:15-18; Wis 18:17), or the revelation of things unknown (Gn 28:12-15; Jb 4:12-21), or promises (3 Kgs 3:5-14).

According to Nm 12:6 dreams and visions were the usual means in which God revealed Himself to the prophets. In fact Dt 13:2 considered prophets to be synonymous with dreamers. Yet, if the great prophets spoke frequently of their visions, they did not seem to make much of their dreams (Jer 23:25-27; 27:9.10; Is 29:7.8). Only the later prophets (Dn 7:1; Jl 3:1) and the authors of the various Apocalypses appealed to the dreams by which God communicated His revelations to them. Dreams must be distinguished from visions or nocturnal auditions (for example, Gn 15:12; 1 Sm 3; Za 1:8), which are perceived while awake.

Greater importance, of course, was attached to dreams in ancient times [1]; it was then believed that they contained light about the future or divine communications. But even in those days it was recognized that the interpretation of dreams could be trusted only if it came from God (Gn 40:8; 41:16; cf. Dn 2:28), and that it had authority and truth only when it was inspired by " the spirit of God " (Gn 41:38; cf. Dn 4:5.6.15; 5:11.14). The Babylonians (Dn 2:2; 4:3; 5:15), the Egyptians (Gn 41:8), the Greeks and other peoples had official dream interpreters who were often priests, yet there is no trace in the Old Testament of such professional diviners, even though they certainly

[1] Critics attribute to the Elohist all the passages of Gn and Jgs 7:13.14 where reference is made to dreams.

were to be found among the lower classes of the Israelite people just as in recent Judaism. They were condemned by the law with all the other magicians and diviners (Lv 19:26; Dt 18:10). The great prophets, from the eighth century to the Exile, showed marked distrust with regard to dreams, and Deuteronomy (13:2-4) warned the people against prophets and dreamers who sought by oracles and prodigies to turn them to other gods. Isaias (29:8) [2] points out the deceptive nature of dreams : " As when a hungry man dreams he is eating and awakens with an empty stomach, or when a thirsty man dreams he is drinking and awakens faint and dry, so shall the horde of all the nations be, who make war against Mount Sion. " Jeremias accuses " prophets who utter lying dreams " (23:26.32), in order to lead people astray with their tales. He does not deny that the dream can be a means of discovering divine communications, but he knows that it is subject to illusion and that many abused it : " Let the prophet who has a dream recount his dream; let him who has My word speak My word truthfully! What has straw to do with wheat? says Yahweh " (Jer 23:28). Jeremias obviously distrusts dreams and places far above them the word Yahweh communicates to His prophets.

The wise men were no less sceptical : " As though they were the dream of one who had awakened, O Lord, so will You, when You arise, set at nought these phantoms (the wicked) " (Ps 73:20); another psalmist describes the happiness of the captives who returned from Babylon, as a form of gladness exceeding all that they hoped for but never dared to believe existed, just as one dared not believe in images seen in a dream (Ps 126:1). Ecclesiastes (5:2) sees in dreams a vain agitation that disturbs sleep and is the result of many occupations. Finally Sirach (34:1-6) warns against dreams which are, like divinations and presages, vain things; but he acknowledges that they can be used by God : " Unless it be a vision specially sent by the Most High, fix not your heart on it " (v. 6).

In spite of all this, in recent Judaism a renewed belief in prophetic dreams is attested by the Apocrypha, Josephus (*Ant.* XVII, 6.4; *Bell. Jud.* II, 7.4; III, 8.3) and the Talmud. The art of interpreting dreams which was practiced by the Essenians (Josephus, *Ant.* XVII, 13.3), was also popular among the Jews. [3]

Some critics believe that they discovered in the Old Testament allusions to *incubatio*, that is to say, to the custom of spending a night

---

[2] Duhm, Cheyne, Marti and Procksch deny the authenticity of this verse which is accepted by Condamin, Guthe, Feldmann, Fischer and others.

[3] Cf. M. Gaster, " Divination (Jewish), " *ERE*, IV, p. 812; many references are given here.

in a sanctuary in order to obtain a divine oracle during a dream. It is possible that the Hebrews, like many other peoples of antiquity, did this. Yet the texts do not provide any proof. In fact whenever there is question of dreams or visions obtained in a sanctuary, there is no indication that the people concerned had any hope or intention of securing an oracle; on the contrary, the divine revelation came to them unexpectedly (Gn 15:12.17 ff.; 28:12-22; 46:1-4; 1 Sm 3; 3 Kgs 3:5-15); and in 1 Sm 21:8 no one knows why Doeg was " detained " in the sanctuary of Nob; he certainly obtained no oracle.

§ 6. *The prophets*

A. van Hoonacker, " De profeten, een maatschappelijke stand in Israel, " *Dietsche Warande en Belfort*, 1912, pp. 1-31; E. Tobac, *Les prophètes d'Israël*, 2 vols., Lierre-Malines 1919-1921; A. Condamin, " La mission surnaturelle des prophètes d'Israël, " *Études*, 118 (1909), pp. 5-32; *id.*, " Prophétisme israélite, " *DA*, IV, cols. 386-425; M. A. van den Oudenrijn, *De prophetiae charismate in populo israelitico libri quattuor*, Rome 1926; H. Juncker, *Prophet und Seher in Israel*, Trier 1927; E. Tobac-J. Coppens, *Les prophètes d'Israël*, Malines 1932; J. Chaine, *Introduction à la lecture des prophètes*, 2 vols., Paris 1932; E. Sellin, *Der alttestamentliche Prophetismus*, Leipzig 1912; A. Causse, *Les prophètes d'Israël et les religions de l'Orient*, Paris 1913; G. Hölscher, *Die Profeten*, Leipzig 1914; H. Gunkel, *Die Profeten*, Göttingen 1917; B. Duhm, *Israels Profeten* ^{2}, Tübingen 1922; J. Skinner, *Prophecy and Religion*, Cambridge 1922; H. W. Hertzberg, *Prophet und Gott*, Gütersloh 1923; J. Hänel, *Das Erkennen Gottes bei den Schriftpropheten*, Berlin 1923; E. Fascher, *Prophètes*, Giessen 1927; A. Lods, *Israël, des origines au milieu du VIIIe siècle*, Paris 1930; A. Jepsen, *Nabi*, Munich 1934; A. Lods-C. Guignebert, *Les prophètes d'Israël et les débuts du Judaïsme*, Paris 1935; J. Ridderbos, *Het Godswoord der Profeten*, 4 vols., Kampen 1930-41; F. Siegman, *The False Prophets of the O. T.*, Washington 1939; I. Seierstad, " Erlebnis und Gehorsam beim Prophet Amos, " *ZAW* 1934, pp. 22-41; H. W. Robinson, " The Psychology and Metaphysic of 'Thus saith Yahweh,' " *ZAW* 1924, pp. 1-15; N. W. Porteous, " Prophecy, " in H. W. Robinson, *Record and Revelation*, Oxford 1938, pp. 216-250; J. Hempel, " Prophet and Poet, " *JThS*, 40 (1939) pp. 113-132; J. Lindblom, " Die Religion der Propheten und die Mystik, " *ZAW* 1939, pp. 65-74; Y. Hoschander, *The Priests and the Prophets of the O. T.*, Washington 1939; A. Guillaume, *Prophecy and Divination among the Hebrew and other Semites*, London 1938; I. P. Seierstad, *Die Offenbarungserlebnisse der Propheten Amos, Jesaia und Jeremia*, Oslo 1946; S. Mowinckel, *Prophecy and Tradition*, Oslo 1946; A. van den Born, *Profetie metterdaad*, Roermond 1947; H. H. Rowley, " The Nature of O. T. Prophecy in the Light of Recent Study, " in *The Servant of the Lord and Other Essays on the O. T.*, London 1952, pp. 89 ff.; " Studies in Old Testament Prophecy, " to T. H. Robinson, Edinburgh 1950.

1. *Terminology.* — The word prophet comes from the Greek προφήτης, which in its turn comes from πρό and φημί, to speak. In this composite, the particle πρό does not have a temporal meaning (foretell), but a local one, to proffer a word. In classical language, a prophet is one who speaks, who makes a proclamation, he is a herald: the poet is the herald of the muses; the philosopher, the herald of nature. Yet the word is most often used in a religious sense: a prophet is the

herald of a god, he who proclaims the words of a god. Sometimes the word denotes the interpreter or the exegete of an oracle or a doctrine; rarely does it mean one who predicts the future. The Greeks referred to certain high-ranking Egyptian temple priests as prophets. In the same way the verb προφητεύω means to speak in the name of a god, to reveal something hidden, or to act as a herald; it is never used in the sense of predicting.

The LXX translated the Hebrew word *nabî'* by the word προφήτης, because, according to the opinion commonly held in Judaism, the nabi is Yahweh's herald, one who speaks in God's name. The etymology of the Hebrew word is uncertain: some derive it from the root *nb'*, to spring up, to flow; others from *nb'*, to proclaim (Akkadian: *nabû*, to proclaim, to name; Arabic: *naba'a*, to announce); and there are those who think that it was borrowed from the Akkadian *nabû*, which is also the name of the god of eloquence and divination. [1] The verb *nâbâ'*, which the LXX translated by προφητεύω, is used only in the *Niphal* and *Hithpael* forms; it is usually translated by to prophesy; but its primary meaning, just as that of προφητεύω, is not to predict. In the oldest texts, in the *Hithpael* form (1 Sm 10:5.6.10.13; 18:10; 19:20.21.23.24; 3 Kgs 18:29), as well as in the *Niphal* (1 Sm 10:11; 19:20), it means to be excited, to become furious or to go into a trance; later this meaning seems reserved to the *Hithpael* form (Nm 11:25-27; 3 Kgs 22:10 and often in Jeremias and Ezechiel), [2] while the *Niphal* means to announce, or to proclaim (Am 2:12; 3:8; 7:12.13.16; 3 Kgs 22:12; Jer 14:16; 20:6; 25:13; 26:20; 28:8, etc.; Ez 6:2; 13:2.16; 36:1, etc.). Lastly, after the Exile both forms of the verb are employed indifferently, in the sense of to proclaim (for example, 2 Par 20:37; Esd 5:1 : *hitnabbê'*; Jl 3:1; Za 13:3 : *hinnâbê'*). [3]

The meaning of the word *nabî'*, which the LXX translated by προφήτης, developed along a line more or less parallel to the word *nâbâ'*. At first it seems to have been reserved for enthusiasts who proclaimed Yahweh's praises, and it was applied to members of a profession, " the sons of the prophets " (Am 7:14; 3 Kgs 20:35, etc.).

---

[1] F. W. Albright (*From the Stone Age to Christianity*, pp. 231 ff.), derives the word from the Akkadian *nabû*, to call. This word is often applied to the king, " he whom the great gods have called, " whence comes *nibitû*, " called by the gods " (cf. *nabî'* = called, in the Code of Hammurabi). He concludes that the fundamental meaning of *nabî'* in Hebrew is " called by God, " one who has received a special mission from God. But if this is true, how could Amos (7:14) refuse this title, when he always insisted so much on his divine vocation?

[2] In Jer 29:26 the verb *mitnabbê'* is parallel to *měšugga'* which means to be insane; just as in 1 Sm 18:10 it denotes a crisis of morbid fury.

[3] This is the opinion of A. Jepsen, *Nabi*, p. 8.

Later it meant a herald of God, an envoy charged to proclaim God's word, a man who speaks in God's name: Jeremias (15:19) calls the *nabî'* "the mouth of Yahweh," and Ex 7:1.2 calls Aaron, the *nabî* (prophet) of Moses, because he announced to Pharao the words that Moses suggested to him (cf. Ex 4:16). This meaning is very clear in the account of the vocation of Jeremias (1:4-10): When Yahweh told him that He had chosen him from his mother's womb and made him a *nabî'* Jeremias cried out that he did not know how to speak, because he was a child. Whereupon Yahweh replied: "Say not: I am too young. Because you shall go to whomever I send you and you shall speak whatever I command you," then He stretched forth His hand and touched Jeremias' mouth, saying: "Behold I place My words in your mouth." Jeremias is made a nabi, because God gave him a mission and placed His words in the prophet's mouth. In the same sense God commanded Ezechiel (3:1-4) to eat a parchment scroll containing His words and added: "Go and speak to the house of Israel." Here the nabi is obviously Yahweh's herald who proclaims the words that God suggests to him. This is why all those are called prophets *(nĕbî'îm)* who, throughout the history of Israel, showed themselves to be heralds of Yahweh's words, from Moses (Dt 18:18; 34:10; cf. Os 12:14) [4] to Zacharias.

Most of them, nevertheless, did not give themselves this name; perhaps Osee (9:7.8) and probably Jeremias (1:5) and Ezechiel (2:5; 33:33) claimed it; while Amos (7:14) and Micheas (3:8) refused it. Isaias (37:2; 38:1) and Jeremias (28:5.6.10.12.15; 42:2; 43:6; 45:1) are called prophets by those who edited certain episodes of their life; Nahum, Habacuc, Aggeus and Zacharias were also given this name by those who collected their oracles.

A gloss added to a very old account (1 Sm 9:1-10.16) explains that in former times when men wanted to consult God, they would say: "Come, let us go to the seer." "For he who today is called a prophet *(nabî')*, used to be called a seer *(rô'eh)*" (v. 9). This remark seems to contain an accurate memory of an ancient custom. In fact, throughout the whole account, Samuel is constantly called the seer, or the man of God, and in this way he is clearly distinguished from the nabis. [5] On the contrary, in a more recent text (1 Sm 3:20), he

[4] Even Abraham is called *nabî'* (Gn 20:7), probably inasmuch as he is the favorite, the protégé of God (cf. Ps 105:15). Contrary to Dt 18:18; 34:10, the account of Nm 12:6.7 distinguishes sharply between prophets (nabis), to whom Yahweh revealed Himself in dreams and visions, and Moses to whom Yahweh "spoke face to face."

[5] An account (1 Sm 19:18b-24), probably of a later date and in an uncertain text (1 Sm 19:20), describes Samuel as "presiding" over a troup of "prophesying" prophets, but not taking part in the same transports. Although here Samuel is associated with the nabis, he is not considered to be one of them.

is called nabi. The two terms " seer " and " nabi " are used as synonyms after the days of Amos (7:12-14; Is 29:10; 30:10).

The seer *(rô'eh* or *ḥôzeh)* is one who " sees " what escapes other men (Is 30:10), is " the man whose eye is open, "[6] " who hears what God says, and knows the thought of the Most High, who sees the visions of Šadday, who faints but has his eyes uncovered " (Nm 24: 16.17). His word will certainly be fulfilled : " All that he says comes certainly to pass " (1 Sm 9:6); for he receives communications from Yahweh (9:15.17). Men turn to him when they wish " to consult God " (1 Sm 9:9), that is to say, to discover by means of an oracle something unknown (9:3-6) or something in the future; and a gift is offered him as the price for his answer (9:7.8; Nm 22:7; 3 Kgs 14:3; 4 Kgs 8:8; Mi 3:5.11). Samuel, " the seer, " played an important role in his town's worship (1 Sm 9:12; cf. 10:8) and presided over the sacrificial meal (9:13); he anointed Saul as king and predicted three signs which were in fact fulfilled (1 Sm 10:1-13). According to a more recent account, he offered a sacrifice to obtain victory (1 Sm 7:8.9), and ordered the sacred lots to be drawn by which Saul was named king (1 Sm 10:17-25). Was it because he was a seer that Samuel's part in worship was important, or was it because of his connection since childhood with the temple of Silo? The second hypothesis is no less likely than the first, because one of the priest's principal functions had always been to give oracles (Dt 33:8; Ex 33:7-11) to those who came " to question God. " On the other hand, it is probable that in addition to the priests, none of whom were formally called " seer " in the ancient texts, there were men, not connected with the cult personnel, who gave oracles (cf. Gn 25:23; Jos 8:14; Jgs 1:1). In ancient times they were called seers.

2. *Professional prophets.* — In ancient times the word *nâbi'* denoted a social class that was composed of men who were nabis by profession. That is why Amos (7:10-16) refused this title. When he announced the destruction of the Bethel sanctuary and of Jeroboam's dynasty, the priest of the royal temple drove him out disdainfully : " Off with you, visionary, flee to the land of Juda. There earn your bread by prophesying. " In other words, he told him to ply his trade of prophet in his own country. The priest spoke to Amos as a prophet who " prophesied " to gain a living. Amos cried out : " I am no nabi,

[6] The meaning of the word *šětum* is doubtful. The Vulgate and several interpreters translate it as " closed "; they understand it of the bodily eye which is deprived of its power in ecstasy. In Nm 24 Balaam is described as an ecstatic; the spirit of God is upon him (v. 2); he falls into catalepsy (v. 4 and 16; cf. 1 Sm 19:24) and his inner eye is open to perceive the visions of the Most High (cf. 23:9; 24:17; Is. 30:10).

nor the son of a nabi; I am a shepherd and a dresser of sycamores." He was not a prophet and does not belong to the nabi class.[7] He is, by profession, a shepherd and farmer. But Yahweh took him from following the flock and sent him to pronounce His word against Israel. Amos distinguished himself from other nabis because of the special mission he had received from God. This implies that professional nabis were not usually called individually by God. Nevertheless, he recognized that, like the nazarites, they have to exercise in Israel a function willed by Yahweh (Am 2:11).[8]

Micheas (3:5-8) is no less categorical: while he announces the punishment of nabis who live and traffic with their oracles, he feels that he has been given power to denounce Israel's crimes. He has nothing in common with prophets who "announce peace, when their teeth have something to bite, but declare war against him who fails to put something in their mouth" (v. 5).

The prophets *(nĕbî'îm)* are counted among the ruling social class; they are often named with priests, wise men and princes (Os 4:4.5; Is 3:2.3; 28:7; Mi 3:11; So 3:4; Jer 2:26; 4:9; 6:13; 8:1; 14:18; 18:18; Ez 13:9). Just as diviners and "wise men" are present at oriental courts (Gn 41:8; Is 19:3.11.12; Dn 1:20; 2:2), so certain nabis seem to be attached to the court of David (Nathan and Gad, 2 Sm 7:1-17; 12:1-15; 3 Kgs 1:8.10.11.22.32; 2 Sm 24:11.18), of Josaphat (4 Kgs 3:11-20), and perhaps of Saul (1 Sm 28:6). Even after the Exile, they appear as the indispensable support of royal pretenders (Neh 6:7).

They are consulted about the future and the outcome of every public or private enterprise (for example, 1 Sm 28:6; 2 Sm 7:1-7;

---

[7] It is possible to translate: "I was no nabi... I was a shepherd... but Yahweh took me," because the verb to be is not expressed. But that does not greatly change the general meaning of the phrase (cf. H. H. Rowley, *The Servant of the Lord*, p. 114, n. 2). In the expression "son of a prophet," the word signifies membership in a group or profession; just as one would say "son of a goldsmith" (Neh 3:31), or "son of a perfumer" (Neh 3:8), to designate a member of the corporation of goldsmiths or perfumers (cf. M. A. van den Oudenrijn, "L'expression 'Fils de prophètes' et ses analogies," *Bb* 1925, pp. 165-171).

[8] Some critics question the authenticity of this passage, because it states that prophets and nazarites were "raised up" by Yahweh (cf. Dt 18:18). But nothing prevents us from attributing this idea to Amos, who lists here all the good things Yahweh has showered on Israel; among these he includes the nabis and nazarites who have been instituted by God. Am 3:7 is more difficult to reconcile with 7:14.15; can Amos look at the nabis as servants to whom God reveals all His secrets? Gressmann (*Die älteste Geschichtsschreibung und Prophetie Israels*[2], Göttingen 1921, p. 340) solves the contradiction by omitting, as a gloss, the word *hannĕbî'îm*. This gives us a text expressing an idea in harmony with what Amos thinks of his vocation, and quite in context. Others reject the whole verse wich interrupts the context and is a late addition.

3 Kgs 14:1-16; 22:5-28; 4 Kgs 6:21.22; 8:7-15; 22:14-20; Is 38:1-4; Ez 14:3-10). On other occasions they intervene, without having been asked, at God's order (for example, 2 Sm 12:1-15; 24:11-14.18.19; 3 Kgs 11:29-39; 13:1-3; 16:1-4; 17:1; 18:1.2; 20:13.14).

At certain times nabis were very numerous (3 Kgs 18:13; 22:6), and at times they appear in bands (1 Sm 10:5.10; 19:20; 3 Kgs 22:6.10); this is especially true of the " sons of prophets. " This expression means quite simply " members of the group of prophets " (Am 7:14; 3 Kgs 20:35 and 20:41), just as " son of man " means a man, and " son of perfumer " means a perfumer (Neh 3:8). Yet it seems that in some passages of the book of Kings (3 Kgs 20:35 ff.; 4 Kgs 2:3.5.7.15; 4:1.38; 5:22; 6:1; 9:1) the " sons of prophets " grouped around Elias and Eliseus, and perhaps " the bands of prophets " (*ḥebel nĕbî'îm*, 1 Sm 10:5.10; *laqahat hannĕbî'îm*, 1 Sm 19:20), in the days of Samuel, were organized associations of prophets, that have been incorrectly called schools of prophets. The sons of the prophets lived together under the authority of a leader (1 Sm 19:20; 4 Kgs 4:38; 6:1; 3 Kgs 22:11.12), whom they treated as " lord " (4 Kgs 6:5; cf. 4:1) or " father " (4 Kgs 6:21; 8:9; 13:14); several of these men were married (4 Kgs 4:1). They wore certain distinctive signs: a hairy mantle, a leather girdle (Za 13:4; cf. 4 Kgs 1:8; Mt 3:4; Mk 1:6), a mark on the forehead (3 Kgs 20:35-41), and scars (Za 13:6) of wounds self-inflicted during their ecstasies (cf. 3 Kgs 18:28).

When the spirit of Yahweh seized them they began " to prophesy, " that is to say, they were transported, they entered into trances; to the sound of the harp, the flute, the tambourine (1 Sm 10:5), they sang religious songs, shouted numerous invocations (3 Kgs 18:26.28; 22:10-12), moved about in rhythmical movements and dances (3 Kgs 18:26; cf. Ex 15:20; 2 Sm 6:5.14), made gestures that often had a symbolic meaning (3 Kgs 22:11). This excitement was contagious (1 Sm 10:9.10; 19:20-24; 3 Kgs 22:10-12) and reached a state that resembled frenzy and delirium (Jer 29:26; Os 9:7; 4 Kgs 9:11).[9] In this state they wounded themselves with their swords (3 Kgs 18:18; Za 13:6), sometimes they stripped off their clothes (1 Sm 19:24; cf. Is 20:2; Mi 1:8), and in the end they fall exhausted and unconscious (1 Sm 19:24; Nm 24:4.16; Dn 8:18.27; 10:8.9).

These groups of nabis are mentioned only in the days of Samuel,

---

[9] In Jer 29:26 the verbs *mitnabbê'* (prophesying) and *mĕšuggâ'* (delirious) are synonymous; Os 9:7: " He is mad, the prophet "; 3 Kgs 9:11: " The son of the prophets " is taken for a fool.

Elias and Eliseus, that is to say, from the last decades of the 11th century until the 9th century B.C., in the Northern Kingdom, although the social class of nabis existed in both kingdoms. Until the Exile and even for some time afterwards these groups of nabis were found in the Southern Kingdom (Za 13:4 ff.). They stayed near the principal sanctuaries: at Gibe'a Élohim (the hill of God, 1 Sm 10:5.10), in the region of Rama (1 Sm 19:18-24), where there was an altar (1 Sm 7:17), at Bethel (the house of God, 4 Kgs 2:3) and at Gilgal (4 Kgs 2:1), two ancient and popular places of worship (Am 4:4; Os 4:15), also at Jericho (4 Kgs 2:5), and at Samaria (3 Kgs 22:10), the civil and religious capital of the Northern Kingdom during the reign of Achab. From this fact it may be concluded that these groups of prophets had some connection with the worship; the Chronicler may be alluding to this tradition when he says that the temple singers were "prophesying" (1 Par 25:1-3; 2 Par 20:14).[10]

The nabis took an active part in the struggle to preserve the religion of Yahweh in Israel. They seem to have supported Samuel's national and religious activity (1 Sm 19:18-24), and he seems to have been the promoter of the authentic tradition (1 Sm 15:16-33). Later they became deeply involved, like Elias and Eliseus, in the struggle against the worship of Baal and the house of Achab (3 Kgs 18:4.13.22; 20:35-42) and for this reason the royal family persecuted them cruelly (3 Kgs 19:2.10.14; 18:4.13.22). It was a "son of the prophets" who, at the order of Eliseus, drove Jehu to revolt against the house of Omri (4 Kgs 9); and, without doubt, the nabis were the allies of the Rechabites (4 Kgs 10:15-17) in the violent reaction of the new king against Baal in favor of Yahweh. It is understandable, therefore, that Amos (2:11) ranks them among the leaders raised up by Yahweh, and that Osee (12:11) looks upon them as the spokesmen of Yahweh.

3. *True and false prophets.* — The custom of offering an honorarium to a nabi (Jgs 13:17) for his oracle (1 Sm 9:7.8; 3 Kgs 13:7; 14:3; 4 Kgs 5:22-27; 8:8.9) was not without disadvantages. The needy nabi might be guided by his immediate interests rather than by truth. Micheas knew of nabis (3:5) who trafficked shamelessly with their oracles. These men without consciences are usually called "false prophets." The LXX already introduced this word (ψευδοπροφήτης) into their translation of the books of Jeremias (for example, 6:13;

---

[10] For the connection between the prophets and the cult, cf. H. Juncker, *Prophet und Seher in Israel,* Trier 1928, pp. 9-42; W. O. E. Oesterley-T. H. Robinson, *Hebrew Religion* ², London 1949, p. 201, and the works listed on p. 140, n. 1; there is no proof that the prophets were among those who usually were attached to the sanctuaries (cf. H. H. Rowley, *op. cit.*, p. 105).

33 [26]:7.8.16) and Zacharias (13:2), to designate one who claims to be a prophet and is not. The word prophet is used here in its relatively recent meaning of God's herald, one who is charged to proclaim the divine word. The Hebrew Old Testament does not use this expression. Jeremias, Micheas, Ezechiel, even when they attack " pseudo-prophets, " refer to their adversaries as nabis, because they are members of that social class. They retain the ancient terminology, which comprises under the name nabi all without distinction who give oracles. The " pseudo-prophets, " therefore, are true nabis, but nabis who preach falsehood (Jer 5:31; 6:13; 14:14; 23:25.26; 27:10.14; Ez 13:8.22.23), who proclaim the imposture of their own heart (Jer 14:14.23.26; Ez 13:2.3.17), who have lying visions (Jer 14:14; Ez 13:9.23; Is 9:14), who speak in Yahweh's name, but have not been sent by Him (Jer 14:15; 23:32; 27:15; 29:9; Ez 13:6). They are charged with lying, with being braggarts and deceivers (So 3:4), with " prophesying " for money (Mi 3:5.11), or to win the favor of the mighty or of the masses (3 Kgs 22:13; Is 30:10; Jer 5:31; Mi 2:11), with " prophesying for Baal " (Jer 2:8; 23:13), with giving themselves to debauchery (Jer 23:14) and to drunkenness (Is 28:7); they are charged with encouraging the wicked to continue their wicked ways (Jer 23:14; Ez 13:22), with deceiving the people by promises of peace and prosperity (Jer 6:14; 14:13; 23:17; 37:19; Ez 13:10.16).

It could not be denied that those nabis had visions and dreams (Jer 23:25.27; Ez 13:6.16; Mi 3:6), but these were considered to be lies (Jer 14:14) and false visions (Ez 13:6). Must we draw the conclusion that the prophets believed quite sincerely that their visions had come from Yahweh, whereas they came in fact " from their own heart " (Jer 23:16)? Or that the nabis took advantage of visions of their own invention (Ez 13:3)? Or did Yahweh Himself deceive them? According to Jeremias, this is the hypothesis that the nabis held: " Alas; Lord God; You deceived the people and Jerusalem, when You said: Peace shall be yours; For the sword will put them to death; " (Jer 4:10).[11] Ezechiel expressed the same thought: " As for the prophet, if he is beguiled into speaking a word, I, the Lord, shall have beguiled the prophet. " And Micheas declared that " Yahweh had placed a lying spirit into the mouths of the prophets " who promised victory to Achab (3 Kgs 22:23). The Hebrews made

[11] In the MT these words are introduced by the phrase " I say, " but we should substitute " they say " which is found in the LXX (" they, " of course, means the nabis, cf. Jer 4:9). They refused to acknowledge their responsibility for the promises of peace by which they had misled the people. Some authors correct the text and suggest the reading: " Thou hast deceived us saying: You will have peace! "

no distinction between what God did and what He permitted, and so they attached little importance to secondary causes, even when they were free agents; they attributed the origin of evil [12] to Yahweh. Therefore the nabis, Ezechiel and the author of 3 Kgs 22 did not hesitate to say that Yahweh deceived the people or Achab and misled the prophet. To explain these shocking expressions we must remember that God is said to be the author of the nabi's error because this was the means He chose to punish previous faults, especially the levity of the nabis (Ez 14:9), the crimes of Achab (cf. 3 Kgs 21:17-19) and of the people (cf. Is 29:10). If this lessens the responsibility of the "lying nabis" in the eyes of the sacred writer, it does not completely exonerate them, since they are punished by Yahweh for their lies (Ez 13:9; 14:9.10; Jer 23:15.30.31).

The Deuteronomist (13:6; 18:20) threatens a prophet with death if he has been given no mission yet speaks in Yahweh's name, or if he turns the people away from Yahweh by his word or wonder-working. Deuteronomy 13:2-6 supposes that such a prophet could support his doctrine with prodigies and his words could be fulfilled by signs, and he explains that in this situation God was testing the loyalty of His people (13:4).

For all these reasons it must be admitted that the existence of "prophets of falsehood" provides a problem, difficult for Israel and for us to solve: How can true prophets, who have been sent by God to His people, be recognized? By what criteria may it be known that a prophet was truly speaking in God's name? Different answers to these questions have been proposed. Let us examine them briefly.

Many Catholic exegetes explain that "true prophets" may be distinguished from "false prophets" by the personal mission they have received from God. Many scriptural passages support this belief (for example, Dt 18:18; Am 7:15; Is 6:8.9; Jer 1:4-8); both Jeremias (for example, 5:13; 14:14; 23:21.32) and Ezechiel (13:6.7) rebuked nabis who prophesied without having been sent by Yahweh. It is obvious that this answer does not completely solve the problem. As a matter of fact the Old Testament states that Yahweh can and sometimes does send "false prophets" (3 Kgs 22:10-28; cf. Ez 14:9; Dt 13:2-6). Furthermore some of the men whom God sent could have been unfaithful to their mission (3 Kgs 13:11-22; Ez 3:17-21). And finally, although all professional nabis did not have a personal mission from God (Am 7:14.15), the people thought of them as belonging to the governing classes "raised up" by God (Am 2:11)

---

[12] Cf. above, p. 70, 83 ff., 127, n. 63.

and believed them to be a permanent institution (Dt 18:15.18) meant to mediate between Yahweh and His people (Dt 18:16; Os 12:11; cf. Neh 9:30; Za 7:12) and to save Israel from divination and magic (Dt 18:9-14).

Several non-Catholic historians [13] do not concern themselves about the distinction between true and false prophets, but prefer the categories of prophets of doom and prophets of bliss. They include all the visionaries and the impostors in the latter group. If it is possible to classify all oracles in promises of bliss and promises of doom, this valid literary distinction still cannot be applied to living reality. All who predicted bliss were not impostors, [14] nor did all impostors predict bliss. It cannot be denied that the nabis with whom Micheas, Jeremias, Ezechiel and Micheas Ben Yimla (3 Kgs 22) contended, foretold peace and happiness. But Micheas (3:5) knew some who predicted war, if they were not properly rewarded. The Deuteronomist (18:22) taught that no faith should be paid to a prophet whose predictions were not fulfilled. Jeremias did not reject on principle every promise of happiness as a false prophecy; on the contrary, he admitted that the fulfillment of a promise of happiness is proof of the divine mission of the prophet who pronounced it (28:9). Ezechiel reproached the nabis, not so much for having promised happiness, but for having soothed the people to sleep by lying promises, instead of urging them " to step into the breach " (13:5); in other words, they were not courageous enough to save Israel from destruction by exhorting them to conversion (cf. Ez 3:17-21; 33:2-9; Jer 23:22).

What really distinguished certain professional nabis [15] and false prophets from the true heralds of God was the idea which the various groups formed for themselves about God and the covenant. The former believed, as did the common people of their day, that Yahweh was bound unconditionally and forever by His covenant with Israel (for example, Mi 3:11; Jer 23:17; 14:13), and that the richer the sacrifices they offered Him, the surer they could be of their salvation. The latter, on the contrary, believed that the God of the covenant was a moral God who preferred mercy to sacrifice (Os 6:6), that the

---

[13] In this they follow H. Gunkel (*Die Schriften des A. T. in Auswahl : Die Grossen Propheten*, Göttingen 1915, p. XXXII).

[14] Cf. J. Hempel, *Gott und Mensch im A.T.* [2], Stuttgart 1936, pp. 158 ff.; H. H. Rowley, *op. cit.*, pp. 125 ff.

[15] There were some authentic envoys of Yahweh among professional nabis, for example Gad (2 Sm 24:11), Ahias (3 Kgs 11:29), the nabi of Bethel (3 Kgs 13:11 ff.), the " son of the prophet " of 3 Kgs 20:35 ff.

covenant was a purely gracious act on His part and was intended to promote the moral and religious development of the people far more than its material well-being and power; and that consequently Israel would be punished for the crimes which violated this covenant (Am 3:2; cf. Os 2:4 ff.; Is 5:1-7; Jer 7:12; 12:7.8; Ez 16, etc.).

There were many different ways of distinguishing authorized prophets from nabis without a divine mission. The first criterion is a negative one: the prophet's fidelity to Yahweh; a prophet who would turn away from Yahweh was certainly not sent by Him (Dt 13:2-6). The second is a test suggested in Deuteronomy 18:21.22: the non-fulfillment of a prophecy; a prophet who foretells a disaster that does not take place, does not possess God's word (cf. 3 Kgs 22:28). Inversely Jeremias recognizes (Jer 32:6-8; cf. Za 2:13) that a prophecy fulfilled comes from God (cf. 28:9). A third criterion, to which some prophets appeal, consists in certain signs or prodigies authenticating their mission (3 Kgs 18:35.38; 4 Kgs 20:8-11; Is 38:7.8), or in prophecies which are soon to be realized and the fulfillment of which will guarantee the fulfillment of other predictions referring to events in the distant future (for example, 1 Sm 10:2.7-9; 3 Kgs 13:3.5; 14:12-14; Is 22:15-25; Jer 28:15-17; 29:29-32). Events, indeed, have proved the truth of many predictions made by the prophets and have convinced their contemporaries of the genuineness of the prophets' divine mission (for example, 3 Kgs 17:1; 20:13.28; 21:19.23; 22:17.25; Is 8:1-4.18; 37:33.34; Jer 20:4.5). There is still a fourth criterion which is the most important and the surest: it is the testimony of the prophets themselves. This testimony cannot reasonably be challenged, if we consider the respectability and sincerity of the prophets whose intellectual, moral and religious standard most notably surpassed that of their age and their contemporaries. The prophets who have left us an account of their vocation attest that their mission was imposed on them by God, often against their own will: Amos was taken away from his peaceful life as a farmer and shepherd and was no more able to resist Yahweh's call than one can repress a tremor of fear when hearing the roar of a lion (Am 3:8; 7:14.15). Isaias declares (8:11) that "the hand of Yahweh took hold of him" and that God warned him "not to walk in the way of the people." Jeremias (1:4-6) hesitated and protested against God's call, alleging his youth and his inability to speak (cf. Ex 3:11.12; 4:10-16); he complains that he has been "seduced," subdued, vanquished by Yahweh, and that he has been forced to announce God's word in spite of the opprobrium it brought him (20:7-9), and that he has to utter predictions contrary to his own hopes (28:6). All recognized that the mission they had received from God imposed on them a painful, even a dangerous task (Am 7:15; Is 6:9.10; 8:11; Mi 3:8; Jer 1:17-19; Ez 3:7-9, etc.), but they accepted it with courage and accomplished it with heroism to the prejudice of their rest, at times of their liberty, even of life itself (Elias, 3 Kgs 19; Micheas Ben Yimla, 3 Kgs 22:22-26; Jeremias, Jer 26:12-15; 32:2 ff.; 38:4-6).

4. *The classic prophets.* — Lacking a more appropriate term, we shall use the title " classic prophets " to denote men who in the Jewish and Christian tradition are considered God's great heralds, charged to announce the divine word: Samuel, Elias, Eliseus, Isaias, Jeremias, Ezechiel, as well as the twelve " minor prophets. " [16] Some of these men (Samuel, Elias, Eliseus) are known to us only through traditions recorded in the books of Samuel and Kings; others are known to us through books containing their oracles which were, as a rule, first spoken, then recorded by auditors or disciples. [17]

These great men are far superior to the average nabi. Most of them did not claim this name for themselves. Some of them (Amos and Micheas) did not consent to be compared with those who gave oracles by profession, and almost all had to fight against them or at least rebuke them vigorously at times.

The great prophets, however, in spite of all that separates them from the professional nabis, resemble them in certain aspects. They give oracles to those who " question God " (1 Sm 9:6.20; 4 Kgs 1:3.4; 2:13-20; Is 37; 38; cf. 7:3 ff.; Jer 37:7 ff.; 42:1 ff.; Ez 20:1 ff., etc.). Even Amos uses the verb " to prophesy " in order to describe his own utterances (Am 3:8; 7:15; Jer 26:12; cf. 19:14; 25:13; Ez 11:13, 13:2, etc.). Just like the nabis (3 Kgs 11:29 ff.; 22:11.12) they performed symbolic actions (Is 20:2; Jer 13:1 ff.; 19:10.11; Ez 4:1-3; 4:9-17; 12:3-7; Os 1), they had visions (Is 6:1 ff.; Am 7:1 ff.; Jer 1:11-14; Ez 1:4 ff.; 37; Za 1:8 ff., etc.), they also knew certain mysterious experiences, [18] analogous to those of the nabis, in particular they experienced ecstasy.

---

[16] This is the usual term and is based on the brevity of the writings attributed to these prophets; it is not a very apt choice.

[17] It is almost certain that most of the prophets did not compose the books that circulate as their works. These books are collections of oracles and narrative passages arranged by their disciples. So it is not surprising that some speeches from other sources found their way into the collections of authentic oracles of a given prophet. Some oracles were written by the prophets themselves (cf. Is 8:1; 30:8; Jer 29; 36:1-5).

[18] It was H. Gunkel who introduced this expression which is made the subject of a thorough study of the psychology of the prophets in his little book *Die Propheten* (Göttingen 1917) and in the introduction to his commentary on the major prophets in the collection: *Die Schriften des A. T. in Auswahl*, II, 2, Göttingen 1915.

a) *The ecstasy of prophets.* — According to Gunkel and his school of thought, [19] ecstasy is " the fundamental experience of the prophets. " Others, on the contrary, deny that the prophets, at least " the great prophets, " were ecstatics. [20] This difference of opinion results from the diversity of phenomena which the term ecstasy comprises. [21] It is of primary importance, therefore, to state precisely all that is meant by ecstasy. According to the definition of P. J. Maréchal, [22] " physical ecstasy is... a faltering adaptation of our somatic mechanisms to the central supertension of high intellectual contemplation. " The phenomena of inhibition, of temporary insensibility, immobility and contraction, of subsequent numbness, of partial subtraction from the laws of weight, of mere mechanical words and gestures, all of which characterize ecstasy, may have very different causes: certain diseases, especially hysteria; in normal subjects, the intense concentration of the intellect on an idea or of the imagination on an image; the use of certain psychic or psychophysical techniques, narcotics, inebriating beverages, etc.

If we admit these notions, it may seem correct that we consider certain phenomena which are in evidence with groups of nabis as ecstatic (1 Sm 10:5.9-13; 19:18-24; 3 Kgs 22:10-12). They are examples of collective ecstasy, [23] induced by intense religious sentiments.

Authors who deny that the " classic prophets " experienced ecstasy, seem to think that ecstasy results from a direct perception of and union with the divinity, as is the case in Christian mystics, and in some Hindu, Arabic and Greek mystics. Among the prophets, as

---

[19] *Die Propheten*, pp. 5 ff.; *Die Schriften des A. T.*, p. XXI and in his article " Die Propheten " (*RGG* [2], IV, pp. 1533-1554); G. Hölscher, *Die Propheten*, p. 23, etc.; R. Kittel, *Hellenistische Religion und das A. T.*, Stuttgart 1924, p. 85; W. Eichrodt, *Theologie*, I, pp. 179 ff. Several Catholic authors also admit that the prophets, especially the professional nabis, were ecstatics or, at least, had ecstasies: for example E. Tobac (*Les prophètes d'Israël*, I, p. 23, n. 1), L. Desnoyers (*Histoire du peuple hébreu*, I, Paris 1922, p. 100), already St. Thomas (*Summa Theol.* IIa-IIae, p. 175, 3 ad 2), J. Maréchal (" La notion d'extase d'après l'enseignement traditionnel des mystiques et des théologiens, " *NRT* 64 (1937) p. 988.

[20] For example J. Hänel (*Das Erkennen Gottes*, pp. 150 ff.); H. Juncker (*Prophet und Seher*, pp. 49 ff.); J. P. Seierstad (" Erlebnis und Gehorsam beim Propheten Amos, " *ZAW* 1934, pp. 22-41). J. Coppens (*Les Prophètes d'Israël*, I, p. 18, n. 1) does not like the expression " ecstatic, " because it is equivocal.

[21] Cf. Oesterreich, " Ekstase, " *RGG* [2], II, cols. 95-97; M. de Montmorand, *Psychologie des mystiques catholiques orthodoxes*, Paris 1920; J. Maréchal, *Études sur la psychologie des mystiques*, 2 vols., Brussels 1937-38; the article by the same author, cited in n. 19.

[22] *Psychologie des mystiques*, I, p. 208.

[23] They have often been compared with whirling dervishes, shamans and even bacchants. There may be some analogy between their psychic and physical phenomena, yet it must be noted that they arise from different religious sentiments.

a matter of fact, no indication can be found that they enjoyed an immediate intuition of God, or that they had any direct experience of His presence, or that they felt united with God or absorbed in Him, traits which characterize the unitive ecstasies of mystics. The prophets, on the contrary, are deeply impressed by God's holiness and transcendence, and, as a result, they are well aware of the distance that separates them from Yahweh. [24] The only feeling of unity with God to which they refer is that of moral unity that links the one who is sent to Him who does the sending : this is the reason why Jeremias (15:19) calls himself " the mouth of Yahweh, " just as Aaron is " the mouth of Moses " (Ex 4:16); and many prophets announce the word of God in the first person singular (for example, Is 1:2 ff.; Am 3:2; 4:6 ff.; Os 9:10), following the custom of messengers who in this way usually introduced the messages of those who sent them (for example, Jgs 11:12.14-17; 2 Sm 3:12.13; 3:5.6; 3 Kgs 20:9; 4 Kgs 18:19-25; 18:28-35). There is quite a distance between this moral unity which preserves the distinction of persons and the identification of mystics with God. The prophets always remained conscious of their own ego in the presence of the holy God. [25]

Nevertheless, if they did not attain to this form of ecstasy, there is no reason to deny that many, if not all, experienced physical ecstasy. In fact, there are several indications which seem to prove this. They did indeed feel that they were impelled by a power over which they had no control. When Yahweh spoke, Amos (3:8) was no more able to refrain from " prophesying, " than a man is able to refrain from trembling at the roaring of a lion. Isaias (8:11), Ezechiel (1:3; 3:14.22; 8:1; 33:22; 37:1; 40:1), Elias (3 Kgs 18:46), Eliseus (4 Kgs 3:15) were under the rule of " the hand of Yahweh. " [26] Jeremias (20:7-9) complains that he has been " seduced " and vanquished by Yahweh who forced him to speak, when he vainly tried to resist; and whenever he tried to resist, he felt " a fire burning in his heart " (cf. 4:19). He stands in Yahweh's presence like a man who is drunk, his heart is broken and his bones tremble (23:9). " Lifted up " and " seized " by the spirit, Ezechiel went to Tel-Abib, filled with bitterness and indignation, while the hand of Yahweh rested upon him; he remained there in a state of

---

[24] Cf. the texts cited in the section dealing with the holiness of Yahweh.

[25] Cf. the visions of Amos (7:1-6) in which the prophet intercedes for Israel; the vision of Isaias (6:1 ff.), of Jeremias (1:4-10; 1:11-13) which are dialogues between the prophet and God (cf. J. Seierstad, *op. cit.*, pp. 28 ff.).

[26] " The hand of Yahweh, " which Ezechiel associates with the spirit of Yahweh (3:14; 37:1), plays the same role in the words of the prophets as spirit does in those of the nabis (cf. below, §7).

stupor for seven days (3:14.15),[27] without being able to speak (cf. 24:27; 33:22). On another occasion he was " bound " by God and lay first on his left side, then on his right side for several weeks (Ez 4:4-8), in order to show the length of the Exile of Israel and of Juda. Daniel (10:2 ff.) described an ecstacy which was given him after twenty-three days of severe penance (cf. 9:3): during a vision, his face grew pale and turned the color of death, his breath became short, he weakened and fell in a faint, face forward to the ground (cf. 8:27), when he heard the words that were addressed to him.

b) *Modes of divine communications.* — The prophets are fully aware and affirm that they receive communications from God, that they perceive His secrets (Am 3:7), that they assist at His council (Jer 23:18.22; 3 Kgs 22:19-23), that God speaks to them. According to Numbers 12:6-8, He speaks to them in dreams and visions, whereas He spoke to Moses " face to face, plainly and not in riddles. " Since revelation by theophanies and dreams has been discussed above, only revelation, inasmuch as it is communicated by visions, will have to be examined here.

The Hebrew words describing visions are derived from the roots *râ'âh*, to see, and *ḥâzâh*, to see, to look, to contemplate, and may, like these verbs, signify the perception either of an exterior object or of an internal image. But it is also said that the prophet " sees " *(ḥâzâh)* a word (Is 2:1; Am 1:1; Mi 1:1), an oracle (*maśśâ'*, Is 13:1; Hb 1:1). It is sometimes asked if the accounts of visions, that abound in the prophets, are not a literary device conveying one simple idea. This opinion is unlikely, granted that the prophets were looked upon as seers (cf. Nm 24:3.4), and that visions occurred at all times. It must be admitted, therefore, that these accounts refer to actual experiences, no matter in what literary form the account may have been redacted.

Several of these accounts stress the divine origin of the visions: " Yahweh showed me " (Am 7:1.4.7; cf. Jer 1:11.13); and there is no doubt that all the prophets were convinced of this origin, although they do not all state it explicitly. On the other hand, it is very difficult to discern whether they believed that they saw exterior objects or only internal images, since the ancients, generally speaking, did not care about such a distinction.[28] They claimed, nevertheless, that

[27] *Měšomêm* (participle *po.* of *šmm* = to be in a stupor) should be read instead of *mašmîm* (*Hiph.* of the same root).

[28] Nm 24:3.16 may perhaps suggest this distinction, if the translation is accepted as it is given in the Vulgate and several modern versions: " The man whose eye is closed... who beholds the vision of the Almighty " (cf. p. 151, n. 6). Ezechiel (11)

their visions were objective in the sense that they were not the product of their imagination, of their "heart" (Jer 23:16; cf. Ez 13:3), and that by these visions they learned realities, revealed by God.

If we consider the visions, as the prophets describe them, from a psychological point of view, most of them were apparently perceptions of internal images which, according to their testimony, came to them from God, "from the mouth of Yahweh" (Jer 23:16), that is to say, they were produced by God's action upon their imagination and were images often referring to future events. [29] Many of these images were visual (for example, Am 7:1-9; 9:1; Jer 1:11-24; Is 6:1 ff.), others were auditive (Is 6:3.9; 40:3; Jer 1:5.7, etc.), some were tactile (Is 6:6; Jer 1:9), or gustative (Ez 3:3); sometimes they were connected with the milieu in which the prophet lived. Isaias (6:1-13), for example, was praying in the temple, when he saw the Lord seated on the throne, with the train of His garment filling the sanctuary (the *hêykal*), as well as the Seraphim and the smoke; he heard Yahweh's voice and the song of the Seraphim, he felt the glowing coal searing his lips and perceived how the frame of the temple's door shook; he heard Yahweh's order and understood the object of his mission. Amos, a shepherd and a dresser of sycamores, saw the locusts, formed by Yahweh, devouring the late growth (7:1.2), and in another vision, a basket of ripe fruit (in Hebrew: *qayṣ*), which signified the end (in Hebrew: *qêṣ*) of the Northern Kingdom (8:1.2). Jeremias felt Yahweh's hand touching his mouth (1:9); another time he saw a branch of an almond tree (in Hebrew: *šâqêd*) which made him understand that Yahweh was watching (in Hebrew: *šoqêd*) over His words in order to fulfill them (1:11.12). Ezechiel saw a hand offering him a scroll, covered with writing, and he heard Yahweh's

---

must have realized that from Babylon he could not see with his bodily eyes what was happening in Jerusalem. St. Paul seems to have insinuated this distinction, because he was sure that like the other apostles he had seen the Risen Christ (1 Cor 15:4-8), and he was convinced that all had seen with their own eyes Christ truly alive; on the contrary, he did not know whether "in the body or out of it" he perceived these ineffable mysteries in a later vision (2 Cor 12:1-4). At any rate he was aware that man can see also otherwise than with bodily eyes.

[29] Unbelievers treat these visions as hallucinations. But an hallucination is a perception that has no object, it is "the spatialized projection of images that are closely similar, if not identical with, to those which our senses perceive" (J. Lhermitte, "Origine et mécanisme des hallucinations," *Études Carmélitaines*, 1933, I, p. 130; cf. also J. Lhermitte-F. X. Maquart, "Le rêve et l'extase mystique," *ibid.*, 1932, I, pp. 19-81). Ezechiel, on the contrary, "seized by the spirit" and taken in vision to Jerusalem, sees from Babylon what was happening in the Holy City (11:1.13.24). He was conscious that he had perceived real facts, but not with the eyes of the body. Many of the prophets had visions which were symbolic in character: the images that they perceived signified future events. It is not a question here, therefore, of perceptions without objects.

command that he should eat the scroll; he ate it and found that it tasted as sweet as honey (2:9-3:3).

Other visions were probably simple auditions of words, perhaps only intellectual visions in which God, without making use of any images, communicated His plans to the prophet (Jer 23:22; Am 3:7). This last mode of divine communications is perhaps indicated by the frequently repeated formulas : " Thus spoke Yahweh " (for example, Am 1:3.6.9.11.13, etc.; Is 3:16), " hear the word " (for example, Am 3:1; 4:1; Is 7:13), or " the word of Yahweh came to me " (Ez 12:21.26; 13:1, etc.). [30]

c) *The modes of expression used by the prophets* were words and actions. There are several examples of symbolic actions performed by the prophets : Isaias (20:2) walked naked and barefoot to proclaim the destitution of the Egyptian exiles. Jeremias (27:2) placed a yoke on his shoulders to signify the Chaldean domination that was to burden down the kingdom of Juda (cf. also 19:10.11; 13:1-11). Ezechiel, goes out with bundles, left his home through a breach in the wall, to predict the ruin of Jerusalem and the exile of its inhabitants (12:3-7; cf. also 4:1-3; 4:9-17). These symbolic actions, it seems, will have to be credited to prophetic ecstasy (cf. Ez 4:4-8).

Most of the prophets were preachers, not writers. The oldest ones uttered, or, as the Old Testament expressed it, " cried out " (Is 58:1; Jer 2:2; 3:12) their messages, in short and rhythmic sentences, similar to the form of the ancient oracles (for example, Gn 25:22-23; 27:27-29); this is true of Amos and Osee, and often of Isaias, although in the work of this latter prophet, who was a great poet, we find messages of several strophes (for example, Is 9:7-10:4). [31] The prophets who ordinarily wrote as poets made use of several poetic forms, especially of the funeral lament (for example, Is 14:4 ff.; Am 5:1-2; Ez 19:27), the hymn (Is 40:22-24; 42:10 ff.; 43:16.17), the lamentation (Jer 3:23-25; 14:2-9), the pilgrim's song (Is 2:2-4), the satire (Is 23:7), the threat (Is 1:2-4; Am 1:3-2:8; Os 2:4-5, etc.).

Since they borrowed their images from their geographical and historical milieu, a knowledge of this milieu is necessary for an understanding of their oracles. Moreover, attention must

---

[30] Cf. O. Grether, *Name und Wort Gottes im A. T.*, Giessen 1934, pp. 89 ff.

[31] The long eruditely composed poems that P. Condamin (*Le livre d'Isaïe*, Paris 1905) thinks he found in the book of Isaias, seem to be artificial constructions, due in part to editors who arranged the oracles in collections which make up the present book.

be paid not only to the literary forms that they adopted, but also to certain special characteristics of their messages [32] :

1. In their discourses the prophets addressed, above all, their contemporaries and referred to specific local and historic circumstances. This explains why their prophecies about the future are often wrapped in preoccupations about their own days : thus in a time of oppression, when neighboring kingdoms were attacking Israel, messianic salvation is presented as the victory over those kingdoms (for example, Is 25:10; 43:3; 63:6; Am 9:12); in the time of the Exile, messianic salvation is described as the deliverance from the captivity and the return to Jerusalem (for example, Is 40:1 ff.; Ez 16:53; 39:27, etc.).

Thence it also follows that the prophets often describe events or persons of the future by using traits of Israel's past or of their own time. The future liberator is thus at times described as a new David (Os 3:5; Jer 30:9, etc.), the universal reign of God as having its center, whence it will spread out, in Jerusalem (Is 2:2 ff., etc.), the religious reform as being necessarily a reform of the worship of the temple (Jer 33:17.18; Mal 1:11, etc.).

These promises of restoration, finally, since they were addressed to the Hebrews and wished to sustain their hope and trust in God, had necessarily to be adapted to their intellectual capacity and moral standard. [33] It is for this reason that the promises announced not only the moral and religious renovation, but also the national restoration, the return of material prosperity and happiness, which Israel considered as the certain consequences of moral conversion and as the only valid proof of God's justice and fidelity. If it is permissible to explain certain traits of these promises of material happiness as metaphors, for example those of Is 25:6.7, we definitely cannot extend this interpretation to all those traits so that we would understand them only as figures of spiritual and religious values of the future.

---

[32] On this delicate question, cf. J. Touzard, " L'argument prophétique, " *Revue pratique d'Apologétique*, 1908, V, pp. 757-772; 1908, VI, pp. 906-933; 1908, VII, pp. 81-116, 731-750; A. van Hoonacker, " La prophétie relative à la naissance d'Immanuel, " *RB* 1904, pp. 213-228; M. J. Lagrange, " Pascal et les prophéties messianiques, " *RB* 1906, pp. 533-560; L. Desnoyers, *Histoire du peuple Hébreu*, III, Paris 1930, pp. 296-328; P. Heinisch, *Theologie des A. T.*, Bonn 1940, pp. 288-298; especially E. Tobac-J. Coppens, *Les prophètes d'Israël*, Malines, I, 1932, pp. 59-95, which is, to our knowledge, the most penetrating study of this subject.

[33] In this context may be recalled the principle which Jesus Himself stated (Mt 19:8 = Mk 10:5) with regard to divorce : the Law of Moses, the divine origin of which is taken for granted, allowed divorce " for your hardness of heart, " that is to say, because of the intellectual and moral incapacity of the Jews to understand and to embrace a more perfect law. Jesus admits that God adapted the revelation to the intellectual and moral capacity of the people to whom He communicated it.

The visions of the prophets were visions of faith and as such retained, even for the seers, a certain mystery. [34] Very likely they were aware of the imperfection of their apprehension of future things and had the presentiment that the new order, which appeared to their eyes in the perspective of earthly things and Israelite institutions, would surpass all that. Thus Jeremias (31:31-34), who predicted the future restoration as the renewal of the covenant of Sinai and described it as an interior regeneration of man as well as a spiritualization of religion, has perhaps vaguely foreseen that this future restoration would break through the Israelite cadre in which he had presented it.

2. The prophets who expressed themselves as oriental poets liked colorful images and hyperboles which must not, and at times simply cannot be understood in the proper sense. In order to describe the peace of the messianic times, for instance, they speak sometimes of the destruction of arms by fire (Os 2:20; Is 9:4), sometimes of their transformation into ploughshares (Is 2:4; Mi 4:3), sometimes of the domestication of wild beasts (Is 11:6-8; 65:25), sometimes of their riddance (Ez 34:25). These contradictory traits cannot be understood literally, and the same must be said of hyperboles, since they often borrow the formal language of oriental courts. [35]

3. The tableaux by which the prophets announce the future often lack perspective, so that it is difficult at times to distinguish if the heralded events, delineated on the same plane, refer to the same epoch or must be separated by centuries. The birth of the Emmanuel is thus brought into relation with the threat of a Syrian invasion in the days of Achab (Is 7:1-14); in another passage (Is 49:5-8) the return of the exiles to their home seems to inaugurate the messianic restoration (cf. Za 9; 12; 14, etc.). "All the prophets envisaged salvation as being near, since salvation formed for them the horizon, and future history, an insignificant track between their days and the day of salvation, did not allow them to measure the duration." [36] This lack of perspective is often the result of the mode in which God communicated to the prophet the knowledge of the future: the successive events of the future are perceived in a vision and appear to the seer as simultaneous; and frequently no indication has been given him as to the distance which separates the events in time. It

---

[34] Cf. Nm 12:8: To Moses God spoke "mouth to mouth, and not in riddles"; as for the prophets, to them God spoke only in visions and dreams. This evidently supposes that the revelations granted to the prophets retained the air of mystery.

[35] As for this last point, cf. L. Dürr, *Ursprung und Aufbau der israelitisch-jüdischen Heilandserwartung*, Berlin 1925, pp. 74 ff.

[36] M. J. Lagrange, *RB* 1905, p. 280.

is not surprising, therefore, that this distance in time is not clearly indicated in the accounts of those visions. Furthermore the prophets often considered the more imminent events they were announcing as the guaranty or the beginning of the messianic salvation, since in their eyes Yahweh will certainly finish what He begins. For this reason they stressed more the bond connecting the imminent event with the final completion than the distance which would separate them in time.

d) *The supernatural character of prophetism.* All times and all peoples have known diviners, seers or sorcerers who pretended to know the future and to discover hidden things by second sight, capable of penetrating all secrets; this second sight was attributed either to a superhuman power or to the presence or inspiration of a spirit or divinity. The exercise of this power is bound to the use of certain means, be it of magic formulas, stimulants, narcotics, psychic techniques, or be it in connection with the cult. [37]

In most of the cults in ancient times divination was officially practiced by priests, versed in the art of predicting the future or the outcome of an enterprise, by examining and interpreting omens: In Babylon were the *bârû* (seer, he who looks), [38] the Aramaeans, the Phoenicians [39] and the Edomites had seers (Nm 22:7.8), among the Arabs were the *kahin*, among the Celts the druids, among the Romans the *haruspices*, in Egypt the high dignitaries of the cult of Amon, called prophets by the Greeks, [40] in Greece Pythia of Delphi, etc.

The Bible mentions prophets of the Phoenician Baal (3 Kgs 18: 19.25.40), attached to the court of Achab and Jezabel (3 Kgs 18:19), prophets among the Edomites, Moabites, Ammonites and Phoenicians, wise men, diviners and magicians in Egypt (Gn 41:8.24; Is 19:3.11), in Babylon (Dn 1:20; 2:2) and in Canaan (Dt 18:9-11). Religious ecstasy, analogous to that of the nabis, was found in Phoenicia, [41] in Babylon, in Greece (bacchants), and still exists among Mohammedan dervishes.

Several religions are presented as having been revealed to their respective founder who declares himself a prophet sent by the divinity: Zoroastrianism in Persia is thus said to have been revealed to the prophet Zoroaster (Zarathustra); Orphism in Greece goes

---

[37] Cf. "Divination," *ERE* IV, pp. 775-830.

[38] Cf. P. Dhorme, *La religion Assyro-Babylonnienne* [2], Paris 1910, pp. 291 ff.; A. Lods, *Studies in O. T. Prophecy*, London 1950, pp. 107.

[39] Cf. the inscription of Zakir which mentions a seer (*AOT* [2], pp. 443 ff.).

[40] Cf. A. Moret, *Le Nil et la civilisation égyptienne*, Paris 1926, pp. 388.

[41] Cf. the Egyptian narrative of Wen-Amon (12th century B.C.) (*AOT* [2], pp. 71-73).

back to Orpheus; Buddhism in India to Buddha; Manichaeism to Mani; Islam to Mohammed.

Egypt, it has been said, has given us very old prophetic texts such as the prophecy of a priest in the time of Snefru, those of a potter, of a wise man, a contemporary of king Amenophis, and of others. [42] They are all phrased according to the same pattern: A wise man announces a period of misfortune, of social troubles, of hostile invasions, of famine, etc., which will afflict Egypt; there will follow a time of restoration, connected with the coming of a new king who will establish order, peace, independence and prosperity. This pattern, it is said, became known to the Hebrew prophets and was taken up by them, particularly by Amos, Isaias, Jeremias and Ezechiel. [43]

Can we compare the prophets of Israel with the diviners of antiquity, or at least with the founders of religions, or with Egyptian prophets? The majority of historians who are not believers have no difficulty in doing so, although several recognize, if not the supernatural, at least the original and even superior character of the Israelite prophets.

With regard to these theories, we must briefly indicate here the proofs of the supernatural character of Hebrew prophetism and point out the essential differences that distinguish them from the soothsayers of other nations. Some points, concerning Old Testament oracles [44] as well as the criteria that distinguish " true prophets " from " prophets of falsehood, " [45] have been developed already above. We refer our readers to those sections.

It is important to emphasize here that the prophets, for example Amos, Osee, Isaias, Micheas, Jeremias and Ezechiel, predicted several years in advance events which were humanly unforseeable and yet really took place. In clear and precise terms Amos and Osee announced the fall of the Northern Kingdom and the exile of its people, they announced it in the days of Jeroboam II, that is to say, during one of the most glorious periods of the kingdom of Israel, when the king seemed to have definitively consolidated the national position by his victories. [46] Isaias (for example, 10:5 ff.) foretold the humiliation

---

[42] Several texts have been published in *AOT* ², pp. 46 ff.; cf. also C. Jean, *Le milieu biblique*, II, Paris 1923, pp. 144 ff.

[43] This opinion has been developed, for example, by E. Meyer (*Die Israeliten und ihre Nachbarstämme*, Halle 1906, pp. 451 ff.).

[44] Cf. pp. 139 ff.

[45] Cf. pp. 157 ff.

[46] E. Meyer (*op. cit.*, p. 453) recognizes the fact, but concludes that, since Amos could not have foreseen the fall of the Northern Kingdom, he must have borrowed his prediction from the pattern of Egyptian prophecies. As if in any of the Egyptian texts a single prediction could be found, comparable in its precision to that of Amos!

of Assyria at the very moment when that kingdom was reaching its apogee, and the destruction of the kingdoms of Israel and Syria (Is 7) by Assyria, when they threatened Juda. Several years later, these two kingdoms fell beneath the blows of the Assyrian colossus which collapsed, in its turn, a century later. When Jerusalem, besieged by Assyrian armies, seemed irremediably lost, Isaias (37) foretold its speedy deliverance; a few days later the siege was unexpectedly lifted. From the beginning of the Exile, Jeremias and Ezechiel promised in clear and precise terms the return of the exiles, the restoration of the nation and of Jerusalem. This promise, made in the darkest hour of the history of Israel, was fulfilled in 538. No other people of antiquity provides, as does Israel, a series of precise prophecies, plainly prior to the events and fully confirmed by them. Is there, apart from the chosen people, a single authentic oracle that clearly foretold contingent future events which in due time occurred? If such oracles exist, they may be due to chance or to the extraordinary clairvoyance of a certain diviner. It is obvious, on the contrary, that neither chance nor clairvoyance can explain a series of fulfilled predictions, like the Israelite prophecies. It must be admitted, therefore, that the prophets received special revelations from God, as they constantly affirmed.

Without doubt outside Israel there were physical ecstasies, similar to those of the nabis, even to those of "classic prophets." But there is nothing surprising in this, because individual or collective ecstasies are in themselves psychic phenomena which are induced by the intense concentration of the intelligence or imagination on a determined object, "a tribute paid...to human fragility," as L. de Grandmaison puts it.[47] Physical ecstasy in itself is not a proof of a special intervention by God, but it does not exclude it, since God, by acting in an extraordinary manner on man's faculties, can induce that intense concentration of his intelligence or imagination. It is not correct, therefore, to liken the Israelite prophets to other ecstatics only on the grounds of their ecstasies.

Nor can the prophets of Israel be placed on the same level with the founders of other religions who present themselves as the bearers of divine revelation. These latter were religious geniuses who knew how to channel and re-orientate the religious tendencies and currents of thought of their time and their world. None of these prophets,

---

Moreover, it would have to be proved that the Egyptian prophecies had been composed before the predicted events. This not only has not been proved, but has been contested by informed Egyptologists.

[47] "La religion personnelle," *Études* 1913, p. 328.

with the exception of Mohammed (who borrowed this doctrine from Judaism), preached true monotheism. The great prophets of Israel, on the contrary, professed the highest form of ethic monotheism. But they could not have derived this doctrine, from either contemporary currents of thought or foreign influences; on the contrary, in order to make the unique and holy God known they had to struggle constantly against the innate tendency of their people toward polytheism as well as against the influence of neighboring religions. Because of their doctrine they surpassed all their contemporaries, the common people of Israel [48] as well as the learned theologians of neighboring nations. It is simply impossible to explain the monotheistic doctrine or the personality of the prophets as a product of their environment. The constant action of God must be recognized in all this.

Nor is monotheism merely the fruit of an ingenious intuition of one or of several prophets. Nor is it the conclusion of philosophical reasoning, such as we find in certain Greek thinkers. The great prophets are anything but philosophers: in their discourses there is not a trace of an argument trying to prove the existence of the one God. They simply state that He is the Holy One, the one Lord of all the people of the earth and appeal to the revelation made to Moses and to themselves. Although they consider God to be transcendent, they do not succeed in refraining from the most glaring anthropomorphisms when they try to praise His greatness and power — this is a fresh proof of their inaptitude for speculation.

As for the Egyptian prophetic texts — and the same may be said of certain Babylonian and Assyrian texts — they are, according to several recent Egyptologists, [49] no true predictions, but the writings of sages who use the prophetic form to cloak their laments about the evils and abuses of their time and to express their hopes that the present king will bring them to an end. This so-called prophecy "is above all retrospective or terminates in the vague and banal hope that the new monarch will be better than his predecessor." [50] The pattern of the so-called Egyptian prophecies may well have exercised some influence upon the disposition of oracles in our present biblical books. It is possible that the redactors may have arranged the oracles in such a way that prophecies of doom are followed by promises

---

[48] Cf. pp. 157 ff.

[49] A. Erman, *Die Literatur der Aegypter*, Leipzig 1923, p. 131; H. Ranke, in the first edition of *AOT*, p. 210, n. 2; cf. L. Dürr, *Heilandserwartung*, pp. 1 ff.; A. von Gall, *Basileia tou Theou*, Heidelberg 1926, pp. 48-82; L. Desnoyers, *Histoire du peuple hébreu*, III, Paris 1930, pp. 300 ff.; A. H. Edelkoort, *De Christusverwachting in het Oude Testament*, Wageningen 1941, pp. 28 ff.

[50] J. Coppens-E. Tobac, *Les prophètes d'Israël*, I, p. 94.

of happiness and of restoration, lest the reader be left with a despondent impression.

From what has been said, it may be concluded that Israelite prophetism is a phenomenon, not only unique in the history of religions, but supernatural in the strict sense of the word.

e) *The origin of Israelite prophetism.* — Following A. Kuenen, [51] most non-Catholic historians declare that ecstatic prophetism, whence all Israelite prophetism is derived, is a Canaanite phenomenon which has been adopted by the Hebrews when they settled in the land of Canaan. This opinion is based on the following arguments: 1) The presence of ecstatics in Canaan as early as the 11th century is attested by the Egyptian account of Wen-Amon, and again in the 9th century by the presence of the prophets of Baal (3 Kgs 18:22.29; 4 Kgs 10:19). 2) Ecstatics were numerous in Syria and Asia Minor, whereas they were unknown in Arabia, whence the Hebrews came. 3) Nabis appeared for the first time in the days of Samuel (1 Sm 10:5.10).

The least that can be said about this thesis is that it has not been proved. The presence of ecstatics in Phoenicia, in Canaan or elsewhere is *a priori* probable, because physical ecstasy is a natural phenomenon; and if it has been claimed that ancient Arabia knew neither prophets nor ecstatics, there is also evidence to the contrary. [52] Besides, it is not ecstasy alone, but rather the oracles, which characterize the nabis. And there were oracles in Arabia and in other places, as well as among the tribes of Israel, long before the conquest of Canaan (Gn 25:23; Jgs 1:1). Before the time of Samuel two prophetesses are also mentioned, Miriam, Moses' sister (Ex 15:20), and Debora (Jgs 4:4), who pronounced judgments and was called " a mother in Israel " (Jgs 5:7), just as the nabis, or at least the leaders of the " sons of the prophets, " were called " fathers " (4 Kgs 6:21; 8:9; 13:14). And Numbers 11:24-30 mentions an example of collective ecstasy in the time of Moses. [53] Furthermore, it has not been proved that the " servants of Baal, " whose ecstasy is described in 3 Kgs 18, have been called " nabis " in Phoenicia, as they are called in the Israelite narrative (18:19.20.22.25.40); this narrative has evidently been redacted in the milieu of the nabis.

Finally, if it is true that organized groups of nabis do not appear

---

[51] *De profeten en de profetie onder Israel*, Leyden 1875.

[52] Cf. H. Juncker, *Prophet und Seher*, pp. 94 ff.; J. Pedersen, *Studies in O. T. Prophecy*, London 1950, pp. 132 ff.

[53] It is true that most of the critics consider this text as recent and deprived of historical value.

before the time of Samuel, it is not very likely that professional nabis, or even " classic prophets " would derive from the Canaanites, since they also manifest ardent zeal for Yahweh, [54] strong attachment to Israelite tradition and constant opposition to the intrusion of Canaanite customs in Israel. Thus the prophet Nathan opposes the construction of a temple for Yahweh, because the Ark had always dwelt under a tent (2 Sm 7:5-7). Ahias instigates an insurrection of the tribes against the despotism in the time of Solomon (3 Kgs 11:29-33) who had tried to imitate that of the Phoenicians and Syrians. The prophets also fight against the cult of the Phoenician Baal in the reign of Achab (3 Kgs 19) and push Jehu to revolt against the dynasty of Omri (4 Kgs 9:1-10) who openly favored the Canaanization of the Northern Kingdom.

§ 7. *The spirit*

P. van Imschoot, " L'action de l'esprit de Jahvé dans l'A. T., " *RScPT* 1934, pp. 553-587; *id.*, " L'esprit de Jahvé, source de vie dans l'A. T., " *RB* 1935, pp. 481-501; *id.*, " L'esprit de Jahvé et l'alliance nouvelle dans l'A. T., " *EThL* 1936, pp. 201-220; *id.*, " Sagesse et esprit dans l'A. T., " *RB* 1938, pp. 23-49; *id.*, " L'esprit de Jahvé, principe de vie morale dans l'A. T., " *EThL* 1939, pp. 457-467; *id.*, " Geest, Heilige Geest, " *BW*, cols. 470-485; P. Volz, *Der Geist Gottes und die verwandten Erscheinungen im A. T., und im anschliessenden Judentum*, Tübingen 1910; H. Gunkel, *Die Wirkungen des heiligen Geistes* [2], Göttingen 1909; E. De Witt Burton, *Spirit, Soul and Flesh*, Chicago 1918; J. Köberle, *Natur und Geist nach der Auffassung des A. T.*, Munich 1901; H. Leisegang, *Der heilige Geist*, Leipzig 1919; *id.*, *Pneuma Hagion*, Leipzig 1922; E. F. Scott, *The Spirit in the N. T.*, London 1923; F. Büchsel, *Der Geist Gottes im N. T.*, Gütersloh 1926; J. Hehn, " Zum Problem des Geistes im alten Orient und im A. T., " *ZAW* 1925, pp. 210-225; A. Lamorte, " La notion de rouah chez les prophètes, " *Études théologiques et religieuses* 1933, pp. 97-111; S. Mowinckel, " The Spirit and the Worth in the Pre-exilic Reformatory Prophets, " *JBL* 1934, pp. 199-227; G. Verbeke, *L'évolution de la doctrine du pneuma*, Louvain 1945; R. Koch, *Geist und Messias. Beitrag zur biblischen Theologie des A. T.*, Vienna 1950.

1. *The meaning of the term.* — The spirit of Yahweh is an active agent of the divine revelation and providence toward Israel. It is this aspect which will be considered here. The consideration of the spirit of God as principle of the physical life in man or in the world, as well as the study of the human spirit, are taken up in the chapter dealing with the human composite.

The Hebrew term, which ordinarily is translated by spirit, is *ruaḥ*, the first meaning of which, just as in the case of the Greek πνεῦμα and of the Latin *spiritus*, is breath or wind. Reliable

---

[54] Cf. above, pp. 154 ff.

authors[1] contend, it is true, that prior to the Exile *ruaḥ* signified breath. The meaning of breath, indeed, is assured[2] by texts the age of which is recognized by all, for example, Os 13:15; Is 30:28; Ex 15:8; 2 Sm 22:16 (= Ps 18:16), where *ruaḥ* of Yahweh or of "the nostrils of Yahweh," designating wind, can only be understood as breath. And since poetic language often retains expressions born from very primitive conceptions, one is tempted to conclude that the primary sense of the term is breath, coming forth from the nose or the mouth, and that this sense has been extended to signify wind, because wind has been thought of as the breath of a very powerful being.

Breath, just like wind (Prv 30:4; Eccl 1:6; 3 Kgs 19:11), is an invisible, mysterious and formidable force (Is 11:4; 2 Sm 22:16). Just as the Old Testament speaks of the arm (Is 40:10), the hand (Is 8:11), the face (Ex 32:14), the mouth (Ps 33:6), the nostrils (2 Sm 22:16), the exhalation (Jb 4:9; 33:4; 34:14) of Yahweh, so it speaks also of His breath *(ruaḥ)*. It is not surprising, therefore, that certain prodigious and superhuman phenomena, which are seen with certain men, are explained by relating them to the action of the *ruaḥ* of Yahweh, that mysterious and penetrating force.

2. *The spirit of Yahweh, principle of psychic phenomena.* — a) In the most ancient texts, with the exception of Gn 6:3,[3] the *ruaḥ* of Yahweh or of Elohim is described as producing prodigious but transitory psychic effects in two categories of men: in warriors, destined to save Israel, and in the nabis. It is interesting to see that, once the hereditary kingship had been established, there is no longer any question of the spirit of Yahweh being conferred upon kings,[4] whose decisions, nevertheless, are considered as oracles (2 Sm 14:17.20;

---

[1] Thus P. Torge, *Seelenglaube und Unsterblichkeitshoffnung im A. T.*, Leipzig 1909, p. 19; E. De Witt Burton, *op. cit.*, p. 61; H. W. Robinson, "Hebrew Psychology," in A. G. Peake, *The People and the Book*, Oxford 1925, p. 360; J. Hempel, *Gott und Mensch im A. T.*[2], Stuttgart 1936, p. 105.

[2] This is also the opinion of H. Leisegang ("Geist," *RGG*[2], II, p. 939), of W. Eichrodt (*Theologie*, II, p. 18), of L. Köhler (*Theologie*, p. 95), of M. Lichtenstein (*Das Wort Nephesch in der Bibel*, Berlin 1920, p. 53), and of others. According to C. Virolleaud ("La déesse Anat," *VAB*, B, col. 2:1.2; *Syria*, XVIII, 1937, p. 86) *ruaḥ* designates the vital breath, for example, of young goats (cf. *npš ʿgl*, the breath of the calf, in I, A, B, 5, 4), already in the texts of Ras Shamra.

[3] The whole passage of Gn 6:1-6 is obscure, but especially verse 3: Is the *ruaḥ* of God the divine element which is in the "sons of God," or the vital breath which God breathed into them (Gn 2:7)? In either case it appears to be a force that was to assure the longevity of men, which God now decides to limit. Gn 7:22 does not mention the *ruaḥ* of Yahweh.

[4] 1 Sm 16:13 and 2 Sm 23:2, it is true, attribute the spirit of Yahweh to David; but they belong to a recent stratum within the books of Samuel. Is 11:1 ff. attributes the spirit to the messianic king, not to the present one.

3 Kgs 3:11.12; Prv 16:10), and that the great prophets, with the exception of Ezechiel, do not refer to the spirit, but to the word of Yahweh, to prove their mission.

When the spirit of Yahweh "came upon" Othoniel (Jgs 3:10), upon Jephte (Jgs 11:29), "enveloped Gedeon" (Jgs 6:34), "came mightily upon Saul" (1 Sm 11:6 ff.), these men, obscure by themselves, became heroes and won unexpected victories against the enemies of Israel. When "the spirit first stirred" Samson (Jgs 13:25), or "came mightily" upon him (Jgs 14:6), the hero tears a lion into pieces with his bare hands (Jgs 14:6), all alone kills thirty men (Jgs 14:19), breaks the ropes which were on his arms, just as one breaks flax that has caught fire, and armed with the jawbone of an ass, kills a thousand Philistines (Jgs 15:14 ff.).

The exaltation and the oracles of the nabis, above all, are attributed to the action of the spirit of Yahweh. The spirit is so characteristic of the nabi that he is called "the man of the spirit" (Os 9:7). The nabis, who with the sound of harps, flutes and tambourines give themselves in common to sacred rapture *(hitnabbĕ'û)*, are under the sway of the spirit of God (1 Sm 10:5-13; 19:20-24; 3 Kgs 22:10-12). Their exaltation is contagious : when Saul meets them, he is overcome by the spirit of Yahweh who "comes mightily upon him"; he is "changed into another man" and begins to "prophesy" (1 Sm 10:9 ff.), that is to say, he enters into a trance. Three groups of messengers, charged with the arrest of David who had taken his refuge with a company of prophets, are carried away by the spirit into similar trances, and Saul, who had come to help, undergoes the same fate: "The spirit of God came upon him also, and as he went he prophesied"; such was his exaltation, that "he stripped off his clothes" and at the end fell exhausted to the ground, "and lay naked all that day and all that night" (1 Sm 19:19-24). Yahweh "took some of the spirit that was upon Moses and put it upon the seventy elders; and when the spirit rested upon them, they prophesied *(yitnabbĕ'û)*, but they did so no more" (Nm 11:25). Moses wishes that Yahweh would put His spirit upon all, and that all the people would become nabis (Nm 11:29).

The examples of oracles, attributed to the action of the spirit, are less numerous : according to Nm 24:2 Balaam pronounced one, when the "spirit of Yahweh came upon him." According to the book of Chronicles, the chief of the thirty, Amasai, uttered an oracle, "when the spirit enveloped him" (1 Par 12:18); Azarias (2 Par 15:1.7), Yahaziel (2 Par 20:14-17) and Zacharias (2 Par 24:20) under the action of the spirit of God addressed exhortations and reproaches of religious and moral order.

The compelling action of the spirit of Yahweh is at times attributed to the "hand" of Yahweh, which "is upon" the prophet (3 Kgs 18:46; 4 Kgs 3:15; Ez 1:3; 3:22; 33:22; 37:1; 40:1), "falls upon him" (Ez 8:1) or takes hold of him (Is 8:11; Ez 3:14). The hand of Yahweh causes even prophetic exaltation: Eliseus, of whom the king of Israel asks an oracle, has a melody played before him on a harp, "and while the minstrel played, the hand of Yahweh came upon Eliseus, and he said: Thus says Yahweh..." (4 Kgs 3:15). Under the impulse of the hand of Yahweh, Elias runs before the chariot of Achab from Carmel to Jezreel (3 Kgs 18:46). Ezechiel (1:3; 3:14.22; 8:1; 33:22; 40:1) introduces the narratives of his prophetic experiences, especially of his visions, with the formula: "The hand of Yahweh came upon me," but associates at times the hand with the spirit of God who lifts up (3:14; 37:1).

The spirit (or the hand) of Yahweh (or of God) explains the abnormal, often violent psychic phenomena, which at times become manifest in certain individuals.

b) Other texts describe the action of the spirit in a different manner: it no longer acts intermittently or by force, but is communicated to certain men as a permanent gift with a view to their function: it is upon Moses (Nm 11:17.25) and is transmitted to his successor, Josue (Nm 27:18; Dt 34:9); a part of the spirit of Moses "reposes" over the seventy elders who had been chosen to assist Moses in the administration of the people (Nm 11:25-30); the spirit penetrates into David from the day he had been anointed (1 Sm 16:13) and speaks through his mouth (2 Sm 23:2); it "reposes" over Eliseus (4 Kgs 2:15), who has inherited the spirit from Elias (4 Kgs 2:9); it "fills" the craftsmen entrusted with the making of the objects for the cult (Ex 28:3; 31:3; 35:31); it is in Joseph and communicates to him exceptional wisdom for the government of Egypt (Gn 41:38-40); it "will repose" on the messianic king and will direct all His activity (Is 11:2 ff.) as well as that of His collaborators (Is 28:6); it is upon the servant of Yahweh (Is 42:1), and upon the prophet destined to bring the good news to the lowly (Is 61:1); and, according to the more recent Sapiential books, it is given to the wise and bestows wisdom on them (Jb 32:8.18; Sir 39:6; Wis 7:7; 9:17).

Finally the spirit appears as a permanent medium who by way of the prophets conveys Yahweh's orders to His people (Za 7:12; Neh 9:30), it appears as the guide and protector of Israel (Ag 2:5; Za 4:6; Is 63:10-13), even as the mentor of pious men (Ps 143:10).

It is possible that Is 59:21, [5] where the spirit of God is closely associated with the divine word, transmitted from generation to generation (cf. Dt 4:40; 30:14), preludes the doctrine which considers the Law as the inspired word of God (cf. Hen 91:1; Apoc. Bar. 10:1).

Although prior to Isaias the spirit has not been considered as a force of the moral, but rather of the psychic order, it is not incompatible, however, as it has been said, [6] with the belief in a moral God. The activity of the spirit, indeed, is neither blind nor arbitrary; on the contrary, it is the manifestation of the benevolent protection of the God of Israel; it exercises itself in men, chosen by Yahweh to save or to guide His people; it is the realization of the engagements which God took toward His people by the covenant of Sinai.

3. *The spirit of Yahweh, principle of moral life.* — The great prophets, from the 8th century onwards, understood that the covenant, which had been intended to make of Israel a holy people (Ex 19:5.6; Dt 7:6), had ended in failure through the fault of Israel who shamefully transgressed the clauses. For this reason the people will be chastised as they deserve. But Yahweh, because He is holy, will save His people (Os 11:8.9), or at least a "remnant" (Am 3:12; Is 10:21; cf. 7:3), and will conclude with them a new covenant. The new covenant will attain its end, for it will bring about a religious and moral regeneration of the chosen people. This conception of the messianic restoration, which is a consequence of a more fully developed notion that the prophets have of the holiness of God, implies a considerable evolution in their manner of understanding and describing the action of the spirit of Yahweh: if it is the force by which the holy God will execute His pledged obligations, it will be in the new covenant, above all, the force which will bring about the religious and moral renewal, implied by this covenant. As the covenant belongs to the future, so also is the moral activity of the spirit reserved for the future.

The idea of the moral renewal, brought about by the spirit in the messianic epoch, appears for the first time in Isaias (4:3 ff.). [7] After

---

[5] This verse is probably a late addition to the book of Isaias. It may be asked whether the words of Yahweh are addressed to the community of the new covenant or to a prophet; in the first case, the spirit would be given to all as in Joel 3:1.2; in the second case, these words might announce a series of prophets, as does Deuteronomy 18:15. The expression, however, "my words will not depart from your mouth, nor from the mouth of your children, nor from the mouth of your children's children," which recalls Dt 30:14, makes us think of the Law which is the written word of God. As for this obscure passage cf. P. Volz, *Der Geist Gottes*, Tübingen 1910, p. 97, n. 1; *Jesaia*, II, pp. 14 ff.

[6] E. F. Scott, *The Spirit in the New Testament*, London 1923, pp. 14 ff.

[7] The authenticity of Is 4:2-6 is rejected by several (Duhm, Cheyne, Marti); Procksch rejects the verses 3-6. Skinner, Condamin, Feldmann, Fischer retain 4:2-5.

the catastrophe which will engulf the majority of the nation, those who survive, those who were marked down for life (cf. Ez 13:9), that is to say, who were destined to enjoy the messianic restoration, " will be called holy, " will participate in the holiness, in the inviolability and in the moral perfection of " the Holy One of Israel, " when they will have been purified of their impurities and of the crimes that stained Sion. This purification will be the work of God " by the spirit of judgment and the spirit of purification, " [8] that is to say, by the divine force which, by condemning the guilty, will prune the community and destroy all moral and religious impurities that stained it.

The messianic king will be endowed with the spirit of Yahweh: " Upon Him shall rest the spirit of Yahweh, a spirit of wisdom and of understanding, a spirit of counsel and of strength, a spirit of knowledge and of the fear of Yahweh " (Is 11:1 ff.). In order to make of Him the ideal king, who will establish the reign of justice and of peace, the spirit of Yahweh will rest upon Him, no longer intermittently as upon the heroes of old, but in a permanent way. The spirit will endow Him with superhuman intellectual gifts, with wisdom, understanding, counsel, strength, and with extraordinary moral qualities, with knowledge and with the fear of Yahweh. [9] The collaborators of the messianic king in their exercise of judicial and military power will also be animated by the spirit of justice and strength, for Yahweh Himself " will be a spirit of justice to him who sits in judgment, and strength to him who turns back the battle at the gate " (Is 28:6). [10]

But the spirit will not be the exclusive apanage of the leaders; it will be given to all and will be the principle of physical and moral renovation of the land as well as of the people. In messianic times, the *ruaḥ* will be poured out from celestial heights and will change the earth and the people: the desert will become an orchard; the orchards will be luxuriant as forests. In the desert, where force prevailed, " right will dwell "; in the cultivated regions, where injustice

---

[8] The expression *ruaḥ bâ'er* is translated by *spiritus ardoris* in the Vulgate and LXX; several understand it as a burning wind. The root *b'r* can have the meaning of " to burn "; but it may also mean " to make disappear, " " to remove " (3 Kgs 14:10; Dt 13:6; 17:7, etc.); only this meaning fits into the context which deals with " the washing away " of the stains by this *ruaḥ*. We must, therefore, translate " the spirit which removes, makes disappear "; consequently " the spirit of purification, " the purifying spirit.

[9] The knowledge of Yahweh, according to the use of the term in the Old Testament, is practical knowledge, by which man recognizes God for what He is, and conforms his conduct according to the divine demands (cf. Os 4:1; 5:4; 6:6; Jer 5:4; 8:7; 22:16). It is, therefore, a moral rather than an intellectual quality.

[10] The authenticity of Is 28:5.6 is rejected by Duhm, Brückner, Cheyne, Marti Mowinckel, but upheld by Procksch, Condamin, Feldmann, Fischer, Eichrodt.

held sway, " justice will abide "; so " peace will be the effect of justice, and the fruit of justice will be quietness and security forever " (Is 32:15-18).[11]

Ezechiel (36:23-28) insists even more on the internal regeneration of individuals, which will accompany the restoration of Israel as a nation. Yahweh will begin by washing away the moral and religious impurities of the guilty (v. 25). But this will not suffice to make saints out of those sinners; it is necessary that God radically changes their internal dispositions: He will replace their " heart of stone " with a " heart of flesh, " that is to say, He will replace the hardened hearts, which were insensible to His will, with pliable and docile hearts, and will create in them " a new heart and a new spirit " (v. 26; cf. 11:19; 18:31). Finally, in order to make these renewed hearts capable of observing faithfully His precepts, He will communicate to them His proper strength, His spirit: " I will put My spirit within you, and cause you to walk in My statutes " (v. 27). Thus morally regenerated, sustained in the practice of the good by the divine spirit, " you shall be My people, and I will be your God " (v. 28),[12] the holy people of the holy God.

This is also the doctrine of Jeremias (31:31-34; 32:38-40),[13] who without mentioning the spirit, it is true, announces the day when Yahweh will replace the outdated covenant of Sinai with a new covenant, which is no longer written on tablets of stone, but upon hearts, that is to say, a covenant that will repose no longer upon laws external to man, but on man himself who, having been regenerated by God, has since been enabled, without the help of a master of virtue, to " know God, " that is to say, to recognize Him for what He is and to conform his conduct according to the divine demands (cf. Jer 33:16; 24:7).

This interior regeneration had been promised by the prophets for the future; a psalmist (Ps 51:12-14) asks for it for himself and for his time: " Create in me a clean heart, O God, and put a new and right spirit within me. " Knowing himself to be a sinner and inclined to evil (v. 7; cf. Gn 8:21; Jb 14:4; 15:14; 25:4), the psalmist supplicates

---

[11] Duhm, Cheyne, Marti, Skinner, Procksch consider Is 32:15-18 as post-exilic; Eichrodt, Condamin, Feldmann, Fischer consider it as authentic.

[12] This is the classic expression to designate the object of the covenant (cf. Jer 7:23; 11;4; 24:7; 31:1.33; Ex 19:5 ff.; Dt 29:12, etc.).

[13] The authenticity of this passage, which is rejected by Duhm, Smend, Stade, is rightly upheld by C. H. Cornill (*Das Buch Jeremia*, Leipzig 1905, pp. 248 ff.), J. Skinner (*Prophecy and Religion*, Cambridge 1930, pp. 320 ff.), P. Volz, A. Condamin and F. Nötscher.

God to cleanse him from his faults (v. 3.4 and 11); he has a knowledge of his inborn weakness, which can only be healed by a radical transformation of himself, brought about by God, through the creation in him of a clean heart and a right spirit. For his faults he deserves to be driven far away from God, he deserves to be deprived of the divine spirit which would help him to do good, and of the help of His God who would assure him joy; for all this is the privilege of the just (Ps 11:7; 17:15; 41:13; 140:14; Ez 39:29; Wis 1:4-5). It is for this reason that he continues: "Cast me not away from Your presence, and take not Your holy spirit from me.[14] Restore to me the joy of You help and uphold me with a willing spirit." In this magnificent prayer, unique in the whole Old Testament,[15] the psalmist asks God to confer upon him "His holy spirit," that is to say, His proper strength, without which he would relapse into his faults, and to grant him the divine help which will render his will generous in the accomplishment of the good.

The spirit of God appears elsewhere less as a principle of moral life, communicated to man, than as a mentor who directs through its counsels. Thus in Ps 143:10: "Teach me to do Your will, for You are my God; May Your good spirit guide me on a level path"; the psalmist demands no divine and vivifying strength, but a guide who would instruct and guide him on the paths of virtue and, consequently, of happiness (cf. v. 8; Ps 27:11). The same thought is expressed in Nehemias 9:20: "You gave them Your good spirit to render them prudent,"[16] that is to say, to instruct someone about the divine will is to direct him toward the good. It is very probable that Nehemias is thinking of the teaching given by the divine spirit, through the ministry of "the prophets" (Neh 9:30), as does Zacharias

---

[14] Ps 51:13 and Is 63:11 are the only passages in the Old Testament where the spirit of God is called the holy spirit, literally the spirit of His holiness. The LXX have at times added ἅγιον (Dn 5:12; 6:4); in the deuterocanonical books (Dn 13:45 [Theodotion]; Wis 1:5; 7:22; 9:17), in the Apocrypha (Ps. Sal. 17:37; Asc. Is. 5:14; IV Esdr 14:22) the holy spirit is mentioned more frequently; the expression becomes quite frequent in the New Testament and in the Rabbinic literature. The spirit is holy, because it is the spirit of the holy God (cf. the holy arm, Is 52:10; Ps 98:1; the holy name, Am 2:7; Ez 36:20; the holy word, Jer 23:9; Ps 105:42); holy spirit, therefore, is equivalent to divine spirit (Ez 31:3, LXX). It is possible that the expression "holy spirit" took more and more the place of older phrases like "spirit of Yahweh" and "spirit of Elohim," in proportion as the Jews avoided pronouncing the divine names of Yahweh and Elohim.

[15] H. Gunkel, *Die Psalmen*, Göttingen 1926, p. 224. The same author rightly observes that the psalmists limited themselves ordinarily to asking that God deliver them from evil, or, at the most, that He teach them His will and render their hearts obedient.

[16] The verb *śâkal (Hiphil)* has here, as also in Ps 32:8; Prv 16:23; 21:11; Dn 9:22, the meaning of "to make prudent." But this prudence has the nuance of piety as in Am 5:13; Prv 15:24; 21:11; Dn 11:33.

(7:12; cf. Is 59:21). The spirit of God becomes thus the counterpart of the wisdom found in the Sapiential books, where, with the exception of the book of Wisdom, it plays only an insignificant role.

In the book of Wisdom, " the holy spirit of discipline " (1:5)[17] is a divine power which forms men in wisdom, that is to say, in prudence and piety. Whosoever asks it of God, to him " prudence (φρόνησις) is given, " and " the spirit of wisdom comes to him " (7:7). The spirit, moreover, is identified with wisdom (1:4-6; 7:22-24),[18] and is like her a divine and necessary gift, in order that man may know the will of God: " Who ever knew Your will, except You had given wisdom and sent Your holy spirit from on high? " (9:17). Like wisdom, it " pervades all, " even spirits (7:23.24); and divine wisdom communicates virtues to holy souls (7:27), not only by teaching them (8:7; 9:18; 6:25), but also by producing them: " The fruits of her works are virtues " (8:7); " being on the side " of the wise man, wisdom " works " with him (9:10). She is, therefore, for the wise man a help, descended from heaven (9:10), in order to assist him physically and morally in his works (cf. 10:9-14), to lead him discreetly in his affairs and to safeguard him by her glory (9:11), that is to say, by the unfolding of her power, even to " deliver him from sin " 10:13). These passages suggest that wisdom, just like the spirit, is a divine power which assists the just and fortifies him in the accomplishment of God's will.[19] Wisdom, therefore, just like the spirit, seems to be a divine principle of moral life, communicated to man, or, more exactly, to the just; as a matter of fact, wisdom does not enter into a soul that meditates evil, and does not dwell in a body subjected to sin; for the holy spirit of discipline flees deceit, and sets itself apart from foolish thoughts, and is repulsed when " injustice " enters (1:4.5; cf. Test. Sim. 4:4; Test. Dan. 5:1; Test. Benj. 8:2). Because the spirit is holy, it cannot come into contact with what is stained (cf. Ps 7:25), and, consequently, it is given only to the just (cf. Ps 51:13). It does not transform the

---

[17] πνεῦμα παιδείας is the reading of B ℵ, several minuscules, It., Syr.; πνεῦμα σοφίας, the reading of A 248 Boh. Arm. (cf. 7:7).

[18] 7:22: " she is an intelligent, holy spirit, " is the reading of A 55 106 157 254 296 Euseb. (cf. 1:6: wisdom is a spirit who loves men); but the reading ἔστιν γὰρ ἐν αὐτῇ πνεῦμα which is found in B 23 ℵ 68 248 253 It. Syr. Copt. Arm. seems preferable. One may understand it: " she is in herself (αὐτῇ = αὑτῇ, cf. P. Heinisch, *Das Buch der Weisheit*, Münster im W. 1905, p. 141) a spirit " (cf. 1:6). The identification of wisdom with spirit results from the identity of the effects and the activity attributed to spirit and to wisdom (cf. P. van Imschoot, " Sagesse et esprit dans l'A. T., " *RB*, 1938, pp. 38 ff.).

[19] This idea is more clearly expressed in the Testaments of the Patriarchs (cf. Simeon 4:4; Benjamin 8:2; cf. P. Volz, *op. cit.*, p. 107), in the book of Jubilees (1:21.23 ff.; Ps. Sal. 18:8; cf. Lagrange, *Le Judaïsme avant Jésus-Christ*, Paris 1931, pp. 440 ff.), and especially by Philo (Cherub., X, 6; Leg. all., I, 43 ff., 65; cf. P. Volz, *op. cit.*, p. 106).

sinner into a saint, as the spirit promised by Ezechiel and described by St. Paul (for example 1 Cor 6:11; Ti 3:5).

From the preceding exposition can be seen that the notion of *ruaḥ*, without doubt, developed in the course of the centuries, following, however, a straight line from the very first meaning of the term, namely that of breath. The *ruaḥ* of Yahweh is, at the beginning, a mysterious and penetrating power, the action of which is seen in the extraordinary psychic phenomena that at times become manifest in certain individuals, particularly in the heroes of ancient wars and in the nabis. This divine power is also given by God as a permanent gift with a view to some special function. Before Isaias, however, no effect in the moral field, but only psychic effects, and no action — be it on the normal life of men and animals, or on inanimate nature — have been attributed to the spirit.

But with the prophets the spirit of Yahweh becomes the active principle of moral life and renovation which characterize in their eyes the messianic restoration, or, as Jeremias and Ezechiel put it, the new covenant. As an interior principle of moral life, the spirit of Yahweh exercises its activity only in the messianic future. Only the author of the *Miserere* (Ps 51) dared to ask for this force of moral renovation for his own time. Later, the Greek book of Wisdom, certain Jewish Apocrypha and Philo will take up this idea; but in these works, just as in Ps 51, this divine principle of devout life is accorded only to the just.

Everywhere else, when an activity of the moral order, be it in the past or in the present, is attributed to the spirit of Yahweh, this activity is reduced to that of a mentor who instructs and directs by his counsels. In these texts, all relatively recent, the spirit of Yahweh, more or less personified, plays in the community the role which, according to the Sapiential books of a later epoch, is that of divine wisdom toward individuals.

Several authors conceive, it is true, the evolution of *ruaḥ* in a manner quite different from that outlined above. They assign to it, as its starting point, the animistic or polydemoniac belief. [20] At the beginning *ruaḥ* would be conceived as a demon who takes hold of man and throws him into transports of bellicose or religious enthusiasm. But since

---

[20] B. Stade, *Theologie*, p. 99; R. Birch Hoyle, "Spirit (Holy) of God," *ERE*, XI, p. 785; P. Volz, *op. cit.*, pp. 2 ff.; G. Hölscher, *Geschichte der jüdischen und israelitischen Religion*, p. 16, n. 16; p. 17, n. 25; p. 84, n. 2; likewise J. Schwab, *Der Begriff der Nefesch in den hl. Schriften des A. T.*, Leipzig 1913, p. 76; L. Desnoyers, *Histoire du peuple hébreu*, III, Paris 1930, pp. 147 ff.

certain men seem to be in permanent contact with the supersensible world, the term soon came to include the idea of a supersensible fluid which changes men into "men of the spirit" (Os 9:7) or of Elohim (for example, 3 Kgs 13:1 ff.; 4 Kgs 1:9; 4:7). Neither the *ruaḥ*-demon nor this divine fluid stand in any relation to Yahweh. It became subordinated to Him only when monotheism triumphed in Israel; since then *ruaḥ* serves to designate the immortality, the spiritual majesty and moral perfection of the transcendent God. Isaias was the first to consider the spirit of Yahweh as a spiritual and moral entity; Ezechiel transferred the spirit of Yahweh to man and showed it to be the divine principle of man's moral life. The spirit of Yahweh appears finally as a divine hypostasis which guides and instructs the chosen people in the ways of what is good.

It may be admitted that in very remote times the ancestors of Israel, just like the other Semites, may have shared the animistic belief and believed in the activity of numerous demons throughout the visible world. [21] But the question which arises here is to know whether the most ancient texts of the Old Testament which deal with *ruaḥ* can be understood in the animistic or polydemoniac sense, as the exponents of the above mentioned opinion claim. The answer to this question, it seems, must be negative. In order to convince us, let us see whether the texts present the spirit as a demon, an individual being, or as an impersonal power. We shall then examine what the relation is between the spirit and Yahweh. The examination of these two points will enlighten us on the view which the Hebrews had with regard to the nature of *ruaḥ*.

4. *The nature of ruaḥ.* — Was the spirit conceived in the beginning as an individual being, as a demon? Several indications converge to a negative reply.

a) In the Old Testament the word *ruaḥ* never designates a disembodied soul, [22] nor, at least not in the plural form, demons. Very rarely does the singular signify a spirit (Jgs 9:23; 1 Sm 16:18-23; 18:10; 19:9; 3 Kgs 22:19-23), and in that case it is almost always accompanied by a pejorative determinative (Jgs 9:23; 1 Sm 16:14-23; 18:10; 19:9). [23]

---

[21] Cf. above, II, § 6, B, 1 and 7, pp. 122, 131 ff.

[22] The *ruaḥ* which is in the living man is by no means a double in the animistic sense, cf. below part II, 1, § 4.

[23] For a justification of this opinion, cf. our study in *RScPT* 1934, pp. 559 ff. and M. Burrows, *An Outline of Biblical Theology*, Baltimore 1946, p. 75. It is not excluded, however, that "the evil spirit (coming) of Yahweh" (Jgs 9:29; 1 Sm 16:14, etc.) designates quite simply an evil disposition provoked by Yahweh. It is in this way that we now understand "the spirit of jealousy" (Nm 5:14.30),

b) The word is feminine in nine out of ten cases. But in Hebrew, as in other Semitic languages, the term which designates a person is masculine; the word designating a thing or an impersonal being is feminine.[24] When *ruaḥ* is masculine, it designates at times a personal spirit (3 Kgs 22:21.22 = 2 Par 18:20.21), but more often an impersonal power (Gn 6:3; 3 Kgs 18:12; 22:24; 4 Kgs 2:15; Is 32:15; Ez 1:12.20; 2 Sm 23:2), breath or spirit (Jos 5:1; 3 Kgs 10:5; Is 34:16; 57:13; Eccl 3:19; Ps 51:12; Prv 18:14; Ps 77:7; Jb 20:3), or wind (Ex 10:13.19; Nm 11:31; 3 Kgs 19:11 ff., etc.); on the other hand, when used in the feminine, it may designate a spirit-demon (in Jgs 9:23; 1 Sm 16: 14.23; 18:10; 19:9). The predominant use of the feminine speaks in favor of an interpretation which sees in *ruaḥ* a thing or an impersonal power.

c) None of the verbs which express either the action of *ruaḥ* on man or the action by which God confers the spirit, requires, and several, on the contrary, forbid that *ruaḥ* be interpreted as a demon. The most frequent expression is "to be upon" (*hâyĕtâh ʿal*, Nm 24:2; Jgs 3:10; 11:29; 1 Sm 19:20.23; Is 59:21; 61:1), which suggests the image of a power which envelops and dominates, rather than that of a personal being; the same can be said of the parallel expression "the hand of Yahweh was upon" (3 Kgs 18:46; 4 Kgs 3:15; Ez 3:22, etc.). "To be in," a more rare expression (Gn 41:38; Nm 27:18; Dn 4:5.6.15), can be understood, strictly speaking, of a personal being, but suggests rather the idea of a power. "To come mightily upon" (*ṣâlaḥ ʿal*, Jgs 14:6.19; 15:14; 1 Sm 10:6.10; 11:6; 16:13; 18:10), "to envelop" (or to envelop oneself with, *lâbaš*, Jgs 6:34; 1 Par 12:18; 2 Par 24:20), "to pass" (*'âbar*, Nm 5:14.30; 3 Kgs 22:24; Jb 4:15), "to fall upon" (*nâphâl ʿal*, Ez 11:5), "to enter in" (Ez 2:2; 3:24), "to depart" (*sûr*, 1 Sm 16:14), can be understood of an impersonal power, since these verbs are also used with the name of a thing as subject.[25] On the other hand, "to rest on" (*nûaḥ*,

---

"the spirit of fornication" (Os 4:12; 5:4), "the spirit of impurity" (Za 13:2), because of their analogy with "the spirit of dizziness" (Is 19:14), "the spirit of wisdom" (Is 11:2; Ex 28:3; cf. 31:3; 35:31; Dt 34:9), "the spirit of justice" (Is 28:6), "the spirit of grace and petition" (Za 12:10); these expressions denote the effects of Yahweh's action upon man. This is evident in Is 11:1 ff.

[24] Cf. Albrecht, "Das Geschlecht der hebräischen Hauptwörter," *ZAW* 1895, p. 313; 1896, pp. 41 ff.; the author concludes that *ruaḥ*, just as in Arabic, is *generis communis;* but the feminine clearly predominates. According to Rosenberg (*ZAW*, 1905, p. 338) the term is used only in the feminine form in the Mishna. But in spite of it the expression "an unclean spirit" became current in that time to designate a demon.

[25] *ṣâlaḥ* is said of a weapon which penetrates (Is 53:10; Jer 12:1); "to pass" *ʿâbar*, of the wind (Jb 37:21); "to fall upon," of the hand of God (Ez 8:1); "to enter in," of the vital spirit (Ez 37:10) and of the *nepheš* (3 Kgs 17:21 ff.); "to envelop," of the arm of Yahweh (Is 51:9); "to depart," of the hand of God (1 Sm 6:3).

Nm 11:25 ff.; 4 Kgs 2:15; Is 11:2), " to be poured out " (*'ârâh, Niph.*, Is 32:15) can only be said of a power (cf. Is 25:10 : the hand of Yahweh rests on); the same can be said of : " to be filled with the spirit " (Dt 34:9).

Other verbs indicate the vehemence of the action of the *ruaḥ :* the spirit of Yahweh " stirs " (*pâ'am*, Jgs 13:25) Samson, " lifts up " (*nâśâ'*, 3 Kgs 18:12; 4 Kgs 2:16; Ez 3:12.14; 8:3; 11:1.24; 43:5) or " takes " (*lâqaḥ*, Ez 3:14) the prophet; he can cast him (*šâlâk*, 4 Kgs 2:16) upon a mountain, conduct him (*bô'*, *Hiph.*, Ez 8:3; 11:1.24; 43:5) to a remote place, " make him stand " (*'âmad*, *Hiph.*, Ez 3:24). With the exception of 3 Kgs 22:24 and 2 Sm 23:3 which make the spirit " talk, " no verb suggests the image of a personal being; they rather suggest a breath which dominates or a wind which carries man away like a leaf. [26]

A quite different image, which, however, plainly confirms our conclusion, is evoked by several passages in which the spirit is represented as a fluid : Yahweh " has mixed " (*mâsak*, Is 19:14), as wine is mixed, a spirit of dizziness within the bosom of Egypt; " He pours out " upon Israel " a spirit of deep sleep " (*nâsak*, Is 29:10); " He extends " (*šâpâk 'al)* a spirit of grace (Za 12:10), or His spirit (Ez 39:29; Jl 3:1 ff.; *yâṣaq*, Is 44:3; cf. Is 32:15) over His people. [27] He fills certain men with a spirit of wisdom (Ex 28:3; 31:3; 35:35; cf. Dt 34:9). He " sets aside " *('âṣal)* some of the spirit which is on Moses and " places " *(šîm)* it on the elders (Nm 11:17); He " puts " *(nâtân 'al)* His spirit on His servant (Is 42:1), [28] He " places " *(šîm)* it within His people (Is 63:11), " sends " (*šâlaḥ*, Ps 104:30; Is 48:16) it. All these verbs express clearly the communication of a power; only *šâlaḥ* (to send) can have a personal being as object; the context, however, in which it is used, excludes such a hypothesis.

From all these indications it may be concluded that *ruaḥ*, in ancient texts as well as in others, is a power which is represented most

---

[26] In order to describe the action of the wind, several identical or synonymous verbs are used (cf. Ex 10.13.19; Nm 11:31; Is 40:7; 41:16; 57:13; Ps 1:4; 103:16, etc.).

[27] The image of wine is demanded by the idea of folly which Isaias (19:14; 29:10) represents as drunkenness. In other texts the spirit is figured by water, since the spirit will be the cause of abundance and blessings, but in Palestine water is the source of all abundance, and, consequently, the usual symbol of divine blessings. These verbs, which in the proper sense are said of water, will simply express the abundance of the spirit which God gives profusely. They are used in figures of speech where the proper sense is completely forgotten, for example : to pour out one's wrath (Lam 2:4; 4:11), one's *nepheš* (1 Sm 1:15), one's heart (Lam 2:19), one's malice (Jer 14:16); the figurative sense, therefore, must not be urged too much.

[28] The verb *nâtân* is also used in 3 Kgs 22:23 : " I will put my lying spirit into the mouth of all the prophets, " although in the context the spirit is represented as a personal being. In 4 Kgs 19:7 = Is 37:7 Yahweh " puts " *(nâtân)* a spirit into the king of Babylon; here spirit designates an interior disposition, fear or error.

frequently as breath or wind,[29] more rarely as a fluid. The Hebrews did not reflect on the nature of this power and have not defined it; but it is true that they did not consider it as spiritual, in the philosophical meaning of the word, that is to say, as immaterial and simple. They admit, on the contrary, that this power is divisible (Nm 11:17; 4 Kgs 2:9.15) and measurable (Sir 16:25). It is a concrete and invisible power, analogous to breath and wind[30] which are designated by the same word.

The notion of *ruaḥ* is essentially dynamic[31]: *ruaḥ* is a very strong power, superior to man; it dominates man and is able "to change him into another man" (1 Sm 10:6.9), not only from a psychic point of view — this kind of effects of the spirit are only mentioned in ancient texts — but also from a moral point of view (Ez 36:26 ff.; Ps 51:12 ff.).

5. *The relation between ruaḥ and Yahweh.* The spirit is essentially a divine power. This results clearly from the text of Isaias (31:3): "The Egyptians are men, and not god *('êl)*; their horses are flesh, and not spirit. When Yahweh stretches out His hand, the helper will stumble, and he who has been helped will fall, and they all will perish together." The prophet reproaches the king of Juda because he had been looking for an alliance with Egypt and for the support of the army, particularly of the cavalry of Egypt, instead of placing his trust in Yahweh, the only efficient helper. This conduct is tantamount to relying on what is weak, instead of counting on what is strong, and can only lead to ruin; for Yahweh will punish this defiance directed against Him, and will annihilate at the same time the helper (the Egyptians and their army) as well as the one who had been helped (Juda). The Egyptians are of no help, because they are but "men" and their army is "flesh," that is to say, weak and perishable; *'âdâm* (man) and *bâśâr* (flesh) are strictly parallel and, therefore, equivalent terms; to "man" is opposed "God" *('êl)*, and to "flesh" is opposed "spirit" *(ruaḥ)*; God and *ruaḥ*, therefore, are as equivalent as the other terms and designate what is strong, durable and immortal. Although Isaias does not say formally that God is spirit, or that Yahweh alone is spirit, his thoughts certainly tend to this conclusion (cf. Is 30:1): for him Yahweh "represents all

[29] Cf. M. Burrows, *op. cit.*, p. 76.
[30] The wind has a weight *(mišqâl)* which can be measured (Jb 28:25). Sir 16:25 says of the *ruaḥ*: "I will pour out (literally: I shall make come forth, *nâba'*, *Hiph.*) my spirit by measure (*mišqâl*, literally: by weight), and with discretion (modesty) will I declare my knowledge." As for the concrete character of *ruaḥ* and of word, cf. L. Dürr, *Die Wertung des göttlichen Wortes im A. T. und im antiken Orient*, Leipzig 1938, pp. 144 ff.
[31] M. Goguel, *La notion johannique de l'esprit*, Paris 1902, p. 10.

that can be called *'êl* and *ruaḥ*. "[32] If Yahweh, indeed, is the only help that can save Juda, it is, according to the terms of the anithesis, because only He is God or spirit. He has only to stretch out His hand, and the Egyptians and their powerful army will stumble : for " man " or " flesh " cannot resist God or the spirit (cf. Jer 17:5; Ps 56:5; 2 Par 32:8; Jb 10:4).

Isaias presupposes as already known these anitheses between man and God, and between flesh and spirit. The former is found already in Osee (11:9; 14:4); the second probably in Gn 6:3.[33] He also presupposes as already known the parallelism between man and flesh, and between God and spirit; as a matter of fact, the term " flesh, " in current language, is equivalent to *'âdâm* with the added nuance of weakness (Gn 6:3; Jer 17:5; Ps 56:5; 78:39; Jb 10:4; Sir 14:17 ff.). The same conclusion may also be drawn from the popular expressions which designate the nabis as " men of God " (*'îš 'élôhîm*, 3 Kgs 17: 18.24; 4 Kgs 1:9 ff., etc.), or as " men of the spirit " (*'îš hâruaḥ*, Os 9:7). Isaias, far from introducing new notions or spiritualizing traditional ones,[34] uses only given and proven terms.

From the equivalence of the terms *'êl* and *ruaḥ* it may be deduced that God is spirit and that the spirit is something divine; but it would be forcing the sense of the text to see here only an affirmation of the spiritual, that is to say, the immaterial nature of God (cf. Jn 4:24). The spirit (or God) is here opposed to flesh (or to man), not as something immaterial to something material, but as a powerful and durable element to that which is weak and perishable.

Has this strict relation, which according to Is 31:3 exists between Yahweh and the spirit, always been recognized by the Hebrews?

This is not very probable, for there was a time when the ancestors of the Hebrews " served other gods " (Jos 24:2.14). The spirit was then most likely the divine, supersensible element, pertaining to the world of the gods. But once Yahweh had been recognized as the only God of Israel — and this can be traced back to the times of the patriarchs[35] — He became the only possessor of the spirit. It was not Isaias who introduced this idea; on the contrary, if he does not

[32] B. Duhm, *Das Buch Jesaia*[3], Göttingen 1914, p. 205. This results also from Is 30:1 where the expressions " without Me " (Yahweh) and " without My spirit " are parallel.

[33] Gn 6:3 is extremely obscure; the current translation : " My spirit shall not remain in man forever, since man is flesh " is open to discussion (cf. the commentaries of Heinisch, Procksch, Gunkel, Strack, Skinner, Driver, Chaine).

[34] P. Volz, *op. cit.*, p. 73.

[35] Cf. I, § 5.

think it more important to establish the equivalence of " God " and " spirit " than that of " man " and " flesh, " it is because these notions were currently accepted prior to his time. As a matter of fact, as far back as the texts allow us to go, *ruaḥ* is a divine power, and this divine power is that of Yahweh (cf. Gn 6:3; Jgs 11:29; 13:25; 14:6.19; 15:14; Nm 11:17.25.29; 1 Sm 10:6.10, etc.).

The expression *ruaḥ 'élôhîm* does not prove the contrary. If this expression may, indeed, be understood of a divine spirit in Gn 41:38 (cf. Dn 4:5.6; 5:11.14), it is so because it is found in the mouth of a pagan. Elsewhere it certainly signifies the spirit of God, of the only God (Gn 1:2), or of Yahweh (Nm 24:2; cf. 24:13). The word *'élôhîm* is often used without an article to designate the only God, since it has the value of a proper name. [36]

To affirm that in the narrative concerned with the transmission of the spirit of Elias to Eliseus (4 Kgs 2:9.10), Yahweh plays no part, is to misunderstand the meaning of the narrative. Eliseus shall receive the spirit of Elias, provided that Yahweh will grant him (cf. 4 Kgs 6:17) to witness the assumption of Elias, and not because " he sees an invisible phenomenon and shows proof of pneumatic dispositions. " [37] The witnessing of Elias' assumption is not the reason why Eliseus will receive the spirit, but the sign by which he will know that his petition will be granted by Yahweh; and this sign has been given him by Yahweh, for no man can see a supernatural phenomenon if Yahweh does not open his eyes (4 Kgs 6:17). According to the meaning of the narrative it is Yahweh, " the God of Elias " (2:14), who transmits to Eliseus the spirit which He had given to Elias (cf. Nm 11:17); this transmission does not depend on man: what Eliseus has asked " was a difficult thing " to grant (v. 10).

There remains a last point to be explained: Has the spirit of Yahweh to be conceived as really distinct from Yahweh, or only as a manifestation of His action upon creatures?

To this question it must be answered that the spirit in the Old Testament is not really distinct from Yahweh; it is not an agent that has its proper existence and proper action. This results clearly from the passages in which a parallel is drawn between the spirit of Yahweh and Yahweh Himself, for example, Is 30:1; 31:3; 40:13; Ps 139:7;

---

[36] Cf. *Ges. K.*, No. 125-126.

[37] P. Volz, *op. cit.*, p. 53; the author writes: " It is not because Yahweh judges Eliseus worthy, but because Eliseus has perceived an invisible phenomenon and has shown himself disposed for pneumatic phenomena, that he receives the spirit. "

Ag 2:5 (cf. 2:4). The analogy of the expression " the spirit of Yahweh " with similar expressions indicates that the spirit is nobody else but Yahweh Himself acting in man. Thus " the hand of Yahweh, " to which are often attributed the same effects as to His spirit (3 Kgs 18:46; 4 Kgs 3:15; Ez 1:3; 3:22; 33:22; 37:1; 40:1), signifies the action of Yahweh; " the mouth of Yahweh " (Jos 9:14; Is 30:2) designates Yahweh manifesting His will; " the face of Yahweh " (for example, Ex 33:14 ff.; Dt 4:37; Is 63:9) often signifies Yahweh in person [38]; even " the angel of Yahweh " (Gn 16:7.13; Jgs 13:3.21 ff., etc.) is not distinct from Yahweh in the narratives dealing with theophanies. [39] From these indications it may be concluded that the Hebrews attributed to the spirit of Yahweh neither existence nor action distinct from the existence and action of Yahweh.

If, nevertheless, they present the *ruaḥ* as a concrete entity, separable in some way from Yahweh (for example, Ps 104:30), and capable of acting apart from Him, it is only because they cannot conceive an abstract power or an action without material support. Their thought remains imaginative and attached to sensible impressions, the perception of which is at the very beginning of the formation of their language, which will always be poor in abstract terms and dominated by concrete images. But *ruaḥ*, just like the word, [40] is more external to the person and more separable than the hand, the face, or the mouth; the breath, just like the word, acts when it has gone forth from the animated being. This is the reason why the *ruaḥ* of Yahweh is conceived as an entity operating separately from God, although *ruaḥ* cannot really be distinct from God.

§ 8. *The word*

J. Szeruda, *Das Wort Jahwes*, Lodz 1921; P. Heinisch, *Das Wort im A. T. und im alten Orient*, Münster im W. 1922; H. W. Obbink, *De magische beteekenis van den naam inzonderheid in het Oude Egypte*, Amsterdam 1925; O. Grether, *Name und Wort Gottes im A. T.*, Giessen 1933; L. Dürr, *Die Wertung des göttlichen Wortes im A. T. und antiken Orient*, Leipzig 1938; V. Hamp, *Der Begriff " Wort " in den aramäischen Bibelübersetzungen*, München 1938; O. Procksch-G. Kittel, " Lego, " *ThW*, IV, pp. 89-129.

---

[38] Cf. F. Nötscher, *Das Angesicht Gottes schauen*, Würzburg 1924, pp. 47 ff. J. Hempel, *Gott und Mensch im A. T.* [2], Stuttgart 1936, p. 20.

[39] Cf. above II, § 6, A, 2, b, pp. 109 ff.

[40] In the O. T., as in numerous Egyptian and Babylonian texts, a parallel is often drawn between *ruaḥ* and the word (Is 11:4; 34:16; Ps 33:6; 147:18); for the ancients both terms are concrete and acting entities (cf. J. Hehn, *op. cit.*, p. 218; P. van Imschoot, *RB*, 1935, p. 491; L. Dürr, *Die Wertung des göttlichen Wortes*, pp. 104, 149 ff.

The terms that are generally used in Hebrew to designate the word are derived from the roots *'mr* (to say) and *dbr* (to speak; the verb *dbr* has no *Qal* form). The verbs *'âmar* and *dibber* signify also to think; for to say or to speak is to exteriorize that which one " says in one's heart " (*'âmar bĕlibbô*, Gn 17:17; Is 47:8 ff., etc.). And the term *dâbâr* designates not only the word, but also the thing (Gn 24:66; 3 Kgs 11:41, etc.).

For the ancients and the uncivilized the word is not simply the expression of a thought or of a will; it is something concrete, something existing and active, and is, so to say, charged with the force of the soul of the one who pronounces it. The pronounced word does not only subsist in the conscience of the one who pronounced it and of the one who heard it, it exists in itself and acts just as such a concrete force would act; and breath *(ruaḥ)*, which comes forth from the mouth at the same time as the word, is frequently parallel with it (Ps 33:6; 147:18; Is 11:4; 34:16; Prv 1:23; Jb 15:13; Jdt 16:17).[1] Since the word is an active force, curse (Nm 22:6; Ps 109:18; Za 5:2.3) and blessing are considered as efficacious[2]: the blessing which Isaac uttered subsists and will have its effects, although by mistake it had been addressed to Jacob (Gn 27:35-37); the curse pronounced by Josue (Jos 6:26) still weighs upon Jericho many centuries later (3 Kgs 16:34); a curse can only be rendered ineffective by an opposing blessing (Jgs 17:2) or by a blessing from Yahweh (Dt 23:6; Ps 109:28); the curses inscribed on sarcophagi in Egypt, in Phoenicia[3] and on boundaries in Babylon are meant to protect tombs or fields against profaners or thieves.

The efficacy of the word is attributed either to the formula itself — this is the case of the magic formulas of all countries and times — or to the power of him who says it; also then it may be considered as capable of constraining the gods and remains in the sphere of magic. In Egypt, and even in Babylon, one does not always see clearly whether the word acts by itself or by the power of a god. In Israel, without doubt, the use of magic formulas has existed at all time among the lower classes, but has been reproved by the official religion (Ex 22:17; Lev 20:6.27; Dt 18:9-13; 1 Sm 15:23; 28:3;

---

[1] Cf. the Egyptian and Babylonian parallels quoted by J. Hehn, *op. cit.*, p. 218 and L. Dürr, *op. cit.*, pp. 149 ff. and the note 3, p. 200.

[2] Cf. J. Hempel, " Die israelitischen Anschauungen von Segen und Fluch im Lichte altorientalischer Parallelen, " *ZDMG* 1925, pp. 20-110; *id.*, " Segen und Fluch, " *RGG*[2], V, pp. 388-394; P. Heinisch, *Theologie*, pp. 211-212; P. van Imschoot, " Vloek, Zegen, " *BW*; Beyer, " Eulogeô, " *ThW*, II, pp. 751-763.

[3] Cf. the inscriptions of Itobaal of Byblos (1. 2), of Kilamu (1. 14), of Zakir (B, 1. 16) (*AOT*[2], pp. 440-444) and numerous examples quoted by J. Hempel *(op. cit.)*.

Mi 5:11; Jer 27:9; Ez 13:18-20; Mal 3:5). The efficacy of curses and of blessings is derived from Yahweh (Prv 3:33; Sir 4:6; Gn 12:3; Nm 22:6; 23:8); the curse can be obstructed (Nm 22:22 ff.), weakened (Prv 26:2) or changed into a blessing by Yahweh (Dt 23:6); it is ordinarily pronounced in the form of a prayer (Jer 15:15; 18:19-23; Ps 109, etc.).[4] Also the word of a prophet, because he is "a man of God," is sure to prove true (1 Sm 9:6; cf. 3:19; 3 Kgs 17:24; Is 44:26), that is to say, it will certainly come about; it is deadly (Os 6:5) like a sword (Is 49:2), it devours like a fire (Jer 5:14; 23:29) or it is like a hammer shattering rocks (Jer 23:29). And the word of the messianic king, because the spirit of Yahweh rests upon him, will strike the ruthless, as if with a rod, and will slay him (Os 11:4; Ps. Sal. 17:43; Hen 62:2; cf. 2 Thes 2:8; Hebr 4:12; Ap 19:15.21).[5]

Just as in Egypt and in Assyro-Babylonia the gods produce all things by their word,[6] so in the Old Testament whatever Yahweh says comes to be: "He spoke, and it was made, He commanded, and it stood forth"; "by the word of Yahweh the heavens were made, and by the breath of His mouth all their host" (Ps 33:9.6; cf. 148:5; Lam 3:17; Jdt 16:17; Wis 9:1.2; Sir 39:17; *heb.* 42:15); and in the narrative of the creation "God said: Let there be light, and there was light," etc. (Gn 1:3.6.9.11.14.20.24). "Man does not live by bread alone, but by all that comes forth from the mouth of God" (Dt 8:3), that is to say, by all that God produces by His word (cf. Wis 16:26).[7]

By His word God directs the phenomena of nature, such as snow, frost, winds (Ps 107:25; 147:15-18; 148:8; Jb 37:5-13; Sir 39:31), the stars (Is 40:26), the waters of the abyss (Is 44:27; 50:2), the fate of peoples (Is 44:26.28; Ps 46:7; 107:20) and intervenes on behalf of Israel (Ps 46:7; 106:9; 107:25; Wis 16:12; 18:14-19).

---

[4] As for the imprecatory Psalms, cf. P. van Imschoot, "Vloekpsalmen," *BW*, and *Coll. Gand.* 27 (1940-44), pp. 89-93.

[5] In the Aramaic book of Aḥiqar (col. VII, 1.10) the discourse of the king is "more pointed and more cutting than a sword with two edges" (cf. Hebr 4:12; quoted by L. Dürr, *op. cit.*, p. 103).

[6] For example, an Egyptian text says of Thoth, the spokesman of Ra: "What surges from his heart, arrives at once, and what he says, exists eternally" (quoted by Dürr, *op. cit.*, p. 28); in Assyro-Babylonia: "Your word (that is to say, of Enlil; literally: the aperture of his mouth) is a good breath, the life of the lands" (*Ibid.*, p. 34); by a word Marduk destroys a garment and by a word he creates it anew (*Enuma eliš*, IV, 19-26); other numerous examples are quoted by L. Dürr (*Ibid.*, pp. 22 ff.).

[7] The expressions "that which comes forth from the mouth" or from the lips (*môṣâ' peh*, Nm 30:13), or "that which the lips pronounce" (*môṣâ' šěpâtayim*) designate the word (Jer 17:16; Ps 89:35) and recall the Akkadian expression *ṣit pišu* used in the same sense (L. Dürr, *op. cit.*, p. 49).

Even after it has been pronounced, the word of God remains charged with force : it is sent by Yahweh and " falls " upon Israel (Is 9:7); it stands forever (Is 40:8); it is irrevocable (Is 31:2; Jer 4:28; Ps 89:35.36), it does not return void (Is 45:23; 55:10.11), it " does not fall " (Jos 21:43; 23:14), that is to say, it does not remain without effect, evidently not because it acts like a magic word, but because Yahweh Himself keeps it standing (*hêqîm*, Dt 9:5; Nm 23:19; 1 Sm 3:12; Is 44:26, etc.), He fulfills it (*millê'*, 3 Kgs 2:27; 8:24), He realizes it (*'âśâh*, Nm 23:19; Jer 28:6), because He " watches His word to fulfil it " (Jer 1:12).

In the narratives concerning the prophets, as well as in the prophetic books, the expression " the word of Yahweh " *(dĕbar Yahweh)* occurs often; " a word of God " (*dĕbar 'ělohîm*, Jgs 3:20; 1 Sm 9:27; 1 Par 17:3) or " the word of God " (*dĕbar hâ'ělohîm*, 2 Sm 16.23; 3 Kgs 12:22; 1 Par 16:32) are found less frequently. [8] In most of the cases, as a matter of fact, God transmits His communications to His heralds by His word. In many narratives of theophanies, the voice of Yahweh resounds in their ears (for example, Gn 15:1; 22:1 ff.; Ex 3:4; Nm 12:8, etc.; 1 Sm 3:3 ff.); more frequently, however, His word may have been perceived only interiorly (for example, 2 Sm 7:4; 3 Kgs 6:11; 13:20; 17:2.8; Jer 1:4.11; 2:1, etc.; Ez 3:16; 6:1; 7:1, etc.), and " the word of Yahweh " becomes, so to say, a stereotyped expression to designate a divine revelation made to a prophet, for example : to come, to say, etc., " by the word of Yahweh " (3 Kgs 13:1.2.5.9.17. 18.32); the same applies to the words, probably added by the redactor, which introduce the oracles (for example Os 1:1; Mi 1:1; Jer 1:2; Is 38:4). The characteristic mark of the prophet, according to Jeremias (18:18), is really " the word, " just as " instruction " *(tôrâh)* characterizes the priest (cf. Ag 2:11-14; Ez 7:26) and " counsel " the sage.

By His word, communicated to the prophets, Yahweh directs the events, and, consequently, the history of His people (for example, 2 Sm 7:4; 3 Kgs 11:31 ff.; 12:24; 13:1 ff.; 15:29; 16:12; 17:2.8; 18:1; 20:42; 22:19 ff.; 4 Kgs 9:1 ff., etc.); " He smites them by the prophets and slays them by the words of His mouth " (Os 6:5); for His word not only announces the events, but also realizes them (Is 9:7; Jer 5:14; 23:29; Is 49:2; 55:10.11; Za 9:1) : it accomplishes God's will and achieves the end for which it had been sent (Is 55:11).

---

[8] According to Grether (*op. cit.*, pp. 64 ff.), *dĕbar Yahweh* is found 242 times in the Bible, including ten uncertain texts; 214 times, out of the total number, the expression designates the word as addressed by God to the prophet or as the divine word communicated by the prophets.

The word of God, transmitted by the prophets, has in view determined historical circumstances; it has, therefore, a momentary value; but the Old Testament uses the same expression, rarely in the singular (Nm 15:31; Dt 5:5; 1 Par 15:15; 2 Par 30:12; 34:21; 35:6), [9] ordinarily in the plural, in order to designate the divine laws, that is to say, the revelation of the divine will, a revelation that has perpetual value and is independent from the circumstances in which it had been manifested. The decalogue, which is the fundamental law of the covenant concluded on Sinai, already has been called " the words " (Ex 34:28), " the ten words " (Ex 34:28; Dt 4:13) [10] written on tablets of stone (Ex 24:12; 31:18), because it is the revelation of divine precepts which are at the basis of the covenant of Sinai and the transgression of which will lead to the ruin of the people (Os 4:2.3; Jer 7:9). Likewise, according to Ex 24:4.8, " the words of Yahweh, " which Moses wrote on the occasion of the conclusion of the covenant, designate the laws of " the book of the covenant, " laws revealed by Yahweh (v. 3) and accepted by the people (Ex 24:7). [11]

Deuteronomy, which also calls the decalogue " the ten words " (4:13; 10:4), extends the meaning of this expression, however, to all " the words of the covenant " (28:69), that is to say, to all the laws — moral, civil, criminal, religious — of the code promulgated by Moses before the conquest of the promised land, for example, " these words (6:6), " the words of this law " (17:19; 32:46); it extends the expression even to the exhortations (1:1; 30:1), comprising promises and threats (4:30; 30:1), which were addressed to those who might observe or trangress them. Thus Deuteronomy, which by the way describes Moses as a prophet (18:15-18), combines the legal sense of the expression " the word " (or " the words ") and the sense it has with the prophets, and names the whole Mosaic law by the term " the word " (4:2; 30:14; 32:47), because it is " the incarnation of the divine revelation. " [12]

---

[9] In Dt 5:5 the versions read : " My words. "

[10] Does Ex 34:28, at least in its present wording, belong to the primitive part attributed to the Yahwist (Eissfeldt)? Some attribute it entirely to the deuteronomistic redactor (Beer, *in h. l.*), others only the words " the words of the covenant " (Heinisch, *in h. l.*), others, on the contrary, the phrase " the ten words " (Driver, *in h. l.*), etc. " The ten words, " it seems, did not designate the twelve cultual laws which precede it presently, but rather the decalogue, as Procksch (*op. cit.*, p. 98) and others believe (R. Kittel, Baentsch, MacNeile, P. Karge).

[11] The modern authors call by this name (the book of the covenant) the series of laws grouped in Ex 20:22-23:19, but they do not agree on the original place of this code. 4 Kgs 23:2.3.21 gives this name to the code of laws discovered in the temple during the reign of Josias, that is to say, according to the opinion of most recent authors to the code of Deuteronomy.

[12] O. Grether, *Name und Wort Gottes*, p. 126.

It is in the same sense that certain psalms praise the law of Yahweh or His word (for example, Ps 147:19), in particular Psalm 119 [13] which considers it as a synonym of *tôrâh*; the law is " the word of truth " (v. 43), it is the psalmist's hope (v. 49), his comfort (v. 50), and a source of life (vv.50.144), his light (v. 105), his delight (v. 103), the principle of wisdom (vv. 98-100.104).

There are already instances in Deuteronomy and in later books where the expressions " the word " and " the words " no longer designate only the word spoken by God, but the written word as well, and are applied to the whole Law. The Law is considered as the expression, henceforth fixed, of divine revelation, and it is forbidden to add to it or to subtract from it (Dt 4:2; 13:1). This notion is already that of the holy book, which developed after the Exile and finishes with including not only the Law, but also the books in which the discourses of the prophets were conserved, and much later those of the sages. It seems that 1 Par 15:15; 2 Par 30:12; 34:21; 35:6 already designate the divine precepts contained in the Law and the prophets as " the word. " In the Targums, the word plays a still more important role than in the Hebrew text, [14] because the Aramaic translators have frequently, although not constantly, substituted the divine names Yahweh, Elohim, as well as personal and possessive pronouns referring to God, by the expression " the *memra* of Yahweh " (pronounced Adonay) or " *my memra, his memra,* " etc. The Targum of Onkelos, for example, translates Gn 31:5 : " The God of my father has come to my help, " but writes in verse 3 : " *My memra* will help me "; Lev 26:12 : " I will be God for you " is translated by " *My memra* will be God for you "; the Targum of Onkelos translates Ex 12:29 : " Yahweh struck down all the first-born, " but the Targum of Jerusalem says : " The *memra* of Yahweh struck down all the first-born, " whereas later it writes (Ex 13:15) : " Yahweh struck down.... " Onkelos translates Lev 1:1 : " Yahweh spoke with him (Moses) " by : " The *memra* of Yahweh spoke with him "; Onkelos retains (Nm 10:35 ff.) : " May Yahweh manifest Himself... may Yahweh dwell again "; but the Targum of Jerusalem writes : " May the *memra* of Yahweh manifest itself... may the *memra* of Yahweh

[13] As for the meaning of " the Law " in Ps 119, cf. A. Robert, " Le sens du mot Loi dans le Ps 119 (Vulg. 118), " *RB* 1937, pp. 182-206.

[14] Cf. H. Strack-P. Billerbeck, *Kommentar zum N. T. aus Talmud und Midrasch*, München 1922-28, especially Vol. II, pp. 302-333; F. Weber, *Jüdische Theologie auf Grund des Talmuds und verwandten Schriften* [2], Leipzig 1897; G. F. Moore, " Intermediaries in Jewish Theology, " *Hibbert Theol. Revue*, 15 (1922), pp. 41-85; *id., Judaism in the First Centuries of the Christian Era*, I, Cambridge 1927, pp. 414 ff.; V. Hamp, *Der Begriff " Wort " in den Aramäischen Bibelübersetzungen*, Munich 1938.

return"; the expression *'al pê'* (literally: according to the mouth) is often rendered by "*'al memra* of...," for example, Ex 17:1: "At the *memra* of Yahweh"; the hand of Yahweh becomes "the *memra* of Yahweh" (Targ. Onk. Nm 11:23); "of the hand of Yahweh," "of the hand of the *memra* of Yahweh" (Targ. Jos 23:31).

The meaning of *memra* is word, from the root *'âmâr*, to say, to speak; but the word, when it refers to God, is only employed with a possessive (of Yahweh, or My, His, etc.) and only in the Aramaic versions, not in commentaries or rabbinic writings. It is not even used to translate the word *dâbâr* which is regularly translated by *pitgama* (word). In numerous cases, the original meaning (word) still seems to be preserved and understood by the Aramaic translators of the Bible. [15]

Various hypotheses have been proposed to explain the use of *memra* in the Targums; according to one opinion the Aramaic translators wished, by using this expression, to veil the anthropomorphisms of the Old Testament. [16] It seems, indeed, that this preoccupation is manifest in the Targums as also in the Greek version (LXX); but it is also certain that this alone does not explain the phenomenon and has not removed a great deal of anthropomorphisms from the Aramaic versions. Others [17] see in it a consequence of the transcendency attributed to God: Yahweh, having become transcendent, would act only through intermediaries, of which the *memra* would be one instance. But transcendence has never, either in the Bible or in recent Judaism, separated God from creatures to the extent of forbidding a direct action on them and postulating the introduction of hypostases by which God could act. [18] V. Hamp [19] explains the phenomenon as an exegetical procedure by which the Aramaic translators tried to give greater clarity to biblical texts and to prevent, among the less trained readers, an all too crude and erroneous interpretation. This explanation appears to be just, but insufficient. [20]

---

[15] Cf. V. Hamp, *op. cit.*, pp. 88 ff.

[16] S. Maybaum, *Die Anthropomorphien und Anthropopathien bei Onkelos und den späteren Targumin*, Breslau 1870; M. Ginsburger, "Die Anthropomorphismen in den Targumim," *Jahrbücher für protestantische Theologie*, 17 (1891), pp. 262-281; 430-459, and others quoted by Hamp (*op. cit.*, p. 72).

[17] F. Weber, *op. cit.*, p. 157; W. Bousset-H. Gressmann, *Die Religion des Judentums*, pp. 313-320; L. Bouyer, *La Bible et l'évangile*, Paris 1952, pp. 35 ff.

[18] As for the question of divine hypostases, cf. III, § 10.

[19] L. Bouyer, *op. cit.*, p. 79.

[20] One does not see, for example, how an expression like "to conclude a covenant between the word of Yahweh and men" clarifies the idea of a covenant between God and Israel; nor that "my *memra* will be God for you" explains "I will be God for you."

We must add, it seems, the preoccupation to avoid certain anthropomorphisms that were too hard, and the tendency of Judaism to substitute, on account of respect, divine names Yahweh, Elohim, by periphrases like " the Heaven, " " the Name, " " the Place, " " the Dwelling, " " the Omnipotence, " " the Merciful, " etc. [21]

§ 9. *The name*

F. Giesebrecht, *Die alttestamentliche Schätzung des Gottesnamens und ihre religionsgeschichtliche Grundlage*, Königsberg 1901; H. W. Obbink, *De magische beteekenis van den naam inzonderheid in het Oude Egypte*, Amsterdam 1925; J. Perdersen, *Israel*, I, London 1926, pp. 245 ff.; O. Grether, *Name und Wort Gottes im A. T.*, Giessen 1933; H. Schmidt, " Namenglaube, " *RGG* ², III, cols. 408-410; W. Heitmüller, *Im Namen Jesu*, Göttingen 1903; Bietenhardt, " Onoma, " *ThW*, V, pp. 242 ff.

The name of God plays an important role in the religion of the Old Testament, and in particular in the revelation of God. The name, indeed, is in the eyes of the ancients and of the uncivilized not only that which characterizes, distinguishes, and consequently makes known him who bears it, but also an integrating part of the individual and something which possesses a mysterious force. Whatever has no name, does not exist [1]: an insignificant man is " a man without name " (Jb 30:8); " whatever is, its name was called long ago " (Eccl 6:10); on the contrary, the name of a still-born child is covered with darkness (Eccl 6:3.4; cf. Ps 41:6). The name corresponds to the essence of the thing : " For as his name is, so he is; Nabal (= fool) is his name, and there is folly in him " (1 Sm 25:25). [2]

Given the belief in the force of the name and in the connection existing between the name and the person or its nature, the name is considered as a kind of double of the person (cf., for example, Is 30:27.28), and is even employed as a synonym of the person (Nm 1:2-42): to know someone's name is to have power over him; for this reason in Egypt and elsewhere the gods keep their names

[21] Cf. H. Strack-P. Billerbeck, *op. cit.*, p. 308; cf. for example : Onkelos Ex 33:19 : " I shall proclaim the name Memra Adonay " instead of " I shall proclaim the name of Yahweh "; Onkelos Is 8:5 : " The Memra of Adonay spoke to me " instead of " Yahweh spoke to me. " These examples, which could be multiplied, seem to prove that often the Memra of Yahweh (pronounced Adonay) is hardly more than a respectful periphrase, just as Adonay is a substitute of the same genre for the sacred tetragram.

[1] In order to express in the Babylonian narrative of the creation that the heaven and the earth did not exist, it is said that " they had not yet been named "; " no name had been named, " that is to say, nothing existed.

[2] Cf. the proverb : *nomen est omen*.

concealed (cf. Gn 32:30; Jgs 13:6)[3]; to pronounce the name is to attract the presence or, at least, the power of that person; one is also afraid to pronounce the name of an angry god (Am 6:10).[4] To pronounce the name of a person over another person or over an object, is to establish the power of the person whose name has been pronounced over the object: if the name of Joab would be pronounced over the city he had taken, it would belong to him (2 Sm 12:28); seven women who wish that the name of one man be pronounced over them, wish that he become their master (their *ba'al*, husband, Is 4:1); he who writes the name of Yahweh on his hand, declares himself and really becomes the servant of Yahweh (Is 44:5; cf. Ap 13:16.17; 14:9, etc.); to change the name of an individual is to change his personality and to submit him to the power of him who gives the name; victorious kings do this when they impose a new name on vanquished kings (4 Kgs 23:34; 24:17). Finally, pronouncing the name of a powerful being assures the protection and the action of that being: thus, when the priest blesses the assembly, "he places" *(śîm)* the name of Yahweh over the people, and Yahweh really gives His blessing (Nm 6:27); "the name of Yahweh is a strong tower," where the just will find safety for himself (Prv 18:10; cf. Ps 20:2). It is for this reason that the exorcisms among the Jews are performed "in the name of Yahweh," that is to say, by pronouncing His name (cf. Acts 19:13; Lk 9:49).[5]

In view of all this it can be understood that the name played an important role in the magic of all peoples, at all times, and also in polytheistic religions, since it was indispensable to know the name of the god whom one wanted to invoke, and to pronounce his name in a loud voice in order to attract his attention (3 Kgs 18:16-28), his power and his presence. A trace of that belief has been preserved by the Old Testament in the expression *qârâ' běšem Yahweh* (Gn 4:26; 12:8; 13:4; 21:33; 26:25), which is ordinarily translated by "to invoke the name of Yahweh," but which literally signifies "to appeal (cry) by the name of Yahweh," that is to say, to call on Yahweh by pronouncing the divine name with a loud voice in an act of public worship. With regard to the public worship of Yahweh, however,

---

[3] For the same reason, among certain uncivilized peoples, men keep their true name concealed.

[4] There perhaps remains some trace of that fear in the care which the Jews took to avoid the pronunciation of the name of Yahweh; but here it is rather a case of reverential fear; this care may in part be due to an extension of Ex 20:7 and of Dt 5:11 which forbid the misuse, that is to say, principally the magic use, of the divine name.

[5] Cf. the formulas of exorcisms including the name of 'Ιαω (Yahweh) in W. Baudissin, *Kyrios*, II, pp. 189-236.

the Israelite knows that the invocation of the divine name does not force God, for he is aware of the prohibition which forbids the misuse of the sacred name (Ex 20:7; Dt 5:11), that is to say, the use of the name for magic purposes (cf. Ex 22:17).[6] The expression *qârâ' běšem Yahweh* eventually signified to worship Yahweh (often in a sacred place), or, quite simply, to invoke Him in prayer or in a cultic act (Is 12:4; 41:25; Jer 10:25; Ps 80:19; 105, etc.), just like the parallel expression *qârâ' 'el Yahweh* (Ps 4:4; 28:1), to cry to Yahweh, to invoke Him, and *qârâ' šem Yahweh* (Dt 32:3; Ps 99:6; Lam 3:55), to invoke (to proclaim) the name of Yahweh.

The traditions recorded by Exodus insist on the revelation of the name of God who manifested Himself to Moses on Sinai : by revealing His proper name " Yahweh " (Ex 3:14.13; 6:3), God manifested not only His person, but also His very Being, sovereignly independent and efficient. The God of Sinai has nothing to fear, as do the gods of Egypt and elsewhere, by making His name known, precisely because He is who is,[7] and is not exposed to succumbing to the domination and constraint of the magicians. If he forbids, nevertheless, the misuse of His name (Ex 20:7; Dt 5:11), He does it because the use of the names of gods or of demons was a frequent magic practice, deeply anchored in the people (cf. Ex 22:17; Lev 20:27; Dt 18:9-13; 1 Sm 28:3), although it was a less virulent practice in Israel than among other Semites and the Egyptians (Nm 23:23). The name of Yahweh holds a considerable place in the cult and the religious life of Israel because " at every place, where Yahweh records His name, He comes and blesses " (Ex 20:24), that is to say, at every sanctuary where He wishes and ordains that His name be remembered, Yahweh is present and blessed.[8] It is " in the name of Yahweh " *(běšem Yahweh)*,

---

[6] The expression *laššâw'* signifies : in vain, or badly; *šâw'* is said of what is unreal, vain, useless, false, without value : for example " a false witness " (Dt 5:20), " a false report " (Ex 23:1). In Ex 20:7 and Dt 5:11 it is better to translate " badly " *(frevelhaft)* than " deceitfully " *(lügenhaft; GB, s. v.)*. Every misuse of the name of Yahweh is forbidden, and especially, the misuse of the divine name in magic practices (cf. P. Heinisch, *Das Buch Exodus*, Bonn 1934, p. 153; G. Beer, *Exodus*, Tübingen 1939, p. 101; E. M. T. Böhl, *Exodus*, Gröningen 1928, p. 147; Böhl quotes also O. Eissfeldt, " Jahweh-Name und Zauberwesen, " *Zeitschrift für Missionskunde*, 1927, pp. 161-185).

[7] Cf. above, pp. 15 ff.

[8] According to the Massoretic Text the initiative in the cult and in the invocation of the divine name is attributed to God; it is not man who, by invoking the name and by the cult, provokes and constrains God to be present and to come to his help. In the Old Testament the magic conception of the power of the name is effaced. The Syriac version interpreted : " Where you will record My name "; but this reading which attributes to man the initiative of the cult, cannot be preferred, it seems (Beer, *in h. l.*, quoting Merx, Procksch), to that of the M. T., upheld by the LXX and the Vulgate.

that is to say, by pronouncing the divine name, that the Hebrew prays and offers his sacrifices, swears, blesses, curses, fights and triumphs (Gn 4:26; 13:4; 1 Sm 20:42; 2 Sm 6:18; 4 Kgs 2:24; 1 Sm 17:45; Ps 20:6.8). He knows, indeed, that the invocation of the sacred name will guarantee him the presence and the help of Yahweh; he does not believe, however, as most of the ancients and uncivilized do, that he can constrain his God, because he has the very clear and profound awareness of his own dependence (cf. Dt 33:3; Jb 23:14-16) and of the grandeur of the Most High, his Lord, [9] before whom he feels himself " dust and ashes " (Gn 18:27).

Since the name supposedly corresponds to the reality of the thing or the person, the name really manifests what that reality is. " A man of name " (Gn 6:4; Nm 16:2; 1 Par 5:24) is a man who appears and is recognized as a powerful personality. The name, in this case, assumes the meaning of renown, of glory, of honor; it designates not only the esteem acquired among others, but signifies above all, like the Hebrew word *kabôd* (glory : from the root *kbd*, to have weight), the intrinsic value of the individual. Yahweh acts " for His great name " (Jos 7:9) or " for His holy name " (Ez 36:22), that is to say, in order to assert Himself and to be recognized as great and holy. One asks Him not to reject the prayer of His people " because of His name " (Jer 14:21), because one is convinced that the renown or the glory of Yahweh is identified with the prosperity and the power of His people (cf. Ez 36:20-22). The name, therefore, is often associated or considered as parallel with the glory of Yahweh (for example, Is 42:8; 59:19; Ps 102:16). [10]

The intimate connection which exists between God and His name already appears in the ancient and strictly synonymous expressions " to swear by the name of Yahweh " (for example, 1 Sm 20:42) and " to swear by Yahweh " (Jos 2:12; 3 Kgs 1:17), " to curse by the name of Yahweh " (4 Kgs 2:24) or " to curse by God " (1 Sm 17:43). For this reason a parallel is frequently drawn between the name of Yahweh and Yahweh Himself (Is 25:1; 56:6; Ps 9:2.11; 18:50; 68:5; 74:18; 86:12, etc.) so that the name of Yahweh is used as the equivalent of Yahweh; and expressions like " to profane His name " (Am 2:7; Lev 18:21; 19:12), to sanctify it (Is 29:23), to love it (Ps 5:12), to praise it (Ps 7:18; 9:3), to exalt it (Ps 34:4), etc., signify to profane, sanctify, love, praise, exalt Yahweh. Among the Rabbis, finally, " the name " becomes one of the periphrases which designates God.

---

[9] As for the antiquity and the meaning of the divine names El, ʿelyôn, Adon Melek, cf. above pp. 7, 21 ff.
[10] On glory, cf. below III, § 10, pp. 199 ff.

The name itself can be presented as a double of Yahweh : the name comes from afar, burning in anger (Is 30:27), the name is in the angel who guides, protects Israel and gives them orders (Ex 23:20.21), the name is a strong tower (Prv 18:10), the name protects (Ps 20:2) and helps (Ps 54:3; 3 Kgs 8:42, where the name is associated with the hand and the arm; cf. Ps 89:25). The name thus designates God inasmuch as He manifested Himself to men.

In Deuteronomy and in several texts of the same school or which derive therefrom, the " name " is used in order to avoid an expression that might be too gross when speaking of God's presence in the temple or in the holy city, since the transcendent God cannot be contained in a sanctuary or in a determined place (3 Kgs 8:27)[18bis] : the temple is the place where Yahweh makes His name dwell (Dt 12:5.11; 14:23; 16:2.6.11; 26:2; Neh 1:9), the place He has chosen for His name to dwell (Dt 12:5.21; 14:24; 2 Par 6:20; cf. 3 Kgs 9:3; 4 Kgs 21:7); " His name is in " the temple 3 Kgs 8:16.29; 4 Kgs 23:27) and in the holy city (2 Par 6:6; 33:4). In these expressions the name is less a double of Yahweh than a literary device, aiming to explain that although the presence of God is not limited either to the temple or to Jerusalem, God manifests especially His presence and His benevolent protection there, because the temple is the place which He has chosen for His cult, and which He has appropriated for Himself, or, as 3 Kgs 8:43 (cf. Jer 7:10.11) says, because His name has been pronounced over that house. For this reason one no longer naively says that God dwells in the temple (cf. 3 Kgs 8:10-12), but that His name resides there.

§ 10. *The glory*

G. B. Gray-I. Massie, " Glory, " *HDB*, II, pp. 183-186; A. Marmorstein, " Iranische und jüdische Religion, mit besonderer Berücksichtigung der Begriffe ' Wort, ' ' Wohnen ' und ' Glorie ' im IV Evangelium und in der rabbinischen Literatur, " *ZNW*, 1927, pp. 231-242; A. von Gall, *Die Herrlichkeit Gottes*, Giessen 1900; H. Kittel, *Die Herrlichkeit Gottes*, Giessen 1934; G. Kittel-G. von Rad, " Doxa, " *ThW*, II, pp. 236-258; E. S. Owen, " Doxa and Cognate Words, " *JThS*, 33 (1931), pp. 132-150; 265-279; B. Stein, *Der Begriff Kebod Jahweh und seine Bedeutung für die alttestamentliche Gotteserkenntnis*, Emsdetten 1939; P. van Imschoot, " Heerlijkheid, " *BW*, cols. 613-169.

1. The Hebrew word which is generally translated by glory *(kabôd)*, is derived from the verb *kdb* which properly signifies to be heavy. Glory, in its primary sense, is that which gives weight, importance, which imposes esteem and gives prestige : the term *kabôd* may thus signify wealth (Gn 31:1; Ps 49:17), pomp, luxury (Est 1:4), might

[18bis] This verse interrupts the context and is a late addition.

(Is 16:14; 21:16), the remuneration paid to a soothsayer (Nm 24:11). The primary meaning of this term is concrete, but it is used also in an abstract sense and often signifies glory, honor, majesty (for example, Ps 8:6; 21:6; Prv 25:2; Is 14:18); but even in this sense it does not signify only the esteem paid by another or external splendor, but also the intrinsic value of the individual.

What gods and men appreciate *(jĕkabdû)* in an olive tree, is its oil which constitutes its value (*kabôd*; Jgs 9:9); Samuel " is esteemed " *(nikbâd)*, for he truly is what his name implies, " a man of God " (1 Sm 9:6); David " is honored " *(nikbâd)* in the house of Saul, because he is faithful and the son-in-law of the king (1 Sm 22:14); " the glory " of Joseph is the power and the high position which he obtained in Egypt (Gn 45:13); " the glory of Lebanon " (Is 35:2; 60:13) is that which makes its splendor and its wealth, it is the mighty forest of cedars; the ark of Yahweh is " the glory of Israel, " that which constitutes its strength and its honor (1 Sm 4:22); Yahweh " is the glory of Israel " (Ps 106:20; Jer 2:11), that is to say, that which gives power and prestige to Israel. The *kabôd* of man is so intimately united with his intrinsic value, that a parallel may be drawn between man's *kabôd*, his soul (Gn 49:6), his person (Ps 30:13), his heart (Ps 16:9; 57:9; 108:2), his life (Ps 7:6).

2. The *kabôd* of Yahweh is that which gives weight, prestige, and inspires man to respect and fear. The glory of Yahweh, therefore, is originally something intrinsic to God, but manifested externally. It is, indeed, what constitutes God as God, that is to say, according to the idea of the Hebrews, His holiness and His power, but manifested. Thus, in order to express that God reveals what He is, namely holy and mighty, one says that " He glorifies Himself " or " He sanctifies Himself. " [1] " He will glorify Himself in Pharao and in his whole army " (Ex 14:4.17.18), that is to say, He will manifest by His miracles what He is, namely almighty, " and that one may know that He is Yahweh "; " He glorifies Himself " by increasing Israel (Is 26:15), or " He sanctifies Himself " by restoring His people (Ez 36:24); by showing His might against Sidon, " He will glorify Himself in her midst " or " He will sanctify Himself in her " and " one will know that He is Yahweh " (Ex 28:22.23); destroying Abiu and Nadab by fire, " He sanctified Himself among those who were near Him " and " He glorified Himself in the eyes of Israel " (Lev 10:3).

One may, therefore, define the glory of God: the divinity manifested, or more precisely: divine holiness and power manifested.

---

[1] The two verbs are parallel and used as synonyms by Ez 28:22; Lev 10:3.

If, instead of placing the accent on divine holiness and power, one places it on their manifestation, one will define the glory of Yahweh by " manifestation of the holiness and of the power of God. " This manner of conceiving the glory of Yahweh, which is frequently found in the Old Testament, will form the object of point 4 of this article.

3. The glory of Yahweh, understood as divine holiness and power manifested, is often mentioned, especially in the Psalms and prophetical books. Yahweh is " the king of glory, " that is to say, " the strong, the mighty in battle " (Ps 24:7.8.10) : this Psalm praises the power, the grandeur and the majesty of the warrior king of Israel, who is making his triumphal entry into his palace, that is to say, into the temple. Isaias (6:3) contemplates the King — Yahweh, the Holy One — seated on a high throne, surrounded by Seraphim who acclaim Him : " Holy, holy, holy is Yahweh Sabaoth, all the earth is full of His glory. " The glory is the holiness and the majesty of the holy God, of the King of the universe.

Often the glory of Yahweh is the royal majesty and the power which He manifests through His works and miracles, be it as the author of created nature (Ps 19:2; 29:1.3; 104:31), [2] be it as the protector of His people (Ex 16:7; Nm 14:21.22; Is 35:2; Ps 66:2; 79:9; 108:6.7) or of the pious Israelite (Is 58:8; Ps 57:6.12; 138:5; 145:5.11), be it as judge of the nations (Is 59:19; Ps 66:2).

The glory of Yahweh, that is the manifested power and majesty of the universal King, assumes in the Psalms of Yahweh's Enthronement (Ps 96:3.7.8; 97:6), an eschatological meaning, which is also found in the second and third part of the book of Isaias : " A voice cries out : In the desert clear the way of Yahweh...let the rugged heights become a valley; then the glory of Yahweh shall be revealed and all flesh shall see it (the salvation wrought by God) " [3] (Is 40:3-5). The glory is the power which the King Yahweh will manifest by bringing about the salvation of Israel. Elsewhere (Is 60:1.2) the glory is represented as a light which rises and irradiates Jerusalem : " Arise, shine, for your light has come, and the glory of Yahweh rises (like a sun) upon you.... Upon you Yahweh rises (like a sun) and His glory appears upon you. " Although this description of the glory of Yahweh reminds us of that given by Ezechiel (43:2 ff.), it cannot

---

[2] The whole Psalm 29 insists on the power of the voice, that is to say, of the word of Yahweh, exercising itself in nature (cf. Ps 104); the expression " the God of glory thunders " designates the thunder as the voice of the almighty and terrible God (cf. Ps 18:14). The tempest manifests the might of the terrible and majestic God, and the poet invites " the sons of God " to celebrate Him.

[3] Text corrected according to the LXX.

be understood here in the proper sense: the glory of Yahweh is no more a light which rises like the sun than Yahweh Himself. The light is only a figure of the manifested majesty and power of God, whose protection assures the happiness of restored Jerusalem, or, as the prophet says, irradiates Sion (cf. Is 62:1.2). Is 66:18-19 announces that all nations will come to Jerusalem in order to see the glory of Yahweh, that is to say, His power manifested by a sign which will consist in the reunion of dispersed Israel; "and Yahweh will send messengers to all the nations which have not heard His fame, nor seen His glory," that is to say, His power and His majesty. "To see the glory" of Yahweh is to recognize His power by the sign which He accomplishes.

Ps 73:23-26, finally, which expresses very high sentiments of confidence and love toward Yahweh, seems to insinuate the hope that the Psalmist will be "received" by God into the glory (cf. Ps 49:16). Must this text be understood in an eschatological sense, and must we recognize there an analogous idea to that which is found in the New Testament? Several believe so[4]; others deny it and correct the text of verse 24 which is not certain.

In other texts one speaks of "the glory of the name of Yahweh," or one considers the two terms "glory" and "name" as parallel: thus Ps 29:1 invites the "sons of God" to "give to Yahweh glory and strength," to "give Him the glory of His name" (cf. Ps 66:2), that is to say, to recognize Him for what He is, mighty and exalted (cf. Jos 7:19; 1 Sm 6:5; Jer 13:16)[5]; the name seems here to be understood as the manifested personality, as in Is 59:19 and Ps 102:16, where "to fear"[6] the name of Yahweh is parallel with "to fear" "His glory," that is to say, to fear the holy God, mighty and terrible.[7] One asks His help "for the glory of His name" or "for His name" (Ps 79:9; Jer 14:21; cf. Jos 7:9; Ez 36:22), that is to say, in order that He may affirm Himself and be recognized as mighty, great and holy. The name and the glory are so intimately

---

[4] This is the understanding of B. Stein (*Der Begriff kebod Jahweh*, pp. 218 ff.), F. Nötscher (*Das Angesicht Gottes schauen*, Würzburg 1924, p. 163), several commentators of the Psalms (R. Kittel, J. Calès, B. Duhm, Briggs, Staerck), whereas H. Gunkel, H. Herkenne, H. Schmidt and others reject this interpretation and correct verse 24; cf. part II, II, 3, 2c.

[5] The expressions *śîm kabôd* (Jos 7:19), *nâtan kabôd* (1 Sm 6:5; Jer 13:16) and *yhb kabôd* (Ps 29:1; 96:7) are synonyms and signify to give glory.

[6] In Is 59:19 and Ps 102:16, instead of *yir'û* = "fear!," certain manuscripts have *yr'û* = "see!" There is no reason to prefer this reading (against Gunkel, *in h.l.*).

[7] Ps 102:16: the nations will fear the name or the glory of Yahweh, "when He will have rebuilt Sion and appeared in His glory," that is to say, in His power.

tied to the person, to the very existence of Yahweh, that He may not give up either the one or the other : " I am Yahweh, this is My name; I will not give My glory to another, nor My honor to carved images " (Is 42:8; cf. 48:4); " the name " expresses the essence of God, His divinity, and since here it is a question of the name of " Yahweh, " it expresses that it is God who effectively manifests His existence (Ex 3:14); " the glory " manifests that which He is, " the holy, " who is absolutely different and above every other being (cf. Is 40:25; 46:5). Yahweh could not give up His glory without giving up that which He is.

It is again the holiness of Yahweh which Is 3:8 underlines, when he declares that the sins of Jerusalem defy " the eyes of His glory, " that is to say, the regard of the holy God (cf. 5:18 ff.), whose eyes cannot endure the sight of evil (cf. Hb 1:12 ff.).

In Jer 14:21 the people supplicate Yahweh to have pity: " For Your name's sake spurn us not, profane not the throne of Your glory. " The destruction of Sion and of the temple, where Yahweh dwells (cf. 3:17; 17:12), would be a profanation of His glorious throne [8] (cf. 17:12) and of His name (cf. Ez 36:22), that is to say, of the holiness of His throne and of His person, the holiness which should render them inviolable. The motives which Yahweh has to save Sion are all personal: the honor of His name, the glory of His throne, the covenant which He had concluded with His people (Jer 14:22). The Levites invite the people to " bless " Yahweh; and " they blessed the name of His glory which is exalted over all blessing and praise " [9] (Neh 9:5). " The name of His glory, " that is to say, His glorious name, is here perfectly parallel with Yahweh Himself and insists on the majesty of God who is above all praise.

4. The glory, understood as a manifestation of the holiness and power of Yahweh, is hardly mentioned except in the narratives referring to Moses and in Ezechiel. It forms part of the descriptions of theophanies and of visions presented as theophanies.

---

[8] In the expression *kissê' kĕbôdekâ*, the possessive pronoun seems to refer to *kissê'* just as in similar expressions : *šem kĕbôdô* = His glorious name (Ps 72:19), *markĕbôt kĕbôdekâ* = Your glorious chariots (Is 22:18), *šem qŏdšî* = My holy name (Lv 20:3), *ruaḥ qŏdšo* = His holy spirit (Is 63:11), etc. Wis 9:10 and Dn 3:53 ff. (Vulg.) name the heaven " the throne of Your glory, " or " of Your holy glory " (cf. B. Stein, *op. cit.*, p. 100, n. 228 and 229). The expression *kissê' kabôd* is also used in profane language to designate an honorable seat (1 Sm 2:8; Is 22:23). Can the expression *miškan kĕbôdekâ* = the temple (Ps 26:8) be understood in the sense of " Your glorious dwelling, " as in Jer 14:21; 17:12, or is it an allusion to Ex 40:34 ff.; 3 Kgs 8:10-13 and does it designate the temple as the dwelling of the glory of Yahweh?

[9] With the LXX we read *kĕbôdô mĕrômâm* and *wayyĕbirkû* instead of *wibârkû*.

The oldest text (Ex 33:18-23) [10] throws vivid light upon the holiness of Yahweh, whom no mortal can see and live (v. 20; cf. Gn 32:31; Jgs 6:22.23; 13:22; Is 6:5). When Moses asked Yahweh for the favor to see " His glory, " He answered him: " My face you cannot see, for no man sees Me and still lives.... Here is a place near Me, where you shall station yourself on the rock. When My glory passes, I will set you in the hollow of the rock and will cover you with My hand until I have passed by. Then I will remove My hand, so that you may see My back; but My face is not to be seen. " As the face, so also the glory is here identified with Yahweh. [11] Moses cannot see either the face or the glory of Yahweh, because, when it passes before him, Yahweh will cover his eyes with His hand. When Yahweh will remove His hand, Moses will be able to see Him from behind, that is to say, he will see something less distinct than " the face " and something like a reflection that remains after the passage of God's glory. Since the whole narrative, which is naively anthropomorphic, deals evidently with a corporal vision, [12] the glory, although identified with Yahweh, must be a splendor perceptible with the eyes of the body: it is here the splendor of the holy God, whose direct light the eyes of man cannot endure.

In a series of texts attributed to the Sacerdotal Code, " the glory of Yahweh " is a visible phenomenon, similar to a fire (Ex 24:17); it is frequently associated with a cloud, [13] and like it manifests the

---

[10] Most of the critics attribute Ex 33:18-23 as a whole to the Yahwist, or at least to a stratum of it. H. Gressmann (*Die Anfänge Israels* [2], Göttingen 1914, p. 73) detaches verses 20 to 23 (E). But verse 22 evidently belongs to the primitive narrative.

[11] " To see My face " = to see Me (v. 20); " My glory passes " = I pass (v. 22). There is no relation whatsoever between the glory and the ark (against Eissfeldt, *Exateuchsynopse*, p. 274, who refers erroneously to 1 Sm 4:21, where the glory is not the visible manifestation of God).

[12] The eyes of Moses would not be able to endure the light of the glory of Yahweh; for this reason Yahweh covers his eyes with His hand (cf. F. Nötscher, *Das Angesicht Gottes schauen*, Würzburg 1924, p. 45). The same author interprets thus the idea which the narrative expressed anthropomorphically: " It is not given to man to understand God completely; he can only perceive interiorly, as from afar and from behind, the effects of the power of God, inasmuch as they are produced by the divine manifestation " (*op. cit.*, p. 46).

[13] The cloud, in all the strata of the Pentateuch, is the sign of the presence of Yahweh on Sinai — Horeb (Ex 19:9; 34:5 J; 19:6 E; 24:16-18 P; Dt 4:11; 5:22.[19]). It hides Him, for man cannot see Him and live (Ex 33:20; Jgs 6:22; 13:22; Is 6:5, etc.), although it manifests His presence (Ex 16:10). The column of cloud, which is fire during the night (Ex 13:21 J; Nm 9:16; 14:14 P), is only mentioned in texts attributed to J and to E. According to J (Ex 13:21 ff.; 14:19b.20; cf. Nm 14:14; Dt 1:33; Neh 9:12.19; Ps 78:14), Yahweh guided His people by it in the desert. According to E, it remained at the entrance of the " meeting tent, " when Moses approached to consult Yahweh (Ex 33:7-11; cf. Nm 11:25; 12:5; Dt 31:15; Ps 99:7). According to P, the cloud as well as the glory of Yahweh covered during seven days Mount Sinai (Ex 24:16-18). The cloud is ordinarily associated with the " meeting tent, " except in Ex 16:10 and in Nm 10:34; Ps 105:39, where

presence of the almighty and terrible God. It appears on Sinai: "The glory of Yahweh rested on Mount Sinai and the cloud covered it for six days" (Ex 24:16).[14] "On the seventh day He[15] called Moses from the midst of the cloud. The aspect of the glory of Yahweh appeared to the eyes of the children of Israel like a consuming fire on the summit of the mountain" (cf. Dt 5:22.23). The cloud and the glory are here sensible phenomena manifesting the presence of the holy God, who reveals Himself to Moses on the holy mountain. The idea of the holiness of God is still more apparent in Ex 40:34.35, which closes the narrative of the erection of the "meeting tent": "The cloud covered the meeting tent, and the glory of Yahweh filled the dwelling. Moses could not enter the meeting tent, because the cloud settled down upon it and the glory of Yahweh filled the dwelling" (cf. 3 Kgs 8:11; 2 Par 5:14; 7:1.2). Neither Moses nor the priests (3 Kgs 8:11) can enter the sanctuary when the cloud covers it, and when the glory, that is to say, the visible manifestation of the holy God, fills it. The glory of Yahweh is still associated with the cloud in Ex 16:10: the glory "appears in the cloud," and in Nm 17:7, where the glory appeared when the cloud covered the meeting tent and manifested the presence of Yahweh who announced a terrible chastisement against Israel in rebellion.

When the glory of Yahweh is mentioned alone (Ex 29:43; Lev 9:6.23; Nm 14:10; 16:19; 20:6), it is localized near the meeting tent, and only once in its interior (Nm 14:10; cf. Ex 29:43),[16] and it reveals the presence of God who is going to manifest His power by a miracle. With the exception of Ex 29:43, the text of which is uncertain, the glory of Yahweh is not presented as habitually residing in the proximity or in the interior of the sanctuary; on the contrary, the glory appears when Yahweh will manifest His power by some

---

it stands over the Israelites and seems to protect them; it covers the tent constantly (cf. however Nm 17:7) ever since the moment of its erection, when the glory filled it, hindering Moses from entering (Ex 40:34 ff.; cf. 3 Kgs 8:11). Whenever the cloud was lifted, the Israelites used to set out on their journeys; wherever the cloud came to a standstill, there they erected their tents (Ex 40:36.37; Nm 19:15-22).

[14] The masculine pronoun attached to the verb *wayyĕkassêhû* may refer to *kabôd* or to *har* (mountain). If it is referred to *kabôd*, it seems that the cloud was destined to temper the light of His glory; cf. Ex 16:10 "the glory of the Lord appeared in the cloud."

[15] The LXX insert here "Yahweh."

[16] The text of Ex 29:43 is not certain: the subject of the verb *niqdâš* is not expressed; in the present context it seems to be the meeting tent, which will be consecrated by the glory of Yahweh; certain critics affirm that this text is no longer in its primitive place and assume that the altar is the subject. The Greek (LXX) and Syriac versions, and Targum Onkelos read *wĕniqdaštî* = I shall sanctify myself by My glory, that is to say: I shall manifest My holiness by My glory.

striking action. Ps 26:9 alludes perhaps [17] to 3 Kgs 8:11 (Ex 40:34.35), but no longer understands "the glory of Yahweh" as a visible manifestation of God; the expression "the dwelling of Your glory" designates the temple as the residence of the almighty God, whose protection is invoked (v. 1) and whose presence in the temple is looked for (cf. Ps 63:3).

That which characterizes "the glory of Yahweh" in Ezechiel (1:4-28) is its igneous, luminous character; it is like a dense cloud, enveloped in brightness from the midst of which shoot forth lightnings; it is like a mass of fire or of gleaming metal (1:4), and is associated with a brilliant, radiant human form. "Above the firmament... something like a throne could be seen, looking like sapphire; on that which looked like a throne, One was seated who had the appearance of man. And...upward from what resembled His waist I saw what gleamed like electrum; downwards from what resembled His waist I saw something like fire, and He was surrounded by splendor... Such was the vision of the glory of Yahweh" (1:26-28; cf. 8:2.3). At the sight of this grandiose scene and of this luminous figure which symbolized the majesty of the most holy, most high and most powerful God, the prophet "falls on his face" (1:28). The mystery and the transcendence of God are indicated at the same time by the luminosity of the figure which the prophet perceives, and by the accumulation of terms which insist on the approximative character of the description of God, whom no man can perceive distinctly nor describe adequately.

This luminous mass rises over the Cherubim and stays above them, it moves (10:4), leaves the threshold of the temple and returns again to its place over the Cherubim (10:4.18); the Cherubim transport it to the East of the temple (10:19) and finally out of the holy city to a high mountain east of the city (11:23). This exodus of the glory presages the departure of Yahweh about to leave His temple before the destruction of it and of Jerusalem. All this passes in a vision.

In the description of the messianic temple, the glory of Yahweh appears to the prophet under the same figure (43:3) as in the vision which he had near the river Chobar (1:1 ff.; 9; 10); the glory comes from the East (cf. 11:23) with a sound "similar to that of many waters" (43:2), and while the prophet falls on his face (43:3; cf. 1:28; 3:23; 44:4), it enters into the temple by the eastern gate (43:4; cf. 10:19), and the whole temple is filled with the glory of Yahweh (43:5). Here the glory is conceived, as in Ex 40:34.35 and 3 Kgs 8:11, as a luminous phenomenon, manifesting the presence of God (cf. Ez 43:1; 44:4;

---

[17] Cf. p. 202, note 4.

10:4), who returns to His temple. In Ez 39:21, however, the glory of Yahweh is employed abstractly and designates the terrible power which Yahweh manifests in His judgments against the nations (cf. Ez 28:22).

The glory, the sensible manifestation of the holy and mighty God, is constantly distinguished from the cloud, although the cloud often plays the same role, be it mentioned alone (Lv 16:2; Nm 11:25), particularly in the theophany of Sinai (Ex 34:5; 19:9.16; Dt 4:11; 5:19), be it associated with the glory (Ex 16:10; 24:16; 40:34.35; 3 Kgs 8:11; 2 Par 5:14; 7:1.2). The glory, furthermore, is not identified either with the column, luminous during the night, nebulous during the day, which guided Israel in the desert (Ex 13:21.22; cf. Nm 14:14; Dt 1:33; Ex 14:19.24), or with the column of cloud appearing intermittently at the door of the meeting tent (Ex 33:7-11; Nm 12:5; Dt 31:15), nor with the cloud, which, according to Ex 40:36-38; Nm 9:15-22; 10:11.12, covered the tabernacle, although the cloud, under all these three aspects, was a visible symbol of Yahweh.

§ 11. *The face of Yahweh*

J. Böhmer, *Gottes Angesicht*, Gütersloh 1908; W. Baudissin, " ' Gott schauen ' in der alttestamentlichen Religion, " *ARW*, 18 (1915), pp. 173-240; P. Dhorme, " L'emploi métaphorique de noms de parties du corps en hébreu et en accadien, " *RB* 1921, pp. 374-399, separate print, Paris 1923; F. Nötscher, " ' *Das Angesicht Gottes schauen* ' *nach biblischer und babylonischer Auffassung*, " Würzburg 1924; F. Altheim, " Persona, " *ARW*, 27 (1929), pp. 35-52; N. Greitemann, " Aangezicht, " *BW*, cols. 1-3.

The face (in Hebrew: *pânîm*) is in the eyes of the ancients " the visage, " that is to say, " the part of the body which sees and which is seen. In order to know a man, one looks at his visage, and if one wishes to grasp what he feels, one looks for an answer again to his visage. " [1] One covers one's face, either in order not to see (Ex 3:6; Is 53:3), or in order not to be seen (Jb 24:15; 34:29). Joy " illumines the face " (for example, Ps 104:15); the interior sentiments manifest themselves in the face: " a glad heart makes the face good, " that is to say, healthy, serene (Prv 15:13); " the sign of a joyous heart is a radiant face " (Sir 13:26); benevolence " illumines the face " (Prv 16:15; Ps 67:2; Nm 6:25). On the contrary, anger makes the face " fall " (Gn 4:5), that is to say, makes it depressed, cast down; sadness " makes the face bad " (Neh 2:2: " Why is your face bad,

[1] P. Dhorme, *op. cit.*, p. 43.

since you are not sick? It is nothing else but sorrow of heart "). In the changed face of Laban Jacob discovers the changed sentiments of his father-in-law toward him (Gn 31:2).

Since the face reveals the person, one can easily understand that " the face of Yahweh " plays an important part in the revelation of God.

Since man cannot see the holy God and live (Ex 32:31; Jgs 6:22; 13:22; Is 6:5), Moses cannot see " the face of Yahweh "; it has been granted to him to see God only from the back (Ex 33:20-23)[2]; Jacob is surprised that his life has been spared (cf. Ex 24:11; Jgs 13:22.23), although he " has seen God face to face, "[3] and in memory of that marvelous event he calls the place which had witnessed it by the name *Pĕnî-'El* (face of God). On the occasion of his encounter with Esau, whom he tries to appease with presents, he rejoices that he can present himself before his brother and find favor with him, as he has found favor with God whom he had seen at Peniel : " If I have found favor in your sight, accept my present from my hand; for truly to see your face is like seeing the face of God, and you have favorably received me " (Gn 33:10).

Although in the official sanctuaries of Yahweh there was no image of the divinity,[4] as there were in Babylonian, Egyptian and maybe

---

[2] Ex 33:20-23 contrasts with Nm 12:8 : " I speak to him (to Moses) mouth to mouth, plainly and not in riddles, and he beholds the form *(tĕmûnâh)* of Yahweh. " This passage opposes the direct, clear vision that was given without intermediary, with which Moses had been favored, to the revelations by visions and dreams accorded to the prophets. But the *tĕmûnâh* which he contemplates is less determined and reveals less about the person than the face; to speak mouth to mouth is to converse without intermediary (cf. Dt 34:10). According to Ex 33:11, " Yahweh used to speak to Moses face to face, as one man speaks to another "; this passage which belongs to a different source, insists on the intimate, familiar and direct character of the communications made by God to Moses; " to speak face to face, " however, or " to appear eye to eye " (Nm 14:14) does not necessarily imply the physical perception of the face or of the person, since Dt 5:4 declares that Yahweh spoke face to face with the people on Sinai, although it had been said previously (4:12) : " Yahweh spoke to you from the midst of the fire; you heard the sound of the words, but saw no form *(tĕmûnâh)*. " From the comparison of the two texts it can be concluded that " to speak face to face " (or " Mouth to mouth ") signifies simply to speak without intermediary (cf. Ez 20:35.36) (cf. F. Nötscher, *op. cit.*, p. 23).

[3] Gn 32:31 and Jgs 6:22 are the only narratives of theophanies where the expression " to see face to face " is used; in other texts we find expressions like " to see God " (Ex 24:10.11; Jgs 13:22; Is 6:5; cf. Gn 16:13 ff.) or " to see the form of Yahweh " (Nm 12:8); " to see face to face " can be understood as " to see with one's own eyes, without intermediary " (cf. F. Nötscher, *op. cit.*, p. 55).

[4] Neither in the portable sanctuary of the desert, nor in that of Silo, nor later in that of Jerusalem, was there any image of Yahweh, whose presence was associated with the ark (cf. Nm 10:35.36; 1 Sm 4:4; 2 Sm 6:2; Is 37:16; Ps 80:2). Neither the bronze serpent preserved in Jerusalem (4 Kgs 18:4; cf. Nm 21:8 ff.), nor the ephod, nor the teraphim mentioned in certain sanctuaries of Yahweh (Jgs 18:17; 18:5; 1 Sm 21:10; Os 3:4) were images of Yahweh. In the temples of Bethel and of Dan (3 Kgs 12:28-32; cf. Ex 32:1-6), on the contrary, the " golden calves " which

Canaanite temples,[5] the Bible often uses currently the expression "to see the face of God"[6] in the meaning of presenting oneself in the sanctuary (Ex 23:15.17; 34:20.23.24; Dt 16:16; 31:11; Is 1:12; Ps 42:3), which is the dwelling of Yahweh (2 Sm 6:17; 7:6.7; 15:25; 3 Kgs 6:1 ff., etc.), just as one said "to see the face of the king" (for example, Gn 43:3.5; 44:23.26; Ex 10:28.29; 2 Sm 14:24.28.32), with the meaning of "to present oneself before the king," "to be received in audience." In the Old Testament, therefore, the expression "to see the face of Yahweh" is taken in an improper sense.[7] One ordinarily approaches an important person to pay homage (cf. Ex 23:15; 34:20: "No one shall appear before Him (God) emptyhanded"), and to obtain a favor; and the fact that one is received by a great person is already a favor. Similarly the expression "to see the face" implies the idea of recourse to the benevolence or to the protection of him whom one visits in the palace. This idea is very predominant in Ps 42:3, where the pious Psalmist, who is in exile, aspires to the happiness of "seeing the face of God," that is to say, to enjoy the divine presence and protection in the temple (cf. v. 5; Ps 23:6; 27:4.5; 63:2.3; 95:1.2; 100:2). The expression "to see the face of Yahweh," which is used independently of any corporal perception of a statue or divine figure, eventually becomes detached even from the sanctuary where God resides, so as to designate the enjoyment of the divine presence, the communion with God by prayer and contemplation; for example, in Ps 17:15: "In justice I shall behold Your face" (cf. Ps 11:7; Jb 33:26).

Similarly the expression "to seek the face of God" signifies

---

were perhaps in the thought of the king only pedestals of the invisible God (cf. H. T. Obbinck, "Jahwehbilder," *ZAW*, 1929, pp. 264 ff.), were considered by the common people as images of Yahweh (cf. Os 8:5; 13.2).

[5] The old Canaanite sanctuaries did not contain any images of the divinity. But in Betshan a great mutilated statue has been found, numerous figurines of Astarte, and stelae dedicated to the god Mikal and the goddess Anat (cf. *RB* 1928, pp. 126; 512 ff.; 544); in Transjordan, a stele, of Egyptian style, representing Anat who presents a king to Kamos (*RB* 1932, pp. 422-444; 1933, pp. 353-365) (cf. "Beeld," *BW*, cols. 134-135; K. Galling, *Biblisches Reallexikon*, Tübingen 1937, cols. 200-234).

[6] On account of a theological scruple the Massoretes replaced the *Qal* (to see, *râ'âh*) with the *Niphal* (*yêrâ'eh* = to be seen, to appear), whenever the object was "the face of God"; the accusative *'et pĕnêy* proves that primitively the verb was active, not passive (P. Dhorme, *op. cit.*, p. 49). Already the LXX made the same correction (Ex 24:11; Ps 17:15) or introduced other changes in order to efface the offensive expressions.

[7] The expression "to see the face of a god" is very often used in Babylon in the proper sense, since in the temple one saw the statue of the god before whom one prostrated oneself; but sometimes it is used in a figurative sense: to have recourse to a god in order to obtain his help, and even to obtain the guarantee of his favor (cf. F. Nötscher, *op. cit.*, pp. 72 ff.). One says in the Babylonian language "to see the face of the king" and "to look toward the king" in the sense of having recourse to his protection (cf. F. Nötscher, *op. cit.*, pp. 77 ff.).

sometimes to have recourse to God in His sanctuary in order to obtain His protection (Ps 24:6; cf. 1 Par 21:30) or to consult Him (2 Sm 21:1), at other times it simply signifies to invoke Him apart from any act of cult, that is to say, to return to Him in sincere conversion (Ps 105:4; Os 5:15; 2 Par 7:14; cf. Am 5:6; Jer 29:12.13). The metaphorical meaning is evident in the expressions: "May Yahweh let His face shine upon you, and be gracious to you; may He lift up His countenance upon you and grant you prosperity" (Nm 6:25.26; cf. Ps 4:7; 31:17; 67:2; 80:4.8.20; 119:135; Dn 9:17); the light of the face of Yahweh signifies His benevolence (cf. Ps 89:16; 44:4). The same applies to the expression "to appease the face of Yahweh" *(ḥillâh 'et pânîm)*, which signifies to pacify Yahweh or to implore His mercy, be it by sacrifices (1 Sm 13:12; Mal 1:9), be it by prayer (Ex 32:11; 3 Kgs 13:6), or by repentance and conversion (Jer 26:19; 2 Par 33:12; Dn 9:13; Ps 119:58.59).

Finally "the face" is sometimes simply the equivalent of the person [8]: thus in Prv 7:15: "I looked for your face and I found Thee"; in Ez 6:9: "They will loathe their faces," that is to say, they will loathe themselves; and in 2 Sm 17:11: "Your face will march," that is to say, You will march in person. For this reason a psalmist (Ps 139:7) draws a parallel between the face and the spirit of Yahweh: "Where can I go from Your spirit, where can I flee from Your face?" The meaning of the psalmist's question is: No matter how far away from God he goes, God knows all and is present everywhere (vv. 8-12).

In the same sense we must understand Ex 33:14-15, a text which would cause no difficulty if we could abstract from its context [9]: Moses had asked Yahweh for the name of him whom He would send along to guide the people on the march across the desert, and Yahweh replies: "My face will go along and I will give you

---

[8] This is also true in the Egyptian language (cf. H. Grapow, *Die bildlichen Ausdrücke des Aegyptischen*, Leipzig 1924, pp. 113 ff.).

[9] Ex 32-34 is clearly an "amalgam" of different traditions, the separation of which is almost impossible. Cf. p. 111, note 10. The verses 12-15 are attributed to J (Driver) and attached to 33:1-3 by Driver and Heinisch. — Baentsch attributes the verses 1a.3a.4 to J; 1b.2.3b to Rje; 5-11 and 34:1 to E; 12-14.18.20-23 to J*; 15-17 to J²; 19 to Rje; 34:2 and 3 to J. — Eissfeldt attributes verses 3b.4 to L; 1-3a and 34:1a.2.3.4b.5, etc. to J; verses 12-23 and 34:1b.4a.6.7.9.10, etc. to a secondary stratum of J; verses 5-9 to E. — Gressmann (*Die Anfänge Israels*, pp. 72 ff.) adopts a still more complicated division; Beer attributes 33:5-11 to E; verses 1.3a.4 and 34:1a.2 ff. to J² (with the exception of some parts which are attributed to Rje); 33:12-23 to Js. He is inclined to admit the opinion of K. Galling (*RGG* ², II, col. 1103) who sees in "the face of Yahweh" (Ex 33:14; 34:29) a metallic mask which the priest as a spokesman of the divinity used to wear (cf. G. Hofmann-H. Gressmann, *ZAW* 1922, pp. 82 ff., who propose the same opinion). This opinion has no support in the text which deals neither with priest nor oracle.

rest." [10] Moses answered: "If Your face does not come with us, do not make us depart from here." In this passage it is clear that "My face will go" signifies "I will go in person" (cf. 2 Sm 17:11), "My face" being parallel with "I" (cf. Ex 33:20). [11] The difficulty arises from the context: in fact, after the episode of the golden calf, Yahweh refuses to guide the people henceforth, "to go up in their midst" (33:3; cf. 33:5); yet previously He had announced that He would send an angel to guide the people (33:2; 32:34). It is evident that these different declarations are incoherent. If it must be, one can attach the verses 14 and 15 to 33:1.3, for these verses 14 and 15 suppose that Yahweh will no longer go up with Moses (33:1.3), since Moses asks for the name of him who henceforth would guide the people. [12] One can suppose, as a matter of fact, that Yahweh allows Himself to be persuaded by the prayer of Moses and by His own condescension (33:12b.13) and, consequently, renounces His plan to separate Himself from Israel (33:3) and even promises to go along in person in order to guide Moses (and the people) toward a place of rest (33:14). Whatever may be said of this hypothesis, there is no reason to consider here "the face of Yahweh" as a hypostasis, distinct in some way from Yahweh Himself and parallel with the angel, who in the actual text (33:2 and 32:34) will be sent instead of Yahweh to guide Moses. We have to deal with two different, even incompatible conceptions, of which one (the angel taking the place of Yahweh) is probably due to a gloss. [13]

In Deuteronomy 4:37: "He brought you out of Egypt by His face and His great power," the expression "by His face" can only

---

[10] Instead of "I will give you rest" *(haniḥoti)*, Ehrlich proposes "I will guide you" *(hinḥitîka)* (cf. Beer, *Exodus*, p. 158).

[11] The LXX expressed well the sense when they translated "My face" by αὐτός.

[12] The text of Ex 33:12: "You say to me: lead this people up" recalls 33:1: "Depart from here, you and the people whom you have brought up from the land of Egypt to the land...," although the order of departure is not given in the same words. But 33:2 and 32:34 (I will send an angel) are incompatible with the actual narrative (cf. p. 112, note 14).

[13] Cf. p. 112, note 4. The angel who is mentioned in the present text of Ex 32-33 is not "the angel of Yahweh," that is to say, an external manifestation of Yahweh Himself as in Jgs 2:1-4; he is also not so intimately united with Yahweh as the messenger in whom the name of Yahweh dwells (Ex 32:20) (cf. p. 111); in Ex 32-33 the angel is placed in opposition to Yahweh Himself (33:3), which is not the case in Ex 23:20 (against Baudissin, *op. cit.*, p. 198; Kautzsch, *Theologie*, p. 88; Baentsch, *in h.l.;* Eichrodt, *Theologie*, II, p. 13; König, *Theologie*, p. 135) (cf. F. Nötscher, *op. cit.*, pp. 48 ff.; Dhorme, *op. cit.*, pp. 59 ff.; J. Hehn, *Gottesidee*, p. 289; P. Heinisch, *Exodus, in h.l.*). S. Driver (*The Book of Exodus*, Cambridge 1911, p. 357) rightly remarks that verse 2 interrupts the phrase begun in verse 1: "to the land which I have promised on oath to Abraham...," and which continues in verse 3: "a land flowing with milk and honey"; verse 2, furthermore, is incompatible with verse 12, where Moses would ask God to tell him what He had told him already in verse 2.

mean " in His own person " (cf. Dt 7:10); it is impossible to understand here " face " as a synonym of " power, " since *pânîm* cannot be used in this sense. [14]

Is 63:9 (LXX), finally, where the allusion to Ex 33:14 seems quite evident, declares : " It was no messenger or angel, but His face that saved us, " [15] that is to say, He Himself saved them, Yahweh in person. These words are parallel to the following : " He Himself redeemed them. "

Ps 21:10 speaks of " the time of Your face, " an expression which probably signifies, according to the context, the time when Yahweh will manifest Himself to chastise (cf. Ps 80:17). [16] Lam 4:16 : " The face of Yahweh has dispersed them, it does no longer look at them, " [17] signifies : Yahweh Himself has dispersed them and has turned His face, His eyes away from them.

With the biblical expression " the face of Yahweh " has been compared a similar expression, which in Phoenician inscriptions designates the goddess Tanit as *pn B'l (pĕnêy Ba'al)*, " the face of Baal, " [18] that is to say, the representative of Baal, the faithful image in which Baal in person manifests himself and acts, in other words, Baal in person. [19] But this Phoenician expression " the face of Baal " tends to unify two divinities each of which has its proper personality; in Hebrew, on the contrary, the expression referred to designates the personality of the one God.

§ 12. *Hypostases*

M. Hackspill, " Études sur le milieu religieux et intellectuel contemporain du N. T., " *RB* 1901, pp. 200 ff.; 377 ff.; 1902, pp. 58 ff.; J. Göttsberger, *Die göttliche Weisheit als Persönlichkeit im A. T.*, Münster W. 1919; A. Vaccari, " Il concetto della Sapienza nell'A. T., " *Gregorianum*, 1920, pp. 218 ff.; P. Heinisch, *Personificationen und Hypostasen im A. T. und im alten Orient*, Münster im W. 1921; *id.*, *Das Wort im A. T. und im alten Orient*, Münster W. 1922; *id.*, *Die persönliche Weisheit des A. T. in religionsgeschichtlicher Beleuchtung*, Münster im W. 1923; J. Lebreton,

[14] Cf. P. Dhorme, *op. cit.*, p. 67; see above p. 112, note 13.

[15] Cf. p. 112, note 12; cf. the commentaries of Duhm, Condamin, Volz, Feldmann, Fischer, Van Hoonacker; Dhorme, *op. cit.*, p. 60; Nötscher, *op. cit.*, p. 50.

[16] Gunkel and Schmidt *(in h.l.)* correct " the time of Your face " *(panĕykâ)* to " the time of anger " *('apkâ)*; similarly some authors correct " before the menace of Your face " (Ps 80:17) to " of Your mouth " *(pîkâ)*.

[17] It seems preferable to read the verb in the plural *(BH)*.

[18] Cf. *Répertoire d'Épigraphie sémitique*, II, 1907-1914, p. 452, quoted by F. Nötscher (*op. cit.*, p. 51). C. Virolleaud (*Syria*, XV, 1934, p. 311) points out that in Ras Shamra a certain Yadid, son of El Gzr, is called *pn Mot*, that is to say, face of Mot.

[19] Cf. F. Nötscher, *op. cit.*, p. 51; J. Hehn, *Gottesidee*, pp. 113 ff.; Hehn quotes this expression of " *Astarte šm B'l*, " name of Baal (inscription d'Ešmunazar, 1. 18, *ERS* ², p. 483), which designates the goddess as the counterpart, the equivalent of Baal. F. W. Albright (*From the Stone Age to Christianity*, p. 228) understands the Phoenician expression in the sense of presence, power.

Histoire du dogme de la Trinité [7], I, Paris 1927, pp. 122 ff.; B. Botte, " La Sagesse dans les livres sapientiaux, " *RScPT* 1930, pp. 83 ff.; P. van Imschoot, *La Sagesse dans l'A. T. est-elle une hypostase?*, *Coll. Gand* 1934, pp. 1 ff.; 85 ff.; F. Ceuppens, " De conceptu Sapientiae divinae in libris didacticis V. T., " *Angelicum*, 1933, pp. 333 ff.; J. Fichtner, " Die Stellung der Sapientia Salomonis in der Literatur- und Geistesgeschichte ihrer Zeit, " *ZNW* 1937, pp. 113 ff.; W. L. Knox, " The Divine Wisdom, " *JThS*, 38 (1937), pp. 230 ff.; P. Humbert, " Weisheit, " *RGG* [2], V, col. 1801 ff.; *id.*, *Recherches sur les sources égyptiennes de la littérature sapientiale d'Israël*, Neufchâtel 1929; W. Baumgartner, *Israelitische und altorientalische Weisheit*, Tübingen 1931; W. Bousset-H. Gressmann, *Die Religion des Judentums* [3], Tübingen 1926; G. Foot-More, *Judaism*, Cambridge 1927, I, pp. 400 ff.; *id.*, " Intermediaries in Jewish Theology, " *Harvard Theological Review*, 15 (1922), pp. 41 ff.; S. Mowinckel, " Hypostasen, " *RGG* [2], II, cols. 2065 ff.; Strack-Billerbeck, *Kommentar*, II, pp. 302 ff.; Articles under the heading of " Personification, " *ERE*, IX, pp. 781 ff.; G. Boström, *Proverbiastudien. Die Weisheit und das fremde Weib*, Lund 1935; A. Ringgren, *Word and Wisdom; Studies in the Hypostatization of Divine Qualities and Functions in the Near East*, Lund 1947.

Almost all exegetes speak of hypostases with respect to the divine wisdom, the spirit, the name, the word, the glory, the face and the angel of Yahweh. Several call hypostases the wisdom, the spirit, etc., [1] at least in the post-exilic texts of the Old Testament and in the writings of later Judaism; others reject this idea completely [2]; still others admit that the wisdom, the word and the spirit are hypostases, [3] or are at least on the way to becoming such, [4] but not the name, the glory, the face or the angel of Yahweh.

Before taking up the discussion about the problem of hypostases in the Old Testament, it is important to clarify the meaning of this term, which all exegetes use, but in very different meanings.

For the greater number of Catholic authors, as also for Scholastic theologians, hypostasis is synonymous with person, that is to say, according to the classic definition, a *rationale suppositum*, an individual substance of rational nature. [5] On the contrary, some Catholic [6] and Protestant critics speak of hypostasis where the term " person "

---

[1] Almost all Protestant authors, for example, Bousset-Gressman, Humbert, Mowinckel, Volz *(Der Geist Gottes)*, Grether *(Name und Wort)*, Smend *(Theologie)*, Stade *(Theologie)*, Eichrodt *(Theologie)*, Kautzsch *(Theologie)*, Procksch (*Theologie*, pp. 479 ff.), F. W. Albright (*From the Stone Age to Christianity*, pp. 283 ff.), Ringgren, (*op. cit.*, pp. 89 ff.), etc.; among the Catholics, Heinisch, Dürr *(Die Wertung des Wortes)*.

[2] Among non-Catholic authors, especially Foot-More and Strack-Billerbeck; M. Burrows (*An Outline of Biblical Theology*, Baltimore, pp. 78 ff.); among Catholics : Botte, P. van Imschoot, V. Hamp *(Der Begriff Wort)*, Ceuppens.

[3] Some Fathers and many of the ancient commentators, U. Lattanzi, " Il primato universale di Cristo secundo le S. Scrittura, " *Bb*, 1937, pp. 466 ff.

[4] Lebreton, Hackspill, Vaccari.

[5] L. Billot, *De Deo uno et trino* [4], Romae 1903, p. 425.

[6] For example P. Heinisch (*Personificationen*, p. 18), who defines hypostases as " entities *(Gestalten)* who are midway between fully independent persons and simple attributes, who are less graspable than angels, but endowed with reality and divine power. "

would seem misplaced to them. Hypostases, according to their opinion, are " more or less hybrid beings, " halfway between a personification and a person. " They are the creations of a still puerile spirit, incapable of arriving at a complete abstraction. " [7]

It must be recognized, indeed, that the spirit of the Hebrews is less inclined to abstractions; their thought remains imaginative and is incapable of conceiving a purely abstract concept, for example power, quality, action. They conceive power as a concrete and active substance; action is for them something which is supported, so to speak, by a material substratum. This is the reason why an Israelite scribe describes the *ruaḥ* (breath or spirit), the word, the name, even the glory and the wisdom of man and of God, as concrete and active entities, capable of acting even apart from the subject, without conceiving them, however, as agents really distinct from man or from God, or as having an independent existence and activity. This manner of speaking does not imply a proper personification, although these entities are conceived as efficient and active, just as there is no personification when we say that fire " gives " heat or that lightning " strikes. " If one wishes, one may give the name " hypostases " to these concrete and active entities, whose subject may be man as well as God; but there is no reason to reserve this name for the spirit, the wisdom, the glory, the name or the face of God, as modern authors do, since these entities in man differ from those of God only by a lesser degree of efficacy, by a less extensive and less powerful activity.

Catholics and Protestants of today, with few exceptions, admit that neither the wisdom, nor the word, nor the spirit, nor the name, nor the glory, nor the face of Yahweh are hypostases in the Scholastic sense of the term, that is to say, persons, in all reality subsisting and distinct from God. Those who consider the angel of Yahweh as a messenger distinct from Yahweh, [8] must renounce calling him a divine hypostasis, in no matter what way they understand it; in this hypothesis, he is not more than an angel of special rank among the messengers of God. Catholic authors generally content themselves with proving that the wisdom, the word, and the spirit of Yahweh in the Old Testament are not hypostases, that is to

[7] B. Botte, *La Sagesse*, p. 84. One may also compare the definition of S. Mowinckel (*op. cit.*, col. 2065) : " a divine entity conceived half as subsisting in itself, half as a manifestation of a superior divinity; this entity is a personification of an attribute, of an activity or of a member of a superior divinity. One speaks often of personifications of abstract concepts; but if for us the name, the power, the qualities of a person are abstractions, it is not so for the primitive mentality which considers qualities and actions as entities, relatively independent from the subject. "

[8] Cf. above II, § 6, A, 2, b, p. 112.

say, divine persons,[9] but they fail to question whether they could be hypostases in a religious sense. For the sake of completeness two questions must be asked: 1) Must we admit in the Old Testament hypostases in the Scholastic sense of the term? 2) May we admit at least hypostases in a religionistic sense?

1. The first question has been sufficiently answered in the paragraphs dealing with the spirit, the word, the name, the glory, the face and the angel of Yahweh. None of these entities appears as a real person, distinct from God, as an agent having his own existence and his proper activity independently from God.

It will suffice to examine, whether the divine wisdom in the Old Testament is a divine person, and if so, at what moment wisdom becomes a person. Those who admit that the divine wisdom is a real person ordinarily describe the development of this doctrine as follows: in the books of Job (28) and of Baruch (3:9-4:4) wisdom is only a simple personification of a divine attribute (Jb 29:12.20; Bar 3:15); but afterwards wisdom develops into a hypostasis. For some wisdom is already a hypostasis in Proverbs 8, for others in Ecclesiasticus, for others finally in the book of Wisdom.

Prior to any discussion of these opinions, it is important to note that all the passages dealing with wisdom have one common trait, namely "their practical character: moral exhortations seem to be their only intention."[10] The authors of the Sapiential Books are moralists who write as poets, not philosophers who speculate on the nature of God or on His relations with the world. Lest we misinterpret their thoughts, we must keep in mind at the same time the general context, the essentially practical purpose of their writings and the poetic character of their descriptions, where highly colored images and picturesque traits abound.

In the book of Proverbs, without doubt, wisdom appears as a popular preacher who stations herself in the intersection of the streets and calls the passers-by, invites them to enter her house and sit down at her table to listen to her (Prv 9:1 ff.); but she is no more a real person than the woman "Folly," her counterpart and opponent,

---

[9] Thus F. Ceuppens and B. Botte; Hackspill (*RB* 1901, pp. 211, 215), Vaccari (*op. cit.*, p. 238), Lebreton (*op. cit.*, pp. 125 and 127) admit that the divine wisdom is no hypostasis (or personality), but is on the way to becoming one; Vaccari (p. 251) even says that the sacred writers did not need any foreign influence in order "to make of wisdom a hypostasis," a hypostasis, without doubt, in the modern sense of the term; Heinisch (*Personificationen*, p. 17 ff.) and Dürr (*op. cit.*, pp. 122 ff.) make it a hypostasis in the religious sense; likewise H. Ringgren (*op. cit.*, pp. 89 ff.), O. Procksch (*Theologie*, pp. 479 ff.).

[10] B. Botte, *op. cit.*, p. 85, who insists rightly on this point.

who offers " stolen waters, " that is to say, spurious doctrines and enjoyments which lead to death (Prv 9:13-18). When the sacred writer represents wisdom as formed by God before all creatures, playing before Him when He established the heavens and separated the earth from the waters (Prv 8:22-31), he thinks of the divine attribute which manifests itself in the order and beauty of the divine work (cf. Prv 3:19.20; Ps 104:24; Sir 1:8-10), and exalts the divine origin (cf. Prv 2:6) and the antiquity of the moral teachings of which he is the depositary and which he communicates to his disciples (Prv 3:32-36); he does not intend to open up new perspectives on the intimate nature of the divinity. Here divine wisdom is poetically personified, and nothing more. [11]

The book of Sirach, a little later than Proverbs 1-9, pursues the same practical end. If Sirach develops the doctrine, he does it by explicitly identifying wisdom with the Law of Moses (Sir 15:1; 19:20; 20:23; cf. Bar 4:1.2; 4 Mc 1:16; Dt 4:6), but not by putting more emphasis on wisdom's personality.

The book opens with a description (Sir 1:1-10) of the origin of wisdom, created by God before all things (1:4.9; 24:3), inaccessible for man (1:6.8; cf. Jb 28:20-27; Bar 3:29-38), unless wisdom be communicated to man by her Author (1:10).

Later on wisdom takes care of her children like a mother, assures them the blessings of God (4:11-15) and sings her own praise on account of her divine origin (24:1-23). This latter chapter (Sir 24, 1 ff.) is a hymn to wisdom which, having come forth from the mouth of the Most High (v. 3), dwells in the highest heavens (v. 4), and after having traveled across the sky and the earth, has come, by the order of God, to live in Israel, where she exercises the sacred ministry (v. 4-10); and like a vigorous tree, wisdom refreshes the people of God with her shade and nourishes them with her fruits (v. 12-17), in order to preserve them from sin (v. 22). This eulogy is evidently addressed to the divine wisdom, identified with the Law, which spreads floods of understanding for future generations, as it is expressly said in verses 23-24 (cf. 15:1; 19:20; Bar 4:1.2; Dt 4:6).

Since Sirach makes wisdom speak in " the assembly of the Most High " and " in the presence of His power, " that is to say, in the presence of His angels (Sir 24:2), some maintain that here wisdom has a more pronounced personality and is no longer a prosopopoeia. [12] But this conclusion is based on a debatable interpretation : the ἐκκλησία

---

[11] Cf. J. Lebreton, *op. cit.*, pp. 127 ff.; M. Hackspill, *art. cit.*, *RB* 1901, p. 211.
[12] J. Lebreton, *op. cit.*, pp. 127 ff.; M. Hackspill (*art. cit.*, *RB* 1901, p. 211).

of the Most High is parallel with the δύναμις and with " Your people, " and designates, as in Ps 74:2; Nm 27:17; 31:16, the Israelite people convoked for the cult; the δύναμις of God is His army (cf. Ex 6:26; 7:4), that is to say, the people which upholds His cause; the people of the wisdom is that of Sion, over which she exercises her power (v. 11) and which is her inheritance (v. 8). Besides, " one does not see why wisdom should deliver a discourse in a heavenly assembly, a discourse, the aim of which is to attract men who long for her. " [13]

Neither the role of wisdom in creation, nor that which she exercises among men, requires that one should consider her as a divine person; and her identification with the Law speaks against it.

In the Greek book of Wisdom, the personification of wisdom is a little carried forward. Like God, she is intelligent, all-powerful, immutable (7:22-27); her action is as extensive as that of God: in the creation of the world she acts as His counselor (8:4), and as the artificer of all things (7:21; 8:5.6); she can do all things (7:27), sees all (9:11), penetrates (7:24) and governs all things (8:1); she teaches men (8:7; 9:11), guides them (9:11; 10:10 ff.), protects them (9:11), assists them (9:10) and lives with them like a bride (7:28; 8:2.9). She appears as distinct from God, since she emanates from Him and forms His reflection and His image (7:25.26); she occupies a throne next to the one of God (9:4), and the glory of her birth merits for her the honor to live in God's intimacy like a bride (8:3).

If all this must be understood in the proper sense, it must be concluded that wisdom is here a true divine person, issued from God and equal to Him. But the last trait (8:3) proves quite clearly that the sacred author speaks in metaphors; for it is certain that he never thought of making wisdom into a goddess espoused to God. He accumulates here figures that are not very coherent: wisdom issues from God and is at the same time His bride; she can become, nevertheless, the bride of any man who desires her. If this wisdom were a real person, distinct from God, could she " be given, " communicated to man (9:9.10)? The divine wisdom, who " produces all things " and is " the artificer of all " (7:21; 8:5), does not differ from human prudence by her efficient activity, but only by a more powerful and more extensive efficiency: " If prudence (φρόνησις) works with efficiency, who more than wisdom is an artificer of the things that are? " (8:6). [14] Who thinks to make human prudence

---

[13] B. Botte, *op. cit.*, p. 88.

[14] The context proves sufficiently that human prudence is meant; her activity as well as that of the divine wisdom is described by the same verb (ἐργάζεσθαι).

into a person on account of her activity? Why then should such a conclusion be drawn when divine wisdom is concerned? Just as φρόνησις designates here a human quality, so does wisdom signify a divine attribute manifested by the activity of the almighty God.

In the book of Wisdom we find the personification of divine wisdom more vigorously presented than in Proverbs and Ecclesiasticus. Divine wisdom is identified with the holy spirit, that is to say, with the divine spirit (1:4-6; 7:22-24; 9:17)[15]; but neither in earlier books of the Old Testament nor here is the spirit conceived as a real person. If the author of Wisdom, who writes as a poet and moralist, following the example of his predecessors, likes to describe wisdom sometimes as an artificer who fashions the world and governs it as its master, sometimes as an educator who teaches men and guides them as their guide, he does so in order to praise wisdom of which he is the prophet (7:27) and for whose cause he wishes to gain his contemporaries. He took special care to inform his readers about his intent when he assumed the role of Solomon and invited the princes to put themselves into his school, and when he promised to expose to them straightforwardly the doctrine which he had received from God and to reveal to them the divine origin of wisdom which he professed (6:22).[16] His aim is not to speculate on the intimate life of God or on God's action in the world; it is, as in the books of the Proverbs and of Ecclesiasticus, essentially practical: to teach wisdom which he receives from God, a wisdom which has her origin in God and is, in his eyes, the divine wisdom herself, that is to say, the divine attribute which is manifested in the creation and government of the world (7:22-8:1).[17]

From what has been said so far, we may conclude that the descriptions which present wisdom as a person, if placed in their context, amount only to prosopopoeias. If a divine origin is attributed to wisdom, it is because in all recent sapiential collections the wisdom of the wise is considered as a gift of God (Prv 2:6.7; Eccl 2:26; Ps 32:8; Jb 11:6; 32:8.18-20; Sir 1:1; 24:8 ff.; 39:6.7; Wis 7:7.27; 8:21; 9:17; Bar 3:27) in whom "reside wisdom and power," with whom "are

---

[15] Cf. above p. 180.

[16] Wis 6:22: "What wisdom is, and how she came to be (ἐγένετο), I shall relate, and I shall hide no secrets from you, but from her very beginning I shall search out (αὐτῆς is proposed and referred to γενέσεως, cf. Heinisch, *Das Buch der Weisheit*, Freiburg im B. 1905, p. 124); others propose αὐτὴν and translate: since the beginning of creation I will bring her understanding to the light of the day, and I will not pass over the truth in silence.

[17] "None of the three authors apparently suspected that it is incoherent to pass from one aspect of wisdom to another; for them wisdom is one" (B. Botte, *op. cit.*, p. 89).

counsel and understanding" (Jb 12:13; Sir 1:8). God possesses her fully (Jb 21:22; Is 31:2; 40:13) and manifests her in His works (Jb 28; Ps 104:24; Prv 3:19.20; Sir 1:9 ff.; Wis 9:2). Since divine wisdom appears in the world as created by God, and is communicated to the wise, she is represented as detachable from God and as capable of acting apart from Him; and, if one writes as a poet — which is the case of all the texts concerned — one makes her appear as a person. But this is nothing more than a figure of speech, which the context forbids understanding in the proper sense.

2. There remains the second question: Can we admit hypostases in the religionistic sense of the term? If by this one understands concrete and active entities that have no proper existence and activity independent from the subject who possesses them, one must, it seems, give an affirmative reply. But, as it has been said already, this kind of hypostases is found in the human as well as in the divine world: the name, the word, the spirit, the face, the glory and the wisdom of man are in the eyes of the ancients no less real (that is to say, they are concrete things) than the name, the word, the spirit, the face, the glory and the wisdom of God; they only differ by a degree of greater or lesser activity and power.

But it is not in this sense that modern authors understand the hypostases: for them they are uniquely divine entities, intermediaries between a superior divinity and the world, conceived as partly subsisting in themselves and partly simple manifestations of this divine superior divinity, in other words: they hold the middle between persons in the strict sense and simple attributes of God; they are not yet persons, but are on the way to becoming persons. [18]

They affirm that in the last centuries preceding our era Yahweh had become a transcendent God and, according to some, almost an abstraction. Yahweh could no longer act directly on the world and men, and the hypostases, destined precisely to re-establish an indirect contact between God and creatures, were introduced.

The alleged reasons do not seem to prove the existence of such hypostases as some modern authors understand them.

The transcendency of the one God, without doubt, appears clearly in the post-exilic books of the Old Testament and in the writings of later Judaism. But this transcendency has never effaced or modified the personal character of Yahweh, nor that of Elohim, when the proper name of God was substituted by the common name or by

---

[18] J. Lebreton, *op. cit.*, pp. 125-127; M. Hackspill, *loc. cit.*, *RB* 1901, pp. 211-215.

Adonay, and eventually by the different circumlocutions like the Word *(memra)*, the Glory *(yĕqarâ')*, the Dwelling *(šĕkinâ')*. [19] The God of Judaism has never become an abstract essence as conceived by Philo, who in this was greatly influenced by Greek philosophy. God never ceased to act personally in the created world; He had no need of intermediaries such as the "powers" and the "Logos" of Philo. He remains, even in the Alexandrian book of Wisdom, the creator of all things (1:14; 9:1.3.9), the artisan (τεχνίτης, 13:1), whose almighty hand has fashioned the universe from formless matter (11:17) and who governs the world with mercy (9:3; 15:1). [20] He provides for men (6:7); He is "the witness" of their reins (1:6; cf. Jer 11:20; 12:2 ff.; Ps 7:10, etc.), "the sure observer of their hearts" (1:6); He hears and receives directly their prayers (1:6; 9:1 ff.); He Himself teaches them the knowledge of existing things (7:15.17); He shelters them with His right hand, and protects them with His arm (5:16); He is so close to His faithful (cf. Sir 42:18 ff.), that the faithful becomes aware of being "in His hand" (3:1; 7:16).

Judaism does not need any hypostases, in the modern sense of the term, in order to establish contact between the transcendent God and the world. When Judaism thought of intermediaries between God and His creatures, they multiplied the angels; but the angels were never more than messengers or executors of the divine will, and as really distinct from God as the creature is from his Creator, as clearly subordinated to God as the servant to his master. Besides, the rigorous monotheism of the Jews was opposed to all division as well as to every multiplication of the divinity, and must have hindered them from transforming the divine

---

[19] The name Yahweh is found neither in Job nor in Eccl; only three times in Dn 9. The collector of the second and third book of Psalms removed it categorically. On the contrary, the name is used in all parts of Prv, in Lam, Par, Esdr, Neh, Sir, and also in Test. Nepht. The LXX translated it generally by κύριος; but this term served also as translation for El and Adon. They translated Lv 24:16 : "Whoever blasphemes the name of Yahweh, will be put to death" by "whoever names (ὀνομάζων) the name of the Lord, let him die." According to rabbinic narratives the priest pronounced "Yahweh" in the temple; elsewhere he said Adonay (*Sota*, VII, 6, cf. Philo, *Vit. Moisi*, II [III], 115). The name Yahweh was frequently used in magic formulas. As for the progressive disappearance of the name of Yahweh and the substitution of Yahweh and Elohim by circumlocutions like The Heaven, the Name, the Blessed, the Place, the Dwelling, the Glory, in recent Judaism, cf. G. Foot-More, *op. cit.*, I, pp. 429 ff.

[20] Holmes (in Charles, *The Apocrypha and Pseudoepigrapha of the O. T.*, Oxford 1913, I, pp. 524, 527; cf. Bousset-Gressmann, *op. cit.*, pp. 342 ff.) opposes the doctrine concerning God of chapter 11 ff. to that of the 10 first chapters, but wrongly, as the texts here quoted prove. As for the unity of the book, cf. the commentaries : P. Heinisch, *Das Buch der Weisheit*, Münster im W. 1912; J. A. Gregg, *The Wisdom of Salomon*, Cambridge 1922; G. Grimm, *Das Buch der Weisheit*, Leipzig 1860; J. Fichtner, *Das Buch der Weisheit*, Tübingen 1938.

attributes, which they personified poetically and also knowingly, into hypostases.

By what right can one forbid that the writers of Israel make use of personifications? This figure of language, common to all times and to all peoples, consists essentially in representing inanimate objects, things or ideas as persons endowed with intelligence, sentiments and will. Can one doubt that it is a deliberate personification, when the prophet invites the mountains to rejoice and the trees to clap their hands (Is 55:12; cf. 14:7.8), when a psalmist speaks of the envy of the neighboring mountains with regard to Sion (Ps 68:17)?[21] The personification is not less deliberate when the author of Wisdom declares that wisdom is of noble birth and dwells with God like a bride (8:3), or becomes the bride of man (7:28; 8:2.9), or when Prv 8:30 makes her play before God like a child. Why should one judge differently when understanding and sentiment are attributed to wisdom (for example Wis 8:4; 7:22) and to the spirit (for example Is 63:10), when the divine word is described as a warrior (Wis 18:14-16) or as the executor of the orders of God (Is 55:11), and when wisdom and spirit act like persons? Are the kindness and fidelity of God (Ps 40:12; 43:3; 85:11.14), divine justice (Is 58:8) and divine anger (Ps 78:38)[22] not also such personifications? And who thinks of making them into hypostases? Nobody, with the exception of Mowinckel, who at least proceeds logically.

The exegetes who make the wisdom, spirit, word, name, face and glory of God into hypostases, are either exaggeratedly impressed by the Philonian Logos, which for them is but a natural development of the teaching of the Old Testament on the word and the wisdom, or by the trinitarian doctrine of the New Testament, which would have been prepared or announced by the speculations of the Old Testament and of Judaism on the spirit, the word and the wisdom, or finally by the numerous parallels which they discover in ancient religions.

But the doctrine of Philo on the Logos " is a deviation due to the Jewish-Alexandrian speculation. "[23] In spite of the continuity which links the Old Testament to the New, the critic has no right to interpret the one only in relation to the other. The historian of Old Testament

[21] Cf. numerous examples in J. Koeberle, *Natur und Geist*, München 1905, pp. 104 ff.; P. Heinisch, *Personificationen*, pp. 7 ff.

[22] In Ps 78:49 divine anger is considered parallel with wrath, fury, strife, and finally with " an army of messengers of doom. "

[23] B. Botte, *op. cit.*, p. 94; cf. E. Bréhier, *Les idées religieuses et philosophiques de Philon d'Alexandrie*, Paris 1925, pp. 115 ff.

doctrine must try to grasp the individual thought of the particular sacred author. Now in the literal sense, which is the one which the sacred writers perceived and wished to convey to their Jewish readers, the wisdom, the word, etc., are nowhere real divine persons, nor entities on the way to becoming persons; these entities, who in God as well as in man are conceived as concrete and active, present themselves in certain passages as simple personifications, more or less alive and picturesque, but always conscious.

It is true that in ancient religions one can discover hypostases in the religionistic sense of the term. But these attributes or divine activities, conceived foremost, it seems, as concrete and active entities, transform themselves into new divinities, who take their place in the pantheon and receive a proper cult. Among the Sumerians, for example, Nigzida, the justice, becomes the vizier of the solar god, the just god. [24] In Babylon, Mesharu (justice) and Kettu (rightness) become divinities subordinate to Shamash, the solar god, guardian of order. [25] In Egypt, Ma'et (rightness) becomes a goddess, a daughter of Ra, the just god. Among the Romans, Victoria, primitively an attribute of Jupiter Victor, Fides, an attribute of Diovis Fidius, the god of oaths, and many others are transformed into divinities, to whom temples and altars are erected. [26] In the Persian religion we have the six Ameshas Spentas, who primitively were hypostases which manifested the moral attributes and the activity of the supreme god Ahura Mazda; they later received the traits of personal beings and had to fulfill determined functions. Thus Spenta Armataï, holy humility or piety, became a kind of goddess, daughter and spouse of Ahura Mazda, mother of the first man and through him of all mankind, and prayers were addressed to her. Vohu Manah, the good thought, whom Plutarch [27] made into Wisdom, was a male being; it was through him that the supreme god created the earth and revealed the law; he was the guardian of heaven and from his golden throne he received the liberated souls. With Ahura Mazda these six Ameshas Spentas constituted the divine powers, and although one never separated them completely from the supreme god, each one of them was honored individually. [28]

---

[24] B. Meissner, *Babylonien und Assyrien*, II, p. 47.

[25] Cf. W. Baudissin, *Kyrios*, III, p. 339 ff. This Babylonian couple has been compared with Ps 89:15.

[26] Cf. *ERE*, IX, pp. 795 ff., which gives several examples.

[27] *De Is. et Osir.*, 47.

[28] Cf. Jackson, " Amesha Spenta, " *ERE*, I, pp. 384 ff.; A. Bertholet-E. Lehman, *Lehrbuch der Religionsgeschichte* [4], Tübingen 1925, II, pp. 321 ff.

Judaism, on the contrary, faithful to the only God, never gave any worship either to the wisdom, the spirit, or to the word of God, or to any of the other divine attributes which had been personified. This confirms the conclusion reached above, that in Israel the divine wisdom, spirit, word, glory, names never passed beyond the point of a fully conscious personification. [29]

[29] One may subscribe to the conclusion of Dom B. Botte (*art. cit.*, p. 94) who defines in these terms the relations between the doctrine of the Old Testament with that of the New : " The light of the Christian revelation has shown in these texts or at least in some of them *a spiritual sense* (typical), intended by the Holy Spirit, but inaccessible to the Jews. By identifying with Wisdom the pre-existent Christ who presented Himself as the Son of God and has been glorified by the Father in His resurrection and in His ascension, a plenitude of sense has been given to these expressions and comparisons which the context alone could not have given them : this personification became, at least in certain aspects, the type of the divine person revealed in Christ. "

CHAPTER IV

GOD AND HIS PEOPLE

§ 1. *The Covenant*

R. Valeton, " Bedeutung und Stellung des Wortes Berith im Priestercodex, " *ZAW* XII (1892), pp. 1 ff.; *id.*, " Das Wort Berith in den jehovistischen und deuteronomischen Stücken des Hexateuchs sowie in den verwandten historischen Büchern, " *ZAW* XII (1892), pp. 224 ff.; *id.*, " Das Wort Berith bei den Propheten und in den Ketubim, " *ZAW*, XIII (1893), pp. 245 ff.; R. Kraetzschmar, *Die Bundesvorstellung im A. T. in ihrer geschichtlichen Entwicklung*, Marburg 1896; Fr. Giesebrecht, *Die Geschichtlichkeit des Sinaibundes*, Königsberg 1900; P. Karge, " Geschichte des Bundesgedankens im A. T. " (*ATA*, II, 1-4), Münster im W. 1910; J. Pedersen, *Der Eid bei den Semiten*, Leipzig 1914; *id.*, *Israel*, I, London 1926, pp. 263 ff.; W. Eichrodt, *Theologie des A. T.*, I, Leipzig 1933, pp. 6 ff.; J. Hempel, " Bund, " *RGG* [2], I, pp. 1360 ff.; M. Höpers, *Der neue Bund bei den Propheten*, Freiburg im B. 1933; G. Quell, " Diathèkè, " *ThW*, II, pp. 106 ff.; M. Buber, *Das Kommende*, I; *Königtum Gottes*, Berlin 1932, pp. 111 ff.; M. Noth, *Die Gesetze im Pentateuch. Ihre Voraussetzungen und ihr Sinn*, Halle 1940; P. van Imschoot, " L'esprit de Jahvé et l'alliance nouvelle dans l'A. T., " *EThL* 1936, pp. 201 ff.; *id.*, " Verbond, " *BW*.

1. *Meaning of the term.* — The etymology of the Hebrew term *(bĕrît)*, which is translated by covenant, is uncertain. Some derive it from a root *brh* with the meaning of " to cut "; others from the root *brh* " to bind, " relating the term to the Assyrian *bîrtu*, band, *bîrîtu*, fetter; others again relate it with the root *brh*, to eat, and think that the primary sense of *bĕrît* is " a meal. " Of these hypotheses the second seems the most likely. [1]

Whatever it may be, the term *bĕrît* has a wider and often more concrete meaning than the ordinary term " alliance, " and not only designates a pact of mutual assistance, but can also be applied to the relation that results from a pact, as in the expressions : " the men of your *bĕrît*, " that is to say, your allies, your next of kin (Abd 7) and " the partners of the *bĕrît* of Abraham " (Gn 14:13), the allies of Abraham; or the term may be applied to the clauses or conditions stipulated by a pact, as in the expressions : " to observe, to keep a covenant " (*šâmar bĕrît*, for example, Gn 17:9.10; cf. " to keep the words of the covenant, " Dt 29:8). From this latter sense are derived the expressions : " the tablets of the covenant " (Dt 9:9.11.15),

---

[1] Cf. Kraetzschmar, *Die Bundesvorstellung*, p. 245; Karge, *Geschichte des Bundesgedankens*, pp. 226 ff.

that is to say, the stone tablets on which were inscribed the clauses of the covenant concluded on Mount Horeb, namely the decalogue (Dt 5:6-19); " the ark of the covenant " (Jos 3:6; 4:9; 6:8) which contained the tablets of the covenant (Ex 40:20) or " the covenant " (3 Kgs 8:21). *Běrît* finally came to signify the religion of Israel, for example, Dn 11:22.28.30.32; or it can be used in the figurative sense as in Jb 31:1 : " a covenant with my eyes, " or Is 28:15.18 : " a covenant with death " (cf. also Os 2:20; Jer 33:20.25).

2. *The concept of covenant.* — As J. Pedersen [2] has well demonstrated, among ancient Hebrews *běrît* designated in the first place the mutual relation of solidarity which united the covenanters and also the rights and obligations which resulted from this relation. The union of peoples, who live under the system of the clan, is assured by the blood-relationship between those who " are one flesh and one bone " (Gn 29:14; 37:27; Jgs 9:2; 2 Sm 5:1), or by " the covenant " which establishes union between those who are not in blood-relationship; the *běrît* establishes fraternity, as the expression " the *běrît* of brotherhood " (Am 1:9) indicates. In reality, " the covenant " assures *šâlôm,* the integrity, the full development and harmony of a human person or group; this is the reason why one speaks of " a *běrît* of *šâlôm,* " a covenant of peace (Ez 34:25; 37:26), or one uses the terms as parallel (Ps 55:21 : " those who are in peace with someone " and his *běrît;* Abd 7 : " the men of your covenant " and " the men of your peace "), or one joins them as synonymous (Gn 26:28.29.31; 3 Kgs 5:6). [3]

" The covenant " also plays an important part in the life of Israel. In private life : for example, the covenant concluded between David and Jonathan (1 Sm 20:8); the covenant between David and Abner (2 Sm 3:12-21) detaches Abner from the house of Saul and attaches him to David. Similarly in public life, the covenant allies the tribes of the North to David (2 Sm 5:1-3) and attaches the warriors of the Carites to the young king Josias (4 Kgs 11:4-8); the king Sedecias concluded with the people a pact *(běrît)* under the terms of which each one pledged to liberate the Hebrew slaves (Jer 34:8-10). The covenant regulates the peace and the relations between Israel and the neighboring tribes, for example between Abraham and Abimelech (Gn 21:22-23), between Isaac and the king of Gerara (Gn 26:26-31), between Jacob and the Aramean Laban (Gn 31:46-48.51-52), between Josue and the Gabaonites (Jos 9:3-27); the covenant establishes the

[2] *Der Eid bei den Semiten,* pp. 31 ff.; *Israel,* I, p. 285; cf. J. Hempel, *Bund,* p. 1360.
[3] Cf. J. Pedersen, *Israel,* I, p. 285.

relations with the neighboring kingdoms and states, for example the covenant of Solomon with the king of Tyrus (3 Kgs 5:15-32), the covenant of Achab with the king of Syria, Ben-Hadad (3 Kgs 20:34); the covenant regulates even the relations between conquerors and conquered, guaranteeing their submission but also their life (Jos 9:3-27; 1 Sm 11:1; Ez 17:13.14).

The covenant supposes an act of will on the part of the covenanters, but not necessarily equality between them nor the equivalence of rights and obligations which it gives to the parties : thus the Gabaonites (Jos 9:3-27), afraid to be exterminated by the Hebrew conquerors of Canaan, think of a rather blunt stratagem in order to obtain " a covenant " with the victors, that is to say, an agreement that establishes peace and union with Israel and assures them at least their life. Their ruse succeeds and " Josue made an alliance with them and entered into an agreement *(bĕrît)* to spare them, and the princes of the community (Israel) sealed it with an oath " (Jos 9:15). The inhabitants of Jabesh Gilead, besieged and oppressed by Nahash the Ammonite, ask for a covenant that would guarantee them their life, but submit them to the victors (1 Sm 11:1). After his victory Nabuchodonosor imposed a new king on Jerusalem and made him his vassal; " He made a covenant with him, binding him under oath (literally : and made him enter into oath with him), so that the kingdom would remain a modest one, without aspirations, and would keep his covenant and obey him " (Ez 17:13.14). A powerful man can offer a covenant to a weak man; thus Jonathan, the son of the king, to David, whose life was in danger (1 Sm 18:1-4). And an inferior may pledge himself by a *bĕrît* to his superior (Ezr 10:3; 2 Par 15:12; 29:10).

Among the Hebrews, as among other ancients, " the covenant " had a sacred character : it is guaranteed by the divinity [4] who chastises the transgressor (for example, Gn 31:53; Jos 9:19.20; 1 Sm 20:23.42; Am 1:9.10). For this reason a covenant was often concluded before Yahweh (1 Sm 23:18; 2 Sm 5:3; 4 Kgs 23:3) and was ordinarily accompanied by oaths (Gn 21:23.24; 26:28.29; 1 Sm 20:9; Ezr 10:5, etc.) or by curses, [5] which would attain him who would violate the pact;

---

[4] This may be the origin of the names Baal *bĕrît* and El *bĕrît* (Jgs 9:4.46), if the name designates, as several critics think, the god guaranteeing the covenant concluded by the Sichemites (cf. L. Desnoyers, *Histoire du peuple hébreu*, I, Paris 1922, p. 171, n. 2, who thinks of the covenant of the Sichemites with the Hebrews, Gn 33:19; Kraetzschmar, *op. cit.*, p. 24, n. 6, who also quotes several authors defending the same opinion; W. Eichrodt, *Theologie*, I, p. 99, who relates *Baal bĕrît* to Zeus ὅρκιος, the guarantor of oaths, etc.; cf. P. Karge, *op. cit.*, pp. 333 ff.). The old pacts often mention the gods as guarantors : several examples are quoted by Karge (*op. cit.*, pp. 240 ff.).

[5] The ancient formula of oath is very often an imprecation or a curse, which

also these expressions were used: "a covenant of Yahweh" (1 Sm 20:8), "an oath of Yahweh" (2 Sm 21:7), or quite simply "an oath" (Neh 6:18: partners of an oath or of "a curse" Gn 26:28; Ez 17:18, that is to say, allies).

3. *Rites of covenant.* — "To conclude a covenant" is expressed in Hebrew *kârat bĕrît*, literally "to cut a covenant"[6] (for example Gn 15:18; 21:27.32; 26:28), *bô* or *hêbî' babbĕrît*, to enter (Jer 34:10; Ez 16:8) or to make enter into a covenant (1 Sm 20:8; Ez 20:37), *'âbar babbĕrît*, to pass into a covenant (Dt 29:11), *'âśâh*, to make a covenant (Dt 4:13), *nâtan*, to give, to grant a covenant (Gn 9:12; 17:2), *nišba'*, to swear a covenant (Dt 4:31; 7:12), *ṣiwwâh*, to order a covenant (Jos 7:11; 23:16), *śîm*, to establish a covenant (2 Sm 23:5), *hêqîm*, to maintain (or institute) a covenant (Gn 6:18; 9:9.11). Several of these expressions are used only with God as subject (to give, to swear, to order, to establish).

The conclusion of a covenant is a religious act comprising certain rites, of which several signify and in the mind of the ancients even produce the union of souls. This applies particularly to certain blood rites used among the Arabs and other peoples, for example, to suck the blood which flows from the incisions which the covenanters inflicted upon themselves, to mix their blood, or to dip the hand into a basin filled with blood.[7] It is possible that similar rites may have been customary among the Hebrews (cf. Ex 24:3-8; 29:20.21), who preserved the expression "the blood of the covenant" (Ex 24:8; Za 9:11) and considered blood as "the soul," that is to say, the vital principle of animal and of man (Lv 17:14; Dt 12:23); and it is precisely for this reason that those who mix their blood or dip their hands into the same blood are meant to become one soul. We must recognize, at any rate, that with the exception of Ex 24:3-8 and perhaps of Gn 15:9.10.17; Jer 34:19 (cf. Ex 29:20.21), the Old Testament does

---

the one who swears pronounces against himself, in case he should not say the truth or should not keep his promise, for example 1 Sm 14:44; 20:13, etc.; the terms oath and curse *('alâh)* are often taken as synonymous (cf. "Eed," *BW*, col. 342; J. Pedersen, *Der Eid bei den Semiten*).

[6] *Bĕrît* is here not logically the direct object of the verb, but expresses the effect that follows the cutting up of the animals (Gn 15:9; Jer 34:19), as in the Greek expression: ὅρκια τέμνειν, and in the Latin: *ferire, percutere, icere foedus*. This expression, which is also the most frequent, is said of man as well as of God (for example, Gn 15:18; Ex 24:8) and is constructed with the prepositions *'im*, *'et* and *l* without any noticeable difference of meaning (cf. the list drawn up by Kraetzschmar, *op. cit.*, pp. 247 ff.). This expression may be compared with the Babylonian expression "to kill an ass" which in the documents of Mari signifies "to conclude a pact" (F. W. Albright, *Archaeology and Religion of Israel*, Baltimore 1947, p. 113, according to Dossin, *Syria* 1938, p. 60).

[7] Cf. W. R. Smith, *Lectures on the Religion of the Semites*, London 1927, pp. 314 ff.; 479 ff.; 691 ff.; J. Wellhausen, *Reste Arabischen Heidentums*, Berlin 1927, pp. 128 ff.

not mention any rite of blood in the narratives that describe the conclusion of a covenant.

On the contrary, the rite of a meal taken in common is mentioned several times (Gn 26:28-30; 31:46.54; Jos 9:14; 2 Sm 3:20), because the consumption of the same food creates a vital unity between those who consume it. "A meal taken in common presupposes and strengthens the psychic community." [8] "Even he who was in peace with me (literally: the man of my peace), in whom I put my trust, who partook of my bread, has raised his heel against me," lamented the persecuted psalmist (Ps 41:10). One cannot imagine a more serious infraction. The common meal and peace are inseparable things. [9] Since he who partakes in the meal of another also "partakes of his salt," one calls it "a covenant of salt" (Nm 18:19; 2 Par 13:5), a covenant of special intimacy.

In the Orient a subject does not appear with empty hands before his superior (1 Sm 10:27); he owes him presents (cf. Gn 43:11) which are an homage of his vassalage (cf. Jgs 3:15.17.18; 2 Sm 8:2.6.10); and the superior for his part must do likewise with regard to his inferiors. [10] The gift "appeases the anger" (Prv 21:14) and is frequently given in order to establish peace (for example, Gn 33; 1 Sm 25:27.35); for this reason gifts are called *šalmonîm* [11] and often accompany the conclusion of a covenant (Gn 21:27.30; 33:8-11); Jonathan goes so far as to give David his own clothes and his arms (1 Sm 18:4), which gifts, since they were considered as integral parts of his person, joined his soul with that of David (cf. 1 Sm 18:3; 20:8). Besides, "to give" is to bring something of one's own self into the life of the other person, so that a solid bond is knotted. [12]

Finally one concludes a covenant by giving one's hand (Ez 17:18; 4 Kgs 10:15) or by shaking hands (Ezr 10:19).

In two solemn circumstances (Gn 15:9.10.17.18 and Ex 24:3-8) a more complicated rite of covenant is mentioned. Gn 15:7-10.12.17.18

---

[8] To eat with an enemy is an unconceivable thing. The prophet, who must keep intact his personal force, refuses for that reason to enter into communion with another man by eating with him (3 Kgs 13:8) (cf. J. Pedersen, *Israel*, I, p. 305).

[9] J. Pedersen, *Israel*, I, p. 305.

[10] The letters of Tell-el-Amarna are filled with demands of Canaanite and Syrian vassals demands which they present to Pharao, their sovereign.

[11] In Akkadian: *šulmânu*, frequently used in the letters of Amarna. In the O. T. the term is only employed by Is 1:23; there is evidently a relation with *šâlôm*, peace (J. Pedersen, *op. cit.*, p. 302).

[12] G. van der Leeuw, *La religion dans son essence et ses manifestations*, Paris 1948, p. 343.

describes a covenant which Yahweh concluded with Abraham (v. 18). Yahweh promises to Abraham the possession of the land of Canaan and pledges His word in a solemn rite : He orders him to take a heifer, a goat, a three-year-old ram, a turtle dove and a pigeon. Abraham cuts the three four-footed animals in two and lays each half opposite the other, leaving a passage between the bleeding halves; he then places one bird on each end of the passage. As the sun was setting a mysterious sleep and a great terror " fell " upon Abraham. Now when it was dark " a smoking oven and a fiery torch passed between the pieces. On that day Yahweh made a covenant with Abraham " (vv. 17 ff.).

This complicated rite is similar to those which were practiced in Assyria, Chaldea, Greece and Rome, [13] and seems to signify the curse which the contracting parties pronounce against any violator of the pact; they wish on each other the fate of the animals cut asunder, if they will not observe the contract. [14] Such is at least the sense which results clearly from the text of Jeremias (34:18) and from that of a treaty concluded between the Syrian king Mati'ilu and Assurnirari, king of Assyria [15] : before a he-goat cut up in pieces, Mati'ilu pronounces the following curse : " If Mati'ilu sins against the oath : as this he-goat is taken away from the fold, so Mati'ilu will be taken away with his sons and daughters...from his land.... This head is not the one of the he-goat, but that of Mati'ilu, the head of his sons... If Mati'ilu perjures : as the head of the he-goat is cut off, so the head of Mati'ilu will be cut off. " Similarly, when a covenant was concluded with the Albans, the Roman plenipotentiary declared : " If the Roman people is first unfaithful... may Jupiter strike the Roman people as I myself today strike this pig, " upon which he killed the pig. [16] The passage of the contracting parties between the bleeding

[13] See the references to the texts in Kraetzschmar, *op. cit.*, pp. 44 ff.

[14] This interpretation is rejected by M. Buber (*op. cit.*, pp. 112 ff.), who relates the rite of Gn 15 to the sacrifice called *fedu'* among the Arabs; this sacrifice, which implies the passage of those who offer it between the pieces of the victim, is offered on the occasion of epidemics or other calamities, in order to turn away misfortune (cf. A. Jaussen, *Coutumes des Arabes au pays de Moab*, Paris 1908, pp. 261 ff.). The context by no means indicates that Abraham was menaced by disaster; on the contrary, the text mentions the benevolence of Yahweh and promises of happiness and of grandeur, which form the object of the covenant concluded with the patriarch. The interpretation which we propose is that of Valeton (*ZAW*, XII, p. 226), of Kraetzschmar (*op. cit.*, pp. 43 ff.), of Karge (*op. cit.*, pp. 238 ff.), of Hempel (*Der alttestamentliche Gott*, Berlin 1926, pp. 31 ff.), and of the majority of recent commentators of Genesis.

[15] The text is quoted and translated by Karge (*op. cit.*, pp. 239 ff.), according to Peiser, *Mitteilungen der Vorderasiatischen Gesellschaft*, 1898, pp. 228 ff.

[16] Tit. Liv., I, 24.

halves of the victims (Jer 34:18.19)[17] seems to signify that they are henceforth exposed to undergo the tragic lot of the victims, if they will be unfaithful, or that on account of the new obligations imposed by the contract they enter into a new state of life. It is probable that the expressions " to cut a covenant, " " to pass " or " to enter into a covenant " originated from those ancient rites of covenant.

The torch and the smoking oven in Gn 15:17, which passed between the pieces of the victims, represented Yahweh, who elsewhere also (Ex 3:2; 13:21; 19:11.13.18) manifests Himself in fire and smoke. This vision, perceived during the sleep (v. 12), signifies that Yahweh " passes into the covenant, " that is to say, that He contracts the engagement with respect to Abraham (v. 18). It will be noticed that Yahweh alone passes between the bleeding pieces, since He alone engages Himself by His promises (cf. Jer 34:18 ff.).

Ex 24:4-8 describes a different rite : Moses builds an altar at the foot of Mount Horeb and erects twelve pillars *(maṣṣēbôt)* " for the twelve tribes of Israel "; these pillars, which belong to the movables of Canaanite and Israelite sanctuaries, seem to be understood here as witnesses of the covenant (cf. Gn 31:45; Jos 24:27). Then Moses makes young men offer up sacrifices : holocausts, in which the whole victim is consumed by fire, and *šělâmîm*, peace offerings, in which a part of the victim is burnt and the rest eaten by the worshippers at a sacred meal (cf. Ex 18:12; Lv 3). He reads " the book of the covenant, " that is to say, the laws of the covenant, before the people and they agree to abide by them. Finally, he sprinkles the people and the altar with the blood of the victims which had been collected in a basin, saying : " This is the blood of the covenant which Yahweh has made with you in accordance with all these words of His. " The blood, which is the soul (Lv 17:14), is splashed on the altar, which represents Yahweh, and is sprinkled on the people, that is to say, over the two contracting parties; by the contact with one and the same " soul, " they become " one only soul. " For this reason the blood is called " the blood of the covenant, " that is to say, the blood which produces the psychic community of the two parties.

4. *The covenant of God.* — The divinity is not only the guarantor of the covenants concluded between men, but can also be one of the contracting parties. Outside of Israel, some examples of these covenants are known : according to a Sumerian text, Urukagina, king of Lagas, about 2400 B.C., declares he has received the kingship from the god Ningirsu, and he imposes on his subjects " the word

[17] The Greek text differs notably from the M. T. which, as it seems, should be maintained.

which his king Ningirsu had pronounced," that is to say, the laws which the god, his sovereign, had imparted to him. He concludes the promulgation of those laws with the words: "with Ningirsu, Urukagina has concluded this covenant."[18] Much later, a Sabean king Kariba'ilu Watar, (about 700 B.C.), performs a cultic, at the same time political and sacred action, namely the renovation of a covenant between the god, the king and the people. By this renovation of the covenant, of which, by his quality as king-priest, he is the mediator, he submits to the god and to the people the lands which he had conquered and declares in the name of the national god that he has become *malik*, king, that is to say, in reality the master of all Southern Arabia.[19] Maybe it is by virtue of a "covenant" that certain Semitic tribes recognize in their god their *malik* (chief, then king). Finally, some historians are of the opinion that the god of Sichem, called Baal *bĕrît* or El *bĕrît* (Jgs 9:4.46), owed his name to a covenant which bound him "to the sons of Hemor" or to the city.[20]

The idea of a covenant which unites Israel with its God is fundamental in the Israelite religion.[21] But what characterizes this covenant is that it is always an initiative of God, a divine intervention in history which occurs at a certain moment in the history of Israel: one says that Yahweh has concluded a covenant with man (for example, Gn 9:9; 15:18; 17:1 ff.; Ex 24:5-8; 34:10.27; Jer 31:31 ff.; Is 55:3; cf. Ex 33:19; Os 2:16-25; 11:1; Am 3:2; 9:7; Ez 16:3 ff.), but not that Yahweh and a man have concluded a covenant,[22] nor that a man has concluded a covenant with God.[23] In the texts which seem to form an exception (4 Kgs 11:17; 2 Par 29:10; Ezr 10:2.3) covenant signifies only the solemn engagement to serve Yahweh which man renews in virtue of a pre-existent covenant.[24]

[18] The text is quoted by Karge (*op. cit.*, pp. 205 ff.), according to Thureau-Dangin, *Les inscriptions de Sumer et Akkad*, Paris 1905 (cf. *VB*, I, Leipzig 1907, pp. 46 ff.).

[19] Cf. M. Buber, *op. cit.*, pp. 56 ff. who refers to N. Rhodokanakis, *Altsabäische Texte* (*Sitzungsberichte der Wiener Akademie, phil. hist. Klasse*, CCVI-VI, 1930, pp. 19 ff.).

[20] E. Meyer, *Die Israeliten und ihre Nachbarstämme*, Halle 1906, pp. 550; R. Kittel, *Geschichte des Volkes Israel* [3], Gotha 1917, II, p. 96, n. 2.

[21] Cf. W. Eichrodt, *Theologie*, I, pp. 6 ff.; J. Hempel, *Gott und Mensch im A. T.*[2], pp. 162 ff.; L. Köhler, *Theologie*, pp. 45 ff.; E. Sellin, *Theologie*, pp. 91 ff.

[22] L. Köhler, *op. cit.*, p. 45. Only Ps 50:5 seems to make an exception; but the sense of "my covenant" is rather the covenant which I have established than "the covenant with me" (Köhler, *loc. cit.*).

[23] In Jos 24:25 it is said that Josue made a covenant with or in behalf of the people, that is to say, a pact according to which all pledge themselves to serve Yahweh alone; similarly in 4 Kgs 23:3 and 2 Par 34:31.32 Josias made a covenant before Yahweh with the people "to walk after Yahweh and to keep His commandments"; in 2 Par 15:12 Asa and the people pledge themselves (literally: they enter into the covenant) to seek Yahweh (cf. Neh 10:30; Jer 34:8).

[24] The text of 4 Kgs 11:17: "Joiada made a covenant between Yahweh and the king and the people that they should be Yahweh's people, and also between the

The covenant, due to the initiative of Yahweh, is therefore the effect of a voluntary act of God, who " shows favors to whom He shows favors and grants mercy to whom He grants mercy " (Ex 33:19), that is to say, who bestows His graces with sovereign independence on whom He wishes (cf. Mal 1:23). The covenant, therefore, is a pure grace on the part of Yahweh, not a consequence of the merits or of the grandeur of Israel (Dt 7:7.8; 9:5). If " among all the families of the earth Yahweh has known Israel alone " (Am 3:2), He is not more tied to Israel than to the Ethiopians, the Philistines or the Syrians (Am 9:7). The covenant and the election of Israel are the effect only of the love of Yahweh (Os 3:1; 11:1; Jer 31:1; Dt 4:27; 7:7.8; 10:15), of a love whose gratuitous nature is described in impressive terms by Ez 16:3 ff. and by the symbolism of the marriage of Osee (1:2 ff.).

From the gratuitous character of Israel's election Amos (3:2) deduces the moral aspect of the covenant; this election imposes moral obligations on Israel: it is because Yahweh " has only known Israel, " that He chastises the iniquities of His people. The divine protection, on which the people counts, is not simply guaranteed because of the election of Israel; it has only been granted under the condition that Israel " would seek the good and not the evil " and practice justice (Am 5:14.15). Osee insists likewise on the moral character of the covenant (6:7; 8:1-3) and on the moral obligations, in particular, on the fidelity to Yahweh which the covenant imposes on Israel (for example 4:1.2.11 ff.; 6:6-8); likewise Jeremias (11:1-8) and Deuteronomy (7:7-10) which deduces the moral and conditional character of the covenant from its gratuitous nature : " Understand that Yahweh, your God, is God indeed, the faithful God who keeps the mercy *(ḥesed)* and the covenant... towards those who love Him and keep His commandments... but He repays with destruction those who hate Him " (cf. Dt 7:12 ff.; 10:12 ff.; 11:26-28; 26:16-19; Ex 19:5).

By these two properties, namely its gratuitous as well as its moral and conditional character, the covenant of Yahweh with Israel differs from covenants and natural relations which unite other peoples with their national gods.

---

king and the people, " differs from 2 Par 23:16 which is perhaps better preserved (cf. Stade, *ZAW*, V, p. 287, n. 1) : " Joiada made a covenant between himself and all the people and the king "; 2 Par 29:10 deals with an engagement by which the king Ezechias and the levites pledged themselves to Yahweh to reform the cult " in order that His fierce anger may turn away from us "; similarly Ezr 10:2.3 : Esdras exhorts the people to make a covenant, that is to say, to pledge themselves to God to send away their foreign women.

The object of the covenant concluded by Yahweh with Israel on Sinai is expressed by the formula which occurs frequently: " You are My people and I shall be your God " (Ex 6:7; Lv 26:2; Dt 29:12; Os 2:25; Jer 7:23; 11:4; 24:7; Ez 11:20; 14:11, etc.). Henceforth Israel is " the special possession " (*sĕgullâh*, Ex 19:5; Dt 7:6; 14:2; 26:18; Ps 135:4) of Yahweh, " the holy nation " of Yahweh (Ex 19:6), a holy people, sacred to Yahweh (Dt 7:6; 14:2.21; 26:19; 28:9), " a kingdom of priests " (Ex 19:6), that is to say, a realm over which the power of Yahweh rules, whose citizens enjoy the right of access to Him (cf. Os 4:6) just as the servants enjoy the right of access to the king (cf. 2 Sm 20:25; 3 Kgs 4:5; Is 61:6). [25] In virtue of the covenant the people assumes certain obligations, which are indicated by the rather general term " to observe the covenant, " that is to say, the clauses stipulated by the contract (for example, Gn 17:9.10; Ex 19:5; 3 Kgs 11:11; Ez 17:14), in the form of laws, namely those of the decalogue (Ex 20:1-17; Dt 5:6-21) written on " the tablets of the covenant " (Dt 9:9.10), or those of " the book of covenant " (Ex 24:7; 4 Kgs 23:2). On His part Yahweh assumes the general engagement to protect Israel, for He is " the faithful God who keeps the covenant and the grace towards His people " (Dt 7:9.12; 3 Kgs 8:23; 2 Par 6:14; Dn 9:4; Neh 1:5; 9:32); and He promises them the possession of the land of Canaan (for example, Gn 15:7; 17:8; Jer 32:22), a numerous posterity (for example, Gn 15:5; 17:4.5), or other material blessings (for example, Dt 7:13 ff.; 11:13 ff.).

5. *The narratives of the covenant of God* are relatively numerous in the Old Testament.

1) If we take these narratives just as we find them, without trying to classify them according to their date of composition and their tendencies, there appears as the most ancient covenant this one which God concluded with the descendants of Noe and with every living creature (Gn 9:1-17): the covenant forbids men and animals to shed human blood, and obliges man to abstain from the eating of the blood of animals; on His part God promises that never again shall the waters become a flood to destroy all living creatures, and He proposes the rainbow as a sign of the covenant.

2) The covenant with Abraham is narrated in two traditions. According to one, the covenant is a solemn engagement expressed by the passage of Yahweh between the bleeding halves of the immolated

---

[25] This is perhaps the primary sense of the root *khn* from which derives the name *kohen*, a sense which seems preserved in 2 Sm 20:25; 3 Kgs 4:5, where the sons of David are called *kohanîm* to David.

victims and promises the possession of the land to the posterity of Abraham (Gn 15:2.7-12.17.16); no obligations in any formal terms are imposed on Abraham who, by the way, does not pass with Yahweh between the halves of the victims. In the second account (Gn 17) no rite of covenant is mentioned; God grants to Abram His covenant, by which He promises him a numerous and powerful posterity, and changes his name into Abraham which is interpreted "father of a multitude"; in return Abraham "will walk in God's presence and be perfect"; he will also accept circumcision for himself and for all his male descendants as the sign of the perpetual covenant. The covenant with "the fathers," that is to say, with the ancestors of Israel or the patriarchs, is recalled by Dt 4:31; 7:12; 8:18 and Jer 11:5, etc.

3) The covenant concluded at the time of the Exodus by the mediation of Moses is narrated in Ex 19:1-34:28 and Dt 5:1 ff. The narrative of Ex 19:1-34:28 is not the work of a single hand and contains several traditions which are interlaced to such an extent that it is impossible to separate and restore them.[26] According to the passages attributed to the Yahwist (for example, Ex 19:11 b.18; 34:2) and the Sacerdotal code (for example, Ex 19:1) the scene is localized on the mountain, called Sinai; the texts, however, which are attributed to the Elohist (Ex 33:6) and the Deuteronomist (Dt 1; 2:6.19; 5:2, etc.), call the mountain "Horeb." There were terrifying phenomena, fire, clouds, lightnings, peals of thunder, trumpet blasts (Ex 19:16-19; 20:18; 24:16.17; Dt 5:19.20), which manifested the presence of God.

All traditions attach to the conclusion of the covenant certain laws, which are the clauses imposed on Israel: according to Ex 34:10-28, it seems, that the cultic laws of Ex 34:14.17-26 are meant; according to Ex 24:7.8 it would be the "book of the covenant," that is to say, in the opinion of many exegetes, the code contained in the laws of the covenant (Ex 20:22-23:19); according to Dt 4:13.23; 5:2.3; 7:9; 29:9 it is the decalogue (Dt 5:6-17; cf. 20:2-17), which had been written on two tablets of stone (Ex 24:12-14; 32:15.16; 34:1.28; Dt 5:22), a circumstance that gave origin to the name of "tablets of the covenant" (Dt 9:9.11.15), "ark of the covenant" (Jos 3:6.8; 4:9; 6:6), "the covenant of Yahweh" (Nm 10:33; 14:44; Dt 10:8; Jos 3:3) and "covenant of God" (1 Sm 4:4; 2 Sm 15:21, etc.). Several indications seem to show that Deuteronomy has kept the tradition more purely

---

[26] An attempt has been made with regard to Ex 19-24 by M. Haelvoet ("La théophanie du Sinaï. Analyse littéraire des récits d'Ex. XIV-XXIV," *EThL* 1953, pp. 374 ff.).

than the other texts : the introduction (" I am Yahweh, who brought you out of the land of Egypt, that place of slavery, " Ex 20:2; Dt 5:6), which attaches the decalogue to the manifestation of Yahweh as liberator of the Israelite tribes under the guidance of Moses [27]; the presence of the decalogue, called " the words " (Ex 20:1; 24:3.8; Dt 4:12; 5:4.5) or the " ten words " (Dt 4:13; Ex 34:28), and placed at the head of the narrative of the covenant (Ex 20:1-17), the connection established between " the tablets of stone " written by God Himself on the mountain (Ex 24:12-14; 34:1-4; Dt 4:12.13; 5:19) and the covenant concluded at the foot of the mountain; the name itself of " the tablets of the covenant " and of " the ark of the covenant " which are found in ancient sources others than Deuteronomy.

On the other hand, the expression " the book of the covenant " (*sepher habbĕrît*, Ex 24:7) does not necessarily designate the " code of the covenant " (Ex 20:22-23:19), and can just as well be understood of " the writing of the covenant, " that is to say, of the decalogue (cf. Dt 5:9 ff.). Finally, the expression " the ten words " in Ex 34:28 cannot be applied to the twelve cultic laws (Ex 34:14.17-26) which precede; this seems to indicate that these twelve laws written by Moses (Ex 34:27) are not at their proper place in the present context which deals with the preparation of the stone tablets written by Yahweh (Ex 34:1-4) and with the covenant concluded on Sinai by the mediation of Moses (Ex 34:10.28). [28]

The accounts of Ex 34:10-28 and of Dt 5:1 ff. do not mention any rite of covenant; Ex 24:4-8, on the contrary, describes in detail the sacrifice and the rite of blood performed by Moses on that occasion, [29] a rite which makes of the contracting parties " one soul "; another tradition (Ex 24:1.2.9-11) tells that Moses, Aaron, Nadab, Abiu and seventy elders had been asked by Yahweh to climb the mountain, where they saw God without suffering death and ate and drank, undoubtedly before God (cf. Is 25:6; So 1:7 ff.) : here the sacred meal, it seems, was presided over by God and was, therefore, a rite of covenant, as in numerous other examples of covenants contracted between men. [30]

The significance of the covenant concluded by the mediation of Moses [30bis] is stated in Ex 19:3-6 (cf. Dt 26:17-19) : Yahweh, who has

---

[27] Cf. L. Köhler (*Der Dekalog, Theologische Rundschau*, 1929, p. 179) who defends the antiquity and historicity of this introduction, cf. O. Eissfeldt, *Einleitung zum A. T.*, Tübingen 1934, pp. 241 ff.; A. Weiser, *Einleitung in das A. T.*, 1939, pp. 91 ff.

[28] Cf. P. Karge, *op. cit.*, pp. 358 ff.

[29] Cf. above p. 230.

[30] Cf. above p. 228.

[30 bis] Cf. H. H. Rowley, *The Biblical Doctrine of Election*, Leiden, 1950, pp. 45 ff.

demonstrated His power and His love by liberating Israel from Egypt, chose this people to be His special possession (*sĕgullâh*, cf. Dt 7:6; 14:2; 26:18; Ps 135:4), He chose it from all the nations — for all the earth is His; Israel shall be to Him a kingdom of priests, that is to say, a realm over which Yahweh will exercise His royal power, and the citizens of which will draw close to Him and serve in His presence, and they will be a holy nation, consecrated to God and belonging to Him (cf. Dt 7:6; 14:2.21; 26:19; 28:9), under the condition that Israel would obey Him and keep the covenant. Yahweh henceforth shall be the *melek* (chief, king; cf. Ex 15:18; Dt 33:5; Jgs 8:23; Nm 23:21), around whom the tribes will gather as around their banner (Ex 17:15.16), He shall be the chief who will lead them to their wars, His wars (Ex 17:16; Nm 21:14; Jgs 5:23; 1 Sm 25:28), and on their journeys (Nm 10:35.36). The covenant of Sinai makes the Israelite tribes into a nation, the leader of whom is Yahweh; they are the people of Yahweh, and Yahweh is their God (Os 2:25; Jer 7:23; 11:4; 24:7; Ez 11:20, etc.).

4) According to Dt 28:69 (Vulg. 29:1) Moses concludes the covenant with the people by the order of Yahweh, in the region of Moab to the East of the Jordan; in a subsequent text (Dt 29:9-14) it is Yahweh who has concluded it " so that He may now establish Israel as His people and be his God, as He swore to Israel's fathers Abraham, Isaac and Jacob " (v. 11.12). The clauses of that covenant are the laws codified in Dt 12-26.

5) In an assembly of the tribes in Sichem, Josue (24) proposes to the people this alternative : either you will serve Yahweh alone, as I have decided to do, or you will serve the gods your fathers served beyond the river, or the gods of Canaan. The people decided in favor of Yahweh. After that Josue required the destruction of the strange gods. The people consented and promised to serve Yahweh and to obey His voice. " On that day Josue concluded a covenant with the people and made statutes and ordinances for them at Sichem " (v. 25); he also set up a stone under the tree that was in the sanctuary as a witness to the obligations resulting from the covenant. It is probable that this covenant is an extension of that of Sinai to include certain clans who had not yet been incorporated into the Israelite amphictyony. [31] Certain exegetes think that the laws given at Sichem are those of the code of the covenant (Ex 20:22-23:19).

6) The text of 4 Kgs 11:17 (2 Par 23:16) narrates that Joiada " made

---

[31] Cf. M. Noth, *Das Buch Josua*, Tübingen 1938, pp. 108 ff.; *id.*, *Geschichte Israels*, Göttingen 1950, pp. 80 ff.

a covenant between Yahweh and the king and the people that they would be the people of Yahweh, and (a covenant) between the king and the people." The text which seems corrupt,[32] distinguishes two "covenants," that is to say, two solemn promises which the high priest Joiada induces them to make, the first one between the king and the people in order that the people may recognize the young Josias as king (cf. 2 Sm 5:3), the second one engaging the king and the people to God, so that Yahweh may be acknowledged as the only God of Israel (cf. Neh 10:30 and Jer 24:8, where an engagement is mentioned which the king and the people took in order to give liberty to the Hebrew slaves).[33]

7) After the discovery in the temple (4 Kgs 22; 23; 2 Par 34:8-33) of "the code of the covenant" (4 Kgs 23:2), that is to say, probably the code preserved in Dt 12-26, the king Josias assembled the people in the temple, read to them "the book that had been found" and "concluded a covenant before Yahweh," that is to say, made the solemn promise "to walk after Yahweh and to keep His commandments... and to fulfill (literally: to maintain) the words of the covenant that were written in this book. And all the people confirmed the covenant (literally: entered)" (4 Kgs 23:3). As a consequence of this covenant Josias undertook a serious reform of the cult.

8) In 444 B.C. Esdras assembled the people and read before them "the book of the law of Moses" (Neh 8:1); afterwards he and the leaders of the people took the solemn engagement *('ămânâh)*, written and sealed (Neh 10:1), confirmed by oaths and curses, "to walk in the law of God...to observe and do all the commandments of Yahweh" (Neh 10:30).

9) Finally Dt 33:9 (cf. Nm 18:19; Jer 33:20-22; Mal 2:1-9) mentions a covenant concluded by Yahweh with the sacerdotal tribe, and 2 Sm 23:5 (cf. 7:8-17; Ps 89:4.5; Is 16:5) a covenant with the house of David.

6. *Evolution of the idea of the covenant of God.* — Certain critics[34] maintain that Jeremias and the Deuteronomistic school presented first the relation uniting Yahweh with Israel as a covenant, that is to say, as a mutual relation that resulted from an agreement on certain rights and obligations of the two contracting parties. According to Kraetzschmar,[35] prior to Deuteronomy, the composition of which

---

[32] Cf. p. 231, n. 24.

[33] Cf. p. 231, notes 23 and 24.

[34] Particularly R. Kraetzschmar *(op. cit.)*. Cf. also R. Smend (*Alttestamentliche Religionsgeschichte*, pp. 117 ff.); B. Stade (*Theologie*, p. 254).

[35] Cf. R. Kraetzschmar, *op. cit.*, pp. 40 ff.; 142.

is placed toward the end of the 7th century B.C., *bĕrît* designated only the ritual act by which two parties contracted a pact, not the relation which united them. Later the Sacerdotal school (P), among whom the idea of *bĕrît* is entirely detached from the concrete rite or from the historic act out of which the relation originates which unites the two contracting parties, is said to have extended the covenant of God to the entire mankind.

This theory starts from a faulty interpretation of the " covenant, " and does not take into consideration certain facts and texts, certainly older than the 7th century.

In effect the word *bĕrît* designates, in its primitive sense, less the concrete rite than the mutual relation of solidarity with its rights and its obligations. This results from the expression *kârat bĕrît* (literally : to cut a covenant) in which the term *bĕrît* designates the effect of the rite, that is to say, the relation brought about by the rite, which consists in the cutting up of the animals (Gn 15:9.10); similarly the old name of the god honored in Sichem, Baal *bĕrît* (Jgs 9:4), signifies the partner of the relation, not of the rite, since *baal bĕrît* designates " ally " in Gn 14:13 and " the man of my *bĕrît* " signifies " my ally " in Abd 7 (cf. Ps 55:21). And when Osee accuses Israel of having " violated the covenant " (6:7; 8:1), evidently he is not refering to a violation of the ritual act of the covenant but means a violation of the obligations that resulted from the fact that Israel belonged to Yahweh.

The most ancient legal codes, the decalogue (Ex 20:2-17), the dodecalogue (Ex 34:11-26), the code of the covenant (Ex 20:23-23:19) as well as the Deuteronomistic and Sacerdotal codes are addressed to a community of which Yahweh is the God on account of the bond which He contracted with that community by certain events of the past [36]; and it is for the same reason that in the ancient song of Debora (Jgs 5:3.5) it is said that Yahweh is the God of Israel, and Israel " the people of Yahweh, " and that the people has the obligation to " come to the help of Yahweh " (Jgs 5:23), just as Yahweh would come to its aid (5:4). There is no reason to doubt that since the time of Moses, or even of the patriarchs, the bond that united Israel and Yahweh had been conceived as a covenant, that is to say, as a mutual relation of solidarity, originated by a pact, concluded at a given time (cf. Ex 24:7.8; 34:10.27); in this way is the covenant understood by Deuteronomy (5:2.3; 29:1.12.13.25, etc.), which insists more on its conditional character (Dt 11:13-17.26-32; 26:17-19). In

[36] Cf. M. Noth, *op. cit.*, pp. 64 ff.

effect, the idea of a covenant with God agrees perfectly with the social and cultural state of the most ancient Hebrews, among whom the covenant of man to man or of clan to clan occupied a large place in social life.

Among older prophets, prior to Jeremias, the covenant, it is true, is rarely named in explicit terms. But Osee (6:7; 8:1), at any rate, refers to it, although he presents the relation which unites Israel to his God rather under the figure of a marriage, which is also a form of voluntarily contracted union. He describes, however, the effects of this union in the same terms which are used with regard to the covenant: " I will say to Lo-ammi (that is to say, " to him who is not my people ") : You are My people; And he shall say : My God " (Os 2:25).

Amos and Isaias do not mention the covenant with Yahweh; but although the word is not found in their oracles, the idea is certainly found : Amos (3:2) alludes to it very clearly, when he declares that among all the families of the earth, Yahweh " has only known, " that is to say, He has only loved and chosen Israel, and that Yahweh will " be with you, as you say, " only, if you seek good and practice justice (Am 5:14.15). Isaias thinks probably of the marriage which unites Sion with Yahweh (Is 1:21), and proclaims, at any rate, that Israel belongs to Yahweh, and announces the moral obligations which bind " this people to Yahweh " (Is 1:3; 3:15; 5:13.25), since they belong (Is 5:1-7) to " the Holy of Israel " (Is 1:4; 5:19.24; 10:17.20). He thinks most likely of the covenant which is the foundation of Israel's confidence (cf. Ex 33:12 ff.; 34:9; Mi 3:11; Am 5:14), when he promises salvation to Ariel " the city where David encamped " (Is 29:1-8), and announces the future glory of Sion (2:2-4; cf. Mi 4:1-5), the dwelling of Yahweh (Is 8:18); he seems to describe the covenant as the unshakable foundation of confidence in salvation (cf. 7:8-9), when he says that Yahweh has placed in Sion as foundation a sure and precious cornerstone, a stone placed solidly according to the measuring line of right and the level of justice (Is 28:16.17). [37]

It is not exact, therefore, to say [38] that the prophets prior to Jeremias ignore the covenant of Sinai. It is, however, true that they do not mention the covenant concluded with the patriarchs (cf. Os 2:16.17; 11:1; 12:10; 13:4), as do Jeremias (11:5) and

---

[37] Cf. B. Duhm, *in h.l.;* Feldmann, *in h.l.;* Procksch *(in h.l.)* prefers the old interpretation, which identifies the cornerstone, the foundation of confidence, with the Messias (cf. Immanuel, God with us, Is 7:14).

[38] Kraetzschmar, *op. cit.*, pp. 100 ff.

Deuteronomy (7:8; 9:5, etc.), and that generally they do not make a great issue out of the covenant. But this can be explained by the fact that their contemporaries understood the covenant as a pact assuring the protection of Yahweh under any hypothesis (Am 5:14.18; Is 28:14; Mi 3:11; Jer 14:13; 23:17) and binding God indissolubly to His people, or as a contract of *do ut des*, that imposes upon Israel only cultic obligations, which, once fulfilled, would guarantee the favors of God. But it is precisely against these false conceptions that the prophets never ceased to protest.

After the discovery of " the book of the covenant " (4 Kgs 23:2.21), that is to say, according to all probability, the book of Deuteronomy, which in imitation of the older prophets (Am 3:2; Os 3:1; 11:1; 12:10; 13:4; Is 5:1 ff.) insists on the gracious and gratuitous character of the covenant (Dt 7:7-9.12; 9:4-6; 10:15; cf. 4:32-40), the idea of the covenant occupies a considerable place in the doctrine of the exilic prophets and sacred writers. The book of Deuteronomy did not introduce a new doctrine; it only popularized and systematized a doctrine which existed already. When it attaches the covenant concluded in the time of Moses to " the oath " by which Yahweh has engaged Himself to the ancestors (Dt 7:8.12; 9:5, etc.; Jer 11:5), it takes up the tradition already consigned by the Yahwist and the Elohist (for example, Gn 12:2.3; 15:5.7-10.18; 26:24); it is the same when it presents " the laws and ordinances " (Dt 5:1; 12:1), that is to say, either the code of Dt 12-26, or the decalogue (Dt 5:2-17) as the clauses imposed upon Israel by the covenant (cf. Ex 24:4-8; 34:27), clauses which Amos (5:14), Osee (6:7; 8:1; cf. 4:1.2) and Micheas (6:8) indicated in more general terms (cf. Jer 7:23). From this intimate connection between the covenant and its clauses originates the usage of *bĕrît* as parallel with law (Os 8:1; Ps 78:10), with precepts (Ps 25:10; 132:12), with ordinances of God (Ps 103:18), and in particular the identification of the covenant with the decalogue (Dt 4:13.23) which occasioned the names " tablets of the covenant " (Dt 9:9; 3 Kgs 8:9), " the ark of the covenant " (Jos 3:6.8; 4:9) and " the ark of the covenant of Yahweh " (Nm 10:33; Dt 10:8; Jos 3:3, etc.).

In the passages attributed to the Sacerdotal code it has been noted that the covenant with Yahweh is presented in a slightly different fashion.[39] The old expression " to cut the covenant " has been

[39] Cf. Kraetzschmar, *op. cit.*, pp. 183 ff.; Eichrodt, *Theologie*, I, pp. 18 ff.; Sellin, *Theologie*, p. 95.

avoided and other expressions have been substituted, for example, " to give the covenant " (Gn 9:12; 17:2; Nm 25:12), a term which insists more on the gracious character of the covenant, or " to maintain the covenant " *(hêqîm)*[40] which indicates the permanence of it (Gn 6:18; 9:9.11.17; 17:7.19.21; Ex 6:4; Lv 26:9; Dt 8:18; Ez 16:60), underlined yet by the qualitative *'ôlâm*, perpetual, added to *bĕrît* (Gn 9:16; 17:7.13.19; Ex 31:16; Lv 24:8; Nm 18:19; 25:13). In this way is brought to light the unity of relation which God has established with His people since the origin, that is to say, since Abraham[41]; but by this very fact the covenant of Sinai passes to a second place and appears only as the consequence and the renewal of that which had been established at the time of the ancestors (Ex 6:4-8; Lv 26:45).[42]

The reciprocity of the obligations and rights has also been attenuated : the circumcision imposed on Abraham and his posterity is only " a sign " of the covenant (Gn 17:11), that is to say, an indication of being a possession of God, just as the Sabbath (Ex 31:13.17; Ez 20:12) is " the sign " manifesting the sanctification, that is to say, the separation and the consecration of the holy people to God (cf. Is 58:13.14). This ensemble of facts gives to the idea of covenant a modality quite different from that which it had in ancient writings and often still in Deuteronomy; the juridical aspect of a bilateral pact freely agreed upon by two contracting parties is toned down under the aspect of a relation graciously granted by the sovereign God on behalf of man.[43]

The covenant, moreover, is no longer restricted to Abraham, but is extended to all the descendants of Noe, that is to say, according to the sense of the account, to all mankind, even to all living creatures and to the whole earth (Gn 9:8-17). This gives to the covenant,

---

[40] Such seems to be the sense of the verb when used in expressions similar to *hêqîm dâbâr*, to keep the word (Dt 27:26; 1 Sm 15:11.12, etc.), cf. Kraetzschmar, *op. cit.*, pp. 200 ff.

[41] This idea appears already in Deuteronomy, in Jeremias (11:5) and in Ezechiel (20:5).

[42] We must not exaggerate : the covenant of Sinai does not disappear from the theory of the Sacerdotal code; that covenant had been announced in Ex 6:4-8, recalled in Lv 26:45 and is evidently presupposed in the expressions " the tablets of the testimony " (Ex 31:18; 32:15) and " ark of the testimony " (Ex 25:22; 30:6.26, etc.), which designate the tablets of the covenant given on Sinai (Ex 19:1.2) and the ark of the covenant.

[43] It is not exact to say that the covenant has no longer a bilateral character, since in Gn 17:1 God requires from Abraham that he walk before Him and be irreproachable, and in Gn 9:4-6, He imposes upon the descendants of Noe the abstinence from blood and homicide. But evidently the juridical aspect of a bilateral pact is much less apparent than in Deuteronomy (especially 26:16-19).

which thus far had a distinctly chauvinistic sense, a universalistic significance (cf. Is 24:5), which almost exclusively belongs to the views of the prophets concerning the future. In this sense not only the history of Israel (cf. Ps 105:7 ff.; 106:45), but that of all mankind and of the world is presented as the realization of the plan of salvation which God executes by His covenant, that is to say, by the relation which He graciously established between Him and mankind and which is constantly actuated under His protection (cf. Ps 111:5.9).

7. *The new covenant.* — Since the covenant is a mutual and voluntary relation, imparting obligations as well as rights, it can be broken by the fault of one of the two contracting parties. This is the reason why several prophets accuse Israel of having broken *(hâpar)* the covenant by its crimes and infidelities (Is 24:5; Jer 11:10; 31:32; Ez 16:59; 44:7; cf. Os 6:7; 8:1). In effect, in their eyes, the covenant should have made Israel into a righteous and just people (Is 5:7; Os 2:21.22), and the divine protection which it guaranteed was conditioned by the submission and the fidelity of Israel with respect to Yahweh (Is 1:16-20; Am 5:14.15; Os 2:21-25; Jer 7:3-10; 11:1-5, etc.). Having abandoned its God, Israel is abandoned by Yahweh (cf. Os 1:2-9; 2:4); what else could Yahweh do but chastise the unfaithful people (Jer 5:7-9)? Yahweh, nevertheless, owes it to Himself, He owes it to His holiness (Os 11:8.9), to His name (Ez 36:22), to His glory (Is 42:8) to take up anew the work compromised by the faults of Israel; He will save a remnant (Is 7:3; 10:20-22; 11:11.16; 28:5; Am 3:12; 5:15) and will restore His destroyed people. This salvation and restoration are presented as a new marriage (Os 2:16 ff.; Jer 31:3; Is 54:2-8; 62:4.5), for Yahweh has never ceased to love His unfaithful wife (Os 11:8.9; Jer 11:15; 12:7; 31:3), or a new covenant (Jer 31:31-34; 32:38.40; Ez 16:60; 34:25; 37:26; Is 42:6; 49:8; 55:3; 59:21; 61:8; Mal 3:1).

This new covenant, announced by the prophets, will replace the one which Israel had broken by its faults, and will differ from it principally because it will bring about an interior regeneration of the people and of the individuals. "Behold the days are coming, says Yahweh, when I will make with the house of Israel and the house of Juda a new covenant. It will not be like the covenant I made with their fathers on the day I took them by the hand to lead them forth from the land of Egypt; for they broke My covenant, and I [had reject them] says Yahweh.[44] But this is the covenant which I will

---

[44] Instead of *ba'âltî*, I was their master, we read *ga'âltî*, I have rejected (cf. LXX Lag), cf. A. Condamin, *in h.l.*

make with the house of Israel after those days, says Yahweh: I will place My law within them, and write it upon their hearts; I will be their God, and they shall be My people. No longer will they have need to teach their friends and kinsmen how to know Yahweh. For all, from the least to the greatest, shall know Me, says Yahweh, for I will forgive their evildoing and remember their sin no more" (Jer 31: 31-34).[45] The new covenant will establish anew the union between Yahweh and Israel: "I shall be their God, and they shall be My people." This covenant will differ from that of Sinai, not by the stipulations, but by the means which it will make available: it will no longer be written on tablets of stone (Ex 24:12-14; Dt 5:19), but in hearts, that is to say, it will no longer rest on an external law, external to man, but on man himself, being engraved in the transformed hearts, renewed by Yahweh Himself and made capable of "knowing Him" (Jer 24:7) and of fearing Him (Jer 32:39.40). The new covenant will be for all a light and an interior force enabling them "to know Yahweh," that is to say, bringing the life of each into conformity with the moral demands of Yahweh, recognized as the just and holy God (cf. Jer 5:4 ff.; 8:7; 22:16; Os 4:1; 5:4; 6:6).

Ezechiel (36:23-28) insists even more on the interior regeneration of individuals, which will accompany the restoration of the nation. He indicates three stages: first the purification of the guilty (v. 25), then the renewal of hearts (v. 26), finally the gift of the spirit which will sustain them in the practice of the good (v. 27). Yahweh will replace the hearts of stone, that is to say, the hard hearts which are insensible to His precepts, by hearts "of flesh," that is to say, docile hearts, or what amounts to the same, He will give to the Israelites "a new heart" and "a new spirit" (cf. 11:19; 18:31; Ps 51:12); in other words, He will renew in them the center and the seat of their moral and intellectual life. This is, therefore, an interior regeneration, one which will make the people, thus purified, renewed, and sustained by the divine spirit,[46] into the holy people of the holy God (v. 28).

The moral and religious renewal of Israel, a renewal quite often attributed to the spirit of Yahweh (Ez 36:26; Is 28:6; 32:15-18; 44:3-5; 49:8; 61:1-3), is without doubt in the eyes of the prophets the essential and charcateristic element of the new covenant, but it is not the only one. The blessings of material order (for example, Is 32:15-17; 44:3-5), in particular the paradisiacal peace (Os 2:20-23;

[45] On the authenticity of this passage, cf. p. 178, note 13.
[46] On the relation between spirit, source of moral life, and the new covenant, cf. III, § 7, 3, pp. 176 ff.

Is 11:6-8; Ez 34:25, etc.), are not forgotten. In addition to these blessings Ezechiel (37:16-26) mentions the return of the dispersed (36:23; 37:21, etc.; Is 49:8.9; 61:1 ff.), the union of the two kingdoms, Israel and Juda, under the scepter of one prince, a new David (Ez 34:23.24; 37:22.24.25; Is 55:3).

The new covenant, finally, clearly has a universalistic character, particularly in the passages concerning the servant of Yahweh " who has been set as a covenant of the people and a light of the nations " (Is 42:6; cf. 49:6). The expression " light of the nations " can only be understood in the sense of " light for the nations " (cf. 42:7 and 42:1 : he shall bring forth justice to the nations, that is to say, " the norm of religious and moral truth "). [47] The first expression " covenant of the people, " showing the same grammatical construction, signifies therefore " the covenant for the people, " that is to say, the servant of Yahweh is either the mediator of " the covenant for the people, " [48] or he is the law for the people (cf. 42:1), if we take *bĕrît* in the sense which it frequently has, namely as the clause of a covenant (for example, Dt 4:13; Ps 78:10). [49] " The people " designates, according to several exegetes, Israel (cf. 49:6a b.8). The context, however, which does not refer to Israel, but to " the people that inhabits the earth " (v. 5), seems to approve those who understand " the people " in the sense of humanity [50] (cf. 49:6 : " I will make you a light of the nations, that My salvation may reach to the ends of the earth "). In either case the mission of the servant of Yahweh, mediator of the covenant or of future laws (that is to say, mediator of the economy of salvation which God will establish), and light of the nations, is not restricted to Israel, but addresses itself to all peoples as the messianic salvation according to numerous oracles (for example, Is 2:2-4; 56:6.7; 60:1-18; Mi 4:1-4; Za 2:14.15; 8:20-23; 14:9.16, etc.).

Although the prophets retain, in order to describe the object of the new covenant, the classic formula applied to the old one: " You will be My people and I shall be your God " (Jer 31:33; Ez 36:28; cf. Za 2:15.16), the juridical character of the bilateral contract, which characterizes the old covenant, disappears in the new: this one, properly speaking, is a gracious unilateral disposition taken by God,

---

[47] Cf. J. Fischer, *Das Buch Isaias*, Bonn 1939, II, p. 51.

[48] J. Fischer, *op. cit.*, p. 53; A. Van Hoonacker, *Het Boek Isaias*, Brugge 1932, p. 241, who interprets *bĕrît* in the sense of salvation; A. Condamin, *Le livre d'Isaïe*, p. 336; F. Feldmann, *Das Buch Isaias*, Münster im W. 1926, II, pp. 58 ff.

[49] P. Volz, *Jesaia*, II, Leipzig 1932, p. 156; J. Van der Ploeg, *Les chants du serviteur de Jahvé*, Paris 1936, p. 31.

[50] P. Volz, *op. cit.*, p. 155; J. Van der Ploeg, *op. cit.*, p. 31; M. Hoepers, *op. cit.*, pp. 64 ff.

that regulates the relation which in the future will exist between God and man.

8. *The Greek version of the Old Testament* seems to have been strongly influenced by the relatively recent conception of the *běrît*, which is almost exclusively translated by διαθήκη. This Greek term rarely signifies a pact, [51] more often a voluntary disposition, particularly a testament. Even when *běrît* clearly designated a contract between two parties (for example, Gn 21:27.32; 1 Sm 23:18), the LXX translated it by διαθήκη, not by συνθήκη (pact); they use the same translation, when *běrît* is used metaphorically (for example, Is 28:18 where διαθήκη is used as parallel with συνθήκη), or when *běrît* designates a covenant concluded between Yahweh and Israel (Gn 15:18; 17:1-22; Ex 24:8; 34:10), or the laws of the covenant (Ps 78:10; 103:18; 132:12).

In the deuterocanonical books of the Old Testament, διαθήκη often designates the permanent relation which unites Israel to his God (cf. Dt 31:16.20), that is to say, the religion of Israel (for example, 1 Mc 1:16; 2:50; 2 Mc 7:36), the clauses of the covenant, that is to say, the Law (for example, Sir 28:7; 38:33; 42:2), or the promises given by God to Israel (for example, Sir 44:20-23; 45:15.24); and the expression " the book of the covenant " (Sir 24:22) is applied to the written law, that is to say, to the Pentateuch, even perhaps to the sacred books of the Jewish Canon.

§ 2. *The chosen people*

Kurt Galling, *Die Erwählungstraditionen Israels*, Giessen 1928; W. Staerk, " Zum alttestamentlichen Erwählungsglauben, " *ZAW* 1937, pp. 1-36; G. Quell, " Eklegomai, " *ThW*, IV, pp. 148 ff.; H. H. Rowley, *The Biblical Doctrine of Election*, London 1950.

The idea of the election of Israel is intimately related to that of the divine covenant. Since election is always due to the initiative of God, it is felt as a privilege by those on whom it bestows the assurance of a special protection by God; and, whereas the covenant imposes on Israel the obligation to serve Yahweh with the exclusion of every other god, since it is He alone who brought Israel out of Egypt (Ex 20:2.3), election suggests to them the impression that they belong to a jealous God (Ex 20:5), that is to say, to a God whose love, without doubt, is demanding and exclusive, but also selective: to be " the people of Yahweh " (Jgs 5:11; 1 Sm 2:24, etc.), " the people of Elohim "

---

[51] Aristophanes, *Av.* 440.

(Jgs 20:2; 2 Sm 14:13, etc.), or, to use a later expression, to be " the holy people " (Dt 7:6; 14:2; 26:19; 28:9; Ex 19:6) is a guarantee of prosperity and a title to glory which places Israel " apart " (Nm 23:9) and makes it " the first, " that is to say, the best of the nations (Am 6:1).

The classic verb that expresses the idea of choice is *bâḥar*, which is used very frequently with God as subject. [1] This verb does not occur, however, prior to Deuteronomy and the writings which underwent its influence. The idea, nevertheless, is much older and certainly goes back to the time of Moses, who indeed was the founder of the religion and at the same time of the nation of Israel. This results from several facts : already in the time of Debora, the only bond which united the Israelite tribes among themselves is the conviction that they belong to Yahweh; they are aware that they form " the people of Yahweh " (Jgs 5:11), who is the God of Israel (Jgs 5:3.5), and that they have toward Him the obligation " of going to His help " (Jgs 5:23), that is to say, to undertake " His war " (cf. Ex 17:16; Nm 21:14). Furthermore, the prophets associated the special bond which united Israel to his God (Am 2:10; 9:7; Os 2:17; 9:10; 11:1; 12:14; 13:4; Mi 6:4.5; Jer 2:6.7; Ez 20:5, etc.) with the interventions of Yahweh in the events of the Exodus. Osee especially returns several times to the fact of Israel's election by Yahweh " in the desert " (9:10), to the love which Yahweh manifested toward Israel as a child, " since Egypt " (11:1; cf. 13:4). The prophet is entirely in line with the tradition indicated by the most ancient documents of the Pentateuch, in particular by the accounts of the vocation of Moses, to whom Yahweh reveals Himself as the liberator of His people (Ex 3:2.3.5.7.9-15.16 ff.; 4:1-4) and as the author of the covenant (Ex 24:3-8; 34:10.28), by which Israel became His people, His particular possession *(sĕgullâh)* among all other peoples, a holy nation (Ex 19:5.6). [2]

It is interesting to see that the prophets prior to Jeremias do not mention the election of the ancestors of Israel, the patriarchs, whereas the accounts attributed to the Yahwist (for example, Gn 9:25 ff.; 12:1 ff.; 25:23; 32:29; 49) and to the Elohist (Gn 15:1-6.13-16; 22:16-18; 27:27.29, etc.), without using the term *bâḥar*, describe how Abraham and his descendants have been placed apart, blessed

---

[1] According to Quell (" Eklegomai, " *ThW*, IV, p. 149), 92 times of 164.

[2] Cf. above p. 233 ff. Since the term *sĕgullâh* is found only in Dt (7:6; 14:2; 26:18) and in Ps 135:4, and since the expression " holy nation " occurs several times in the same book (7:6; 14:2.21; 26:19; 28:9), most of the critics are of the opinion that this passage, which they generally attribute to E, has been rewritten in deuteronomistic style.

and especially protected by God, how they received the divine promises of an innumerable posterity and of the possession of the land of Canaan, where they were only strangers without any fixed dwelling place (cf. Dt 26:5), and how Yahweh sealed His promises by a covenant with Abraham (Gn 15:18; cf. 17:1 ff.).

From this silence of the prophets we may with K. Galling [3] legitimately deduce the existence of two independent traditions, of which the one relates the origin of Israel's election to the Mosaic revelation, whereas the other relates it to the patriarchal time. These two traditions have been united by Deuteronomy, the prophets of the Exile, and the Sacerdotal code into a doctrinal synthesis, which prevailed in all later literature and Jewish piety, a synthesis in which the election of Abraham and of his posterity finally surpasses Israel's election by the events associated with the Exodus; as a result the belief in the divine election came to be expressed by the proud formula of the Jews: " We are of the seed of Abraham " (Jn 8:33.39; Mt 3:9; Rom 2:28.29; 4:12).

According to K. Galling, [4] the tradition which relates the election to the Exodus would be the oldest; the other would have been originated by the Yahwist at a later date, after the division of the two rival kingdoms of Israel and Juda, with a political intention: namely to promote unity and consequently the grandeur of Israel; to this end this ingenious author imagined the theory of the divine election of the common ancestor of all Israelite tribes, namely of Jacob, and especially of Abraham, the father of all believers: one ancestor, one God, one people.

This opinion errs by considering all narratives of the Yahwist as fictions invented with a political purpose, and by ignoring the religious, anecdotical and popular character of his work: he evidently collected popular traditions, preserved probably in the ancient sanctuaries of which the ancestors of Israel had been the founders and where they had been favored with divine communications. These traditions have been transmitted from generation to generation before they could be collected and fixed in writing. Neither the Yahwist nor the Elohist have created the substance and the persons of their accounts; it has been handed down to them by tradition.

---

[3] *Op. cit.*, p. 56; the author goes further and maintains that the prophets (Os 12:4.5; Jer 9:3) have positively rejected the theory of the election of the patriarchs, invented by the Yahwist. There is not the slightest indication which justifies this judgment. Silence is not disapproval; the prophets are not in the habit of combatting by silence the ideas which they disapprove; on the contrary they fight them most directly.

[4] *Op. cit.*, pp. 63 ff.

The God who announces to Moses His intention of liberating " His people " from the Egyptian oppression and of guiding them to a land " where flow milk and honey " (Ex 3:7.8), and who then concludes a covenant with His people on Sinai (Ex 34:10.28), is, for the Yahwist who represents the patriarchs as adoring Yahweh (Gn 12:7.9; 21:33; 26:25; 28:16, etc.), identical with Yahweh, " the God of the fathers, the God of Abraham, of Isaac and of Jacob " (Ex 3:16). For this reason the Yahwist asks no question about the continuity of the divine election : Israel is the object of it since the day when Yahweh separated Abraham from his land and his family in order to make him into a great nation and a source of blessings for all the families of the earth (Gn 12:1-3) and to give to his posterity the land of Canaan (Gn 12:1; 13:14-17; 24:7; cf. 26:24; 27:29; 28:13.14).

Maybe the Elohist has suspected the existence of the tradition that relates the origin of Israel's election [5] to the Mosaic revelation, since he supposes that the people dwelling in Egypt ignored the name of God who manifested Himself to Moses as the liberator (Ex 3:13), an ignorance which is formally affirmed by Ex 6:3 (P.). According to the narrative of Ex 3:13-15, it is to Moses that the God of the fathers reveals His name of Yahweh (cf. Ex 6:2-8 P). Is it because the idea of Israel's election is traditionally associated with the name of Yahweh that Ex 3:13-15 (cf. Ex 6:4 ff. P) insists on the identity of Yahweh, who manifests Himself to Moses, with the Elohim of the fathers whose election, according to the accounts of Gn 15:1.3-6.13-16; 22:16-18; 27:29; 48:15-16, precedes that of the time of Moses? In effect, the God of Abraham, of Isaac and of Jacob, who was or was not invoked under the name of Yahweh, was, in the times of the patriarchs, the God-Protector of the family and of the clan, just as Yahweh was the God of Israel after the union of the tribes into one people. The revelation of the divine name, Yahweh, which, according to Ex 3:13.14 and 6:2-8, dates from the time of Moses, is not understood by those narratives as the revelation of a God heretofor unknown. The idea of having been chosen by the God-Protector can exist in a family or in a clan as well as in a people. This idea does not necessarily imply a clear and explicit notion of the universality of the divine sovereignty [6] such as it is expressed for example by Ex 19:5 and, Am 3:2.

Amos (3:2) affirms very categorically the election of Israel : " You

[5] The Elohist does not speak more than the Yahwist of a covenant with God prior to that which had been concluded at the foot of Mount Horeb (Ex 24:3-8).

[6] Against Köhler, *Theologie*, p. 66. The God of the patriarchs, however, is not only a tribal God (cf. Gn 12:3; 20:17.18; 30:27); cf. pp. 35 ff.

only have I known, of all the families of the earth; therefore I will punish you for all your crimes." To know, in a certain way, is to take possession, to receive for oneself; knowledge implies intimacy, friendship.[7] Among all the nations of the earth, only Israel enjoys this intimacy with Yahweh. But the prophet does not understand the election of Israel in the same way as the people understood it: the people concluded that Yahweh "is with them" (Am 5:14), no matter what they were doing. Amos, on the contrary, deduces from it that Yahweh will chastise the faults of His people, because the election imposed on them moral obligations which Israel had transgressed. The protection on which the people counts because of the election, will only be granted if "it hates evil and seeks good" (Am 5:14.15). Amos seems to associate Israel's election with the Exodus (2:10; 9:7); he sees the effects of it in the very special protection with which Yahweh surrounded His people in the desert, in the conquest of Palestine, and in the course of the following centuries (2:9-11).

For Osee (12:10; 13:4), Yahweh is the God of Israel "since Egypt"; He loved Israel as a child and called His son out of Egypt; He carried him in His arms, and taught him to walk and guided him with bonds of love (11:1-4). It is out of love (cf. 2:16.17; 11:8.9) that Yahweh elected Israel, adopted it and brought it up as His first-born (cf. Ex 4:22). But this divine election imposes on Israel fidelity to Yahweh and moral obligations, the transgression of which will be severely chastised by God (Os 4:1-3; 5:5-9); Yahweh, the father of Israel, will be like "a moth" for Ephraim and like "a lion" to Juda (Os 5:12.14) because of the infidelity and of the faults of His people who "violated His covenant and sinned against His law" (Os 8:1).

Similarly Micheas (6:3-5) describes the liberation from Egyptian slavery and the constant protection by Yahweh during the stay in the desert and the occupation of Oriental Palestine as testimonies of the special benevolence of Yahweh toward His people. But he does not share in the presumptuous confidence of the governing classes, who, while totally violating justice and practising divination, imagine themselves to be safe from misfortune because "Yahweh is in their midst." The prophet, on the contrary, announces that because of their crimes, "Sion will be plowed like a field, Jerusalem reduced to rubble, and the mount of the temple to a forest ridge" (3:11.12).

---

[7] Cf. J. Pedersen, *Israel*, I, London 1926, p. 109.

Isaias alludes only once to the Exodus (10:26); but he insists on the paternal benevolence of Yahweh toward His sons, whom He has nourished and reared, but who have revolted against Him (1:2; cf. 5:1-7).

Like Osee (2:16 ff.), Jeremias (2:2 ff.) presents the covenant of Yahweh with Israel as a marriage concluded between Yahweh and Israel in the desert, at the time of the Exodus. To that period, therefore, Jeremias attributes the election of Israel (cf. 31:32), although he also knows the tradition which traces the covenant back to the times of the patriarchs (Jer 11:5; 33:26). [8]

Ezechiel (20:5.6) attaches the election of Israel also to the Exodus from Egypt (cf. 16:3-8); but he likewise recalls that Yahweh had already given " the land " of Israel to His servant Jacob (28:25; 37:25), at least if Jacob is understood as the ancestor of the people and not as a synonym for the name of the nation, as in 20:5; 39:25.

The book of the consolation of Israel (Is 40 ff.) unites the two traditions and builds on Israel's election its unshakable hope of the deliverance of the people exiled in Babylonia : Yahweh will not abandon " His chosen people " (Is 43:20; 45:4), or " His chosen ones " (Is 65:9.15.22), Israel, His servant, whom He had chosen (Is 41:8.9; 43:10; 44:1.2; cf. 43:1.2; 44:21.24; 48:12), [9] whom He created (Is 43:1-15; 44:2; 45:11; 51:13); in order to liberate His people from the Exile and to bring it back to its home, He will again work those prodigies performed in the time of the Exodus (Is 51:9-11). Gladly are recalled the miracles by which Yahweh manifested His omnipotence in favor of His " chosen one " in the time of Moses (Is 40:1-4; 43:16-19; 51:9.10; 63:7-14; cf. Ps 66:5-12; 77:15-21; 81:9-11; 103:6.7; 136:10 ff.).

Isaias (41:8.9; cf. 29:22; Mi 7:20; Ps 105:6.8.9) retraces the election of Israel or of " the race of Abraham " to the moment when Yahweh went to " take it from the ends of the earth and summoned it from its far-off places "; this can only be understood as referring to the region of Ur in Chaldea, or to Haran, whence Yahweh summoned Israel, in the person of his ancestor (Gn 11:31; 12:1) Abraham, who is here, as in 2 Par 20:7; Dn 3:35 (LXX); Jas 2:23; Jubil 19:9, and in the Koran, decorated with the title of " friend of God. "

---

[8] The authenticity of Jer 11:5 and 33:26 are questioned by several; P. Volz (*Jeremia*, pp. 129 ff.), Heinisch *(in h.l.)*, Condamin *(in h.l.)* defend the authenticity of Jer 11:5, but question that of 33:26.

[9] In Is 49:1 ff. the context proves that " the servant of Yahweh " is an individual; " Israel " must therefore be suppressed in verse 3 (cf. A. Condamin, *in h.l.*; Fischer, *in h.l.*; and others).

The prophets, therefore, have admitted and proclaimed the election of Israel as well as the covenant concluded by Yahweh. In these points they share the popular belief, for they believe, as the people does, that Yahweh revealed Himself to Israel and established by His interventions in the history of this people the relation which made them into " the people of Yahweh. " But, since the prophets conceive Yahweh, the holy God, in a manner quite different from that of the people, they condemn severely the popular conception of Israel's election and of the covenant [10] (Am 5:14.18; Is 28:14.15; Mi 3:11; Jer 14:13; 23:17). According to them, the election of Israel and the covenant should have made Israel into the holy people of the holy God, in other words, election and covenant should have brought about the moral education of Israel (Os 2:21.22; Is 5:7); they imposed on the elected people obligations of justice, of submission and of fidelity to Yahweh (Is 1:16-20; 5:7 ff.; Am 5:14-15; Os 2:21-25; Jer 7:3-10; 11:1-5, etc.). Since Israel transgressed these obligations and thus " violated the covenant " (Os 8:1), it will be severely chastised. From Israel's election and from the divine covenant the prophets thus draw a conclusion diametrically opposed to that of the people: the people sees in those facts an absolute guarantee of happiness and of divine protection: " Is not Yahweh in the midst of us? No evil can come upon us! " (Mi 3:11; cf. Am 5:14.18; Is 28:14.15; Jer 14:13; 23:17); the prophets, on the contrary, find there the reason for a chastisement all the more severe (Am 3:2; Os 8:1-3; Is 5:3-5; Mi 3:12; Jer 7:8 ff., etc.), since the election had been a gratuitous and gracious act on the part of God and had been destined to raise the moral and religious level of Israel.

Deuteronomy as well as the prophets insists on the gratuitous character of the election and of the divine covenant, but attaches the one and the other to the patriarchal period, " because He loved your fathers, He chose their descendants and personally led you out of Egypt by His great power " (4:37; cf. 7:6-8; 10:15; 14:2). Israel is the " people holy to Yahweh, " that is to say, sacred to Yahweh (7:6; 14:2.21; 26:19; 28:9; Ex 19:6), the people whom He has chosen to be a people peculiarly His own (*sĕgullâh*, cf. 7:6; 14:2; 26:18; Ex 19:5; Ps 135:4) from among all the nations. Dt 7:6-8, it seems, wishes to correct a popular opinion of the divine election, since it insists on the gratuity of that election, which is an act of the entirely gracious love of God (cf. 4:32-40; 10:15), not a consequence of Israel's might: " It was not because you are the largest of all nations that

[10] Cf. above pp. 239 ff.

Yahweh set His heart on you and chose you, for you are really the smallest of all nations " (Dt 7:7). It is not because of the justice and righteousness of the heart of Israel that Yahweh places Israel in possession of the land of Canaan, but because of the wickedness of the inhabitants of the land and because of the oath He had made to the ancestors (Dt 9:5).

Deuteronomy is not less explicit in regard to the moral and conditional character of the covenant and the moral and religious obligations imposed on Israel on account of the divine election (cf. 4:3 ff.; 5:9.10; 6:4-19; 7:9.10, etc.); on the observation of the divine commandments depends the divine protection: " As your reward for heeding these decrees and observing them carefully, Yahweh, your God, will keep with you the covenant and the steadfast love (*ḥesed*) which He promised on oath to your fathers " (7:12).

In the narrative of Jos 24, Josue, after having recalled how Israel had been elected by God when " He took your father Abraham from beyond the river and led him through all the land of Canaan " (24:3), how " He brought out Israel from Egypt " (24:5.6), and gave it the possession of the land of Canaan (24:8-13), draws the conclusion that Israel has the obligation to " fear Yahweh and serve Him completely and sincerely " and to cast out the strange gods their fathers served beyond the river (24:14). The orator, therefore, summons the people to pronounce themselves clearly in favor of Yahweh alone (cf. 3 Kgs 18:21) by telling them ironically: " If it does not please you to serve Yahweh, decide today whom you will serve, whether the gods your fathers served beyond the river, or the gods of the Amorrites in whose country you are dwelling; but as for me and my house, we will serve Yahweh " (24:15). The irony of these words is not less lashing than that of Jephte (Jgs 10:14) [11]; if a choice between strange gods is possible since they are innumerable, such a choice, according to Josue and the sacred writer, is no longer reasonable for Israel between Yahweh and strange gods; after all that Yahweh has done for Israel (24:3-13), there remains for Israel nothing else but to fear and serve Yahweh in sincerity and fidelity and to reject every other god (24:14) — for Yahweh is " a jealous God " (24:19) — because it is evidently absurd and criminal to " find it obnoxious to serve Yahweh " (24:15), that is to say, to forsake (24:20) or to " deny " one's God (24:27). When the people proclaim their attachment to Yahweh (24:16-18), Josue replies that they cannot serve Yahweh,

---

[11] Jgs 5:8 seems to express the same idea, but the text is obscure and perhaps corrupt (cf. Lagrange, *in h.l.*; C. F. Burney, *in h.l.*).

for He is a holy God, a jealous God, who will not suffer their transgressions and their sins. As the people reiterates its decision to serve Yahweh, Josue answers: "You are your own witness that you have chosen to serve Yahweh" (24:22). The verb *bâḥar*, used only here with God as object, signifies in the context a decision freely taken [12] to serve Yahweh rather than an election in the strict sense between two persons or two acceptable things. It would be wrong to conclude from this rather unique text that the election of Israel by Yahweh is met by an election of Yahweh by Israel. [13]

Connected with the idea of Israel's election is the idea of the election of the king; in effect the royal power exercised by the elect of Yahweh is the guarantee that Yahweh directs the fate of His people (Ps 28:8; 72:12). Since the commencement of the monarchy, the king is among the Hebrews, as in Babylonia, Assyria and Egypt, [14] the elect of Yahweh; thus Saul, designated by Samuel as the future king (1 Sm 9:16.17; 10:1), is chosen by lot, that is to say, according to the opinion of the time, by Yahweh (1 Sm 10:20-24). The same is the case with David (1 Sm 16:6-13; 2 Sm 6:21; 1 Par 28:4; 3 Kgs 8:16; 2 Par 6:6; Ps 78:70), with Absalom (2 Sm 16:18), with Solomon (1 Par 28:5.6; 29:1), with Zorobabel (Ag 2:23), with any prince (*nâgîd*, 2 Par 6:5); even a foreign king, Cyrus, is called "the shepherd" of Yahweh (Is 44:28), "His anointed one" whose "hand He grasped" (Is 45:1), whom "He has called by His name" and whom He designated (Is 45:4).

The expression "chosen by Yahweh," applied to the king, belongs evidently to the language of the court, since Chusai, the counselor who remained faithful to David (2 Sm 15:32-37), addresses these words to Absalom, whom he considers an usurper (2 Sm 16:18). Besides, we must not forget that "the elect of Yahweh" is also the elect of the people (2 Sm 16:18); it is also said that he is chosen by the people (1 Sm 8:18; 12:13; 2 Sm 16:18); indeed access to the throne in Israel depends on the assembly of the people: the people "appoints Saul king before Yahweh" (1 Sm 11:15) after his victory against the Ammonites; the elders of Israel anoint David as king in Hebron and make a covenant *(bĕrît)* with him (2 Sm 5:3), that is to say, they pledge to recognize him as their sovereign (cf. Jgs 9:6; 3 Kgs 12:20; Dt 17:14-20); without the assent of the tribes, the king could not reign (3 Kgs 12:1 ff.). But of whatever importance the

[12] Cf. similar expressions: to choose the law or the way of God (Ps 25:12; 119: 30.173), to choose the fear of God (Prv 1:29).

[13] Against Köhler, *Theologie*, pp. 64 ff.

[14] Cf. L. Dürr, *Ursprung und Ausbau der israelitisch-jüdischen Heilandserwartung*, Berlin 1925, pp. 28 ff.; H. Gressmann, *Der Messias*, Göttingen 1929, pp. 27, 60.

consent or even the choice of the people may have been, the king could not dispense with divine investiture; this is ordinarily mentioned in the accounts of the enthronement, where the people plays an important role (2 Sm 3:18; 5:2; 16:18); as for the enthronement of the king, Deuteronomy (17:15) distinguishes between the action of the people who " place " *(šîm)* the king over themselves and the action of God who " elects " *(bâḥar)* him (cf. Ps 89:20).

The election of Israel assures for the people certain privileges, among others that of possessing the sanctuary " which Yahweh their God chooses as the dwelling place for His name " (Dt 12:11; cf. 12:5.14.18.21.27, etc.). And the popular opinion saw in " the temple of Yahweh " a pledge of divine protection (Jer 7:4) and reacts violently against Jeremias when he announced the destruction of the temple (Jer 26:2 ff.; cf. Mi 3:12). The prophets, on the contrary, acknowledge the temple as the dwelling place of Yahweh (Is 1:12; 2:3; Mi 3:12; Jer 7:10.11, etc.), but neither the temple, nor Israel's election, nor the covenant are for them an absolute guarantee of divine favors (Jer 7:3-6; Mi 3:9-12; Am 3:2; 5:14.15, etc.). The cult, according to Dt 18:5; 21:5, has been entrusted to the tribe of Levi, which has been chosen by Yahweh to stand before Him and to perform the service in His name.

More rarely, if we except the king, arises the question about the election of an individual; but the idea is not unknown, even in ancient times, since a son of David bears the name Yibhar (2 Sm 5:12; 1 Par 3:6; 14:5), that is to say, El (or Yahweh) chooses or may choose. [15] Even the prophets, who are the object of a special calling by Yahweh, are not called " chosen ones of God "; this title is given only to the servant of Yahweh (Is 42:1; 49:7). Certain recent texts mention the election of Abraham (Neh 9:7) and of Moses (Ps 106:28; cf. 105:26).

For Israel, just as for the Christians (Rom 11:1.28.29; cf. 9:4), the election of Israel is a fundamental and uncontested dogma, which is, without any doubt, an essential element of the originality of the people of God and of their religion. The idea that Yahweh has chosen for Himself this people from among all the nations has really made Israel into a people " apart " (Nm 23:9) and has made their religion different from all those of the ancient East. In those religions the bond which unites each people with their gods originated from the nature of things; in the Old Testament and in Judaism this bond is born from an act of the will and intelligence of the personal God,

[15] Cf. El-yâdaʿ (2 Sm 5:16), the authentic form of which is probably Baal-yâdaʿ (1 Par 14:7), God (or Baal) knows (cf. Am 3:2), name of another son of David.

since it is the result of a gratuitous choice and based solely on love; it began at a given moment of history and is attached to certain historical events, which appear as special interventions of Yahweh in the course of human things and as manifestations of His particular benevolence.

The divine election of Israel, as it has been understood by the prophets and Deuteronomy, has helped to preserve the revelation of moral monotheism; election was not meant to give birth to any presumptuous self-assurance (cf. Mi 3:11, etc.), nor to national pride (cf. Dt 7:6-8), nor to the exclusivism of Israel, since the election is absolutely gratuitous and due neither to Israel's power nor its justice (Dt 7:6-8; 9:5), but solely to the gracious love of Yahweh. But it is equally certain that the doctrine of Israel's election has contributed to orientate Judaism finally toward that national pride, exclusivism and hatred of "the gentiles" which were expressed so frequently by the Rabbis.[16] The Jews, furthermore, forgot that the divine election was addressed to the nation, not to the individuals; they interpreted the love and the promises of Yahweh toward their ancestors (cf. Is 41:8 ff.; Dt 4:37; 10:15; Ex 32:13; Lv 26:44.45, etc.) as a blind partiality and trusted too much in the merits of their fathers, so that eventually they believed that the sole fact of belonging to the race of Abraham would assure the salvation of their descendants (cf. Mt 3:9).[17] Against this deformation of the doctrine of election rose up John the Baptist (Mt 3:7 ff.), and Jesus (Jn 8:33 ff.), and St. Paul (Rom 2:17 ff.; 4:9 ff., etc.).

[16] Cf. G. Foot-More, *Judaism*, I, Cambridge 1927, pp. 398 ff.; J. Bonsirven, *Palestinian Judaism in the time of Jesus Christ*, New York 1963.

[17] Cf. H. Strack-P. Billerbeck, *Kommentar zum N. T. aus Talmud und Midrasch*, Munich 1922, I, pp. 116 ff.

INDEX OF BIBLICAL REFERENCES

OLD TESTAMENT

Deuteronomy

Josue

Judges

Ruth

I Samuel

2 Samuel

3 **Kings**

1 Paralipomenon

2 Paralipomenon

Ezra

Psalms

Ecclesiastes

Wisdom

Sirach (Ecclesiasticus)

Isaia

Lamentations

Baruch

Ezechiel

Zacharia

Malachia

1 Machabees

2 Machabees

NEW TESTAMENT

ADDITIONAL BIBLIOGRAPHY

Introduction :

J. L. McKenzie, *The Two-Edged Sword*, Milwaukee 1956.

E. Jacob, *Theology of the Old Testament*, New York 1958.

E. J. Young, *The Study of Old Testament Theology Today*, London 1958.

Th. C. Vriezen, *An Outline of Old Testament Theology*, Oxford 1958.

A. Gelin, *The Religion of Israel*, (20th Cent. Enc. of Catholicism), New York 1959.

J. Bauer, *Bibeltheologisches Wörterbuch*, Graz 1959.

G. E. Wright, *The Rule of God : Essays in Biblical Theology*, Garden City 1960.

W. Eichrodt, *Theology of the Old Testament*, Vol. I, Philadelphia 1961.

G. von Rad, *Old Testament Theology*, Vol. I, Edinburgh 1962.

X. Léon-Dufour, *Vocabulaire de théologie biblique*, Paris 1962.

F. J. Cwiekowski, " Biblical Theology as Historical Theology, " *CBQ*, 24 (1962), pp. 404-11.

R. C. Dentan, *Preface to Old Testament Theology*, New York 1963.

J. Blenkinsopp, " Biblical and Dogmatic Theology : The Present Situation, " *CBQ*, 26 (1964), pp. 70-85.

J. N. Schofield, *Introducing Old Testament Theology*, London 1964.

J. Dheilly, *Dictionnaire Biblique*, Tournai 1964.

G. A. F. Knight, *A Christian Theology of the Old Testament*, 2nd ed. London 1964.

Chapter I :

J. Gray, " The God YW in the Religion of Canaan, " *JNES*, 12 (1953), pp. 278-83.

E. Schild, " On Exodus 3:14 : ' I am that I am ', " *VT*, 4 (1954), pp. 296-302.

G. R. Driver, " The Interpretation of YHWH as a Participle Form, " *JBL*, 73 (1954), pp. 125-31.

J. P. Hyatt, " YHWH as the God of My Father, " *VT*, 5 (1955), pp. 130-36.

S. D. Goitein, " YHWH the Passionate. The Monotheistic Meaning and Origin of the Name YHWH, " *VT*, 6 (1956), pp. 1-9.

W. F. Albright, *From the Stone Age to Christianity*, 2nd ed. New York 1957, pp. 209-36; 243-49; 258-61.

R. Mayer, " Der Gottesname Jahwe im Lichte der neuesten Forschung, " *BZ*, N. F. 2 (1958), pp. 26-53.

Myles M. Bourke, " Yahweh, the Divine Name, " *The Bridge III*, New York 1958, pp. 271-88.

J. Barr, " Theophany and Anthropomorphism in the Old Testament, " *VT Suppl.*, 7 (1959), pp. 31-38.

D. N. Freedman, " The Name of the God of Moses, " *JBL*, 79 (1960), pp. 151-56.

R. Lack, " Les origines de Elyôn, le Très-Haut, dans la tradition cultuelle d'Israël, " *CBQ*, 24 (1962), pp. 44-64.

R. W. Gleason, *Yahweh the God of the Old Testament*, New Jersey 1964.

Chapter II :

B. W. Anderson, " The Earth is the Lord's : An Essay on the Biblical Doctrine of Creation, " *Interpretation*, 9 (1955), pp. 3-20.

E. T. Mengers, *The Idea of Creation in the Old Testament*, Boston 1957.

M. Ziegler, *Engel und Dämon im Lichte der Bibel*, Origo-Verlag Schweiz, 1957.

T. Ling, *The Significance of Satan : New Testament Demonology and its Contemporary Relevance*, London 1961.

J. de Fraine, *The Bible and the Origin of Man*, New York 1962.

S. G. F. Brandon, *Creation Legends of the Ancient Near East*, London 1963.

H. A. Kelly, " The Devil in the Desert, " *CBQ*, 26 (1964), pp. 190-220.

Chapter III :

J. Guillet, " La révélation progressive du Saint-Esprit dans l'Ecriture, " *Lumen V*, 8 (1953), pp. 18-32.

S. Mowinckel, *He That Cometh*, Oxford 1956.

H. Ringgren, *The Messiah in the Old Testament*, London 1956.

E. Voegelin, *Israel and Revelation*, Baton Rouge 1956.

C. Kuhl, *The Prophets of Israel*, London 1960.

J. L. McKenzie, " The Word of God in the Old Testament, " *TS*, 21 (1960), pp. 183-206.

J. Lindblom, *Prophecy in Ancient Israel*, Oxford 1962.

R. Latourelle, *Théologie de la révélation*, Bruges 1963.

A. Dulles, " The Theology of Revelation, " *TS*, 25 (1964), pp. 43-58.

Chapter IV :

G. F. Mendenhall, *Law and Covenant in Israel and the Ancient Near East*, Pittsburgh 1955.

J. Muilenburg, " The Form and Structure of the Covenantal Formulations, " *VT*, 9 (1959), pp. 347-65.

M. L. Newman, *The Sinai Covenant Traditions in the Cult of Israel*, New York 1960.

M. L. Newman, *The People of the Covenant*, New York 1962.

J. Coppens, " La Nouvelle Alliance en Jer 31, 31-34, " *CBQ*, 25 (1963), pp. 12-21.

D. J. McCarthy, " Three Covenants in Genesis, " *CBQ*, 26 (1964), pp. 179-89.

D. J. McCarthy, " Covenant in the Old Testament : The Present State of Inquiry, " *CBQ*, 27 (1965), pp. 217-40.

An Index of Subjects will be found at the end of Volume III.

N.Y. 28 — Printed in Belgium by Desclée & Cie, Éditeurs, S.A., Tournai — 10.779